DYNAMITE ENTERTAINMENT PRESENTS

ZORRO®

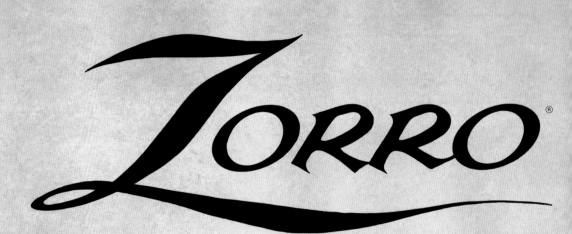

VOLUME TWO: CLASHING BLADES

Dedicated to the works of Johnston McCulley, Isabel Allende and countless film and comic creators who have chronicled the adventures of America's first masked super-hero--the lone and daring adventurer who fought for justice in the wilds of old California. For nearly a century, his tireless blade has rallied against the greedy and malicious, striking terror into the hearts of those who will one day wear his slashing brand... The Mark of ZORRO!

Writer / Art Director:
MATT WAGNER

Artist:
CEZAR RAZEK

Colorist:
SALVATORE AIALA

Letterer:
SIMON BOWLAND

Additional Art:
FRANCESCO FRANCAVILLA

Collection Design:
JASON ULLMEYER

Special Thanks To:
JOHN GERTZ
SANDRA CURTIS
At Zorro Productions, Inc.

This volume collects issues nine through fourteen of the Dynamite Entertainment series, Zorro.

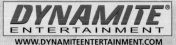

DYNAMITE® ENTERTAINMENT
WWW.DYNAMITEENTERTAINMENT.COM

NICK BARRUCCI • PRESIDENT
JUAN COLLADO • CHIEF OPERATING OFFICER
JOSEPH RYBANDT • EDITOR
JOSH JOHNSON • CREATIVE DIRECTOR
JASON ULLMEYER • GRAPHIC DESIGNER

To find a comic shop in your area, call the comic shop locator service toll-free 1-888-266-4226 or go to WWW.COMICSHOPLOCATOR.COM.

Printed in China

For information regarding press, media rights, foreign rights, licensing, promotions, and advertising e-mail:
marketing@dynamiteentertainment.com

Hardcover ISBN10: 1-60690-115-X ISBN13: 978-1-60690-115-1
Softcover ISBN10: 1-60690-116-8 ISBN13: 978-1-60690-116-8

First Printing 10 9 8 7 6 5 4 3 2 1

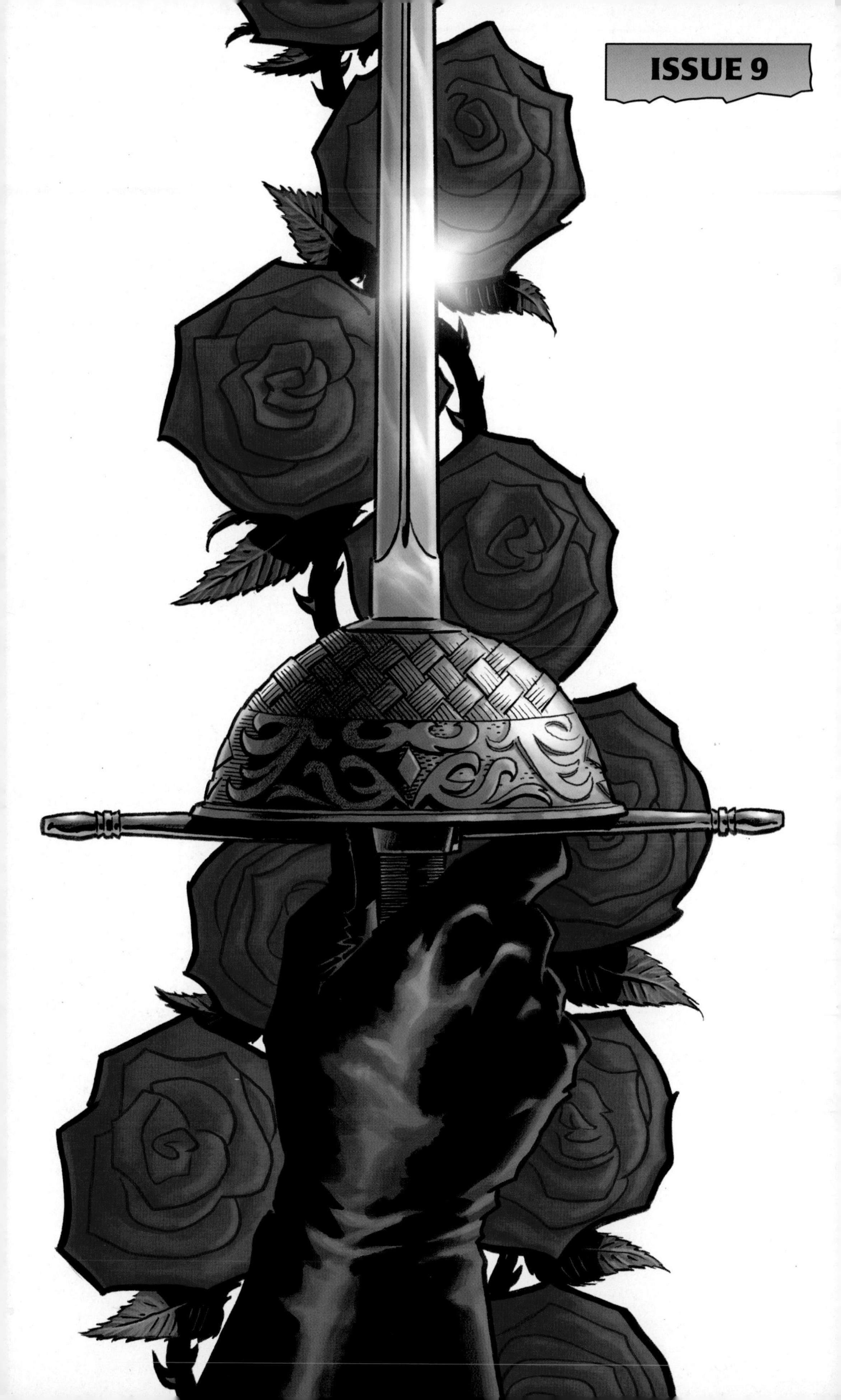
ISSUE 9

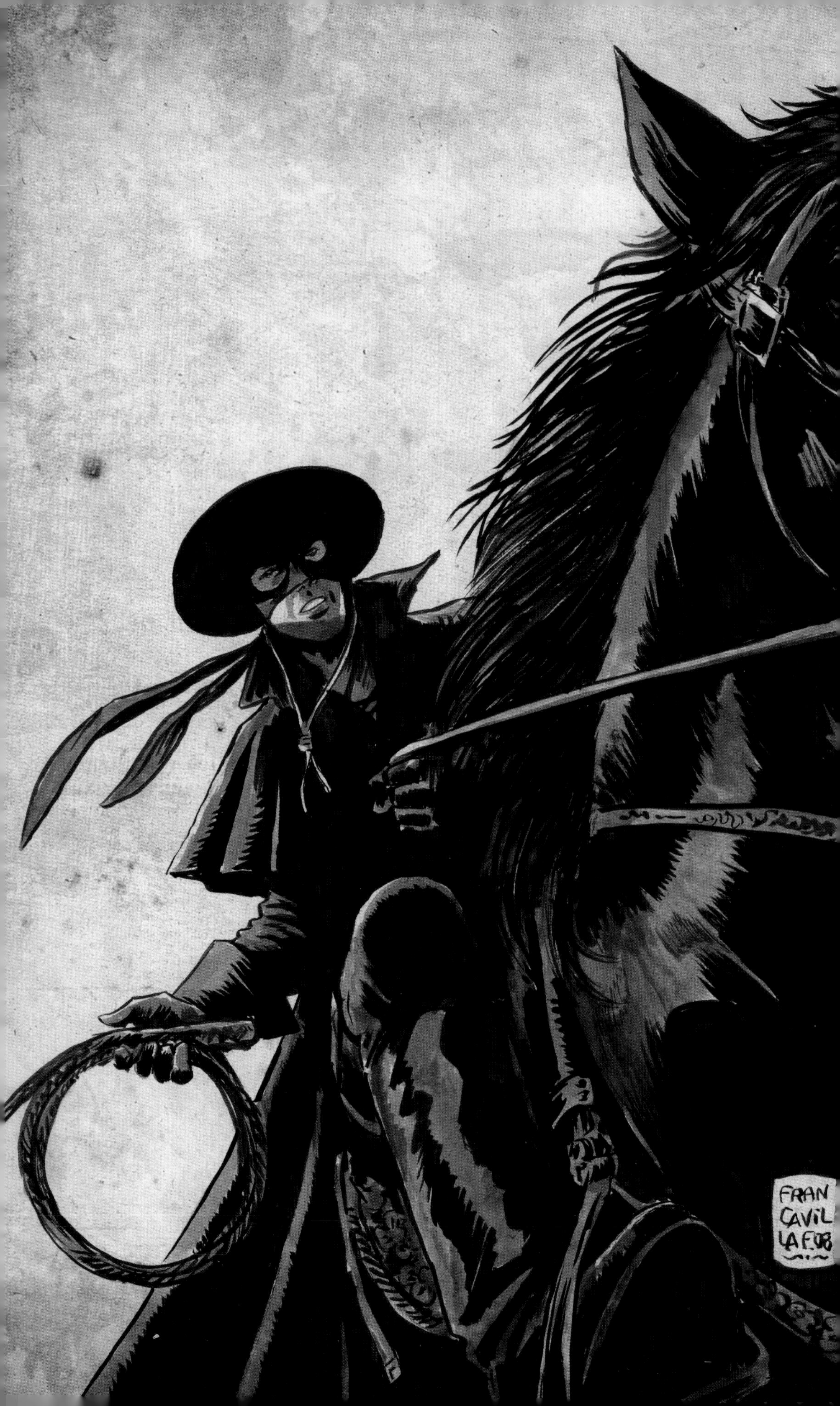
FRAN CAVIL LA F.08

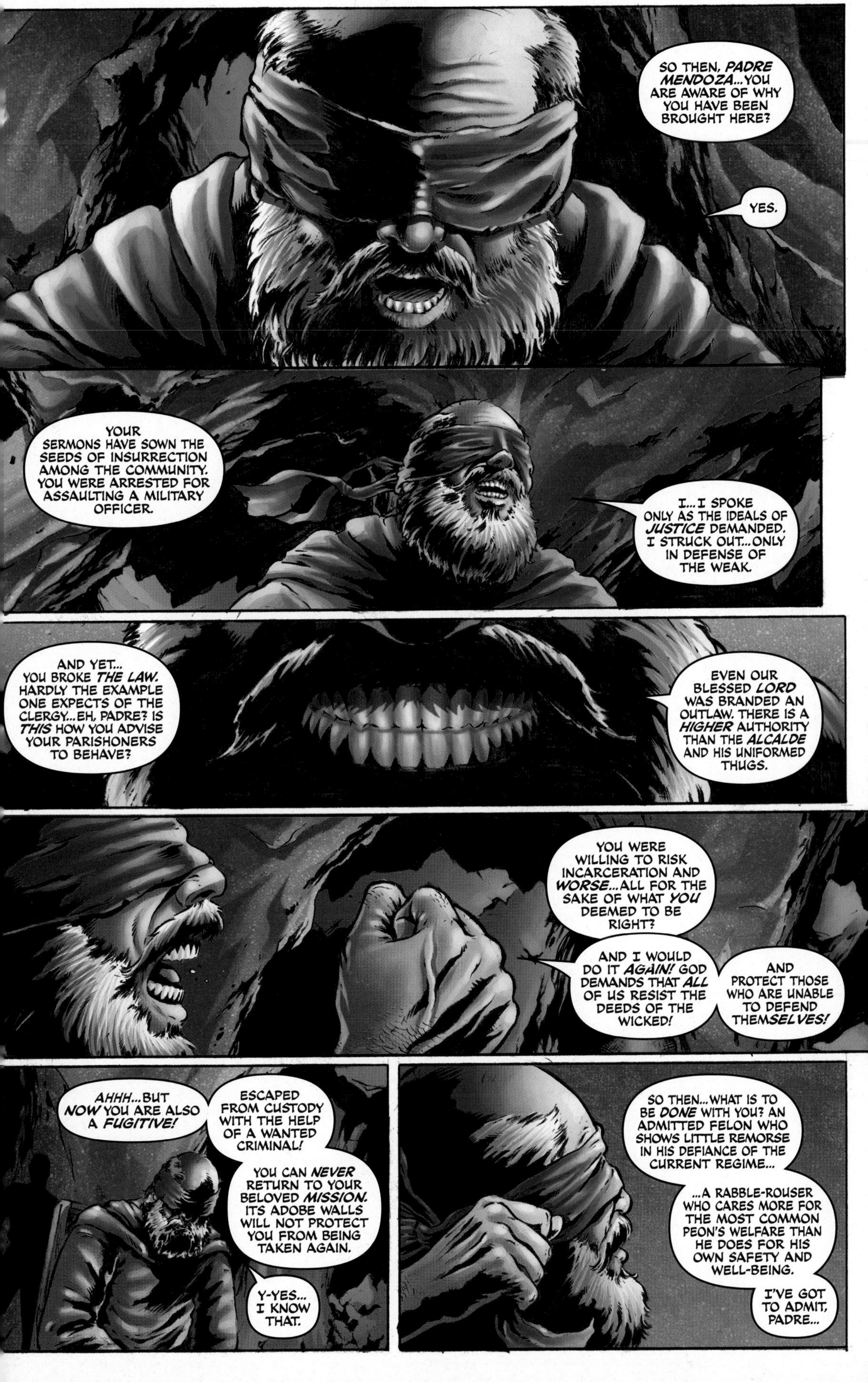

SO THEN, PADRE MENDOZA...YOU ARE AWARE OF WHY YOU HAVE BEEN BROUGHT HERE?
YES.
YOUR SERMONS HAVE SOWN THE SEEDS OF INSURRECTION AMONG THE COMMUNITY. YOU WERE ARRESTED FOR ASSAULTING A MILITARY OFFICER.
I...I SPOKE ONLY AS THE IDEALS OF JUSTICE DEMANDED. I STRUCK OUT...ONLY IN DEFENSE OF THE WEAK.
AND YET... YOU BROKE THE LAW. HARDLY THE EXAMPLE ONE EXPECTS OF THE CLERGY...EH, PADRE? IS THIS HOW YOU ADVISE YOUR PARISHONERS TO BEHAVE?
EVEN OUR BLESSED LORD WAS BRANDED AN OUTLAW. THERE IS A HIGHER AUTHORITY THAN THE ALCALDE AND HIS UNIFORMED THUGS.
YOU WERE WILLING TO RISK INCARCERATION AND WORSE...ALL FOR THE SAKE OF WHAT YOU DEEMED TO BE RIGHT?
AND I WOULD DO IT AGAIN! GOD DEMANDS THAT ALL OF US RESIST THE DEEDS OF THE WICKED!
AND PROTECT THOSE WHO ARE UNABLE TO DEFEND THEMSELVES!
AHHH...BUT NOW YOU ARE ALSO A FUGITIVE!
ESCAPED FROM CUSTODY WITH THE HELP OF A WANTED CRIMINAL!
YOU CAN NEVER RETURN TO YOUR BELOVED MISSION. ITS ADOBE WALLS WILL NOT PROTECT YOU FROM BEING TAKEN AGAIN.
Y-YES... I KNOW THAT.
SO THEN...WHAT IS TO BE DONE WITH YOU? AN ADMITTED FELON WHO SHOWS LITTLE REMORSE IN HIS DEFIANCE OF THE CURRENT REGIME...
...A RABBLE-ROUSER WHO CARES MORE FOR THE MOST COMMON PEON'S WELFARE THAN HE DOES FOR HIS OWN SAFETY AND WELL-BEING.
I'VE GOT TO ADMIT, PADRE...

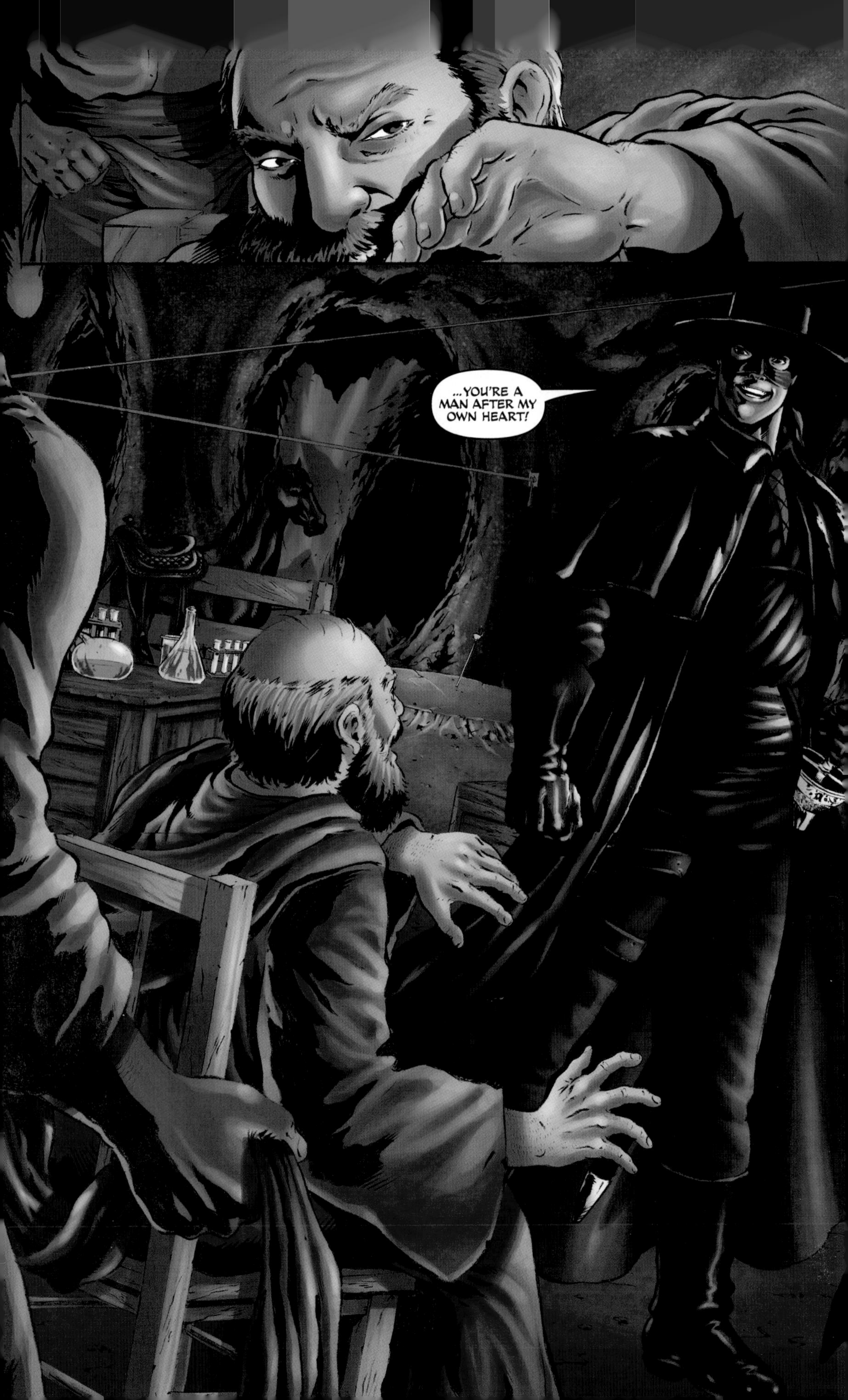
...YOU'RE A MAN AFTER MY OWN HEART!

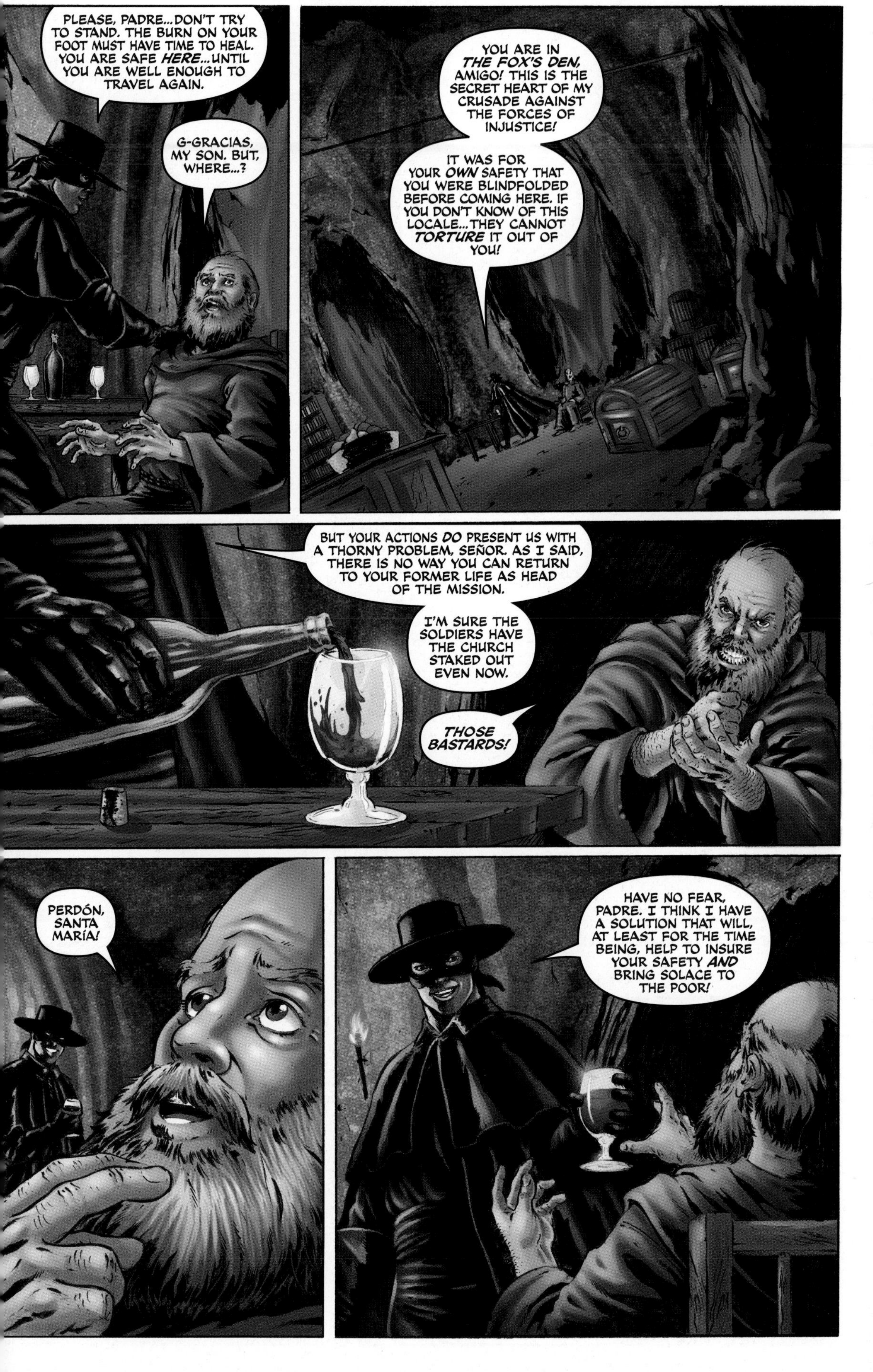
PLEASE, PADRE...DON'T TRY TO STAND. THE BURN ON YOUR FOOT MUST HAVE TIME TO HEAL. YOU ARE SAFE HERE...UNTIL YOU ARE WELL ENOUGH TO TRAVEL AGAIN.
G-GRACIAS, MY SON. BUT, WHERE...?
YOU ARE IN THE FOX'S DEN, AMIGO! THIS IS THE SECRET HEART OF MY CRUSADE AGAINST THE FORCES OF INJUSTICE!
IT WAS FOR YOUR OWN SAFETY THAT YOU WERE BLINDFOLDED BEFORE COMING HERE. IF YOU DON'T KNOW OF THIS LOCALE...THEY CANNOT TORTURE IT OUT OF YOU!
BUT YOUR ACTIONS DO PRESENT US WITH A THORNY PROBLEM, SEÑOR. AS I SAID, THERE IS NO WAY YOU CAN RETURN TO YOUR FORMER LIFE AS HEAD OF THE MISSION.
I'M SURE THE SOLDIERS HAVE THE CHURCH STAKED OUT EVEN NOW.
THOSE BASTARDS!
PERDÓN, SANTA MARÍA!
HAVE NO FEAR, PADRE. I THINK I HAVE A SOLUTION THAT WILL, AT LEAST FOR THE TIME BEING, HELP TO INSURE YOUR SAFETY AND BRING SOLACE TO THE POOR!

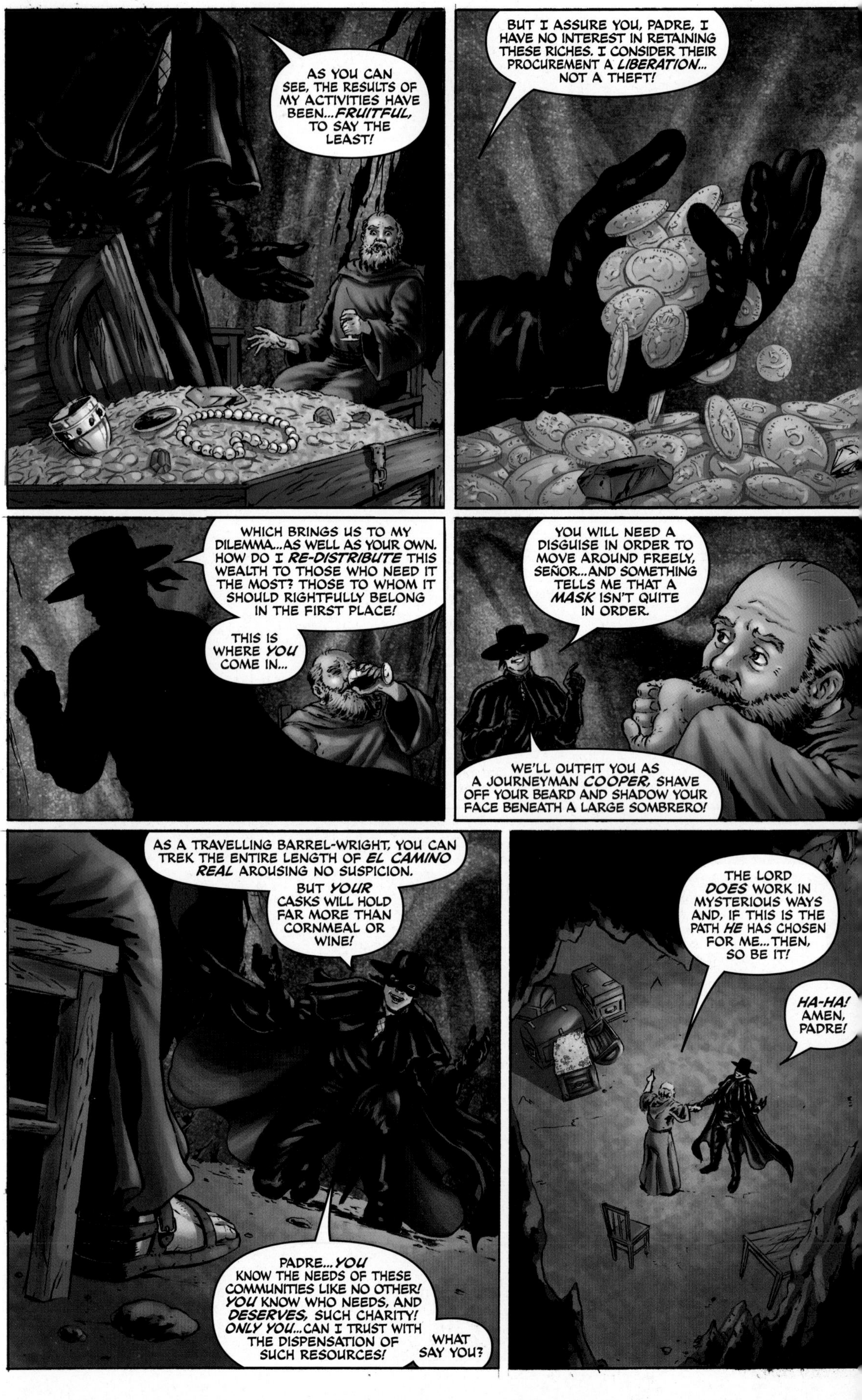
AS YOU CAN SEE, THE RESULTS OF MY ACTIVITIES HAVE BEEN...FRUITFUL, TO SAY THE LEAST!
BUT I ASSURE YOU, PADRE, I HAVE NO INTEREST IN RETAINING THESE RICHES. I CONSIDER THEIR PROCUREMENT A LIBERATION... NOT A THEFT!
WHICH BRINGS US TO MY DILEMMA...AS WELL AS YOUR OWN. HOW DO I RE-DISTRIBUTE THIS WEALTH TO THOSE WHO NEED IT THE MOST? THOSE TO WHOM IT SHOULD RIGHTFULLY BELONG IN THE FIRST PLACE!
THIS IS WHERE YOU COME IN...
YOU WILL NEED A DISGUISE IN ORDER TO MOVE AROUND FREELY, SEÑOR...AND SOMETHING TELLS ME THAT A MASK ISN'T QUITE IN ORDER.
WE'LL OUTFIT YOU AS A JOURNEYMAN COOPER, SHAVE OFF YOUR BEARD AND SHADOW YOUR FACE BENEATH A LARGE SOMBRERO!
AS A TRAVELLING BARREL-WRIGHT, YOU CAN TREK THE ENTIRE LENGTH OF EL CAMINO REAL AROUSING NO SUSPICION.
BUT YOUR CASKS WILL HOLD FAR MORE THAN CORNMEAL OR WINE!
PADRE...YOU KNOW THE NEEDS OF THESE COMMUNITIES LIKE NO OTHER! YOU KNOW WHO NEEDS, AND DESERVES, SUCH CHARITY! ONLY YOU...CAN I TRUST WITH THE DISPENSATION OF SUCH RESOURCES!
WHAT SAY YOU?
THE LORD DOES WORK IN MYSTERIOUS WAYS AND, IF THIS IS THE PATH HE HAS CHOSEN FOR ME...THEN, SO BE IT!
HA-HA! AMEN, PADRE!

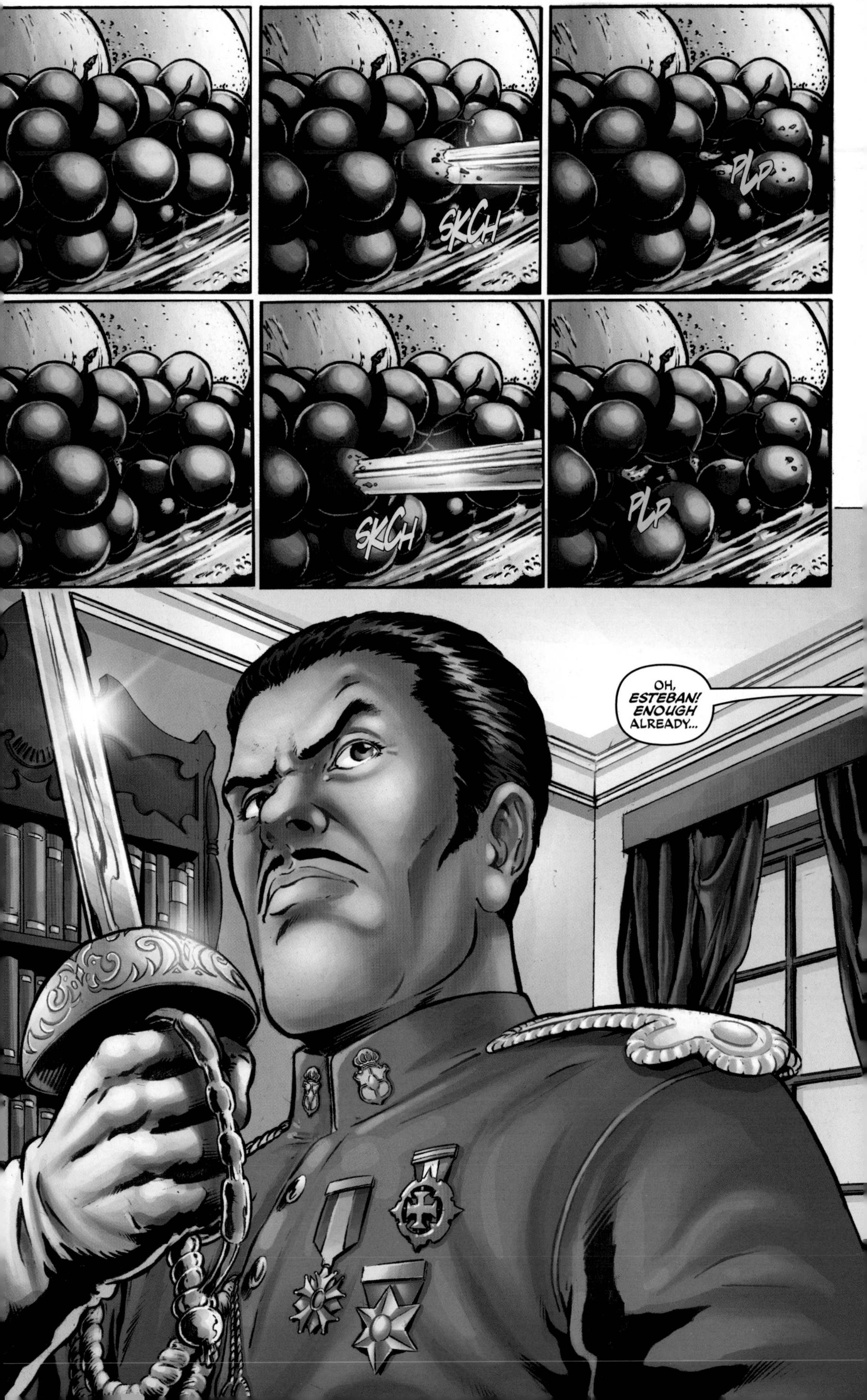
SKCH
PLP
SKCH
PLP
OH, ESTEBAN! ENOUGH ALREADY...

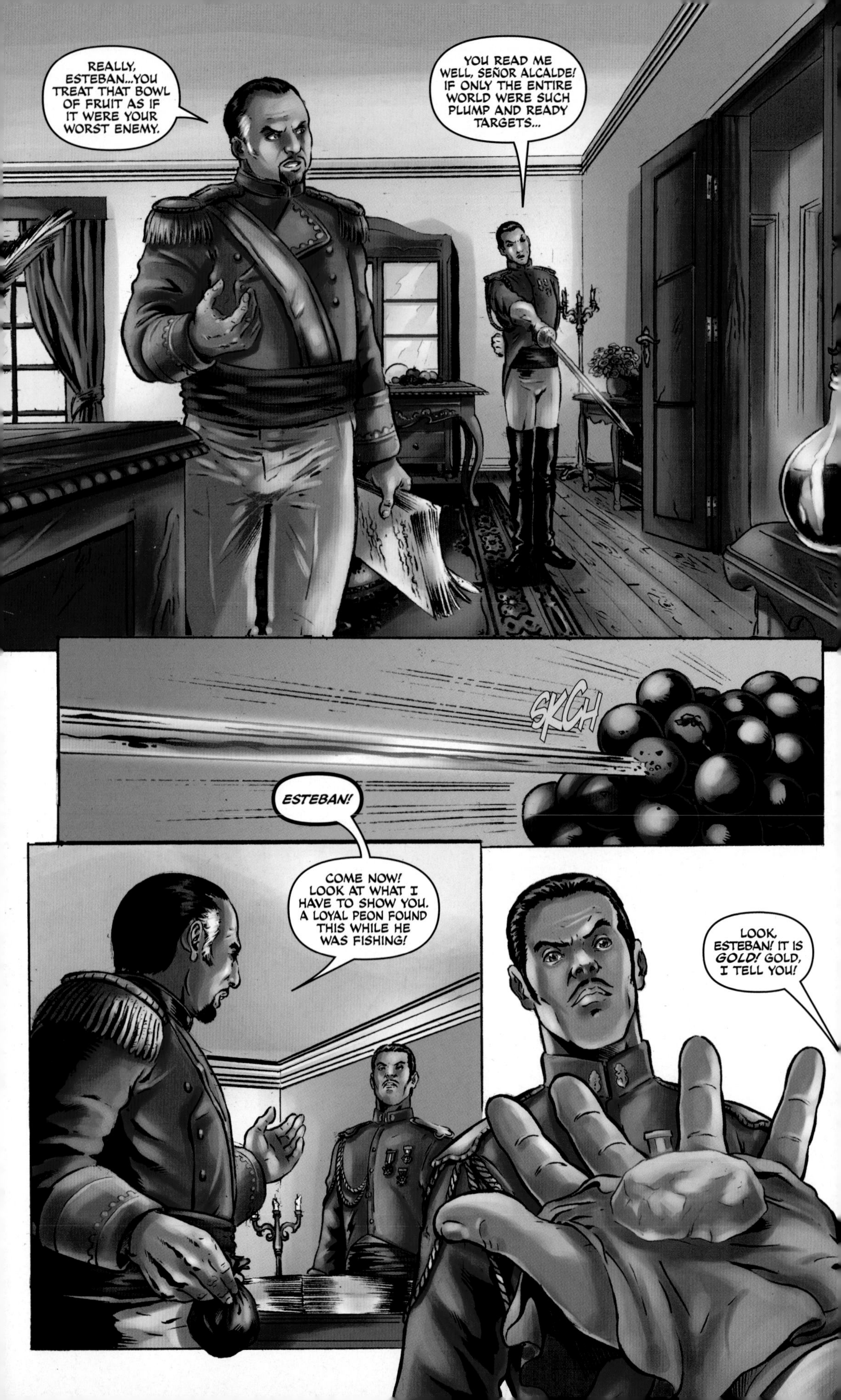
REALLY, ESTEBAN...YOU TREAT THAT BOWL OF FRUIT AS IF IT WERE YOUR WORST ENEMY.
YOU READ ME WELL, SEÑOR ALCALDE! IF ONLY THE ENTIRE WORLD WERE SUCH PLUMP AND READY TARGETS...
SKCH
ESTEBAN!
COME NOW! LOOK AT WHAT I HAVE TO SHOW YOU. A LOYAL PEON FOUND THIS WHILE HE WAS FISHING!
LOOK, ESTEBAN! IT IS *GOLD!* GOLD, I TELL YOU!

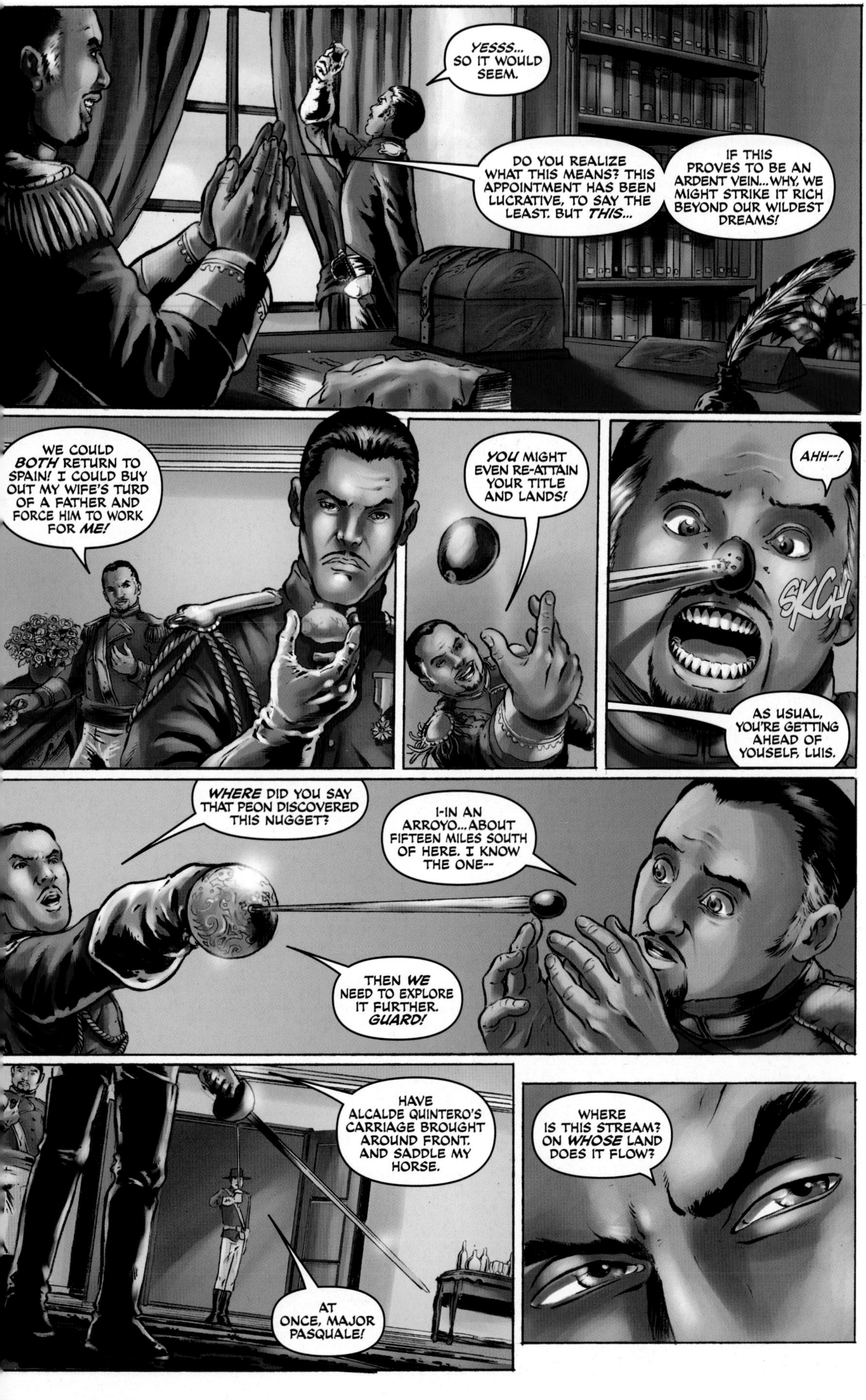
YESSS... SO IT WOULD SEEM.
DO YOU REALIZE WHAT THIS MEANS? THIS APPOINTMENT HAS BEEN LUCRATIVE, TO SAY THE LEAST. BUT THIS...
IF THIS PROVES TO BE AN ARDENT VEIN...WHY, WE MIGHT STRIKE IT RICH BEYOND OUR WILDEST DREAMS!
WE COULD BOTH RETURN TO SPAIN! I COULD BUY OUT MY WIFE'S TURD OF A FATHER AND FORCE HIM TO WORK FOR ME!
YOU MIGHT EVEN RE-ATTAIN YOUR TITLE AND LANDS!
AHH--!
SKCH
AS USUAL, YOU'RE GETTING AHEAD OF YOUSELF, LUIS.
WHERE DID YOU SAY THAT PEON DISCOVERED THIS NUGGET?
I-IN AN ARROYO...ABOUT FIFTEEN MILES SOUTH OF HERE. I KNOW THE ONE--
THEN WE NEED TO EXPLORE IT FURTHER. GUARD!
HAVE ALCALDE QUINTERO'S CARRIAGE BROUGHT AROUND FRONT. AND SADDLE MY HORSE.
AT ONCE, MAJOR PASQUALE!
WHERE IS THIS STREAM? ON WHOSE LAND DOES IT FLOW?

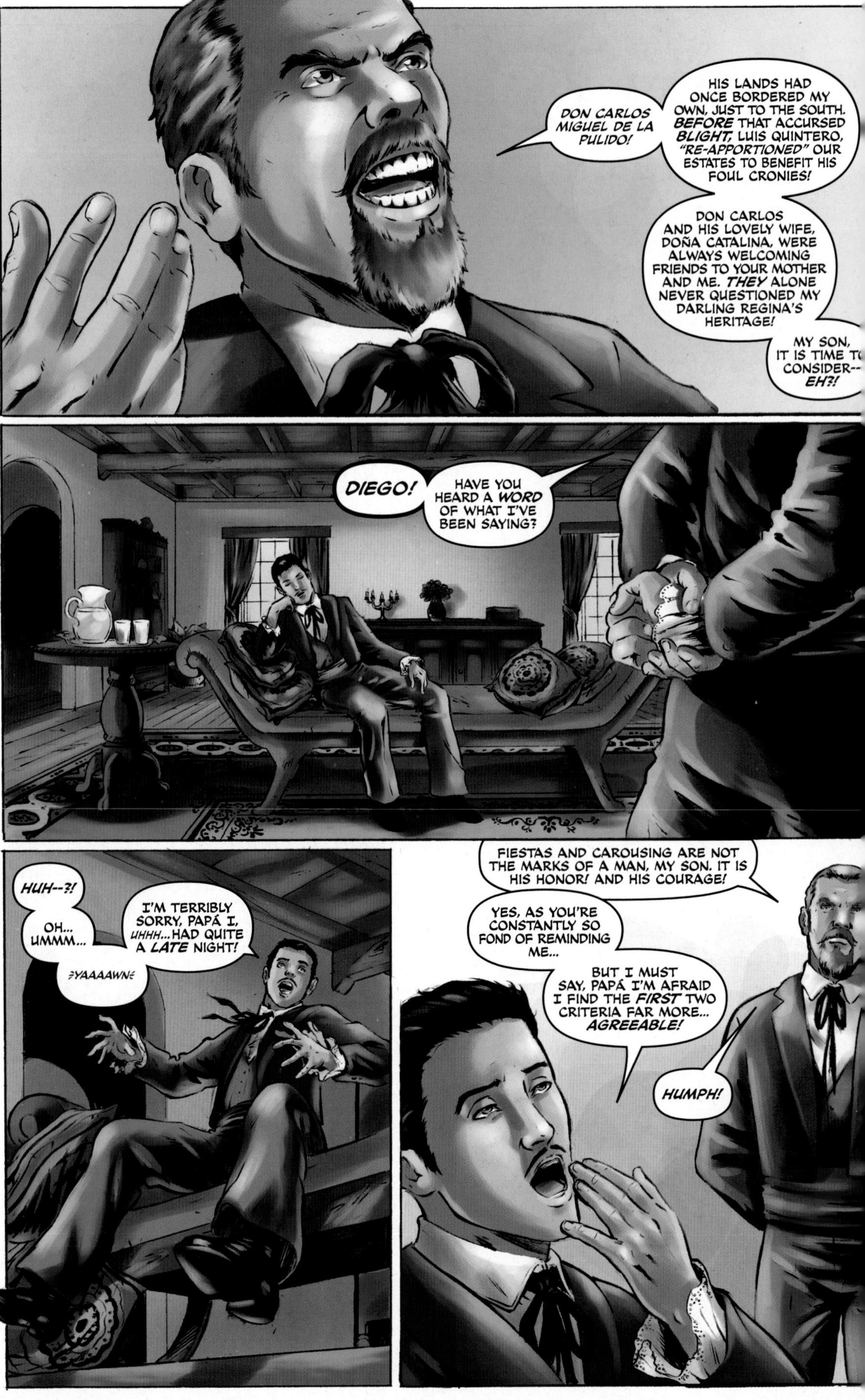
DON CARLOS MIGUEL DE LA PULIDO!
HIS LANDS HAD ONCE BORDERED MY OWN, JUST TO THE SOUTH. BEFORE THAT ACCURSED BLIGHT, LUIS QUINTERO, "RE-APPORTIONED" OUR ESTATES TO BENEFIT HIS FOUL CRONIES!
DON CARLOS AND HIS LOVELY WIFE, DOÑA CATALINA, WERE ALWAYS WELCOMING FRIENDS TO YOUR MOTHER AND ME. THEY ALONE NEVER QUESTIONED MY DARLING REGINA'S HERITAGE!
MY SON, IT IS TIME TO CONSIDER-- EH?!
DIEGO!
HAVE YOU HEARD A WORD OF WHAT I'VE BEEN SAYING?
HUH--?!
OH... UMMM...
I'M TERRIBLY SORRY, PAPÁ I, UHHH...HAD QUITE A LATE NIGHT!
YAAAAWN
FIESTAS AND CAROUSING ARE NOT THE MARKS OF A MAN, MY SON. IT IS HIS HONOR! AND HIS COURAGE!
YES, AS YOU'RE CONSTANTLY SO FOND OF REMINDING ME...
BUT I MUST SAY, PAPÁ I'M AFRAID I FIND THE FIRST TWO CRITERIA FAR MORE... AGREEABLE!
HUMPH!

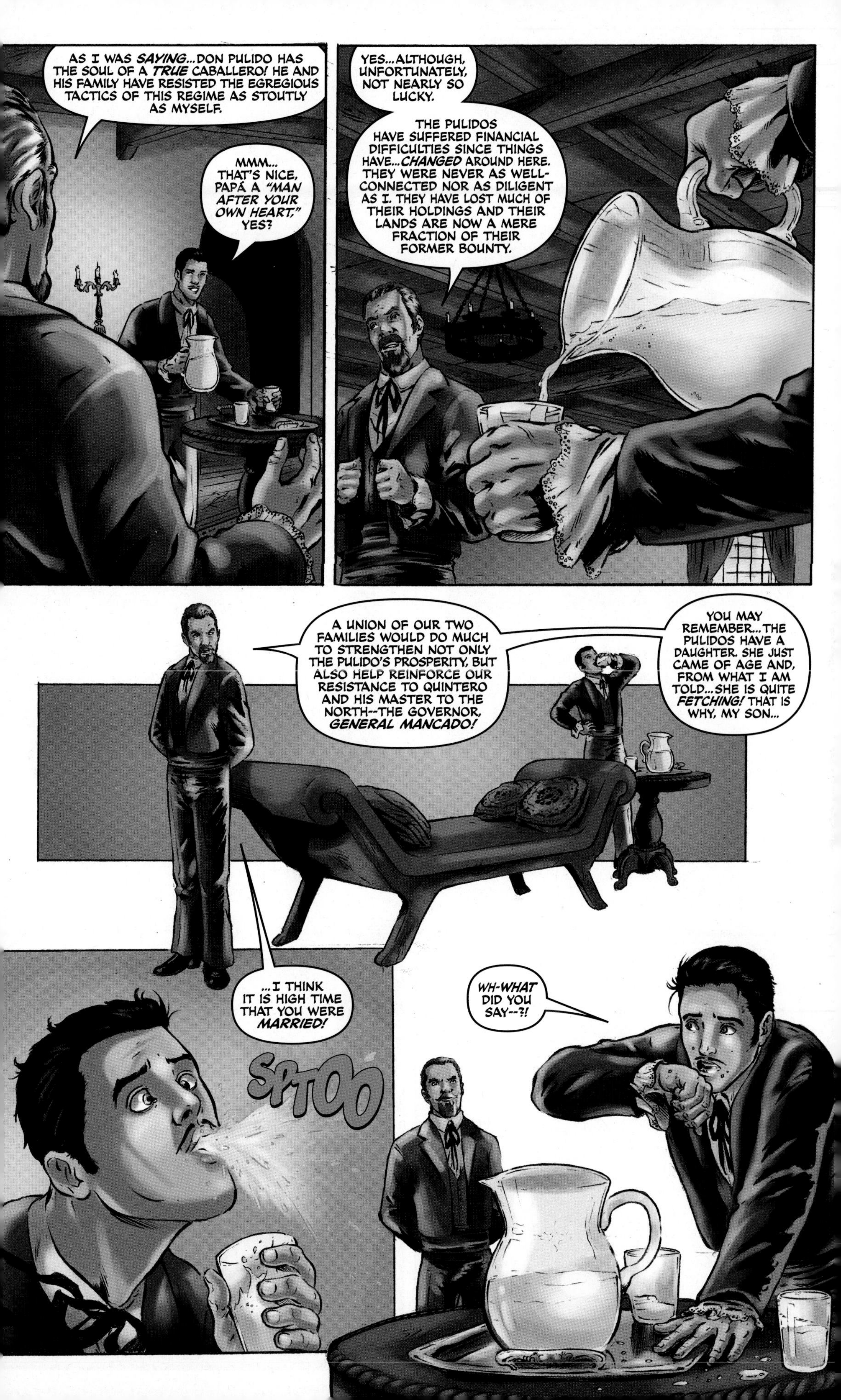
AS I WAS SAYING...DON PULIDO HAS THE SOUL OF A TRUE CABALLERO! HE AND HIS FAMILY HAVE RESISTED THE EGREGIOUS TACTICS OF THIS REGIME AS STOUTLY AS MYSELF.
MMM... THAT'S NICE, PAPÁ A "MAN AFTER YOUR OWN HEART," YES?
YES...ALTHOUGH, UNFORTUNATELY, NOT NEARLY SO LUCKY.
THE PULIDOS HAVE SUFFERED FINANCIAL DIFFICULTIES SINCE THINGS HAVE...CHANGED AROUND HERE. THEY WERE NEVER AS WELL-CONNECTED NOR AS DILIGENT AS I. THEY HAVE LOST MUCH OF THEIR HOLDINGS AND THEIR LANDS ARE NOW A MERE FRACTION OF THEIR FORMER BOUNTY.
A UNION OF OUR TWO FAMILIES WOULD DO MUCH TO STRENGTHEN NOT ONLY THE PULIDO'S PROSPERITY, BUT ALSO HELP REINFORCE OUR RESISTANCE TO QUINTERO AND HIS MASTER TO THE NORTH--THE GOVERNOR, GENERAL MANCADO!
YOU MAY REMEMBER...THE PULIDOS HAVE A DAUGHTER. SHE JUST CAME OF AGE AND, FROM WHAT I AM TOLD...SHE IS QUITE FETCHING! THAT IS WHY, MY SON...
...I THINK IT IS HIGH TIME THAT YOU WERE MARRIED!
SPTOO
WH-WHAT DID YOU SAY--?!

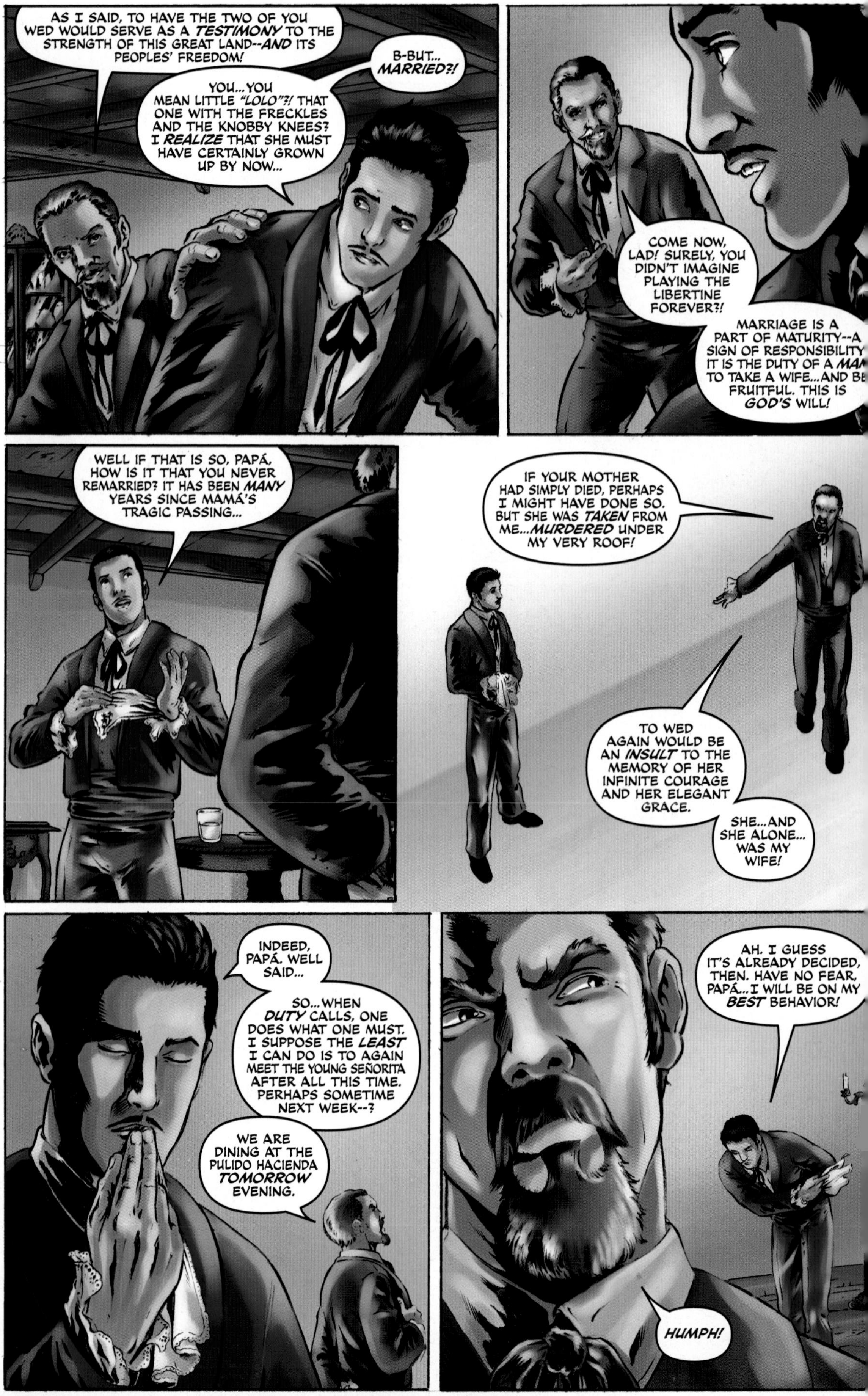
AS I SAID, TO HAVE THE TWO OF YOU WED WOULD SERVE AS A TESTIMONY TO THE STRENGTH OF THIS GREAT LAND--AND ITS PEOPLES' FREEDOM!
B-BUT... MARRIED?!
YOU...YOU MEAN LITTLE "LOLO"?! THAT ONE WITH THE FRECKLES AND THE KNOBBY KNEES? I REALIZE THAT SHE MUST HAVE CERTAINLY GROWN UP BY NOW...
COME NOW, LAD! SURELY, YOU DIDN'T IMAGINE PLAYING THE LIBERTINE FOREVER?!
MARRIAGE IS A PART OF MATURITY--A SIGN OF RESPONSIBILITY IT IS THE DUTY OF A MA TO TAKE A WIFE...AND BE FRUITFUL. THIS IS GOD'S WILL!
WELL IF THAT IS SO, PAPÁ, HOW IS IT THAT YOU NEVER REMARRIED? IT HAS BEEN MANY YEARS SINCE MAMÁ'S TRAGIC PASSING...
IF YOUR MOTHER HAD SIMPLY DIED, PERHAPS I MIGHT HAVE DONE SO. BUT SHE WAS TAKEN FROM ME...MURDERED UNDER MY VERY ROOF!
TO WED AGAIN WOULD BE AN INSULT TO THE MEMORY OF HER INFINITE COURAGE AND HER ELEGANT GRACE.
SHE...AND SHE ALONE... WAS MY WIFE!
INDEED, PAPÁ. WELL SAID...
SO...WHEN DUTY CALLS, ONE DOES WHAT ONE MUST. I SUPPOSE THE LEAST I CAN DO IS TO AGAIN MEET THE YOUNG SEÑORITA AFTER ALL THIS TIME. PERHAPS SOMETIME NEXT WEEK--?
WE ARE DINING AT THE PULIDO HACIENDA TOMORROW EVENING.
AH. I GUESS IT'S ALREADY DECIDED, THEN. HAVE NO FEAR, PAPÁ...I WILL BE ON MY BEST BEHAVIOR!
HUMPH!

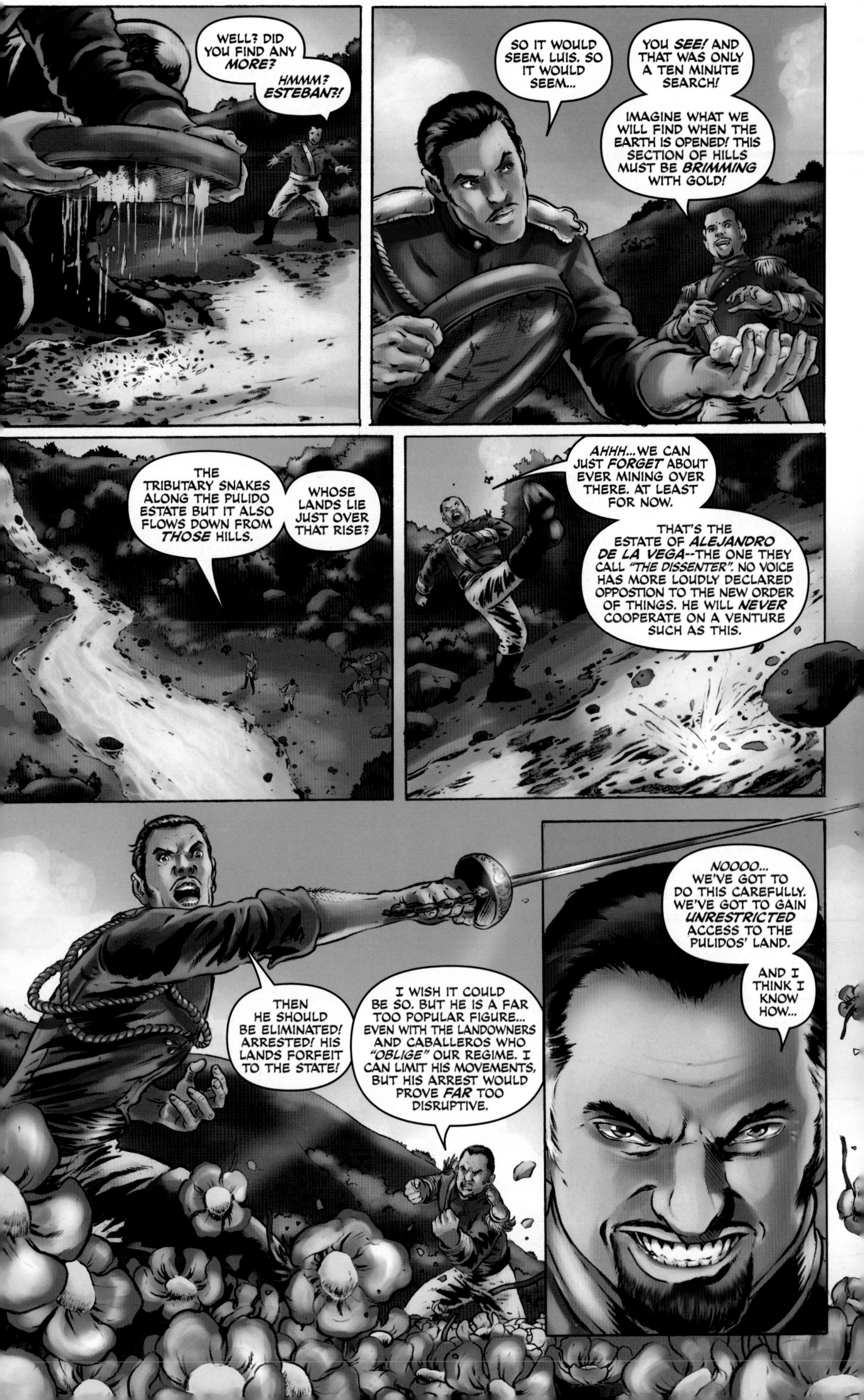

WELL? DID YOU FIND ANY *MORE?*
HMMM? *ESTEBAN?!*
SO IT WOULD SEEM, LUIS. SO IT WOULD SEEM...
YOU *SEE!* AND THAT WAS ONLY A TEN MINUTE SEARCH!
IMAGINE WHAT WE WILL FIND WHEN THE EARTH IS OPENED! THIS SECTION OF HILLS MUST BE *BRIMMING* WITH GOLD!
THE TRIBUTARY SNAKES ALONG THE PULIDO ESTATE BUT IT ALSO FLOWS DOWN FROM *THOSE* HILLS.
WHOSE LANDS LIE JUST OVER THAT RISE?
AHHH...WE CAN JUST *FORGET* ABOUT EVER MINING OVER THERE. AT LEAST FOR NOW.
THAT'S THE ESTATE OF *ALEJANDRO DE LA VEGA*--THE ONE THEY CALL *"THE DISSENTER"*. NO VOICE HAS MORE LOUDLY DECLARED OPPOSTION TO THE NEW ORDER OF THINGS. HE WILL *NEVER* COOPERATE ON A VENTURE SUCH AS THIS.
THEN HE SHOULD BE ELIMINATED! ARRESTED! HIS LANDS FORFEIT TO THE STATE!
I WISH IT COULD BE SO. BUT HE IS A FAR TOO POPULAR FIGURE... EVEN WITH THE LANDOWNERS AND CABALLEROS WHO *"OBLIGE"* OUR REGIME. I CAN LIMIT HIS MOVEMENTS, BUT HIS ARREST WOULD PROVE *FAR* TOO DISRUPTIVE.
NOOOO... WE'VE GOT TO DO THIS CAREFULLY. WE'VE GOT TO GAIN *UNRESTRICTED* ACCESS TO THE PULIDOS' LAND.
AND I THINK I KNOW HOW...

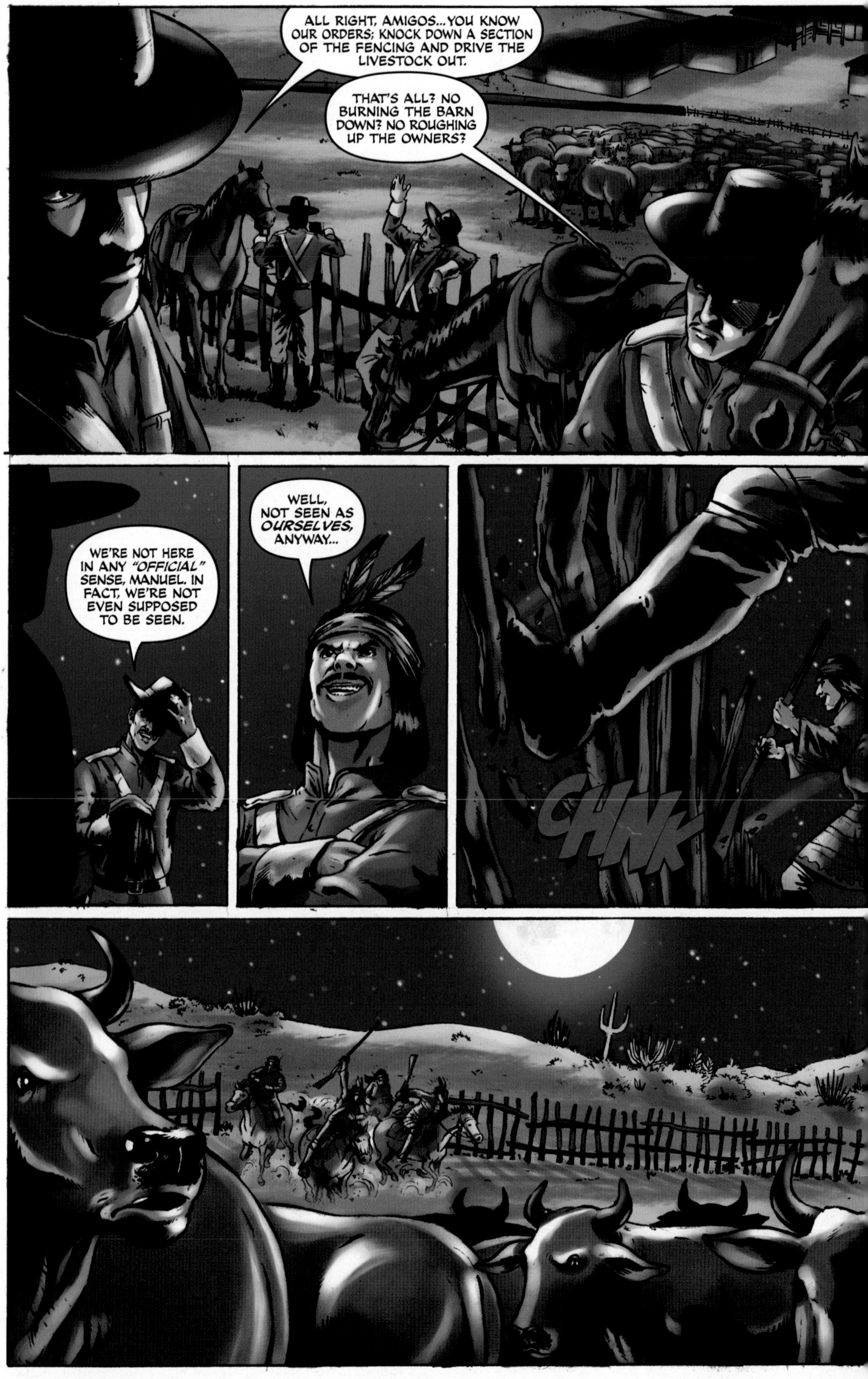
ALL RIGHT, AMIGOS...YOU KNOW OUR ORDERS; KNOCK DOWN A SECTION OF THE FENCING AND DRIVE THE LIVESTOCK OUT.
THAT'S ALL? NO BURNING THE BARN DOWN? NO ROUGHING UP THE OWNERS?
WE'RE NOT HERE IN ANY "OFFICIAL" SENSE, MANUEL. IN FACT, WE'RE NOT EVEN SUPPOSED TO BE SEEN.
WELL, NOT SEEN AS OURSELVES, ANYWAY...
CHNK

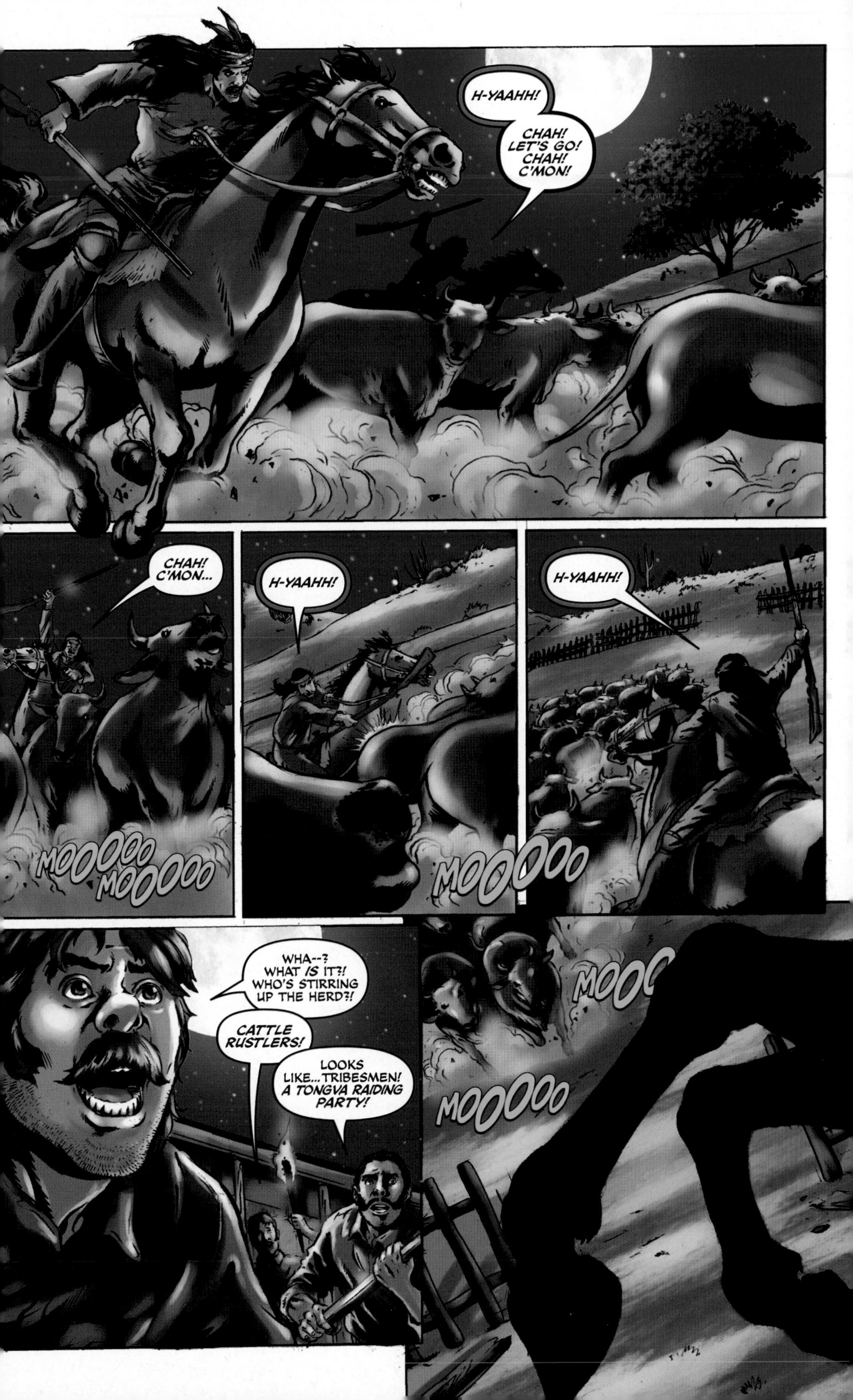
H-YAAHH!
CHAH! LET'S GO! CHAH! C'MON!
CHAH! C'MON...
MOOOOO MOOOOO
H-YAAHH!
H-YAAHH!
MOOOOO
WHA--? WHAT IS IT?! WHO'S STIRRING UP THE HERD?!
CATTLE RUSTLERS!
LOOKS LIKE...TRIBESMEN! A TONGVA RAIDING PARTY!
MOOOOO

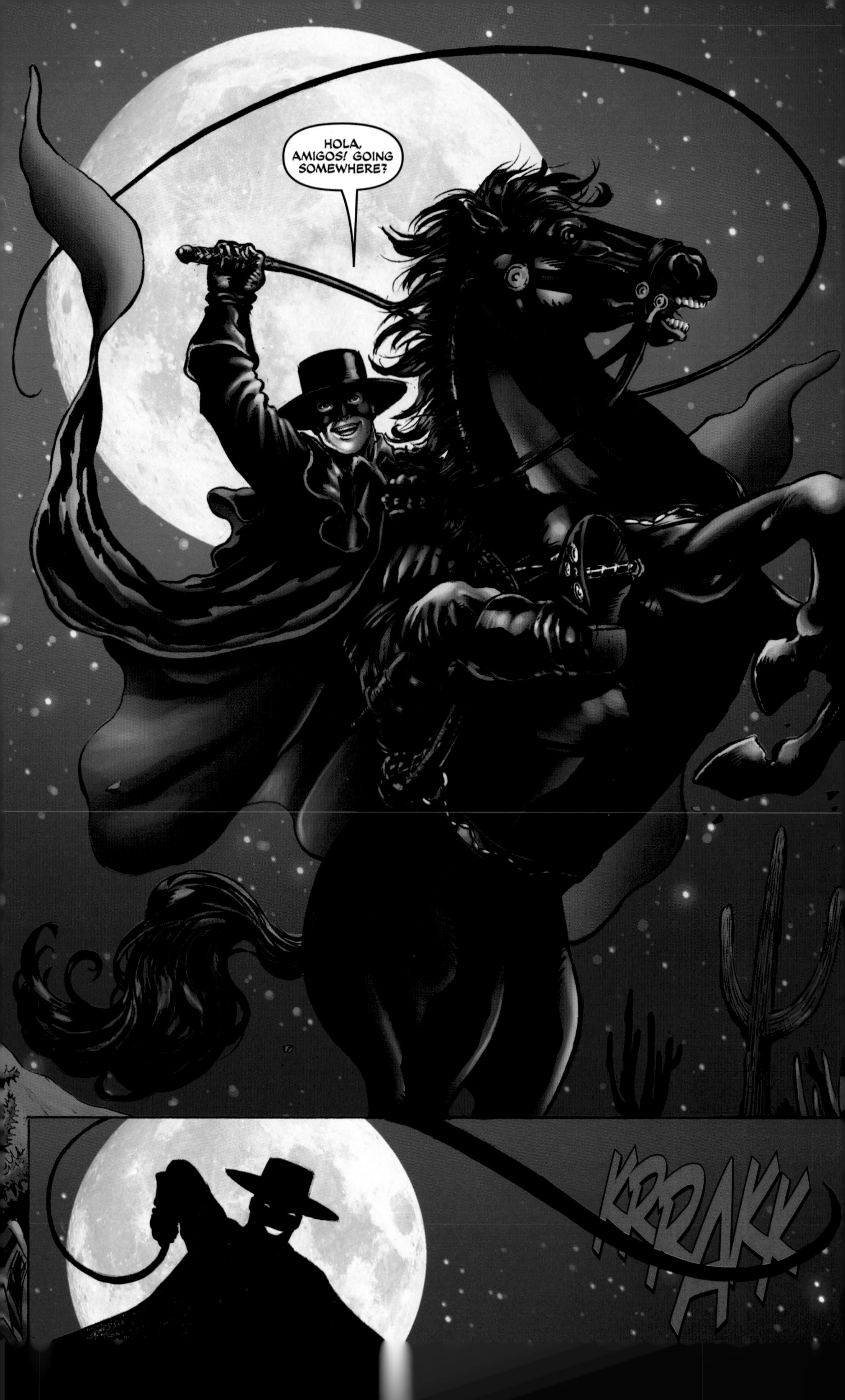
HOLA, AMIGOS! GOING SOMEWHERE?
KRRAKK

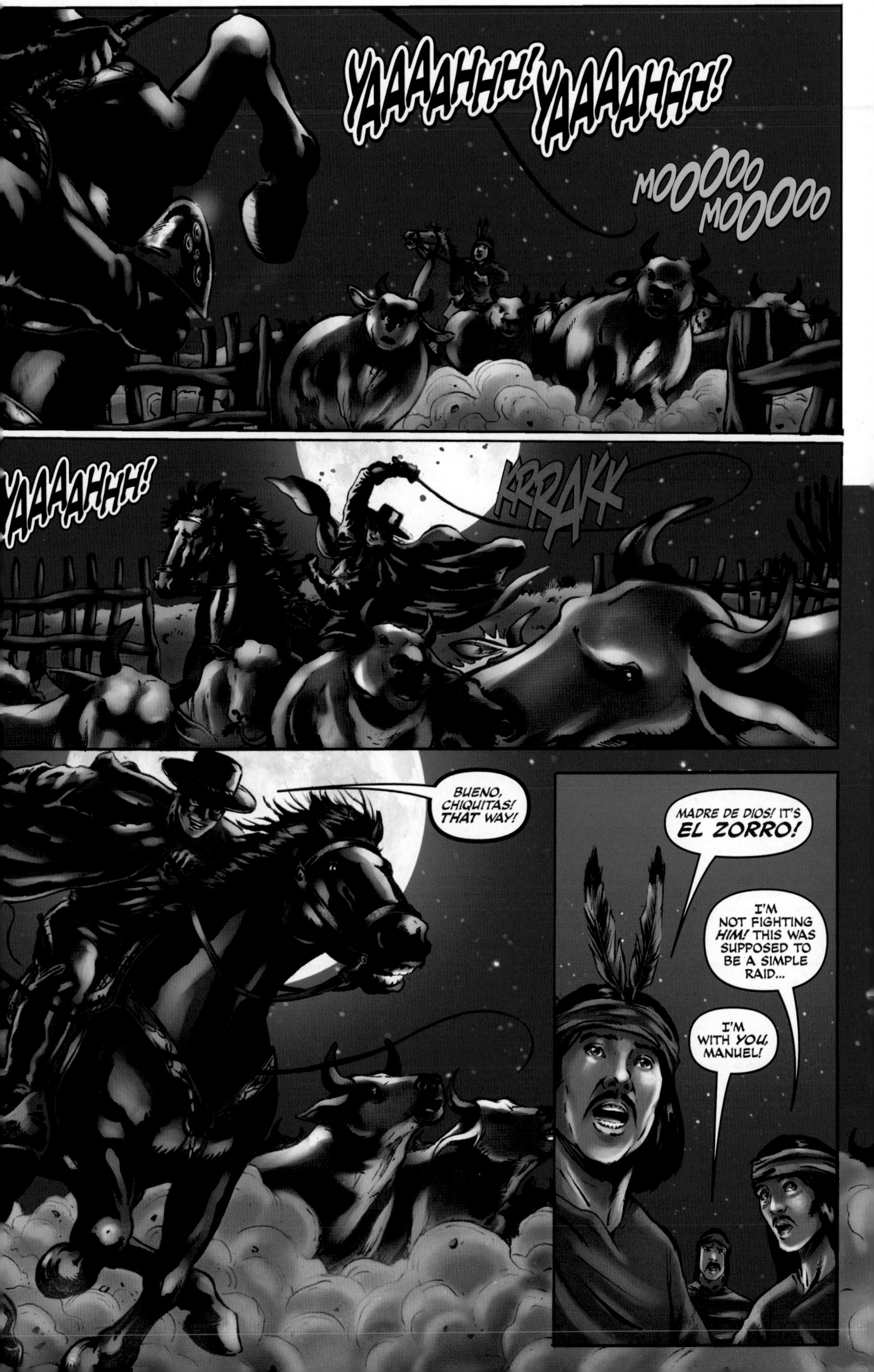

YAAAAHHH! YAAAAHHH!
MOOOOO MOOOOO
YAAAAHHH!
KRRAKK
BUENO, CHIQUITAS! THAT WAY!
MADRE DE DIOS! IT'S EL ZORRO!
I'M NOT FIGHTING HIM! THIS WAS SUPPOSED TO BE A SIMPLE RAID...
I'M WITH YOU, MANUEL!

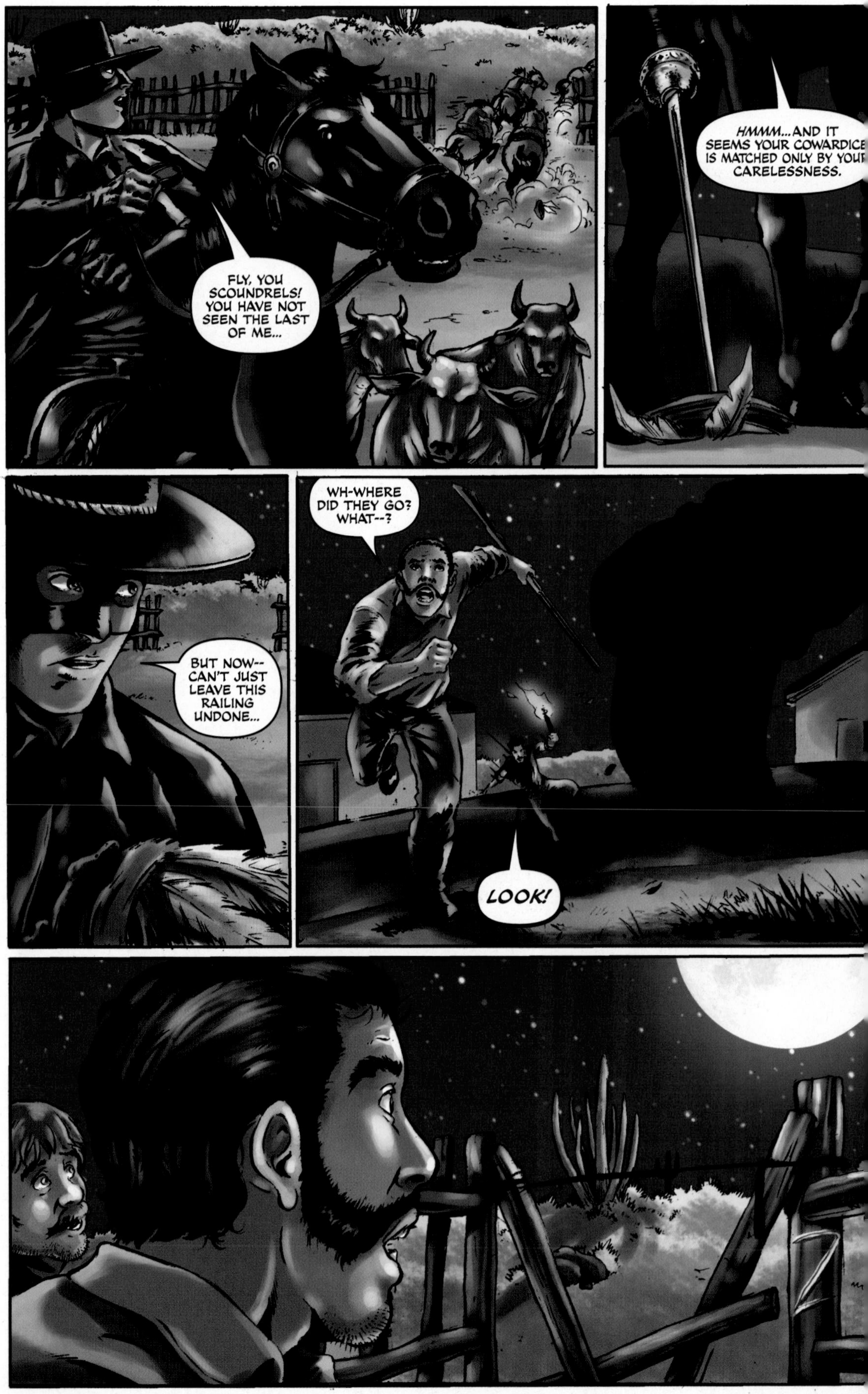
FLY, YOU SCOUNDRELS! YOU HAVE NOT SEEN THE LAST OF ME...
HMMM...AND IT SEEMS YOUR COWARDICE IS MATCHED ONLY BY YOUR CARELESSNESS.
BUT NOW-- CAN'T JUST LEAVE THIS RAILING UNDONE...
WH-WHERE DID THEY GO? WHAT--?
LOOK!

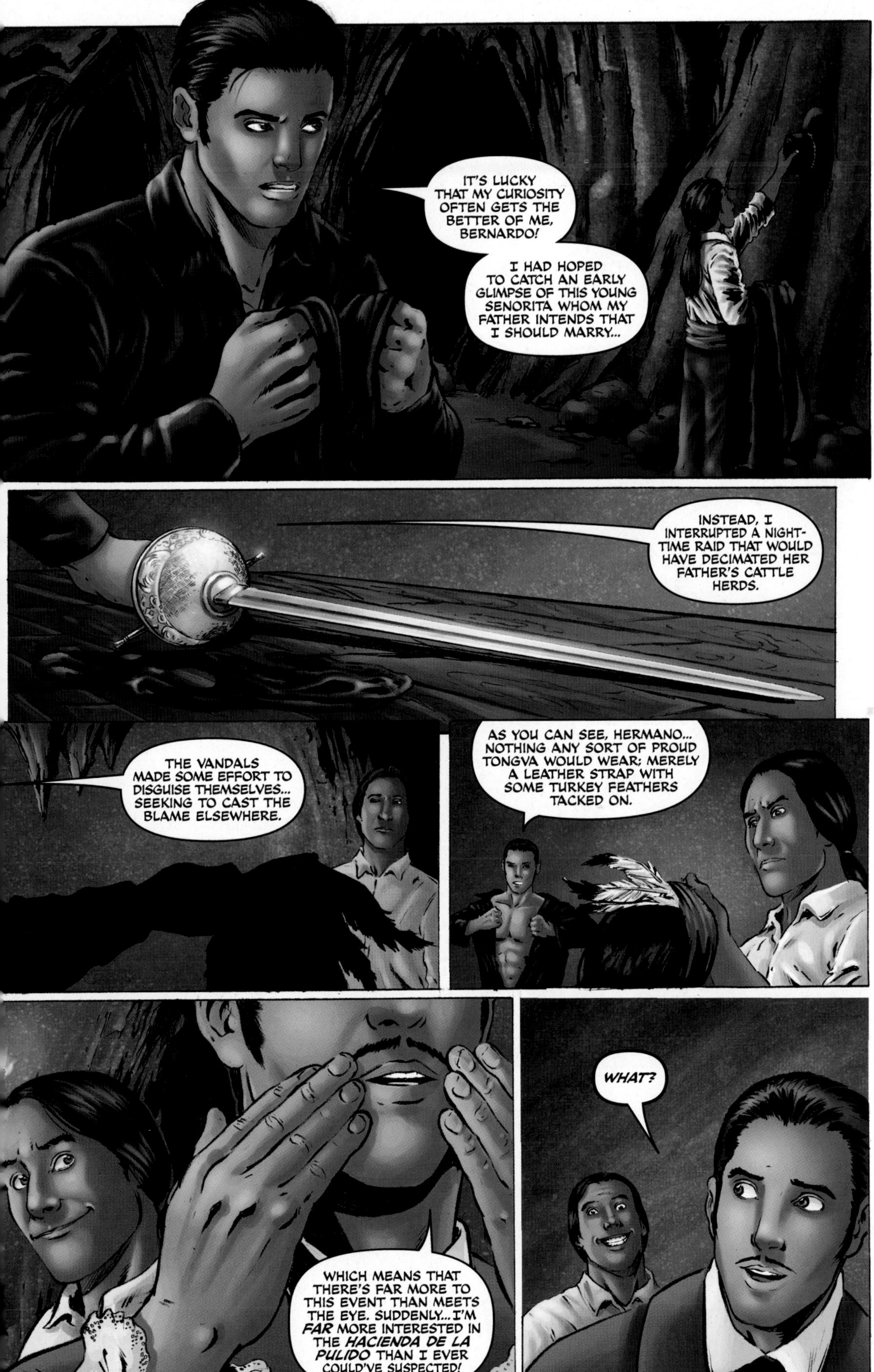
IT'S LUCKY THAT MY CURIOSITY OFTEN GETS THE BETTER OF ME, BERNARDO!
I HAD HOPED TO CATCH AN EARLY GLIMPSE OF THIS YOUNG SENORITA WHOM MY FATHER INTENDS THAT I SHOULD MARRY...
INSTEAD, I INTERRUPTED A NIGHT-TIME RAID THAT WOULD HAVE DECIMATED HER FATHER'S CATTLE HERDS.
THE VANDALS MADE SOME EFFORT TO DISGUISE THEMSELVES... SEEKING TO CAST THE BLAME ELSEWHERE.
AS YOU CAN SEE, HERMANO... NOTHING ANY SORT OF PROUD TONGVA WOULD WEAR; MERELY A LEATHER STRAP WITH SOME TURKEY FEATHERS TACKED ON.
WHICH MEANS THAT THERE'S FAR MORE TO THIS EVENT THAN MEETS THE EYE. SUDDENLY... I'M *FAR* MORE INTERESTED IN THE *HACIENDA DE LA PULIDO* THAN I EVER COULD'VE SUSPECTED!
WHAT?

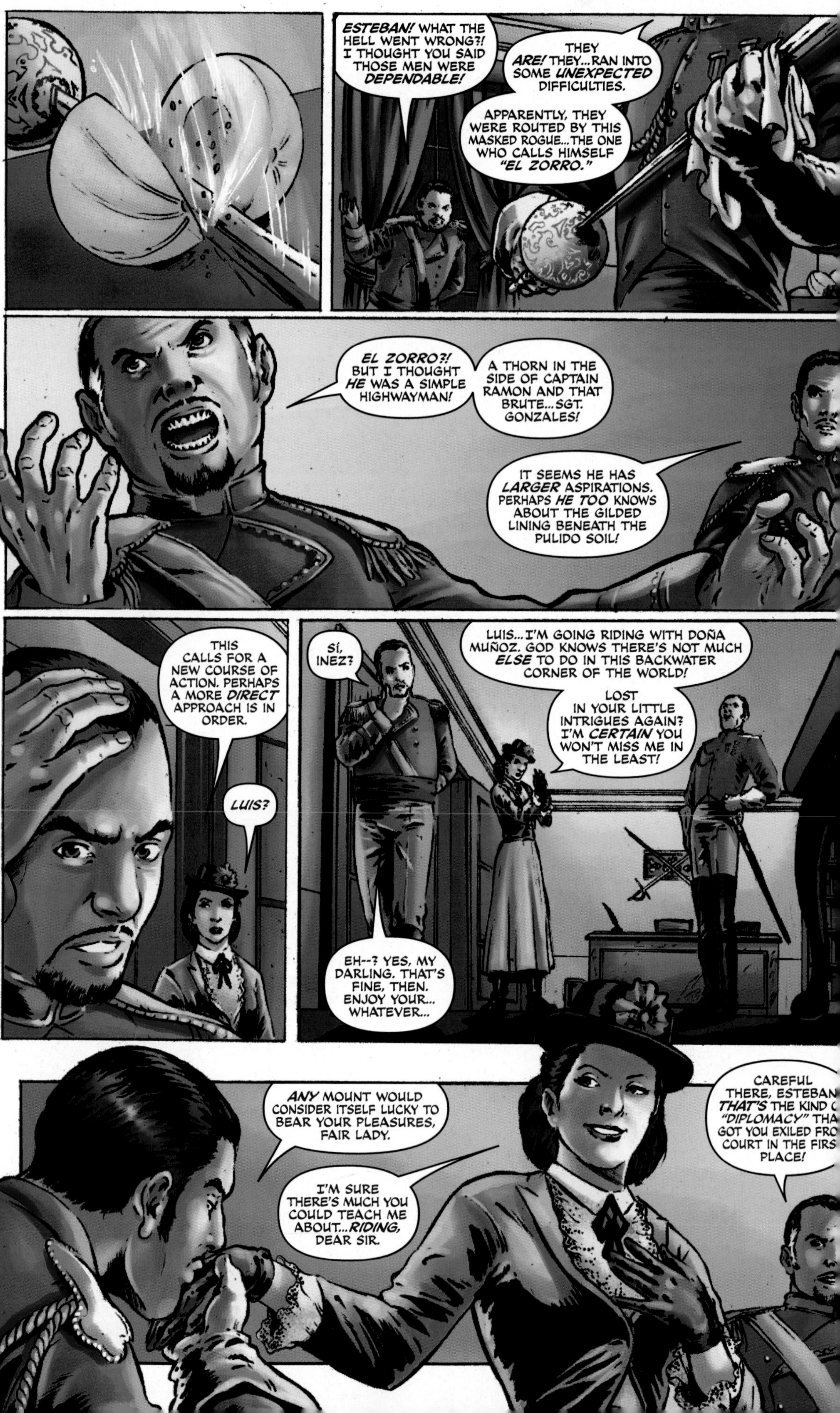
ESTEBAN! WHAT THE HELL WENT WRONG?! I THOUGHT YOU SAID THOSE MEN WERE DEPENDABLE!
THEY ARE! THEY...RAN INTO SOME UNEXPECTED DIFFICULTIES.
APPARENTLY, THEY WERE ROUTED BY THIS MASKED ROGUE...THE ONE WHO CALLS HIMSELF "EL ZORRO."
EL ZORRO?! BUT I THOUGHT HE WAS A SIMPLE HIGHWAYMAN!
A THORN IN THE SIDE OF CAPTAIN RAMON AND THAT BRUTE...SGT. GONZALES!
IT SEEMS HE HAS LARGER ASPIRATIONS. PERHAPS HE TOO KNOWS ABOUT THE GILDED LINING BENEATH THE PULIDO SOIL!
THIS CALLS FOR A NEW COURSE OF ACTION. PERHAPS A MORE DIRECT APPROACH IS IN ORDER.
LUIS?
SÍ, INEZ?
LUIS...I'M GOING RIDING WITH DOÑA MUÑOZ. GOD KNOWS THERE'S NOT MUCH ELSE TO DO IN THIS BACKWATER CORNER OF THE WORLD!
LOST IN YOUR LITTLE INTRIGUES AGAIN? I'M CERTAIN YOU WON'T MISS ME IN THE LEAST!
EH--? YES, MY DARLING. THAT'S FINE, THEN. ENJOY YOUR... WHATEVER...
ANY MOUNT WOULD CONSIDER ITSELF LUCKY TO BEAR YOUR PLEASURES, FAIR LADY.
I'M SURE THERE'S MUCH YOU COULD TEACH ME ABOUT...RIDING, DEAR SIR.
CAREFUL THERE, ESTEBAN THAT'S THE KIND "DIPLOMACY" THA GOT YOU EXILED FRO COURT IN THE FIRS PLACE!

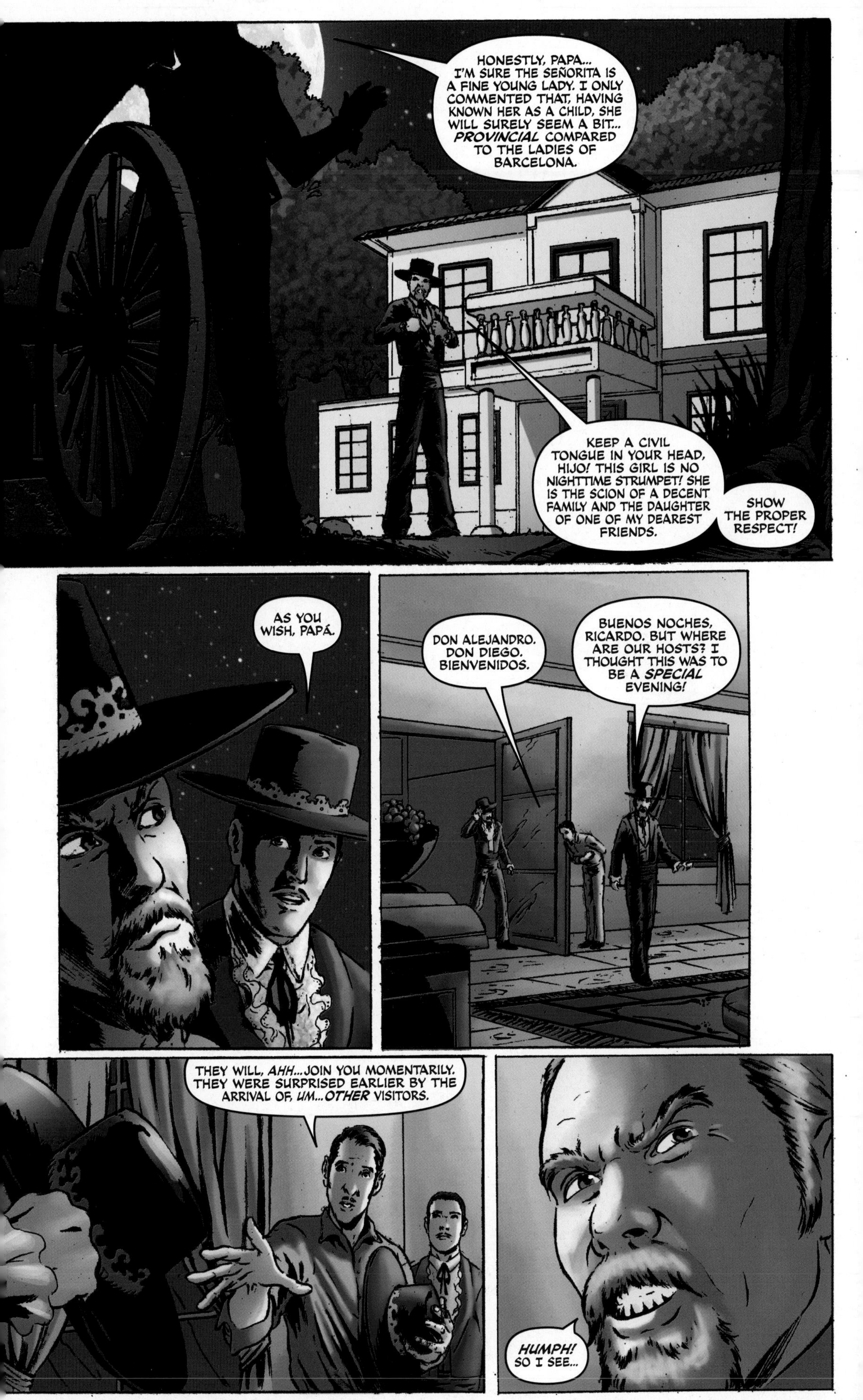

HONESTLY, PAPA... I'M SURE THE SEÑORITA IS A FINE YOUNG LADY. I ONLY COMMENTED THAT, HAVING KNOWN HER AS A CHILD, SHE WILL SURELY SEEM A BIT... *PROVINCIAL* COMPARED TO THE LADIES OF BARCELONA.
KEEP A CIVIL TONGUE IN YOUR HEAD, HIJO! THIS GIRL IS NO NIGHTTIME STRUMPET! SHE IS THE SCION OF A DECENT FAMILY AND THE DAUGHTER OF ONE OF MY DEAREST FRIENDS.
SHOW THE PROPER RESPECT!
AS YOU WISH, PAPÁ.
DON ALEJANDRO. DON DIEGO. BIENVENIDOS.
BUENOS NOCHES, RICARDO. BUT WHERE ARE OUR HOSTS? I THOUGHT THIS WAS TO BE A *SPECIAL* EVENING!
THEY WILL, *AHH*...JOIN YOU MOMENTARILY. THEY WERE SURPRISED EARLIER BY THE ARRIVAL OF, *UM*...*OTHER* VISITORS.
HUMPH! SO I SEE...

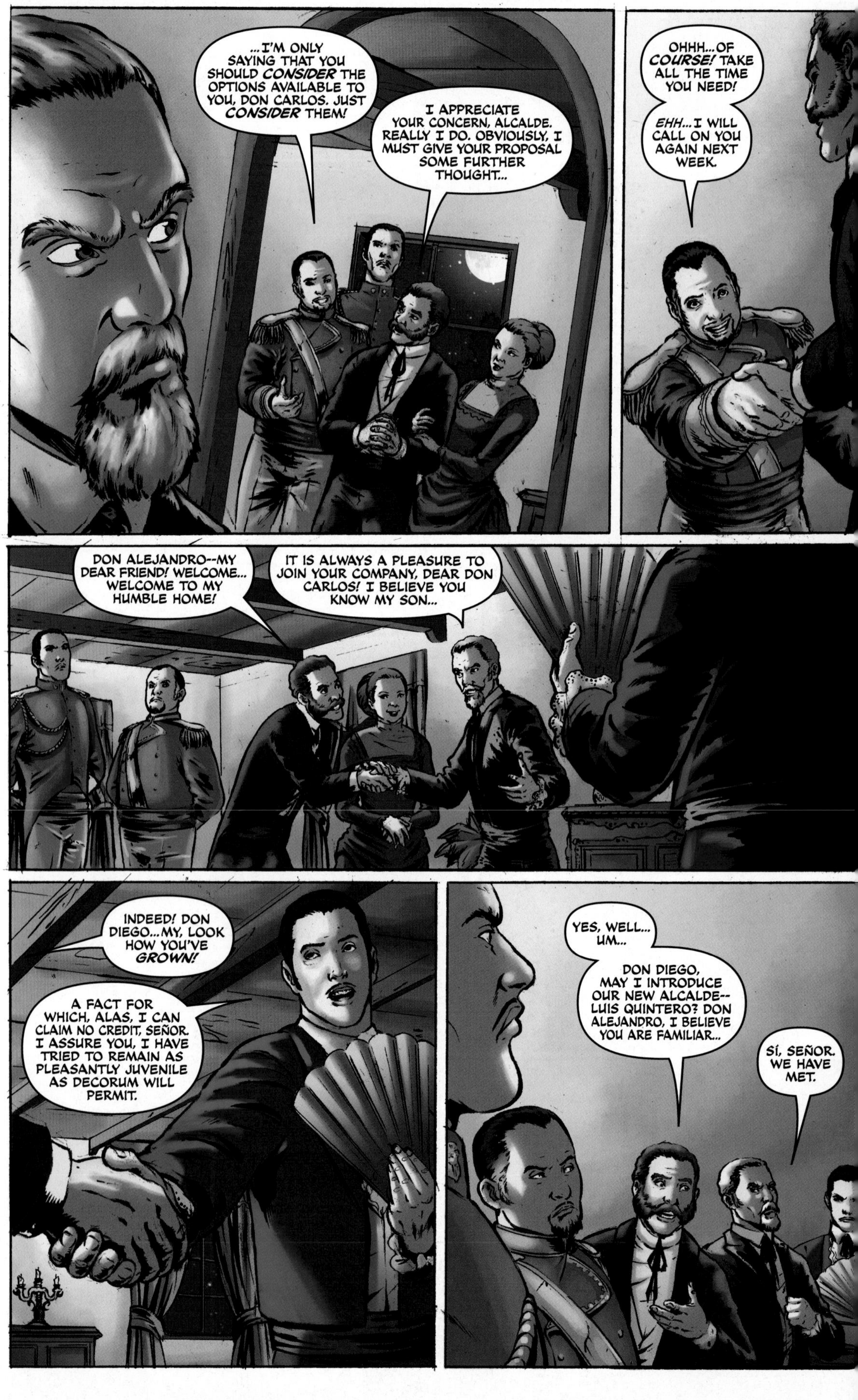
...I'M ONLY SAYING THAT YOU SHOULD CONSIDER THE OPTIONS AVAILABLE TO YOU, DON CARLOS. JUST CONSIDER THEM!
I APPRECIATE YOUR CONCERN, ALCALDE. REALLY I DO. OBVIOUSLY, I MUST GIVE YOUR PROPOSAL SOME FURTHER THOUGHT...
OHHH...OF COURSE! TAKE ALL THE TIME YOU NEED!
EHH...I WILL CALL ON YOU AGAIN NEXT WEEK.
DON ALEJANDRO--MY DEAR FRIEND! WELCOME... WELCOME TO MY HUMBLE HOME!
IT IS ALWAYS A PLEASURE TO JOIN YOUR COMPANY, DEAR DON CARLOS! I BELIEVE YOU KNOW MY SON...
INDEED! DON DIEGO...MY, LOOK HOW YOU'VE GROWN!
A FACT FOR WHICH, ALAS, I CAN CLAIM NO CREDIT, SEÑOR. I ASSURE YOU, I HAVE TRIED TO REMAIN AS PLEASANTLY JUVENILE AS DECORUM WILL PERMIT.
YES, WELL... UM...
DON DIEGO, MAY I INTRODUCE OUR NEW ALCALDE-- LUIS QUINTERO? DON ALEJANDRO, I BELIEVE YOU ARE FAMILIAR...
SÍ, SEÑOR. WE HAVE MET.

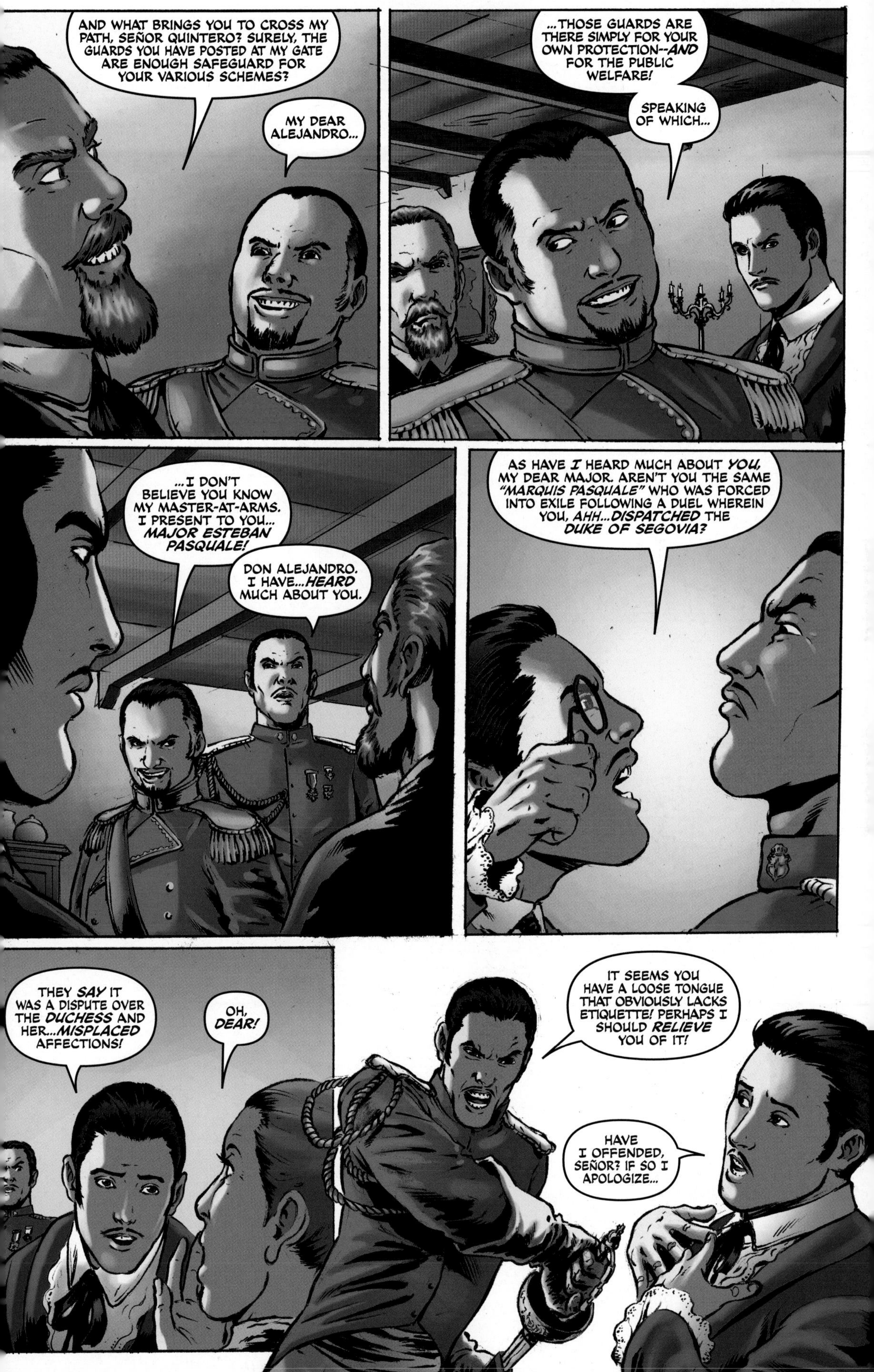
AND WHAT BRINGS YOU TO CROSS MY PATH, SEÑOR QUINTERO? SURELY, THE GUARDS YOU HAVE POSTED AT MY GATE ARE ENOUGH SAFEGUARD FOR YOUR VARIOUS SCHEMES?
MY DEAR ALEJANDRO...
...THOSE GUARDS ARE THERE SIMPLY FOR YOUR OWN PROTECTION--AND FOR THE PUBLIC WELFARE!
SPEAKING OF WHICH...
...I DON'T BELIEVE YOU KNOW MY MASTER-AT-ARMS. I PRESENT TO YOU... MAJOR ESTEBAN PASQUALE!
DON ALEJANDRO. I HAVE...HEARD MUCH ABOUT YOU.
AS HAVE I HEARD MUCH ABOUT YOU, MY DEAR MAJOR. AREN'T YOU THE SAME "MARQUIS PASQUALE" WHO WAS FORCED INTO EXILE FOLLOWING A DUEL WHEREIN YOU, AHH...DISPATCHED THE DUKE OF SEGOVIA?
THEY SAY IT WAS A DISPUTE OVER THE DUCHESS AND HER...MISPLACED AFFECTIONS!
OH, DEAR!
IT SEEMS YOU HAVE A LOOSE TONGUE THAT OBVIOUSLY LACKS ETIQUETTE! PERHAPS I SHOULD RELIEVE YOU OF IT!
HAVE I OFFENDED, SEÑOR? IF SO I APOLOGIZE...

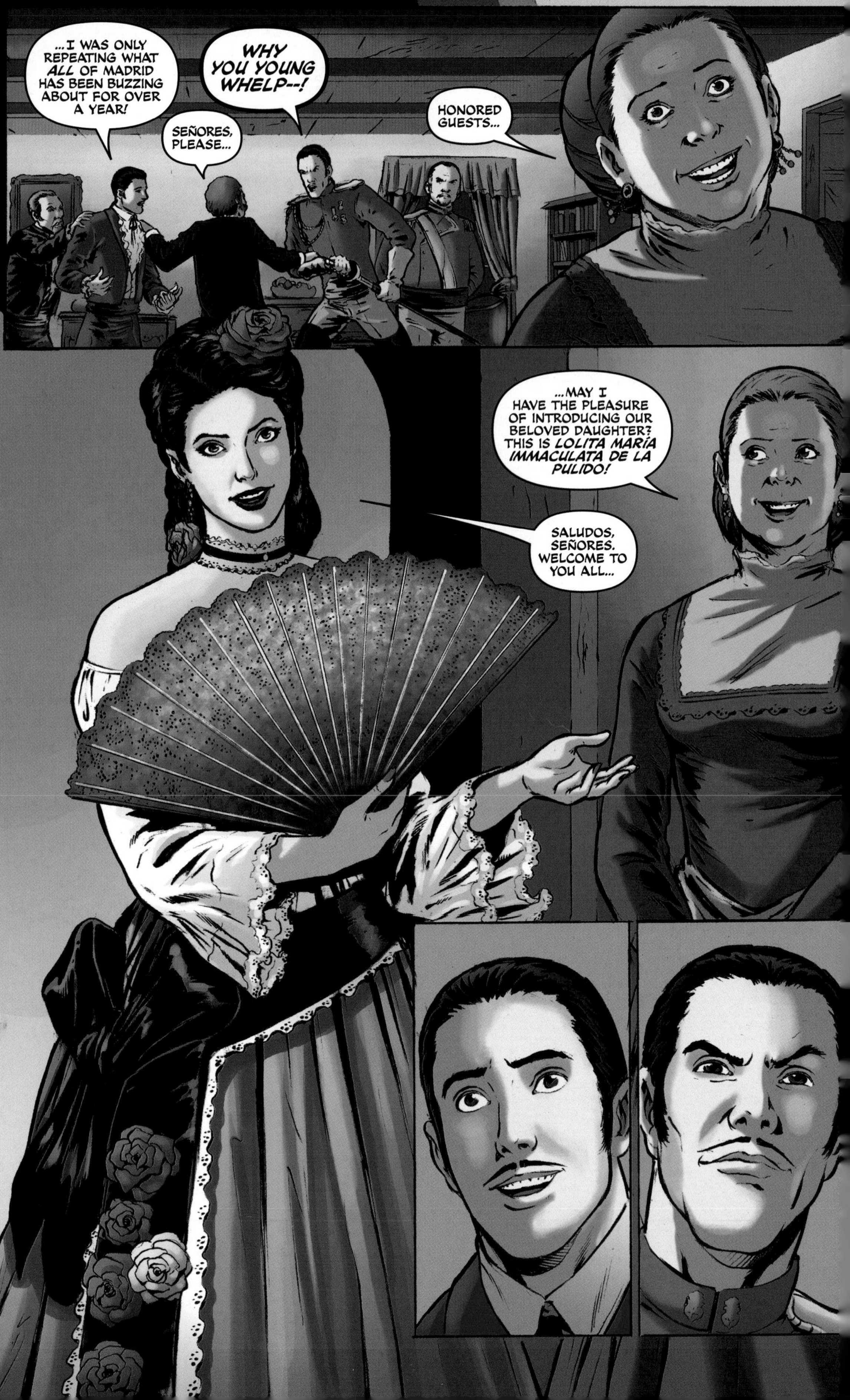
...I WAS ONLY REPEATING WHAT ALL OF MADRID HAS BEEN BUZZING ABOUT FOR OVER A YEAR!
WHY YOU YOUNG WHELP--!
SEÑORES, PLEASE...
HONORED GUESTS...
...MAY I HAVE THE PLEASURE OF INTRODUCING OUR BELOVED DAUGHTER? THIS IS LOLITA MARÍA IMMACULATA DE LA PULIDO!
SALUDOS, SEÑORES. WELCOME TO YOU ALL...

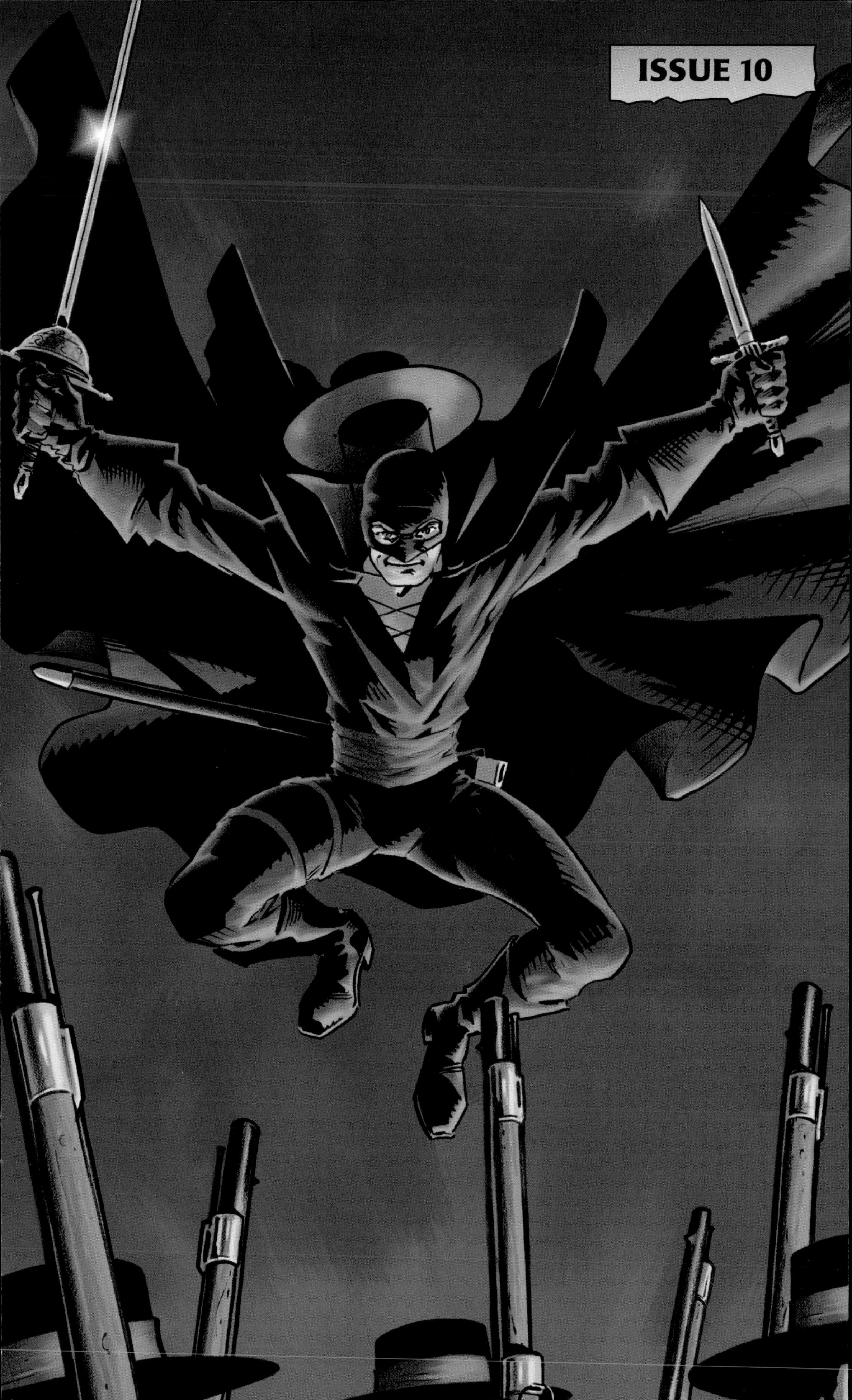
ISSUE 10

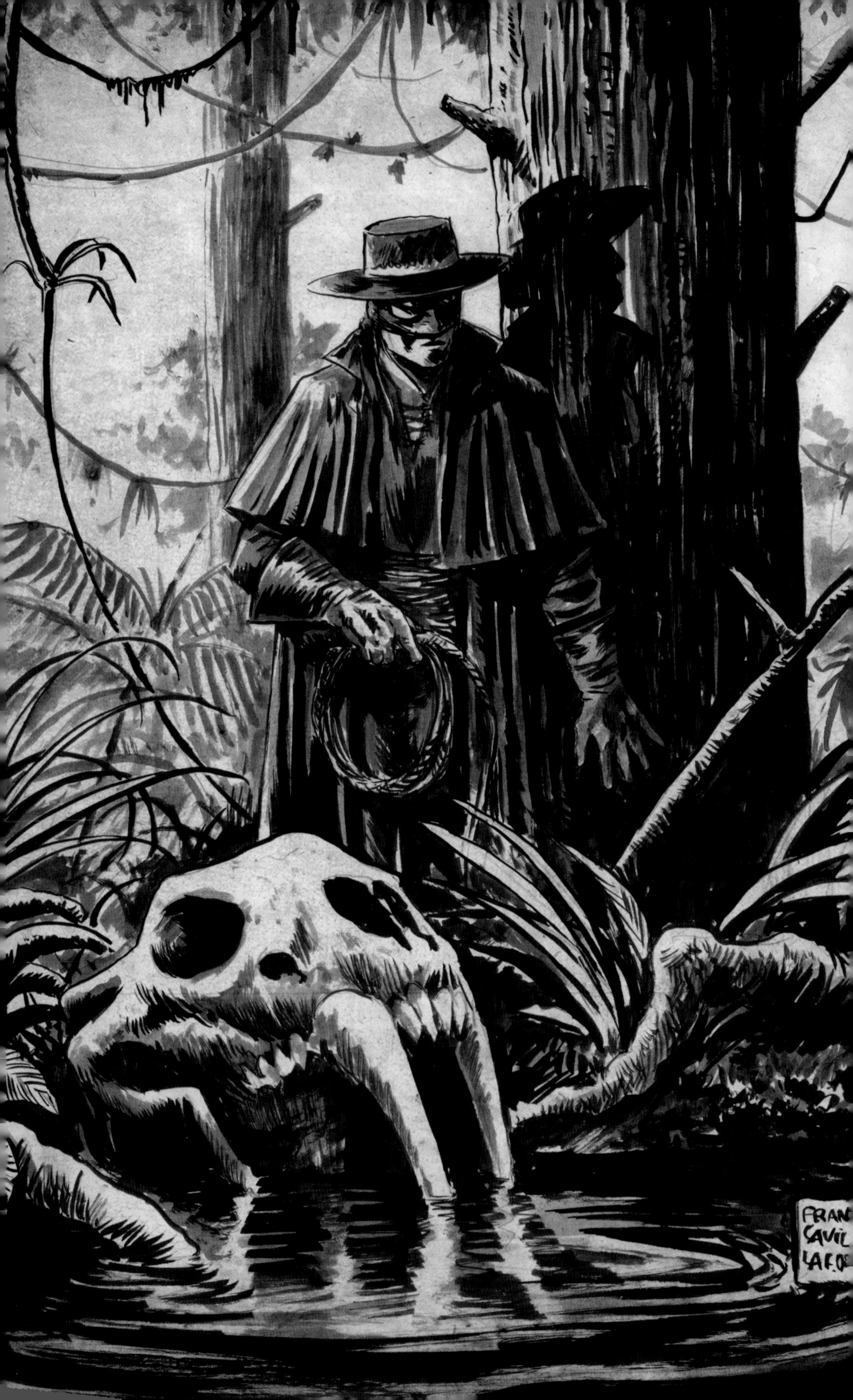
FRAN
ÇAVIL
LA F.0

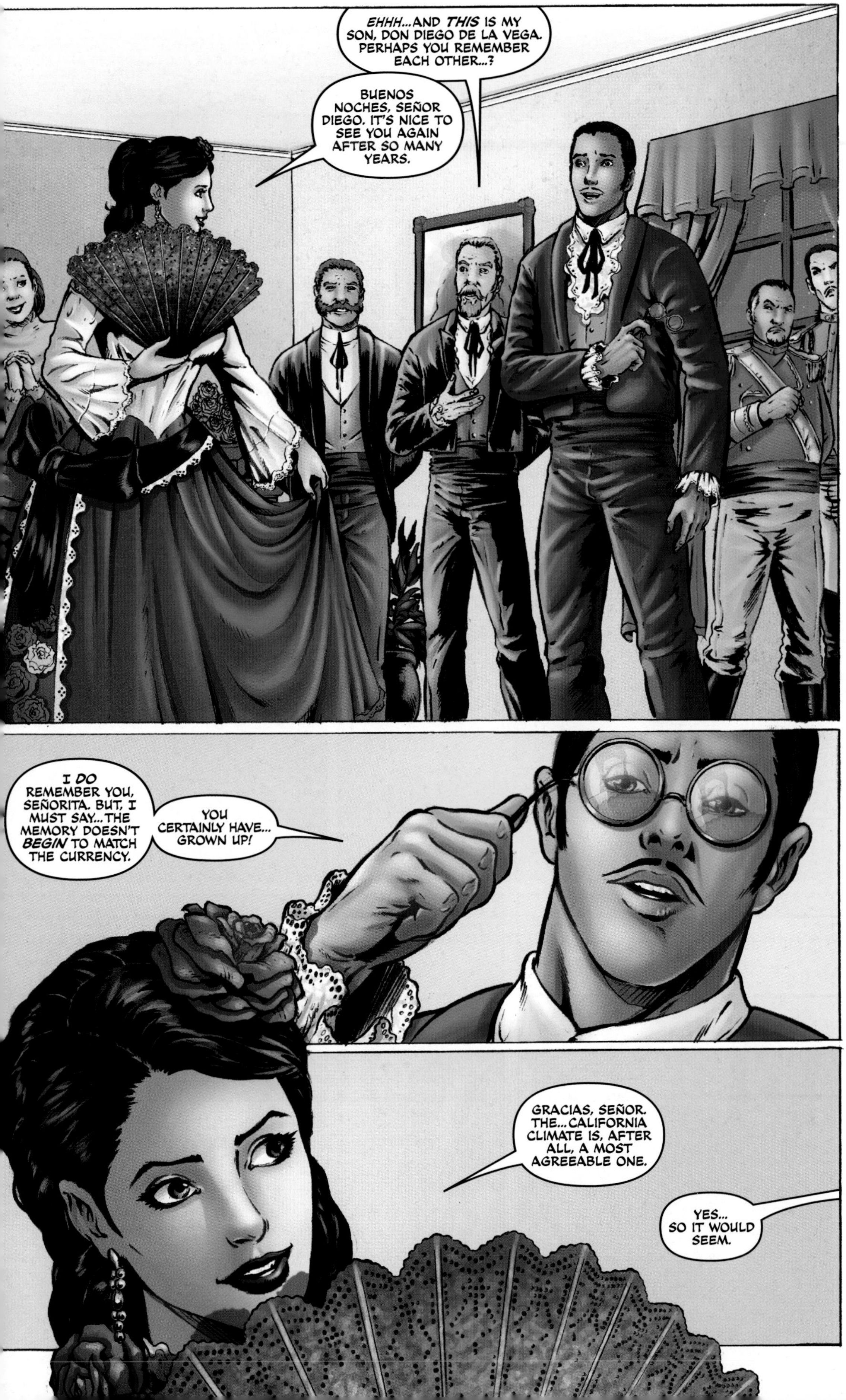
EHHH...AND THIS IS MY SON, DON DIEGO DE LA VEGA. PERHAPS YOU REMEMBER EACH OTHER...?
BUENOS NOCHES, SEÑOR DIEGO. IT'S NICE TO SEE YOU AGAIN AFTER SO MANY YEARS.
I DO REMEMBER YOU, SEÑORITA. BUT, I MUST SAY...THE MEMORY DOESN'T BEGIN TO MATCH THE CURRENCY.
YOU CERTAINLY HAVE... GROWN UP!
GRACIAS, SEÑOR. THE...CALIFORNIA CLIMATE IS, AFTER ALL, A MOST AGREEABLE ONE.
YES... SO IT WOULD SEEM.

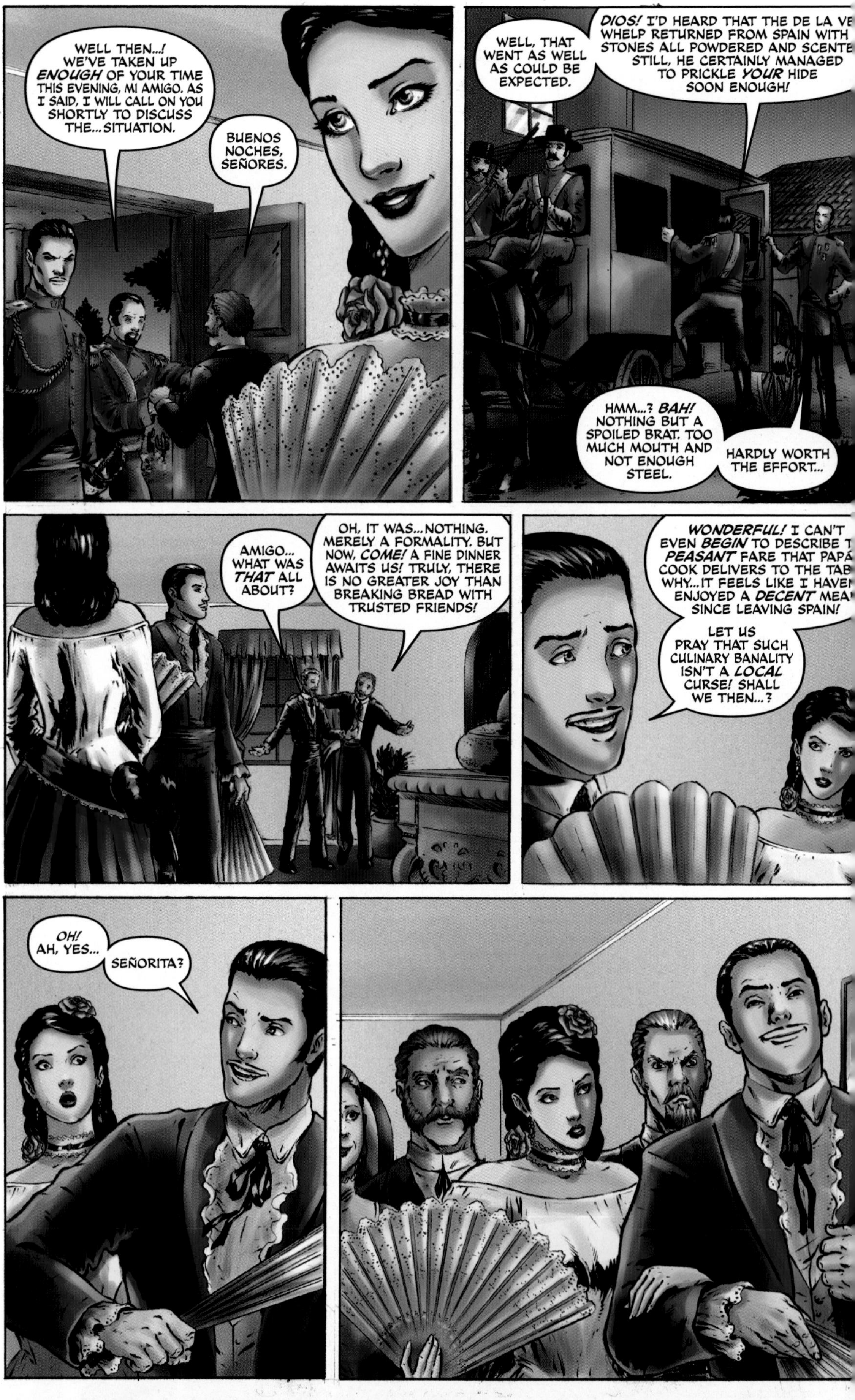
WELL THEN...! WE'VE TAKEN UP ENOUGH OF YOUR TIME THIS EVENING, MI AMIGO. AS I SAID, I WILL CALL ON YOU SHORTLY TO DISCUSS THE...SITUATION.
BUENOS NOCHES, SEÑORES.
WELL, THAT WENT AS WELL AS COULD BE EXPECTED.
DIOS! I'D HEARD THAT THE DE LA VE WHELP RETURNED FROM SPAIN WITH STONES ALL POWDERED AND SCENTE STILL, HE CERTAINLY MANAGED TO PRICKLE YOUR HIDE SOON ENOUGH!
HMM...? BAH! NOTHING BUT A SPOILED BRAT. TOO MUCH MOUTH AND NOT ENOUGH STEEL.
HARDLY WORTH THE EFFORT...
AMIGO... WHAT WAS THAT ALL ABOUT?
OH, IT WAS...NOTHING. MERELY A FORMALITY. BUT NOW, COME! A FINE DINNER AWAITS US! TRULY, THERE IS NO GREATER JOY THAN BREAKING BREAD WITH TRUSTED FRIENDS!
WONDERFUL! I CAN'T EVEN BEGIN TO DESCRIBE T PEASANT FARE THAT PAPÁ COOK DELIVERS TO THE TAB WHY...IT FEELS LIKE I HAVEN ENJOYED A DECENT MEA SINCE LEAVING SPAIN!
LET US PRAY THAT SUCH CULINARY BANALITY ISN'T A LOCAL CURSE! SHALL WE THEN...?
OH! AH, YES...
SEÑORITA?

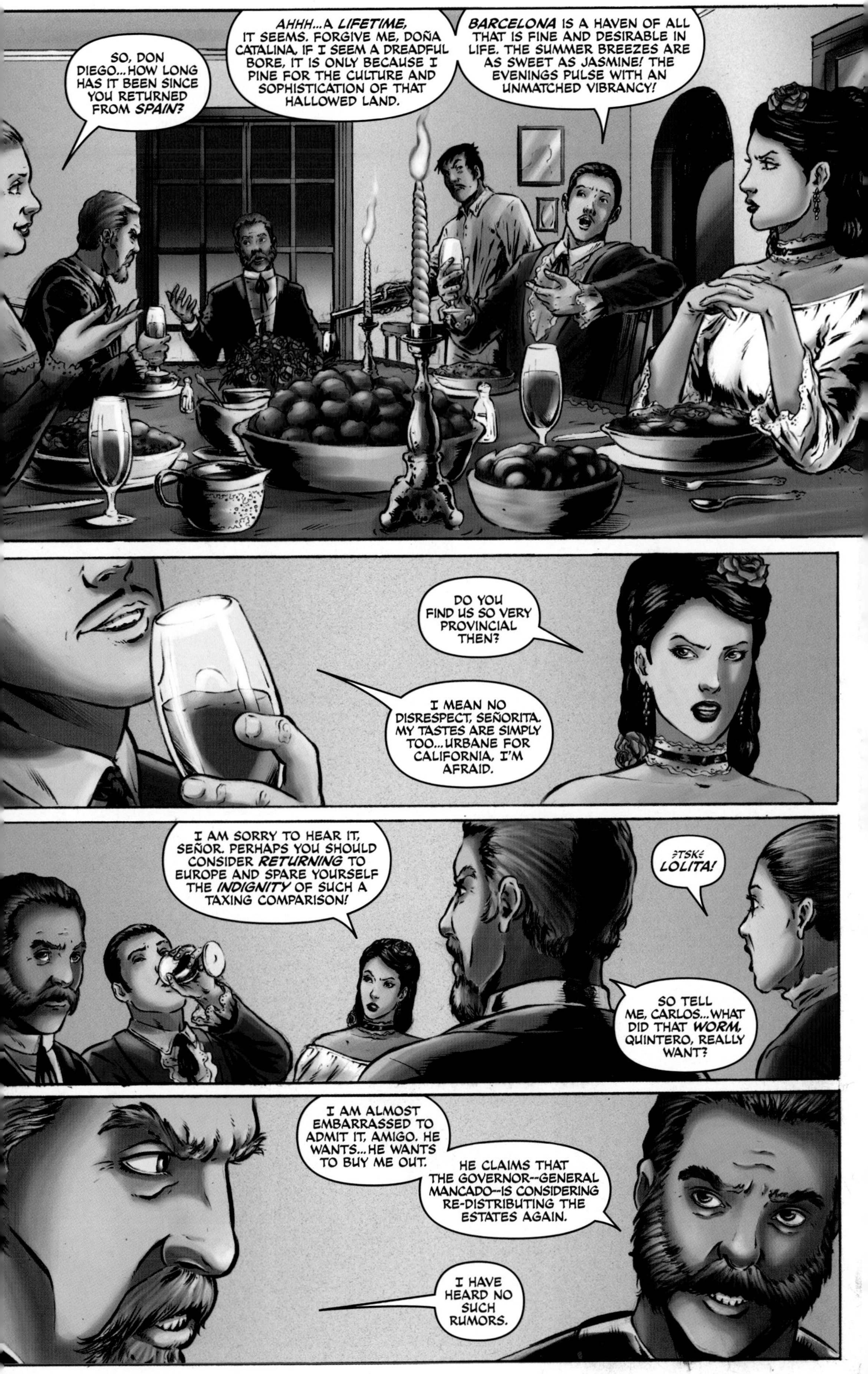

SO, DON DIEGO...HOW LONG HAS IT BEEN SINCE YOU RETURNED FROM SPAIN?
AHHH...A LIFETIME, IT SEEMS. FORGIVE ME, DOÑA CATALINA, IF I SEEM A DREADFUL BORE, IT IS ONLY BECAUSE I PINE FOR THE CULTURE AND SOPHISTICATION OF THAT HALLOWED LAND.
BARCELONA IS A HAVEN OF ALL THAT IS FINE AND DESIRABLE IN LIFE. THE SUMMER BREEZES ARE AS SWEET AS JASMINE! THE EVENINGS PULSE WITH AN UNMATCHED VIBRANCY!
DO YOU FIND US SO VERY PROVINCIAL THEN?
I MEAN NO DISRESPECT, SEÑORITA. MY TASTES ARE SIMPLY TOO...URBANE FOR CALIFORNIA, I'M AFRAID.
I AM SORRY TO HEAR IT, SEÑOR. PERHAPS YOU SHOULD CONSIDER RETURNING TO EUROPE AND SPARE YOURSELF THE INDIGNITY OF SUCH A TAXING COMPARISON!
TSK LOLITA!
SO TELL ME, CARLOS...WHAT DID THAT WORM, QUINTERO, REALLY WANT?
I AM ALMOST EMBARRASSED TO ADMIT IT, AMIGO. HE WANTS...HE WANTS TO BUY ME OUT.
HE CLAIMS THAT THE GOVERNOR--GENERAL MANCADO--IS CONSIDERING RE-DISTRIBUTING THE ESTATES AGAIN.
I HAVE HEARD NO SUCH RUMORS.

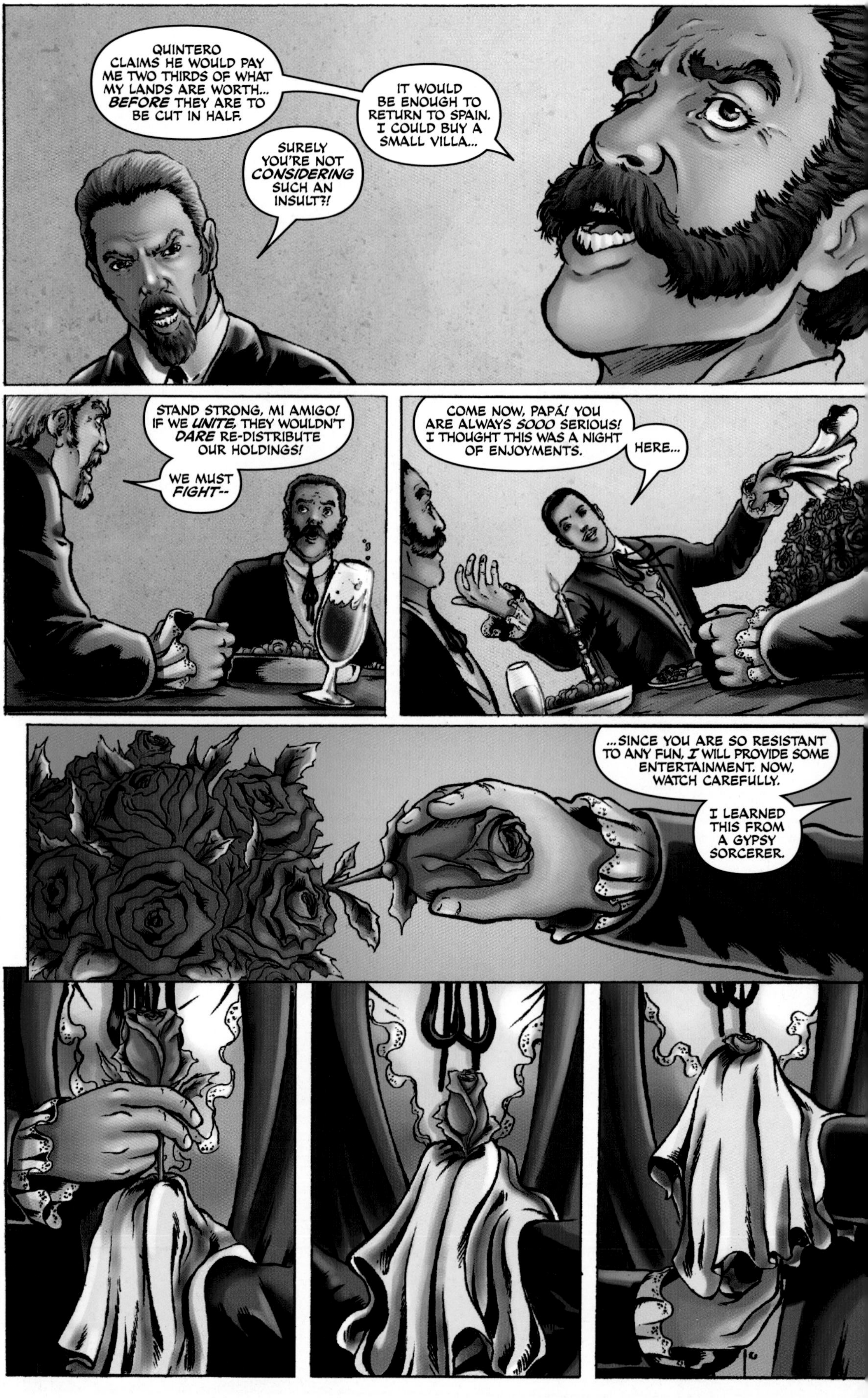
QUINTERO CLAIMS HE WOULD PAY ME TWO THIRDS OF WHAT MY LANDS ARE WORTH... BEFORE THEY ARE TO BE CUT IN HALF.
SURELY YOU'RE NOT CONSIDERING SUCH AN INSULT?!
IT WOULD BE ENOUGH TO RETURN TO SPAIN. I COULD BUY A SMALL VILLA...
STAND STRONG, MI AMIGO! IF WE UNITE, THEY WOULDN'T DARE RE-DISTRIBUTE OUR HOLDINGS!
WE MUST FIGHT--
COME NOW, PAPÁ! YOU ARE ALWAYS SOOO SERIOUS! I THOUGHT THIS WAS A NIGHT OF ENJOYMENTS.
HERE...
...SINCE YOU ARE SO RESISTANT TO ANY FUN, I WILL PROVIDE SOME ENTERTAINMENT. NOW, WATCH CAREFULLY.
I LEARNED THIS FROM A GYPSY SORCERER.

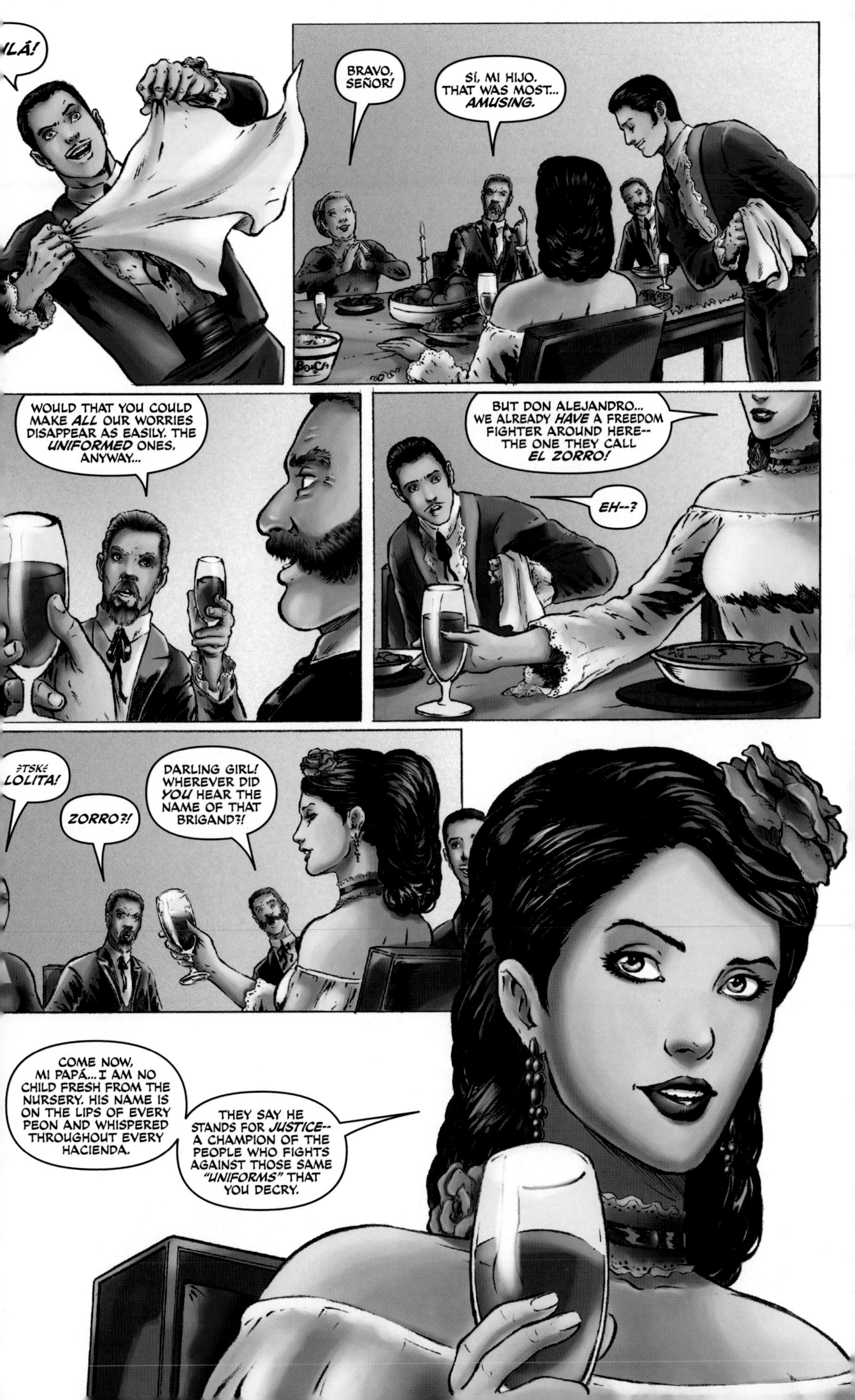

LÁ!
BRAVO, SEÑOR!
SÍ, MI HIJO. THAT WAS MOST... AMUSING.
WOULD THAT YOU COULD MAKE ALL OUR WORRIES DISAPPEAR AS EASILY. THE UNIFORMED ONES, ANYWAY...
BUT DON ALEJANDRO... WE ALREADY HAVE A FREEDOM FIGHTER AROUND HERE-- THE ONE THEY CALL EL ZORRO!
EH--?
TSK LOLITA!
ZORRO?!
DARLING GIRL! WHEREVER DID YOU HEAR THE NAME OF THAT BRIGAND?!
COME NOW, MI PAPÁ... I AM NO CHILD FRESH FROM THE NURSERY. HIS NAME IS ON THE LIPS OF EVERY PEON AND WHISPERED THROUGHOUT EVERY HACIENDA.
THEY SAY HE STANDS FOR JUSTICE-- A CHAMPION OF THE PEOPLE WHO FIGHTS AGAINST THOSE SAME "UNIFORMS" THAT YOU DECRY.

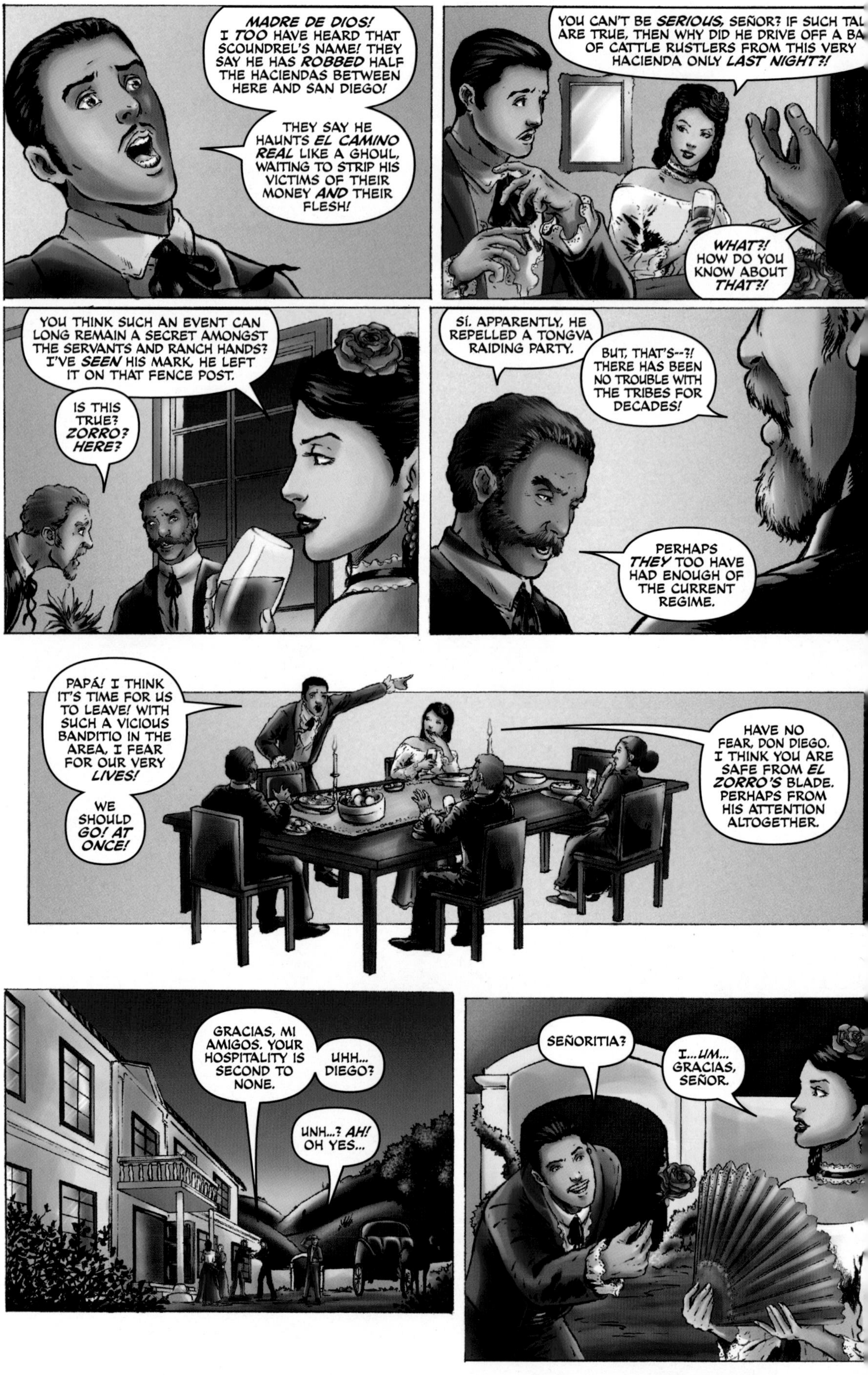
MADRE DE DIOS! I TOO HAVE HEARD THAT SCOUNDREL'S NAME! THEY SAY HE HAS ROBBED HALF THE HACIENDAS BETWEEN HERE AND SAN DIEGO!
THEY SAY HE HAUNTS EL CAMINO REAL LIKE A GHOUL, WAITING TO STRIP HIS VICTIMS OF THEIR MONEY AND THEIR FLESH!
YOU CAN'T BE SERIOUS, SEÑOR? IF SUCH TAL ARE TRUE, THEN WHY DID HE DRIVE OFF A BA OF CATTLE RUSTLERS FROM THIS VERY HACIENDA ONLY LAST NIGHT?!
WHAT?! HOW DO YOU KNOW ABOUT THAT?!
YOU THINK SUCH AN EVENT CAN LONG REMAIN A SECRET AMONGST THE SERVANTS AND RANCH HANDS? I'VE SEEN HIS MARK. HE LEFT IT ON THAT FENCE POST.
IS THIS TRUE? ZORRO? HERE?
SÍ. APPARENTLY, HE REPELLED A TONGVA RAIDING PARTY.
BUT, THAT'S--?! THERE HAS BEEN NO TROUBLE WITH THE TRIBES FOR DECADES!
PERHAPS THEY TOO HAVE HAD ENOUGH OF THE CURRENT REGIME.
PAPÁ! I THINK IT'S TIME FOR US TO LEAVE! WITH SUCH A VICIOUS BANDITIO IN THE AREA, I FEAR FOR OUR VERY LIVES!
WE SHOULD GO! AT ONCE!
HAVE NO FEAR, DON DIEGO. I THINK YOU ARE SAFE FROM EL ZORRO'S BLADE. PERHAPS FROM HIS ATTENTION ALTOGETHER.
GRACIAS, MI AMIGOS. YOUR HOSPITALITY IS SECOND TO NONE.
UHH... DIEGO?
UNH...? AH! OH YES...
SEÑORITIA?
I...UM... GRACIAS, SEÑOR.

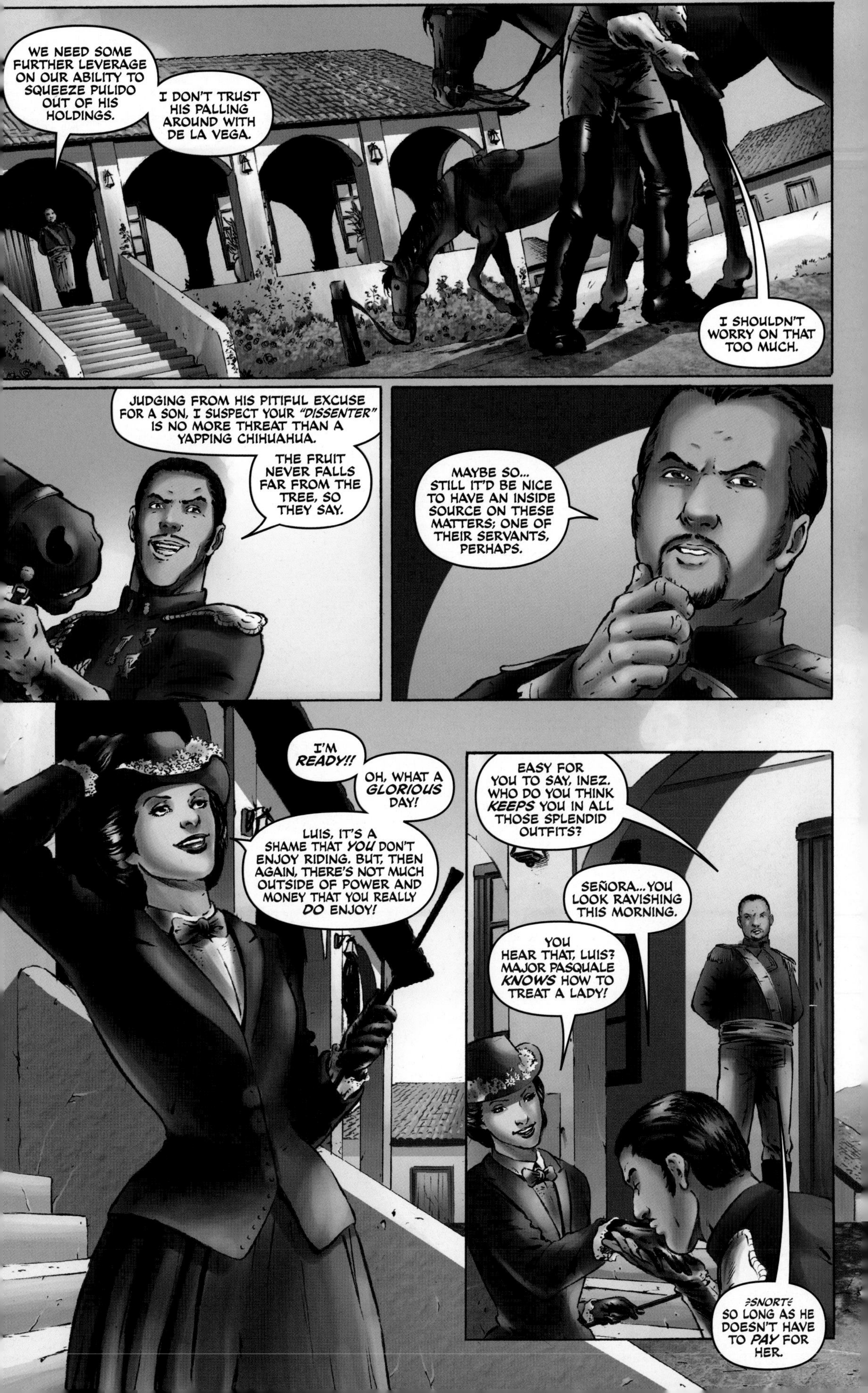
WE NEED SOME FURTHER LEVERAGE ON OUR ABILITY TO SQUEEZE PULIDO OUT OF HIS HOLDINGS.
I DON'T TRUST HIS PALLING AROUND WITH DE LA VEGA.
I SHOULDN'T WORRY ON THAT TOO MUCH.
JUDGING FROM HIS PITIFUL EXCUSE FOR A SON, I SUSPECT YOUR "DISSENTER" IS NO MORE THREAT THAN A YAPPING CHIHUAHUA.
THE FRUIT NEVER FALLS FAR FROM THE TREE, SO THEY SAY.
MAYBE SO... STILL IT'D BE NICE TO HAVE AN INSIDE SOURCE ON THESE MATTERS; ONE OF THEIR SERVANTS, PERHAPS.
I'M READY!!
OH, WHAT A GLORIOUS DAY!
LUIS, IT'S A SHAME THAT YOU DON'T ENJOY RIDING. BUT, THEN AGAIN, THERE'S NOT MUCH OUTSIDE OF POWER AND MONEY THAT YOU REALLY DO ENJOY!
EASY FOR YOU TO SAY, INEZ. WHO DO YOU THINK KEEPS YOU IN ALL THOSE SPLENDID OUTFITS?
SEÑORA...YOU LOOK RAVISHING THIS MORNING.
YOU HEAR THAT, LUIS? MAJOR PASQUALE KNOWS HOW TO TREAT A LADY!
SNORT
SO LONG AS HE DOESN'T HAVE TO PAY FOR HER.

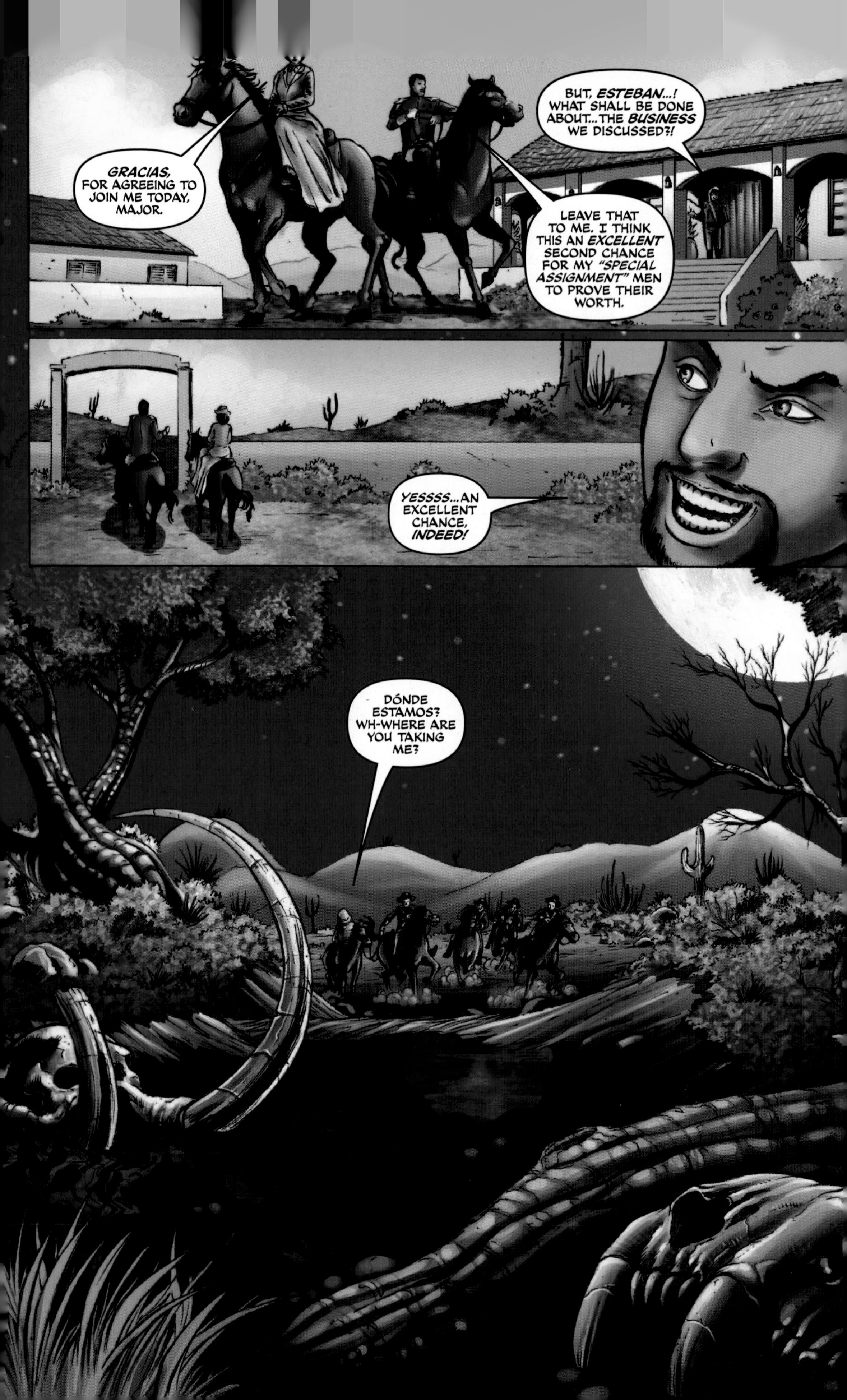
GRACIAS, FOR AGREEING TO JOIN ME TODAY, MAJOR.
BUT, ESTEBAN...! WHAT SHALL BE DONE ABOUT...THE BUSINESS WE DISCUSSED?!
LEAVE THAT TO ME. I THINK THIS AN EXCELLENT SECOND CHANCE FOR MY "SPECIAL ASSIGNMENT" MEN TO PROVE THEIR WORTH.
YESSSS...AN EXCELLENT CHANCE, INDEED!
¿DÓNDE ESTAMOS? WH-WHERE ARE YOU TAKING ME?

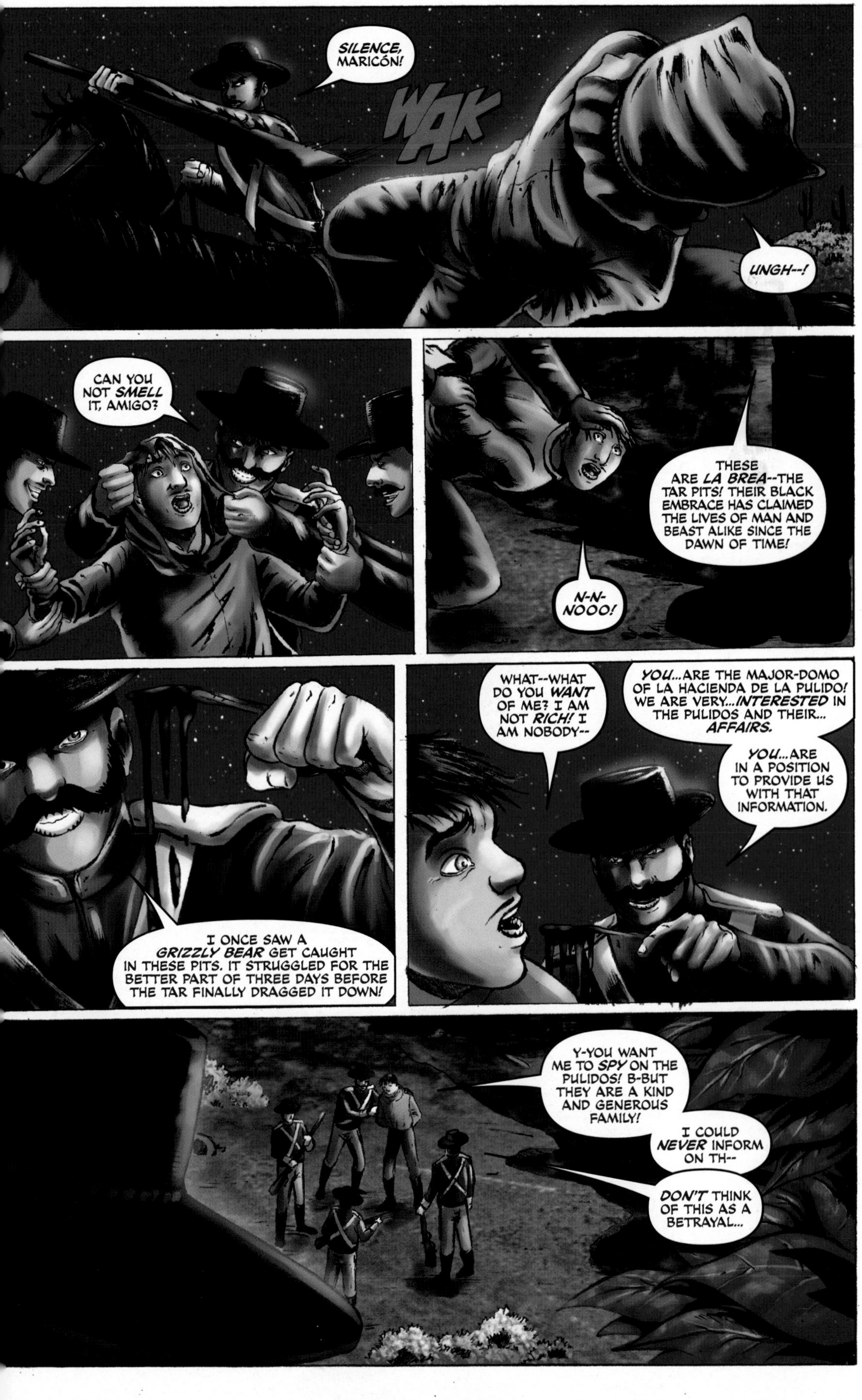
SILENCE, MARICÓN!
WAK
UNGH--!
CAN YOU NOT SMELL IT, AMIGO?
THESE ARE LA BREA--THE TAR PITS! THEIR BLACK EMBRACE HAS CLAIMED THE LIVES OF MAN AND BEAST ALIKE SINCE THE DAWN OF TIME!
N-N-NOOO!
I ONCE SAW A GRIZZLY BEAR GET CAUGHT IN THESE PITS. IT STRUGGLED FOR THE BETTER PART OF THREE DAYS BEFORE THE TAR FINALLY DRAGGED IT DOWN!
WHAT--WHAT DO YOU WANT OF ME? I AM NOT RICH! I AM NOBODY--
YOU...ARE THE MAJOR-DOMO OF LA HACIENDA DE LA PULIDO! WE ARE VERY...INTERESTED IN THE PULIDOS AND THEIR... AFFAIRS.
YOU...ARE IN A POSITION TO PROVIDE US WITH THAT INFORMATION.
Y-YOU WANT ME TO SPY ON THE PULIDOS! B-BUT THEY ARE A KIND AND GENEROUS FAMILY!
I COULD NEVER INFORM ON TH--
DON'T THINK OF THIS AS A BETRAYAL...

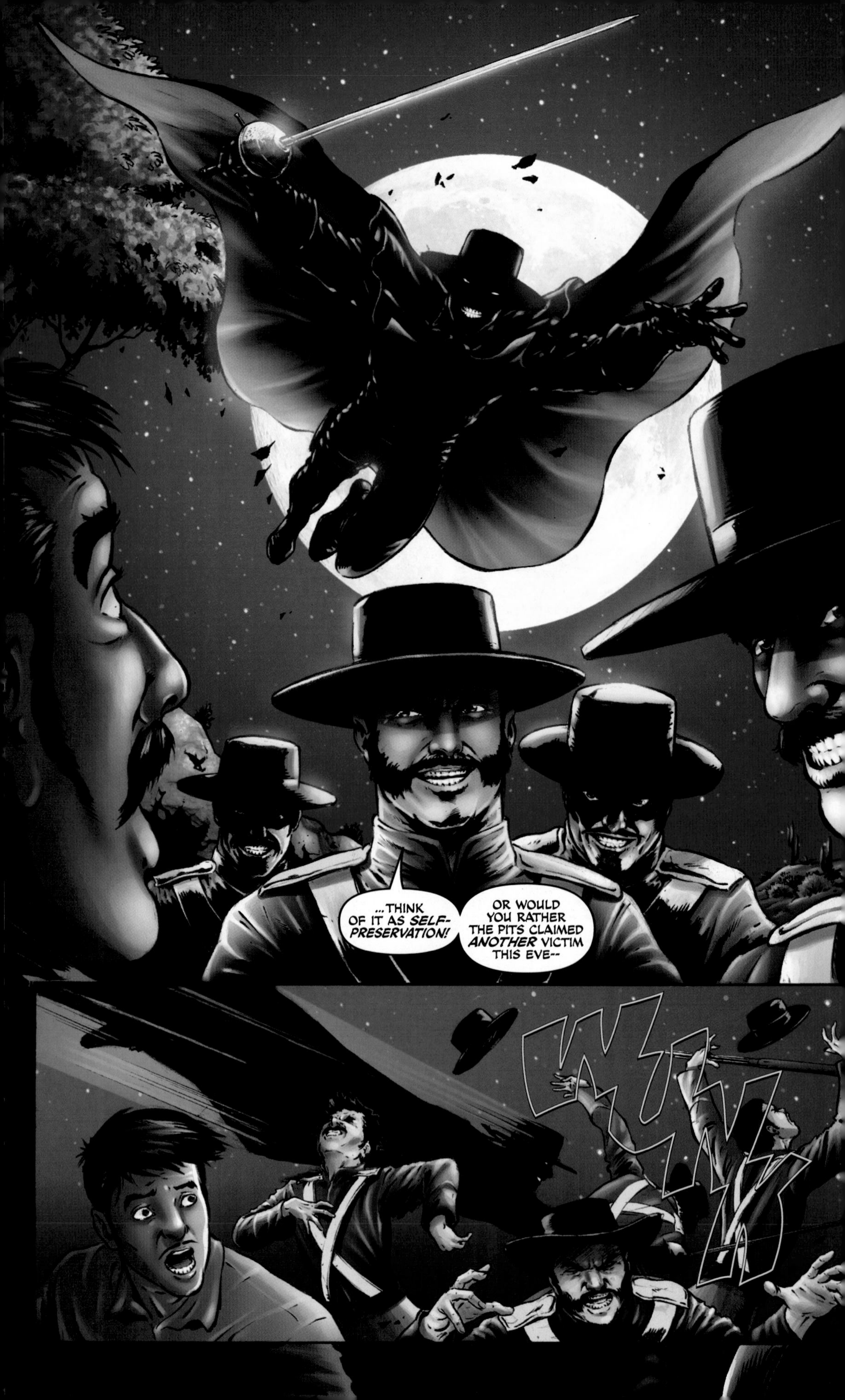
...THINK OF IT AS *SELF-PRESERVATION!*
OR WOULD YOU RATHER THE PITS CLAIMED *ANOTHER* VICTIM THIS EVE--

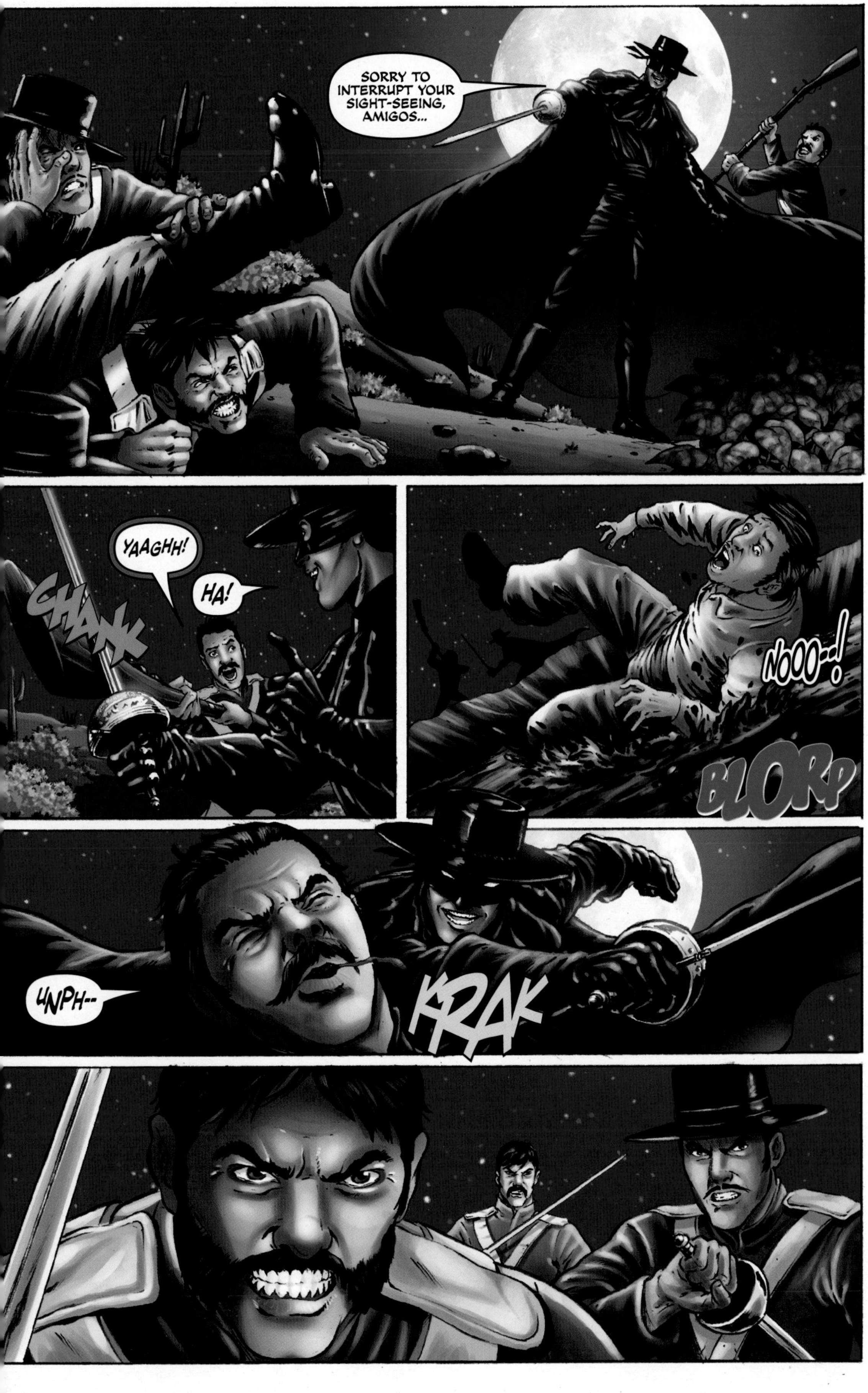
SORRY TO INTERRUPT YOUR SIGHT-SEEING, AMIGOS...
YAAGHH!
HA!
CHANK
NOOO--!
BLORP
UNPH--
KRAK

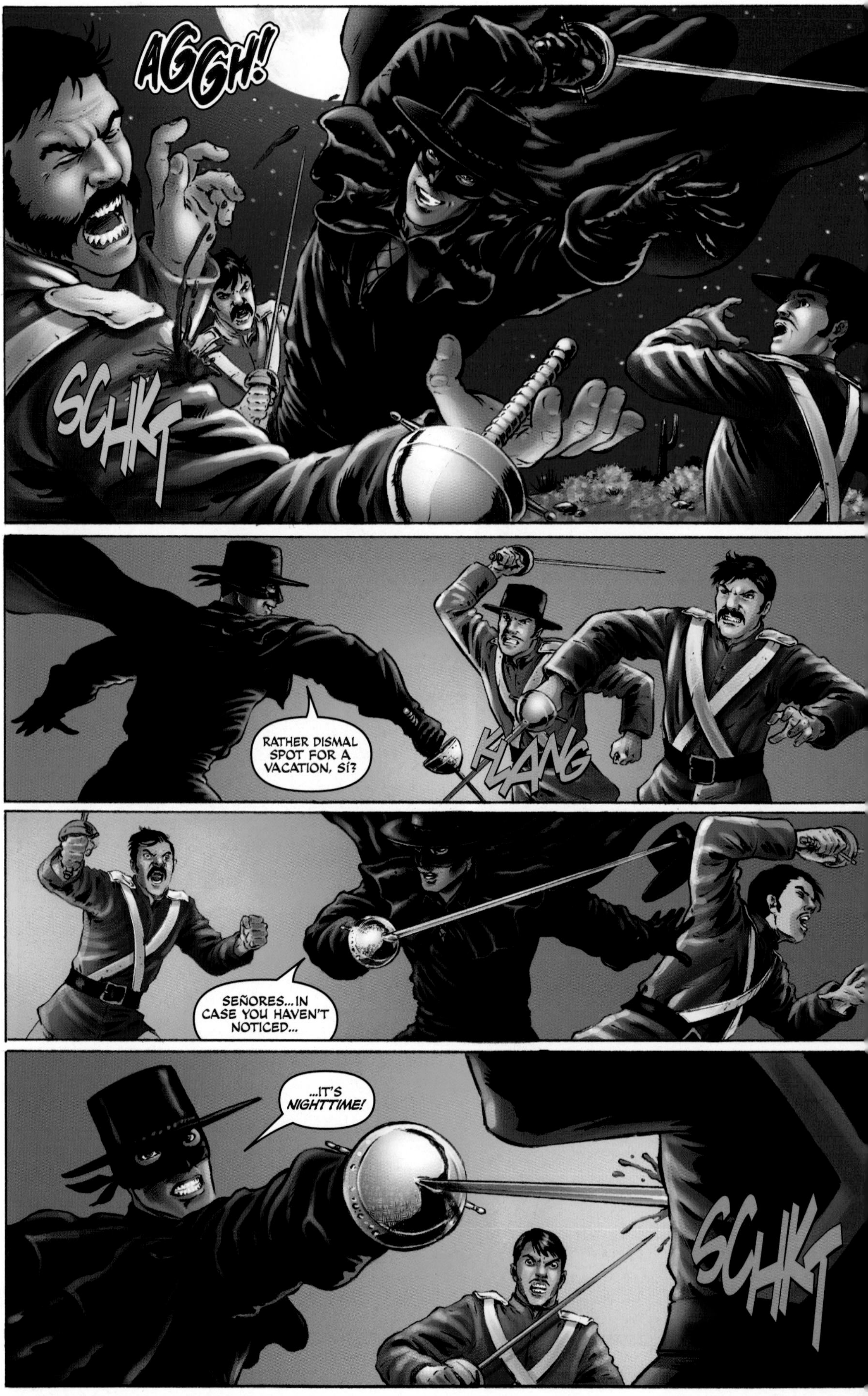
AGGH!
SCHKT
RATHER DISMAL SPOT FOR A VACATION, SÍ?
KLANG
SEÑORES...IN CASE YOU HAVEN'T NOTICED...
...IT'S *NIGHTTIME!*
SCHKT

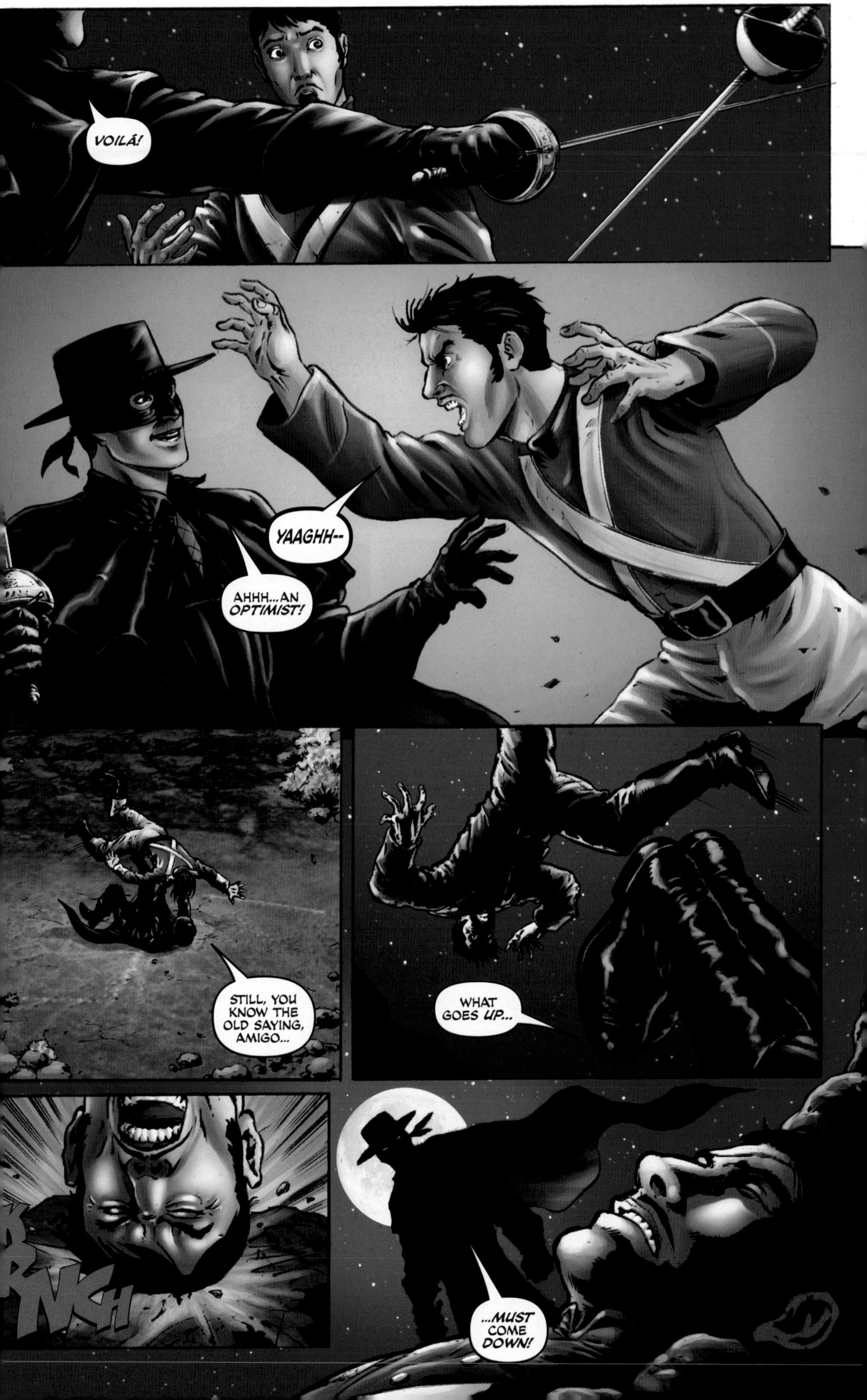
VOILÀ!
YAAGHH--
AHHH...AN OPTIMIST!
STILL, YOU KNOW THE OLD SAYING, AMIGO...
WHAT GOES UP...
...MUST COME DOWN!

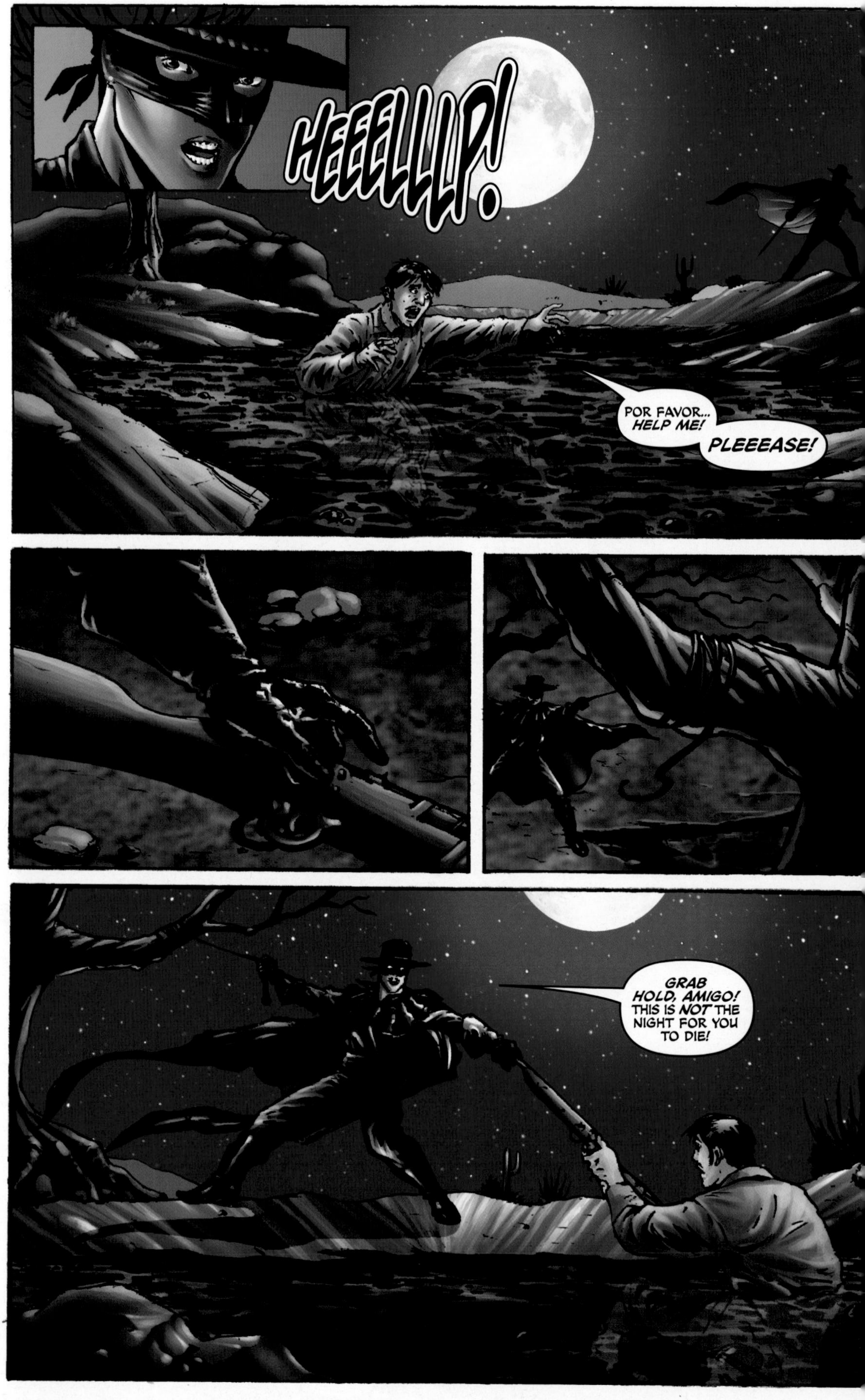
HEEELLLLP!
POR FAVOR... HELP ME!
PLEEEASE!
GRAB HOLD, AMIGO! THIS IS NOT THE NIGHT FOR YOU TO DIE!

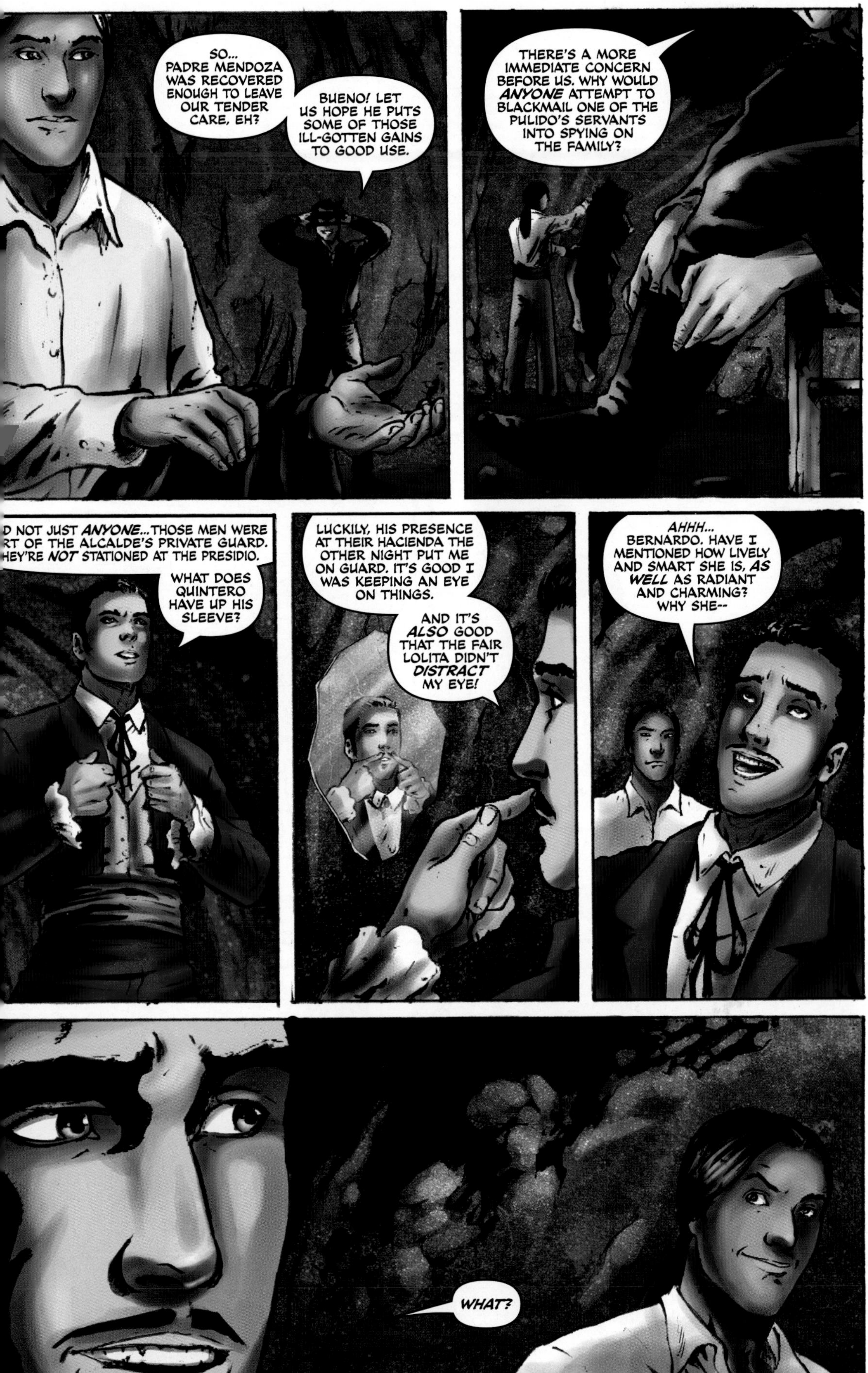
SO... PADRE MENDOZA WAS RECOVERED ENOUGH TO LEAVE OUR TENDER CARE, EH?
BUENO! LET US HOPE HE PUTS SOME OF THOSE ILL-GOTTEN GAINS TO GOOD USE.
THERE'S A MORE IMMEDIATE CONCERN BEFORE US. WHY WOULD ANYONE ATTEMPT TO BLACKMAIL ONE OF THE PULIDO'S SERVANTS INTO SPYING ON THE FAMILY?
D NOT JUST ANYONE...THOSE MEN WERE RT OF THE ALCALDE'S PRIVATE GUARD. HEY'RE NOT STATIONED AT THE PRESIDIO.
WHAT DOES QUINTERO HAVE UP HIS SLEEVE?
LUCKILY, HIS PRESENCE AT THEIR HACIENDA THE OTHER NIGHT PUT ME ON GUARD. IT'S GOOD I WAS KEEPING AN EYE ON THINGS.
AND IT'S ALSO GOOD THAT THE FAIR LOLITA DIDN'T DISTRACT MY EYE!
AHHH... BERNARDO. HAVE I MENTIONED HOW LIVELY AND SMART SHE IS, AS WELL AS RADIANT AND CHARMING? WHY SHE--
WHAT?

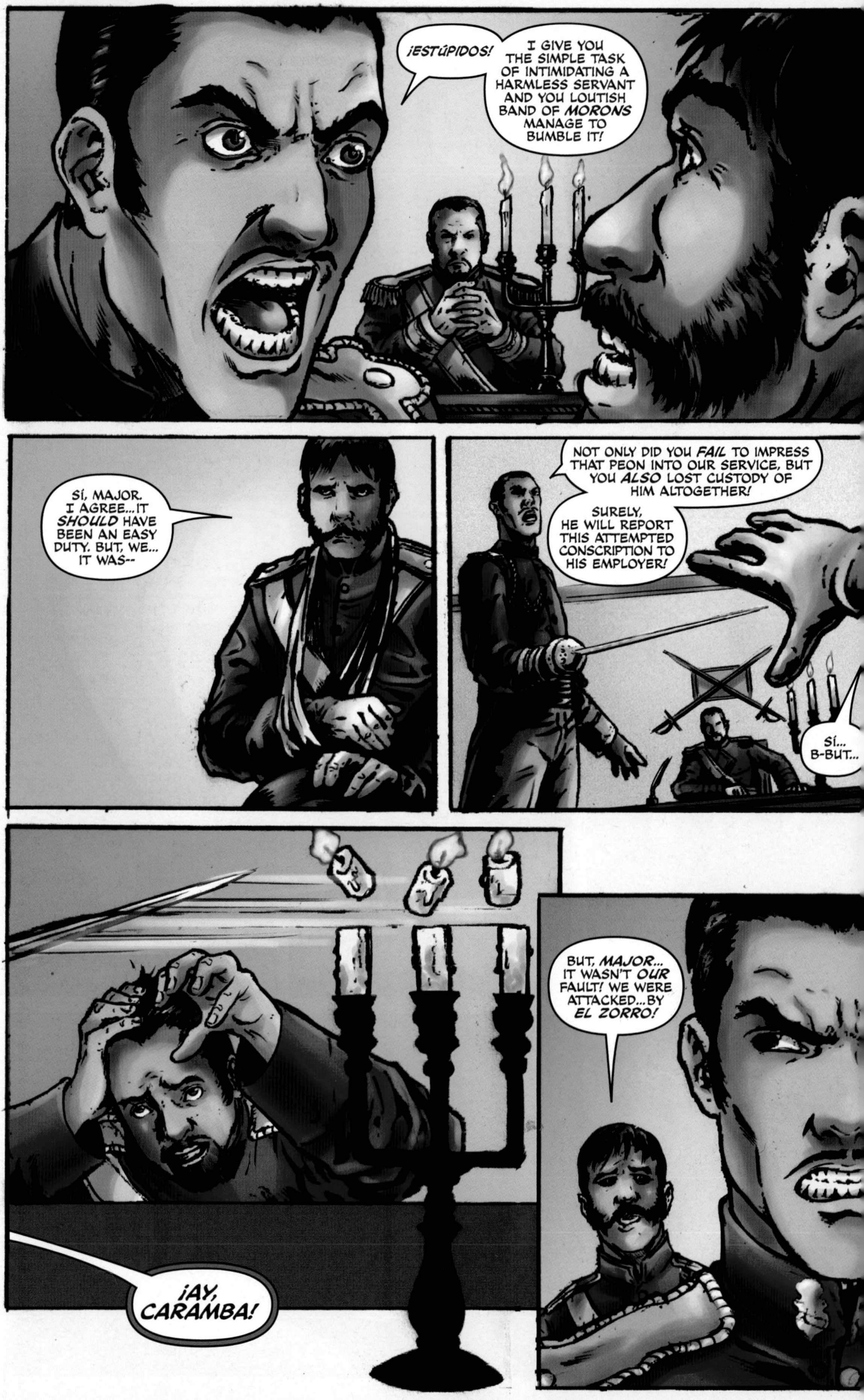
¡ESTÚPIDOS!
I GIVE YOU THE SIMPLE TASK OF INTIMIDATING A HARMLESS SERVANT AND YOU LOUTISH BAND OF MORONS MANAGE TO BUMBLE IT!
SÍ, MAJOR. I AGREE...IT SHOULD HAVE BEEN AN EASY DUTY. BUT, WE... IT WAS--
NOT ONLY DID YOU FAIL TO IMPRESS THAT PEON INTO OUR SERVICE, BUT YOU ALSO LOST CUSTODY OF HIM ALTOGETHER!
SURELY, HE WILL REPORT THIS ATTEMPTED CONSCRIPTION TO HIS EMPLOYER!
SÍ... B-BUT...
¡AY, CARAMBA!
BUT, MAJOR... IT WASN'T OUR FAULT! WE WERE ATTACKED...BY EL ZORRO!

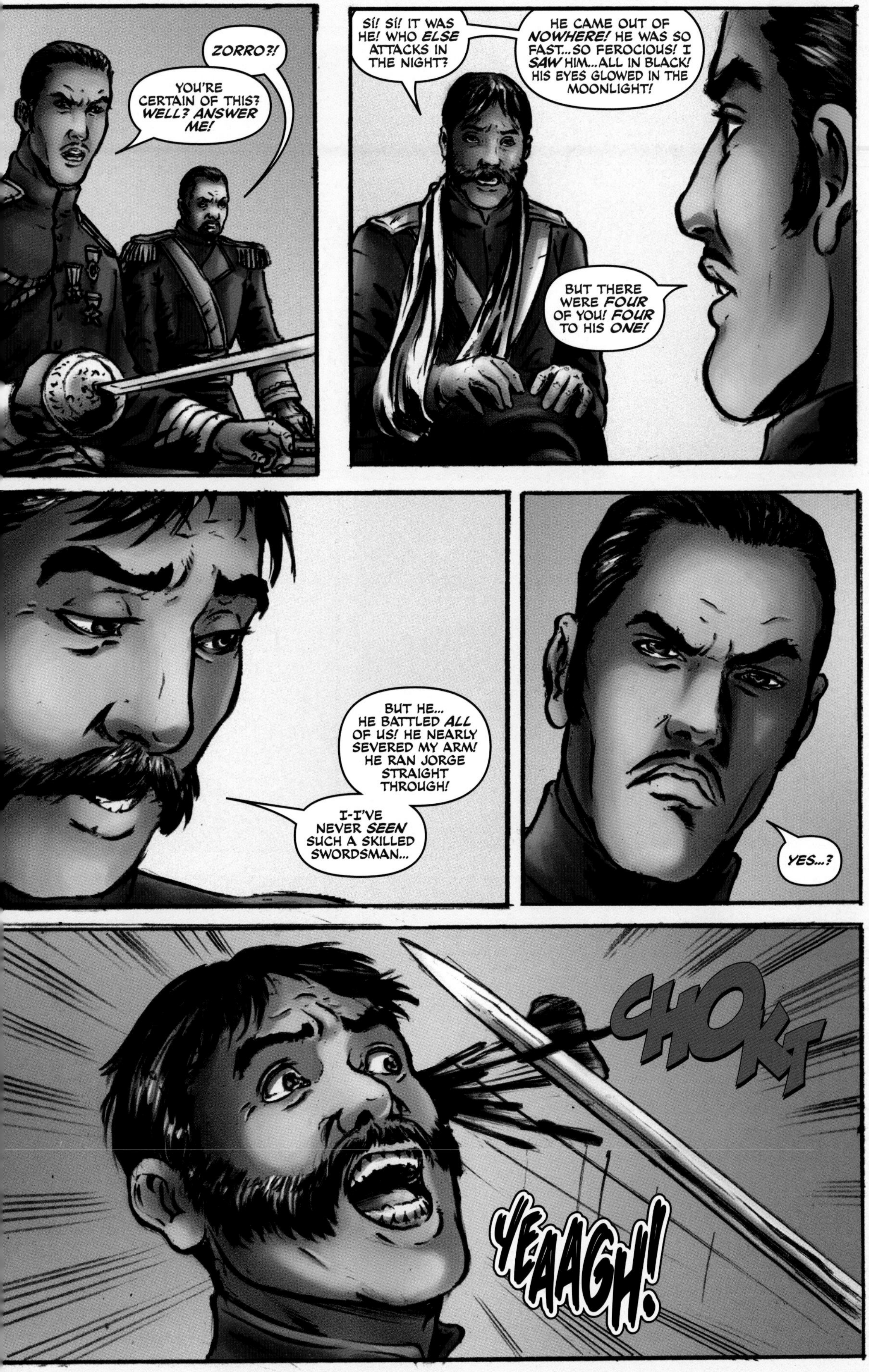
ZORRO?!
YOU'RE CERTAIN OF THIS? WELL? ANSWER ME!
SÍ! SÍ! IT WAS HE! WHO ELSE ATTACKS IN THE NIGHT?
HE CAME OUT OF NOWHERE! HE WAS SO FAST...SO FEROCIOUS! I SAW HIM...ALL IN BLACK! HIS EYES GLOWED IN THE MOONLIGHT!
BUT THERE WERE FOUR OF YOU! FOUR TO HIS ONE!
BUT HE... HE BATTLED ALL OF US! HE NEARLY SEVERED MY ARM! HE RAN JORGE STRAIGHT THROUGH!
I-I'VE NEVER SEEN SUCH A SKILLED SWORDSMAN...
YES...?
CHOKT
YEAAGH!

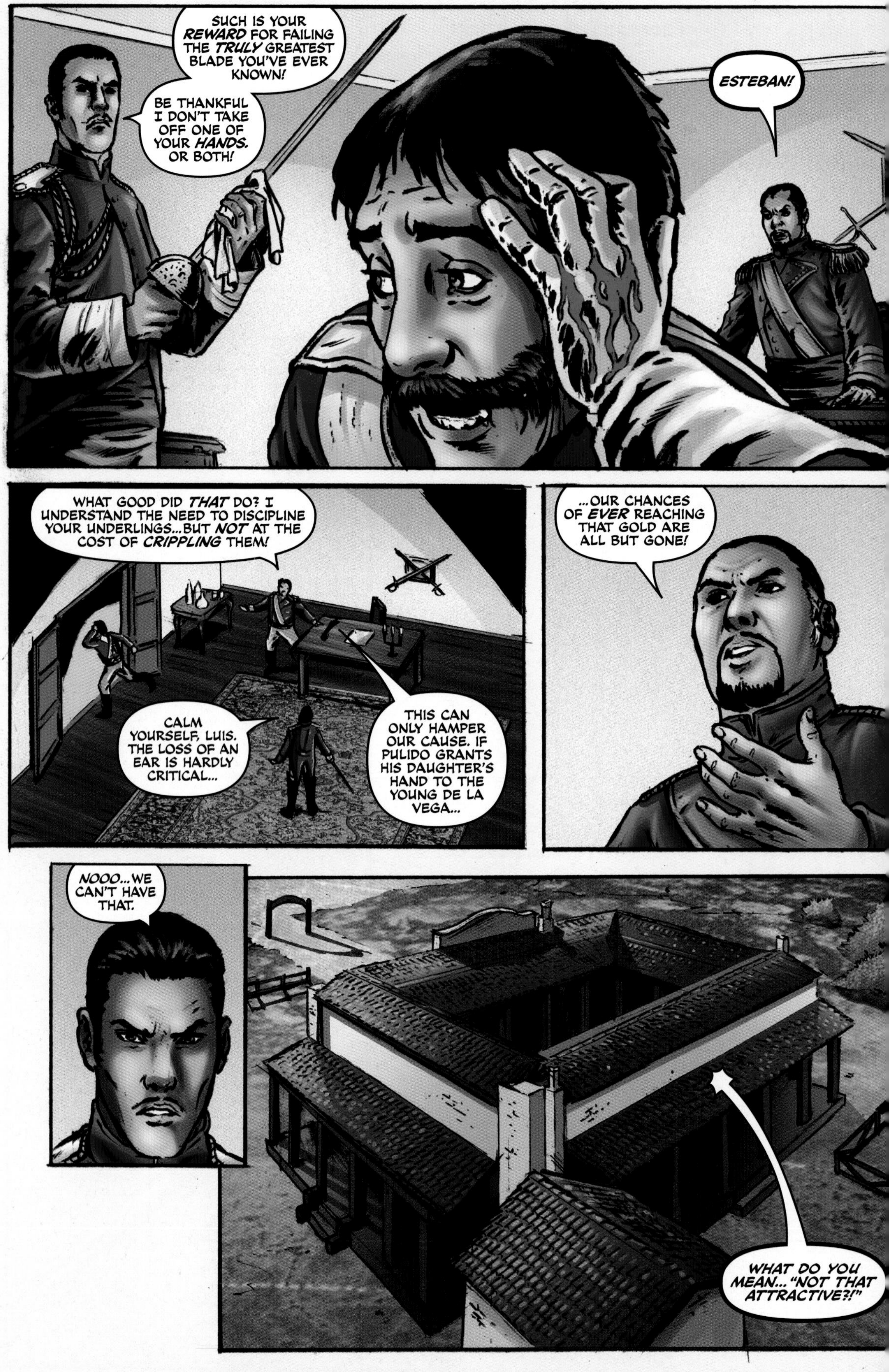
SUCH IS YOUR REWARD FOR FAILING THE TRULY GREATEST BLADE YOU'VE EVER KNOWN!
BE THANKFUL I DON'T TAKE OFF ONE OF YOUR HANDS. OR BOTH!
ESTEBAN!
WHAT GOOD DID THAT DO? I UNDERSTAND THE NEED TO DISCIPLINE YOUR UNDERLINGS...BUT NOT AT THE COST OF CRIPPLING THEM!
CALM YOURSELF, LUIS. THE LOSS OF AN EAR IS HARDLY CRITICAL...
THIS CAN ONLY HAMPER OUR CAUSE. IF PULIDO GRANTS HIS DAUGHTER'S HAND TO THE YOUNG DE LA VEGA...
...OUR CHANCES OF EVER REACHING THAT GOLD ARE ALL BUT GONE!
NOOO...WE CAN'T HAVE THAT.
WHAT DO YOU MEAN... "NOT THAT ATTRACTIVE?!"

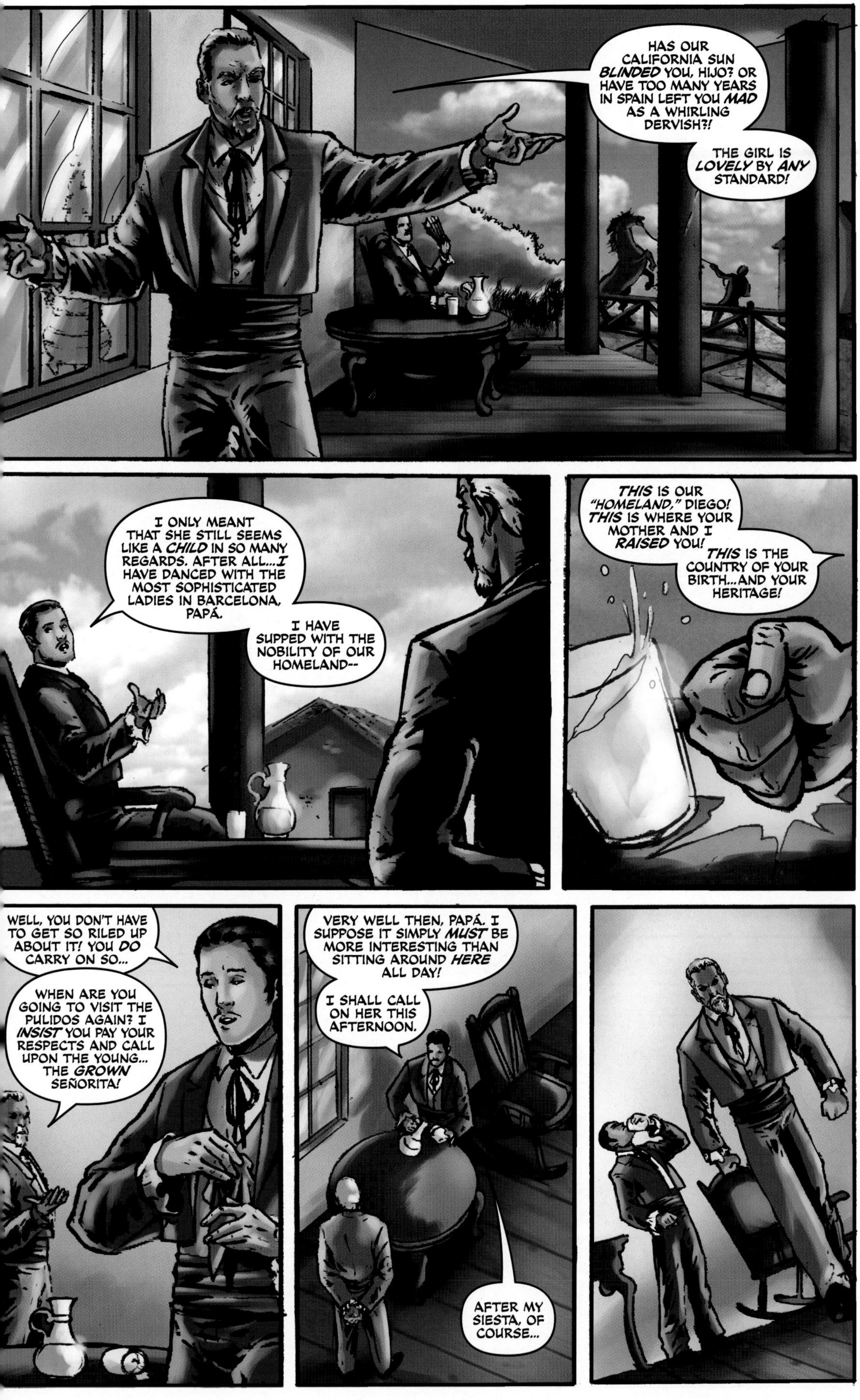
HAS OUR CALIFORNIA SUN BLINDED YOU, HIJO? OR HAVE TOO MANY YEARS IN SPAIN LEFT YOU MAD AS A WHIRLING DERVISH?!
THE GIRL IS LOVELY BY ANY STANDARD!
I ONLY MEANT THAT SHE STILL SEEMS LIKE A CHILD IN SO MANY REGARDS. AFTER ALL...I HAVE DANCED WITH THE MOST SOPHISTICATED LADIES IN BARCELONA, PAPÁ.
I HAVE SUPPED WITH THE NOBILITY OF OUR HOMELAND--
THIS IS OUR "HOMELAND," DIEGO! THIS IS WHERE YOUR MOTHER AND I RAISED YOU!
THIS IS THE COUNTRY OF YOUR BIRTH...AND YOUR HERITAGE!
WELL, YOU DON'T HAVE TO GET SO RILED UP ABOUT IT! YOU DO CARRY ON SO...
WHEN ARE YOU GOING TO VISIT THE PULIDOS AGAIN? I INSIST YOU PAY YOUR RESPECTS AND CALL UPON THE YOUNG... THE GROWN SEÑORITA!
VERY WELL THEN, PAPÁ. I SUPPOSE IT SIMPLY MUST BE MORE INTERESTING THAN SITTING AROUND HERE ALL DAY!
I SHALL CALL ON HER THIS AFTERNOON.
AFTER MY SIESTA, OF COURSE...

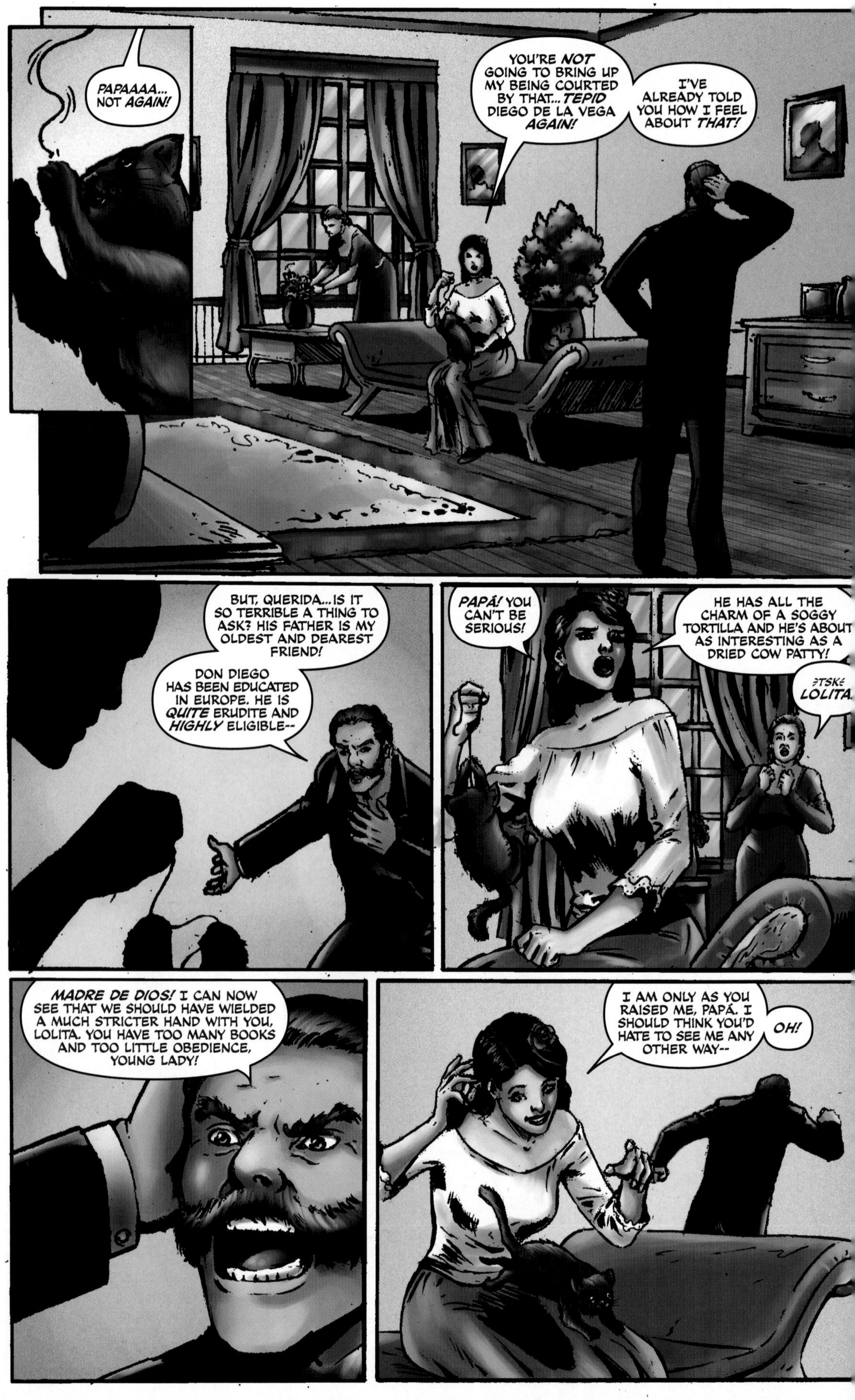

PAPAAAA... NOT AGAIN!
YOU'RE NOT GOING TO BRING UP MY BEING COURTED BY THAT... TEPID DIEGO DE LA VEGA AGAIN!
I'VE ALREADY TOLD YOU HOW I FEEL ABOUT THAT!
BUT, QUERIDA... IS IT SO TERRIBLE A THING TO ASK? HIS FATHER IS MY OLDEST AND DEAREST FRIEND!
DON DIEGO HAS BEEN EDUCATED IN EUROPE. HE IS QUITE ERUDITE AND HIGHLY ELIGIBLE--
PAPÁ! YOU CAN'T BE SERIOUS!
HE HAS ALL THE CHARM OF A SOGGY TORTILLA AND HE'S ABOUT AS INTERESTING AS A DRIED COW PATTY!
TSK LOLITA
MADRE DE DIOS! I CAN NOW SEE THAT WE SHOULD HAVE WIELDED A MUCH STRICTER HAND WITH YOU, LOLITA. YOU HAVE TOO MANY BOOKS AND TOO LITTLE OBEDIENCE, YOUNG LADY!
I AM ONLY AS YOU RAISED ME, PAPÁ. I SHOULD THINK YOU'D HATE TO SEE ME ANY OTHER WAY--
OH!

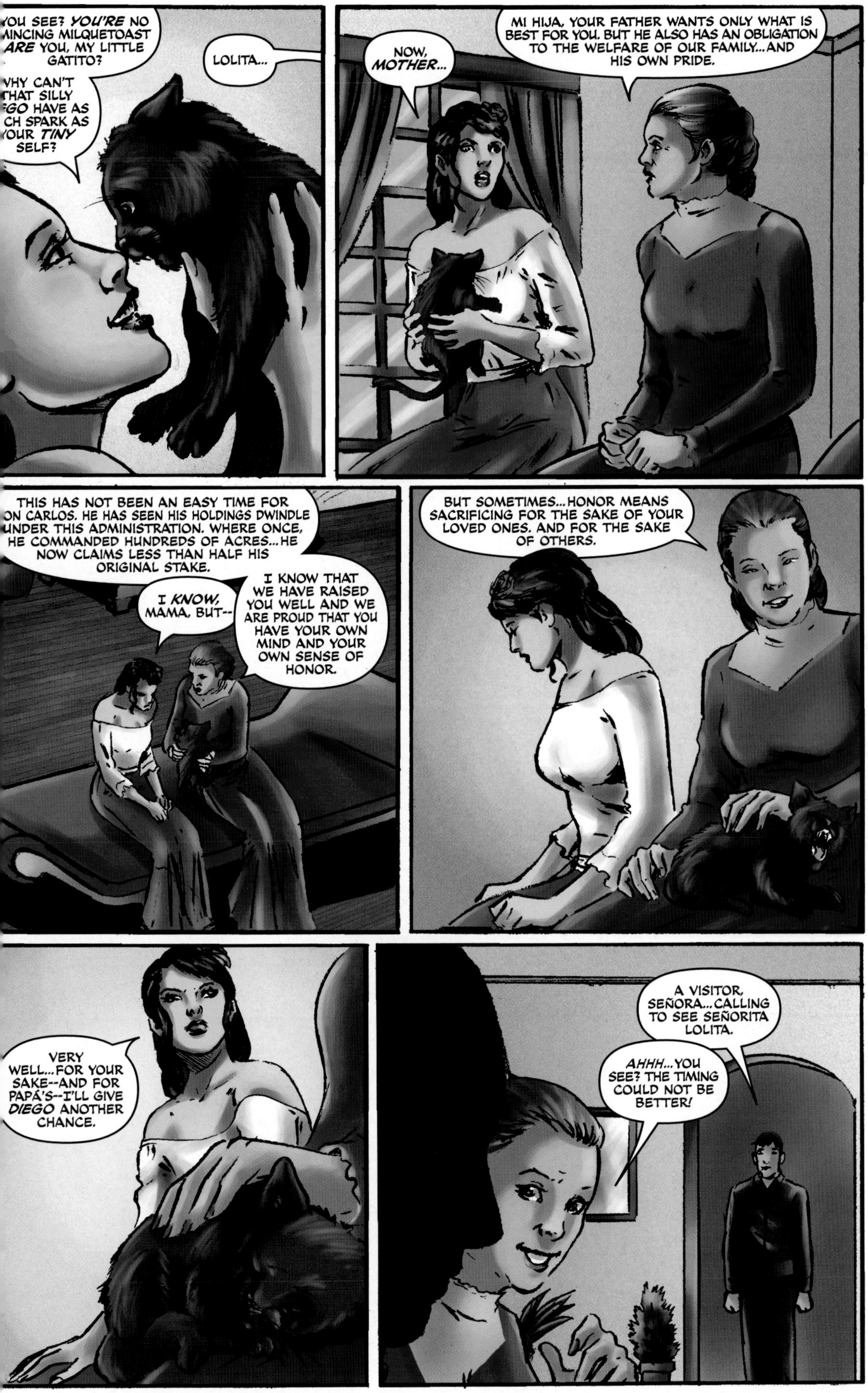

OU SEE? *YOU'RE* NO MINCING MILQUETOAST *ARE* YOU, MY LITTLE GATITO?
LOLITA...
HY CAN'T THAT SILLY GO HAVE AS CH SPARK AS OUR *TINY* SELF?
NOW, *MOTHER*...
MI HIJA, YOUR FATHER WANTS ONLY WHAT IS BEST FOR YOU. BUT HE ALSO HAS AN OBLIGATION TO THE WELFARE OF OUR FAMILY...AND HIS OWN PRIDE.
THIS HAS NOT BEEN AN EASY TIME FOR ON CARLOS. HE HAS SEEN HIS HOLDINGS DWINDLE UNDER THIS ADMINISTRATION. WHERE ONCE, HE COMMANDED HUNDREDS OF ACRES...HE NOW CLAIMS LESS THAN HALF HIS ORIGINAL STAKE.
I *KNOW*, MAMA, BUT--
I KNOW THAT WE HAVE RAISED YOU WELL AND WE ARE PROUD THAT YOU HAVE YOUR OWN MIND AND YOUR OWN SENSE OF HONOR.
BUT SOMETIMES...HONOR MEANS SACRIFICING FOR THE SAKE OF YOUR LOVED ONES. AND FOR THE SAKE OF OTHERS.
VERY WELL...FOR YOUR SAKE--AND FOR PAPÁ'S--I'LL GIVE *DIEGO* ANOTHER CHANCE.
A VISITOR, SEÑORA...CALLING TO SEE SEÑORITA LOLITA.
AHHH...YOU SEE? THE TIMING COULD NOT BE BETTER!

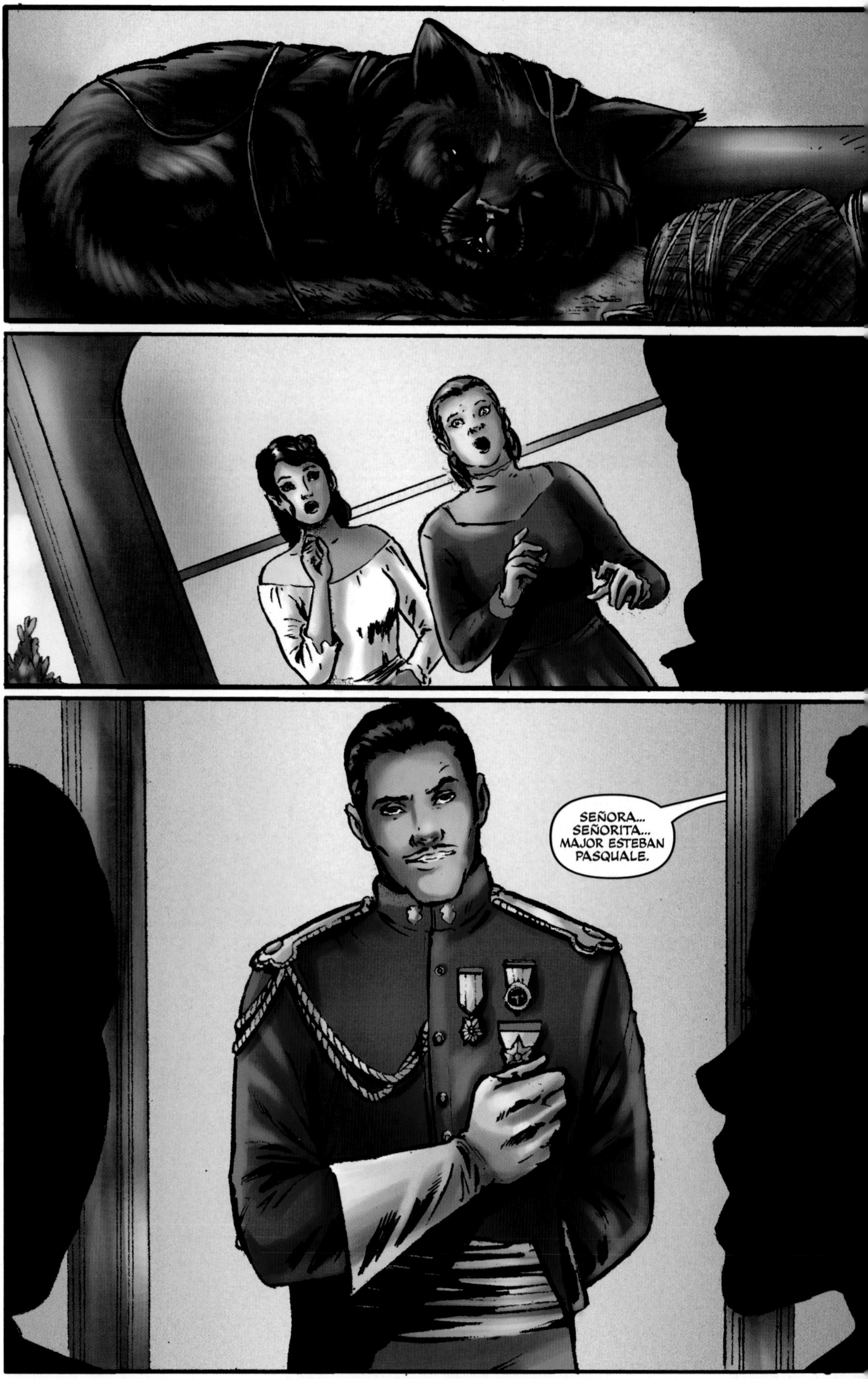
SEÑORA... SEÑORITA... MAJOR ESTEBAN PASQUALE.

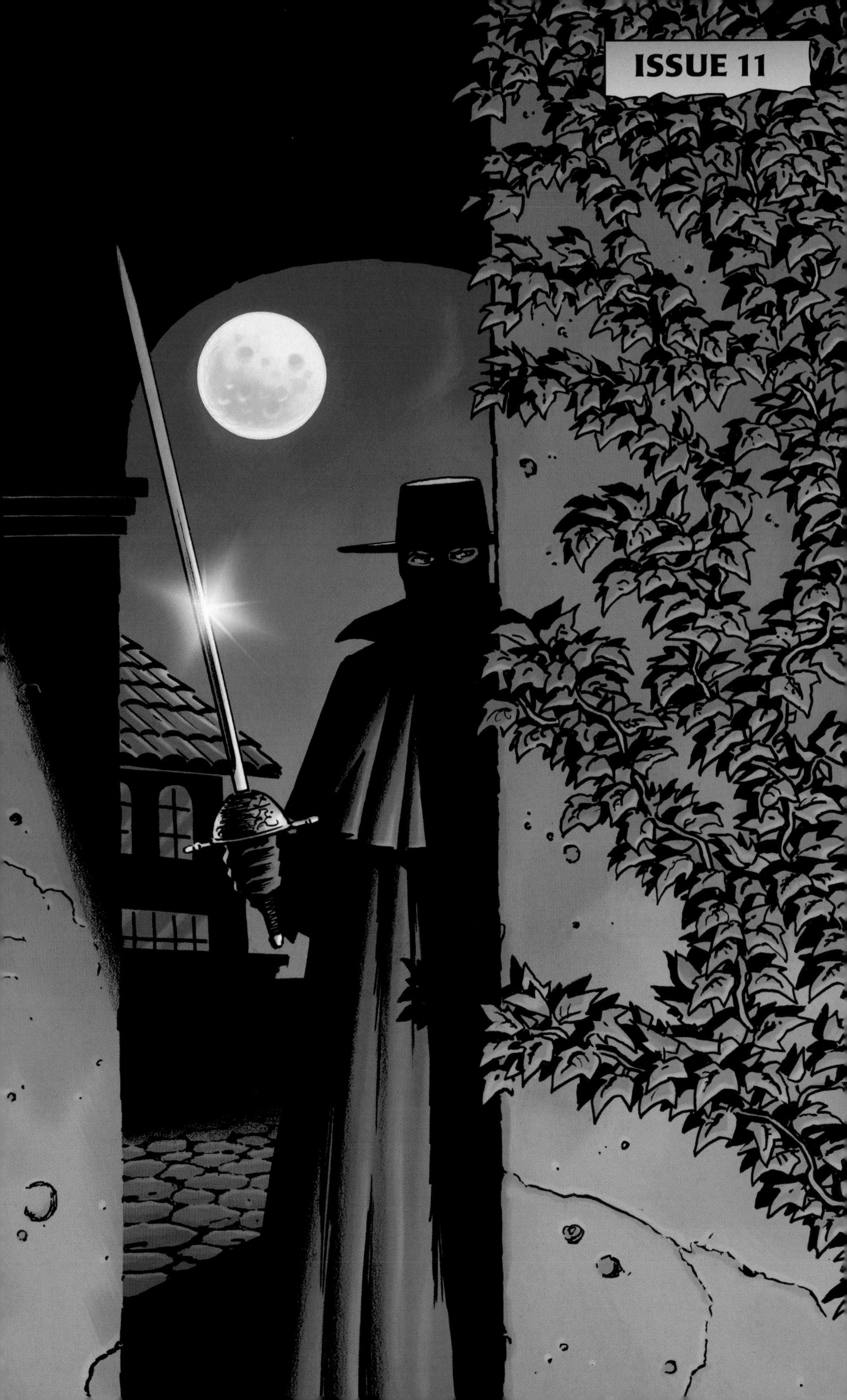
ISSUE 11

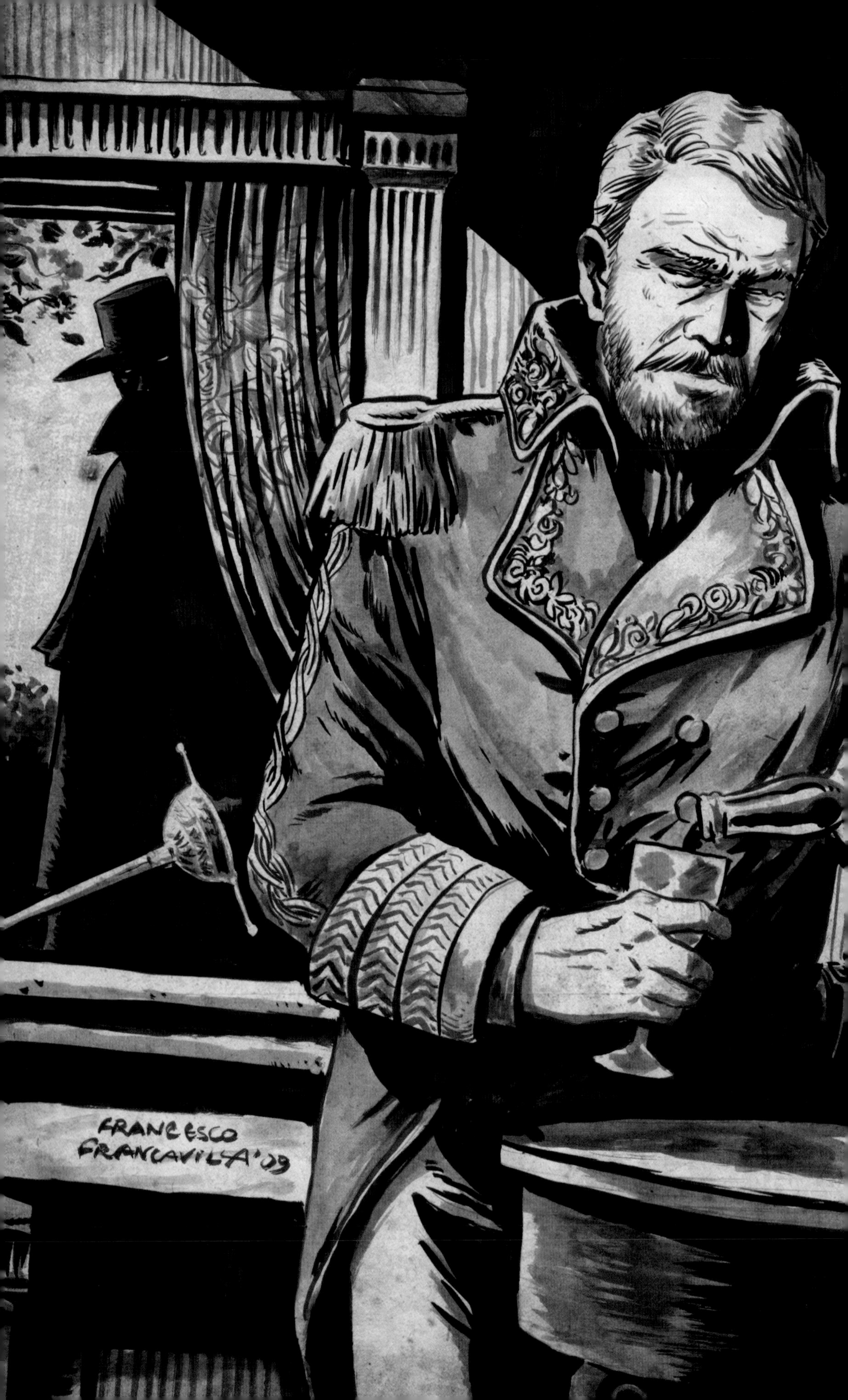
FRANCESCO
FRANCAVILLA '09

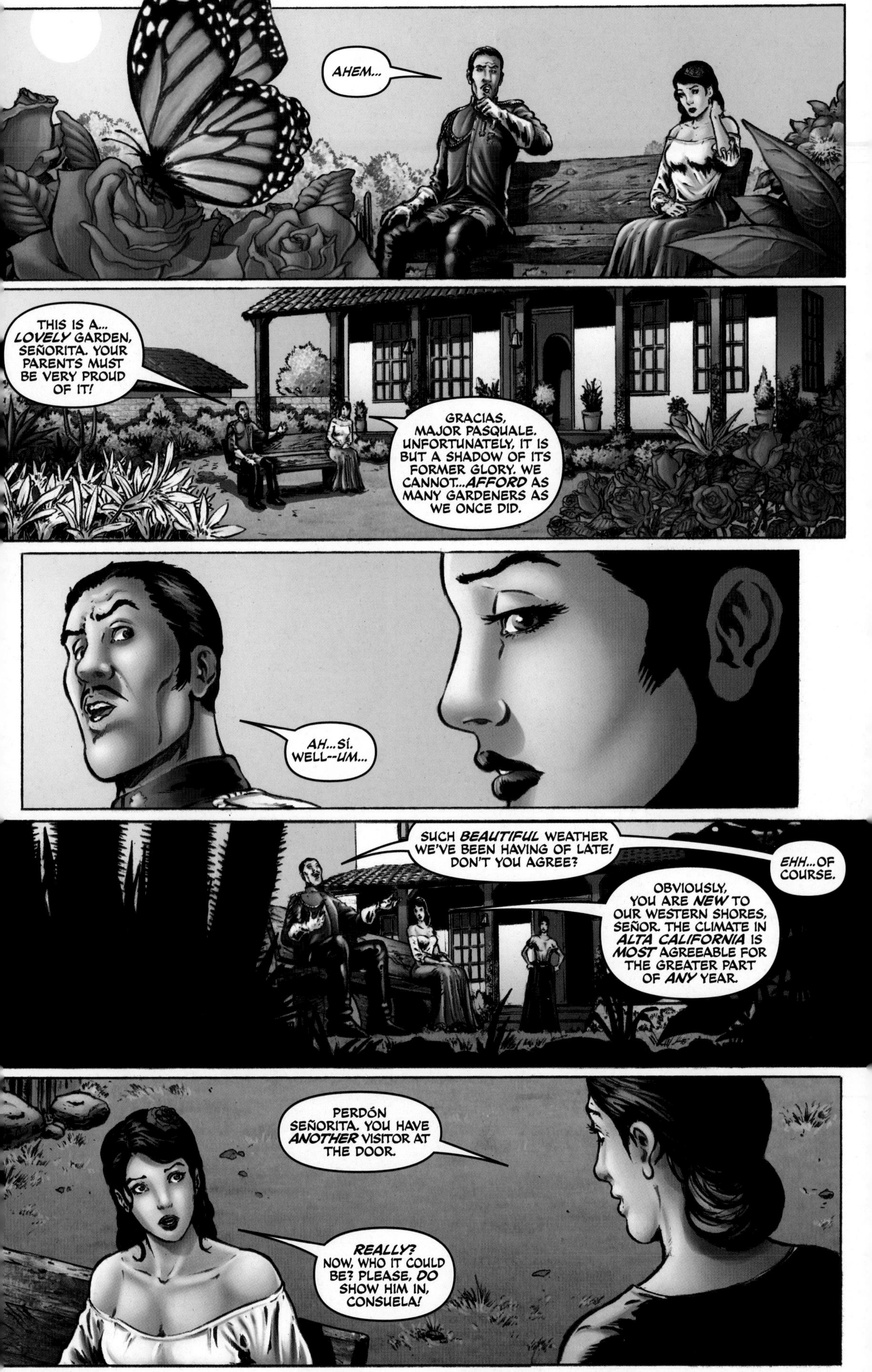
AHEM...
THIS IS A... LOVELY GARDEN, SEÑORITA. YOUR PARENTS MUST BE VERY PROUD OF IT!
GRACIAS, MAJOR PASQUALE. UNFORTUNATELY, IT IS BUT A SHADOW OF ITS FORMER GLORY. WE CANNOT...AFFORD AS MANY GARDENERS AS WE ONCE DID.
AH...SÍ. WELL--UM...
SUCH BEAUTIFUL WEATHER WE'VE BEEN HAVING OF LATE! DON'T YOU AGREE?
EHH...OF COURSE.
OBVIOUSLY, YOU ARE NEW TO OUR WESTERN SHORES, SEÑOR. THE CLIMATE IN ALTA CALIFORNIA IS MOST AGREEABLE FOR THE GREATER PART OF ANY YEAR.
PERDÓN SEÑORITA. YOU HAVE ANOTHER VISITOR AT THE DOOR.
REALLY? NOW, WHO IT COULD BE? PLEASE, DO SHOW HIM IN, CONSUELA!

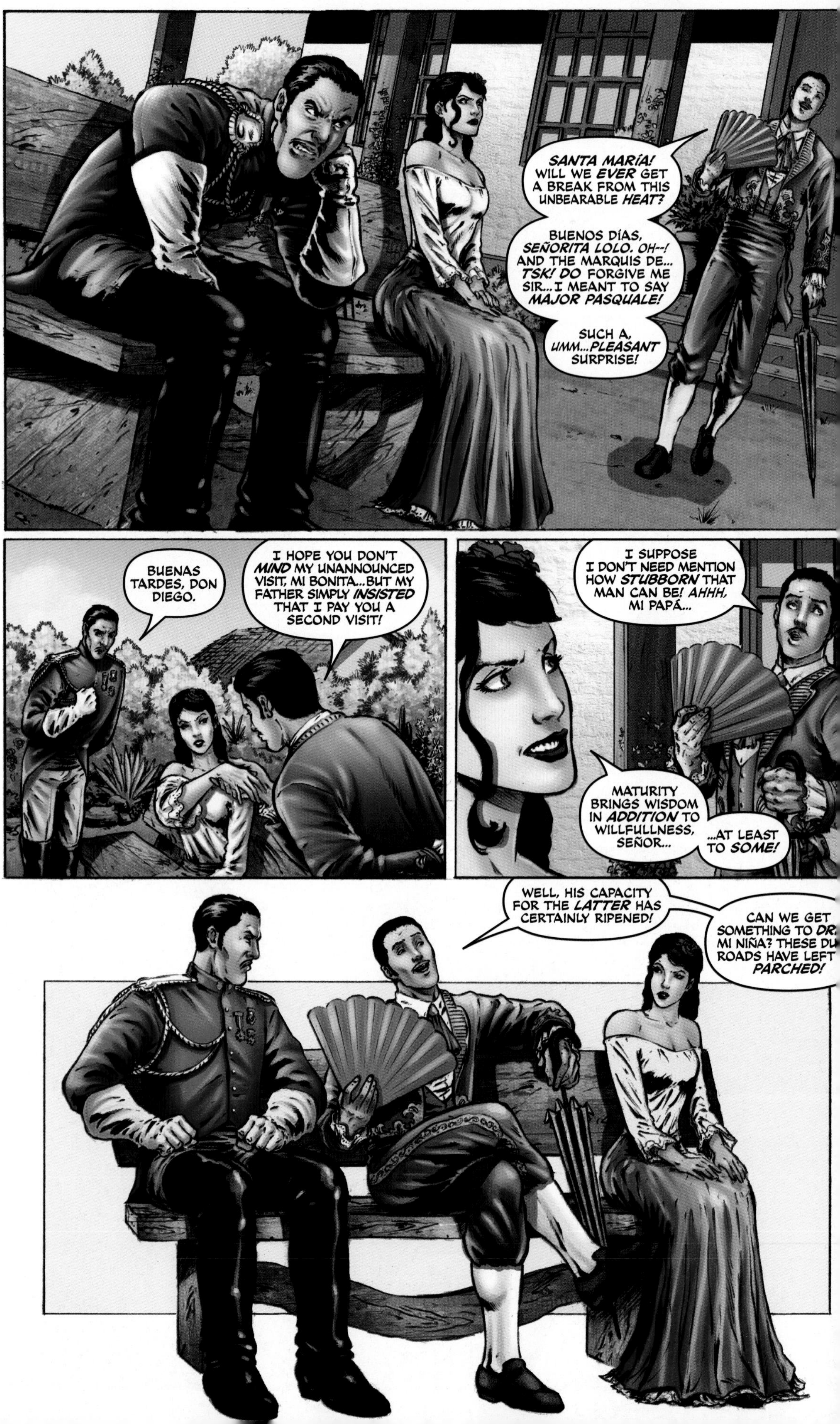
SANTA MARÍA! WILL WE EVER GET A BREAK FROM THIS UNBEARABLE HEAT?
BUENOS DÍAS, SEÑORITA LOLO. OH--! AND THE MARQUIS DE... TSK! DO FORGIVE ME SIR... I MEANT TO SAY MAJOR PASQUALE!
SUCH A, UMM... PLEASANT SURPRISE!
BUENAS TARDES, DON DIEGO.
I HOPE YOU DON'T MIND MY UNANNOUNCED VISIT, MI BONITA... BUT MY FATHER SIMPLY INSISTED THAT I PAY YOU A SECOND VISIT!
I SUPPOSE I DON'T NEED MENTION HOW STUBBORN THAT MAN CAN BE! AHHH, MI PAPÁ...
MATURITY BRINGS WISDOM IN ADDITION TO WILLFULLNESS, SEÑOR...
...AT LEAST TO SOME!
WELL, HIS CAPACITY FOR THE LATTER HAS CERTAINLY RIPENED!
CAN WE GET SOMETHING TO DR MI NIÑA? THESE DU ROADS HAVE LEFT PARCHED!

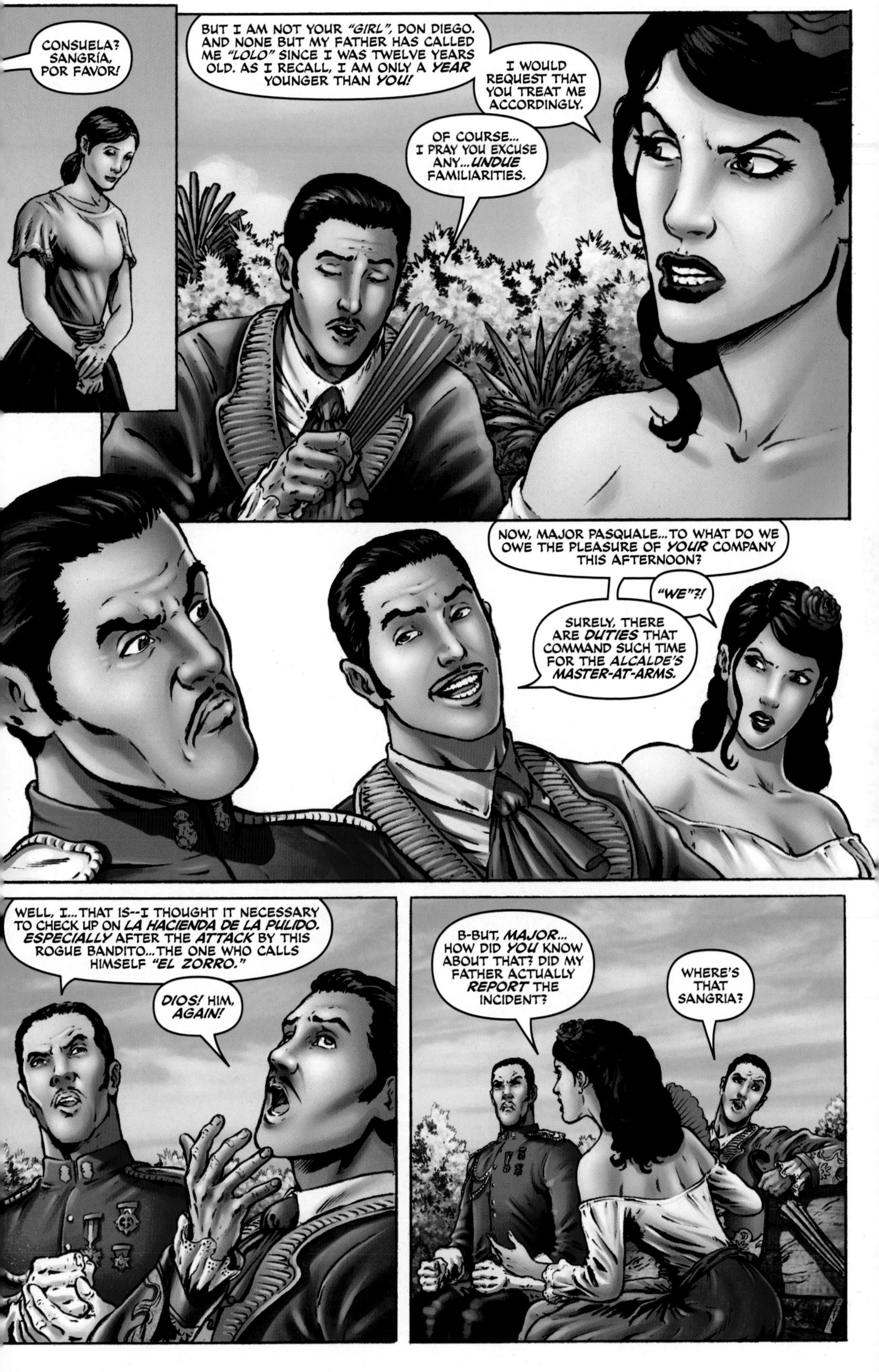
CONSUELA? SANGRÍA, POR FAVOR!
BUT I AM NOT YOUR "GIRL", DON DIEGO. AND NONE BUT MY FATHER HAS CALLED ME "LOLO" SINCE I WAS TWELVE YEARS OLD. AS I RECALL, I AM ONLY A YEAR YOUNGER THAN YOU!
I WOULD REQUEST THAT YOU TREAT ME ACCORDINGLY.
OF COURSE... I PRAY YOU EXCUSE ANY...UNDUE FAMILIARITIES.
NOW, MAJOR PASQUALE...TO WHAT DO WE OWE THE PLEASURE OF YOUR COMPANY THIS AFTERNOON?
"WE"?!
SURELY, THERE ARE DUTIES THAT COMMAND SUCH TIME FOR THE ALCALDE'S MASTER-AT-ARMS.
WELL, I...THAT IS--I THOUGHT IT NECESSARY TO CHECK UP ON LA HACIENDA DE LA PULIDO. ESPECIALLY AFTER THE ATTACK BY THIS ROGUE BANDITO...THE ONE WHO CALLS HIMSELF "EL ZORRO."
DIOS! HIM, AGAIN!
B-BUT, MAJOR... HOW DID YOU KNOW ABOUT THAT? DID MY FATHER ACTUALLY REPORT THE INCIDENT?
WHERE'S THAT SANGRIA?

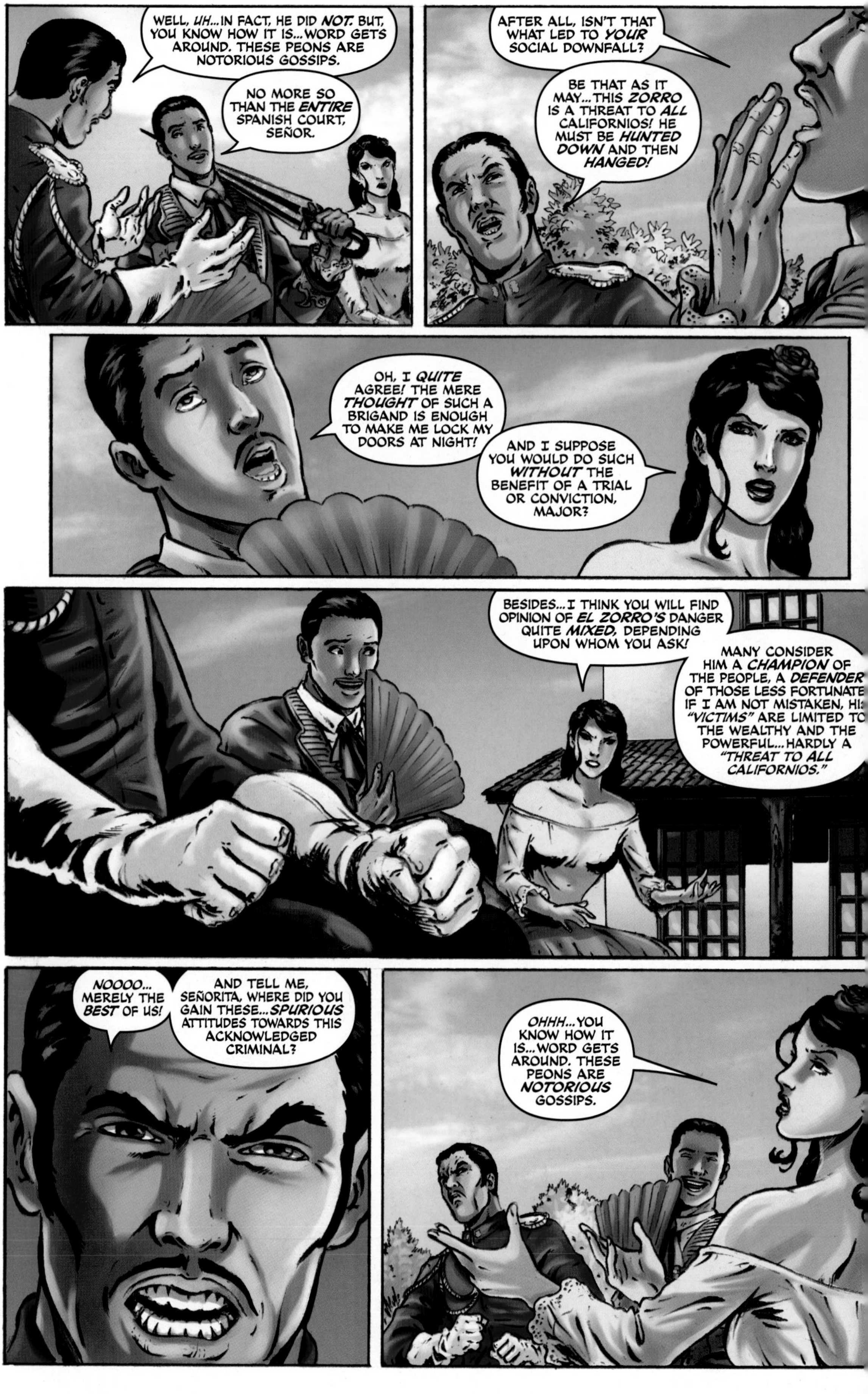
WELL, UH...IN FACT, HE DID NOT. BUT, YOU KNOW HOW IT IS...WORD GETS AROUND. THESE PEONS ARE NOTORIOUS GOSSIPS.
NO MORE SO THAN THE ENTIRE SPANISH COURT, SEÑOR.
AFTER ALL, ISN'T THAT WHAT LED TO YOUR SOCIAL DOWNFALL?
BE THAT AS IT MAY...THIS ZORRO IS A THREAT TO ALL CALIFORNIOS! HE MUST BE HUNTED DOWN AND THEN HANGED!
OH, I QUITE AGREE! THE MERE THOUGHT OF SUCH A BRIGAND IS ENOUGH TO MAKE ME LOCK MY DOORS AT NIGHT!
AND I SUPPOSE YOU WOULD DO SUCH WITHOUT THE BENEFIT OF A TRIAL OR CONVICTION, MAJOR?
BESIDES...I THINK YOU WILL FIND OPINION OF EL ZORRO'S DANGER QUITE MIXED, DEPENDING UPON WHOM YOU ASK!
MANY CONSIDER HIM A CHAMPION OF THE PEOPLE, A DEFENDER OF THOSE LESS FORTUNATE. IF I AM NOT MISTAKEN, HIS "VICTIMS" ARE LIMITED TO THE WEALTHY AND THE POWERFUL...HARDLY A "THREAT TO ALL CALIFORNIOS."
NOOOO... MERELY THE BEST OF US!
AND TELL ME, SEÑORITA, WHERE DID YOU GAIN THESE...SPURIOUS ATTITUDES TOWARDS THIS ACKNOWLEDGED CRIMINAL?
OHHH...YOU KNOW HOW IT IS...WORD GETS AROUND. THESE PEONS ARE NOTORIOUS GOSSIPS.

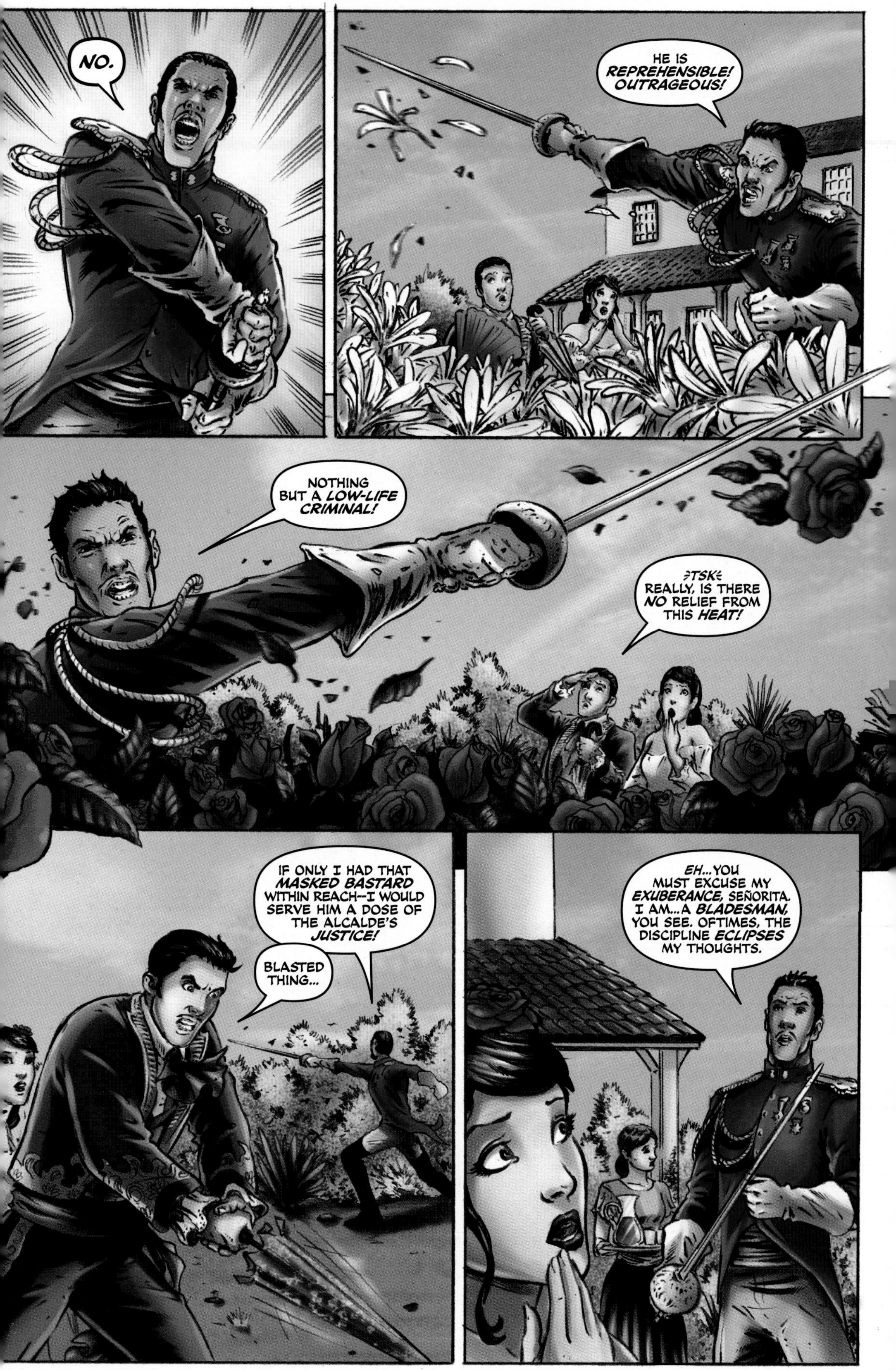
NO.
HE IS REPREHENSIBLE! OUTRAGEOUS!
NOTHING BUT A LOW-LIFE CRIMINAL!
TSK
REALLY, IS THERE NO RELIEF FROM THIS HEAT!
IF ONLY I HAD THAT MASKED BASTARD WITHIN REACH--I WOULD SERVE HIM A DOSE OF THE ALCALDE'S JUSTICE!
BLASTED THING...
EH...YOU MUST EXCUSE MY EXUBERANCE, SEÑORITA. I AM...A BLADESMAN, YOU SEE. OFTIMES, THE DISCIPLINE ECLIPSES MY THOUGHTS.

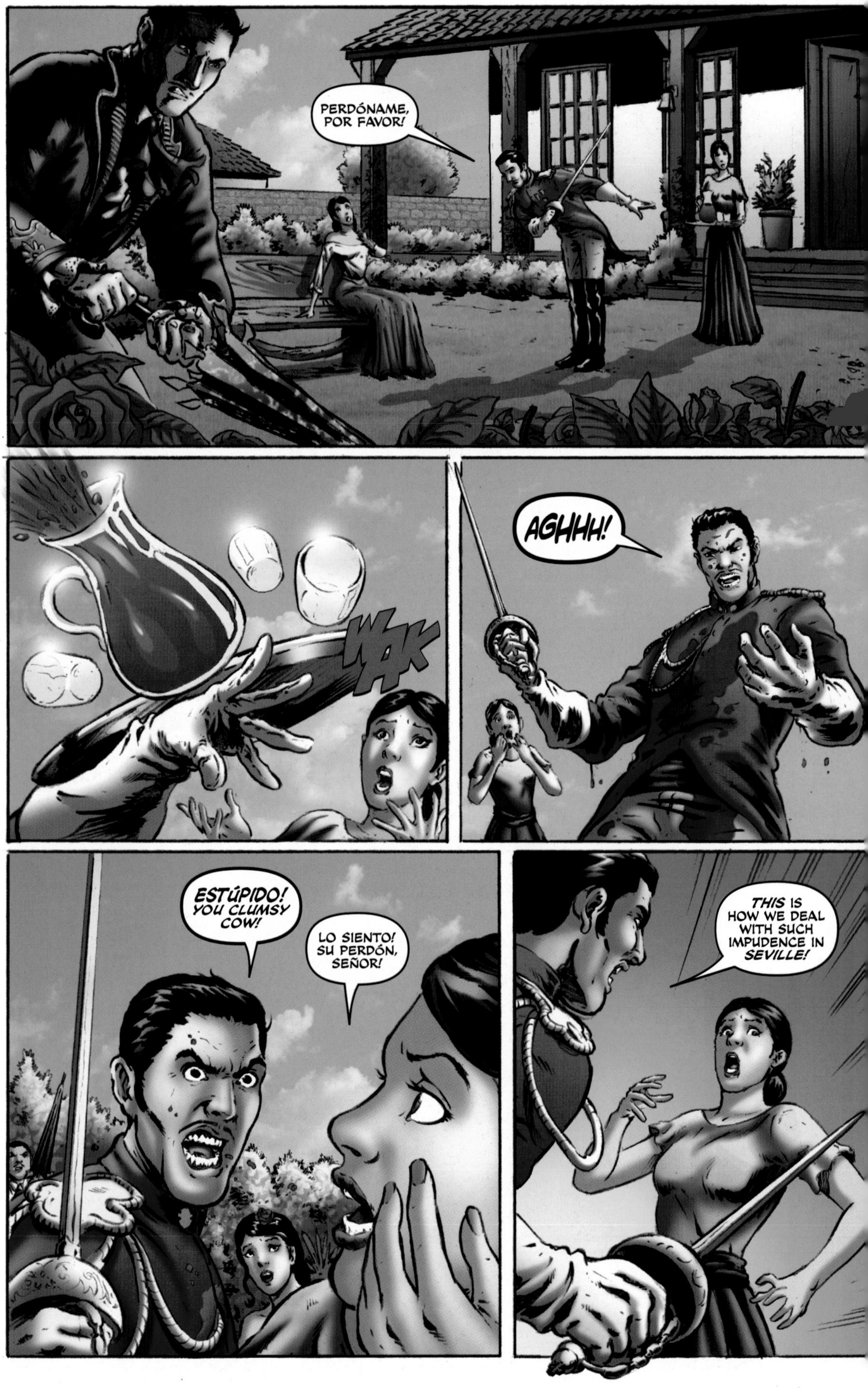
PERDÓNAME, POR FAVOR!
WAK
AGHHH!
ESTÚPIDO! YOU CLUMSY COW!
LO SIENTO! SU PERDÓN, SEÑOR!
THIS IS HOW WE DEAL WITH SUCH IMPUDENCE IN SEVILLE!

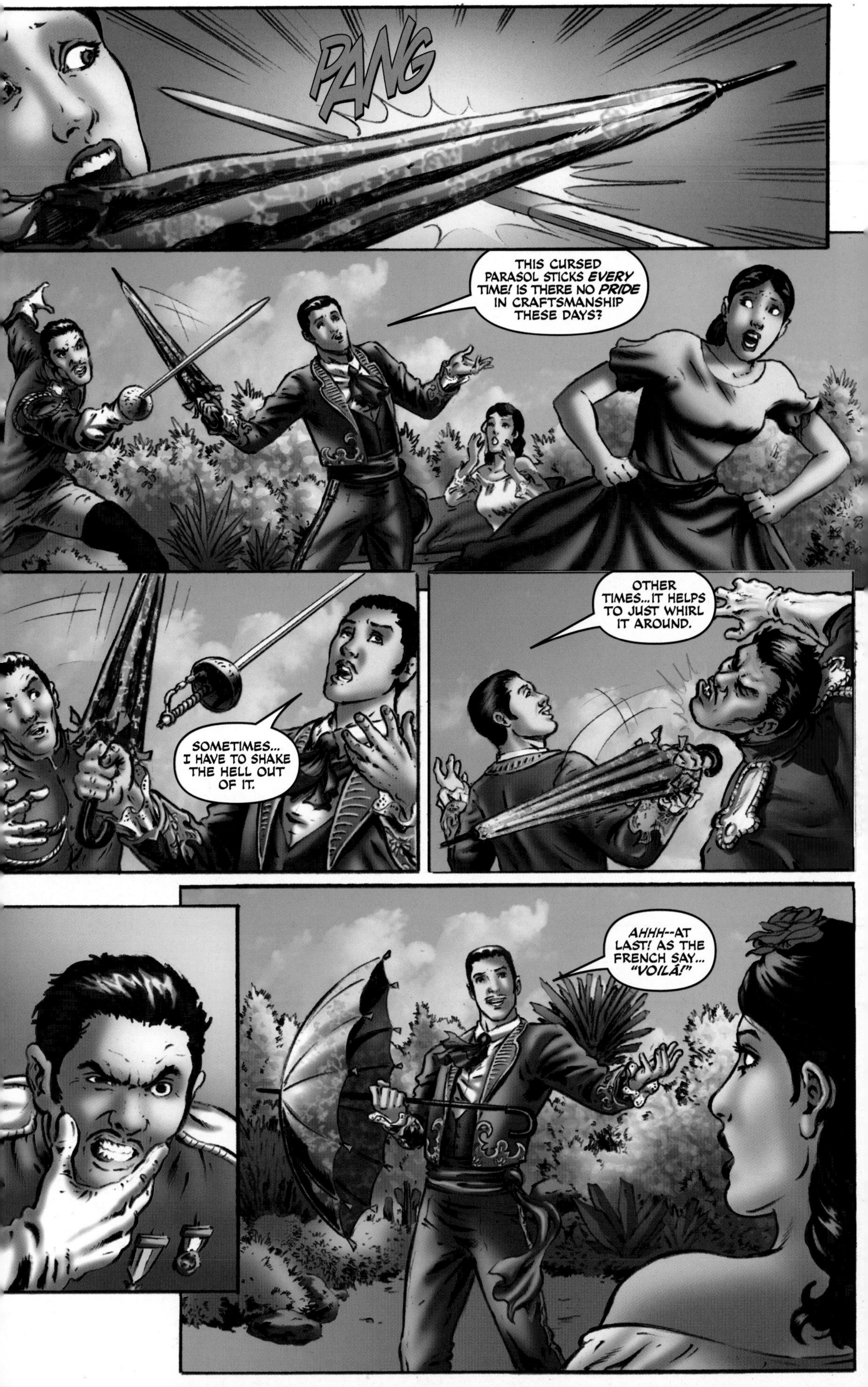
PANG
THIS CURSED PARASOL STICKS EVERY TIME! IS THERE NO PRIDE IN CRAFTSMANSHIP THESE DAYS?
SOMETIMES... I HAVE TO SHAKE THE HELL OUT OF IT.
OTHER TIMES...IT HELPS TO JUST WHIRL IT AROUND.
AHHH--AT LAST! AS THE FRENCH SAY... "VOILÀ!"

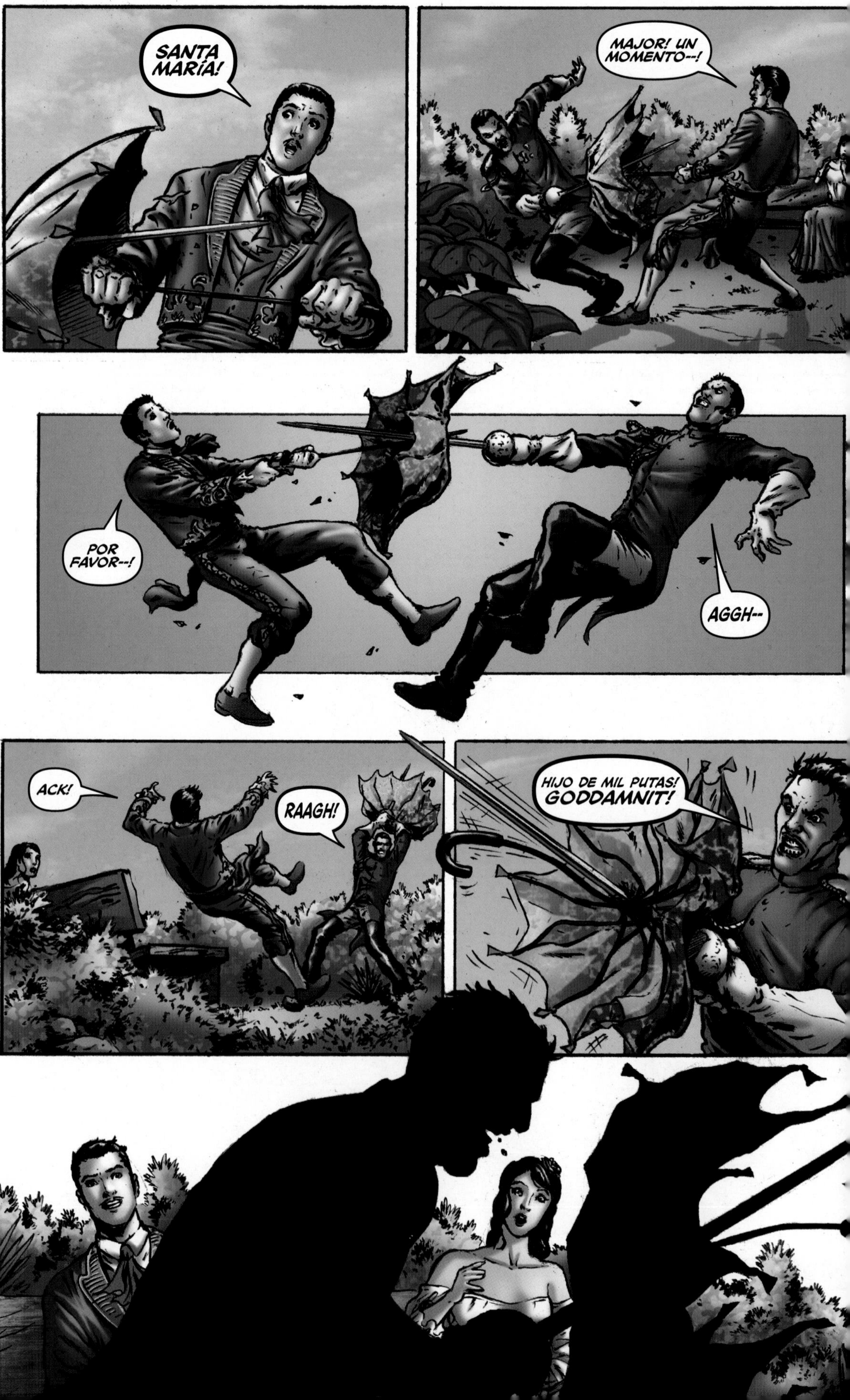
SANTA MARÍA!
MAJOR! UN MOMENTO--!
POR FAVOR--!
AGGH--
ACK!
RAAGH!
HIJO DE MIL PUTAS! GODDAMNIT!

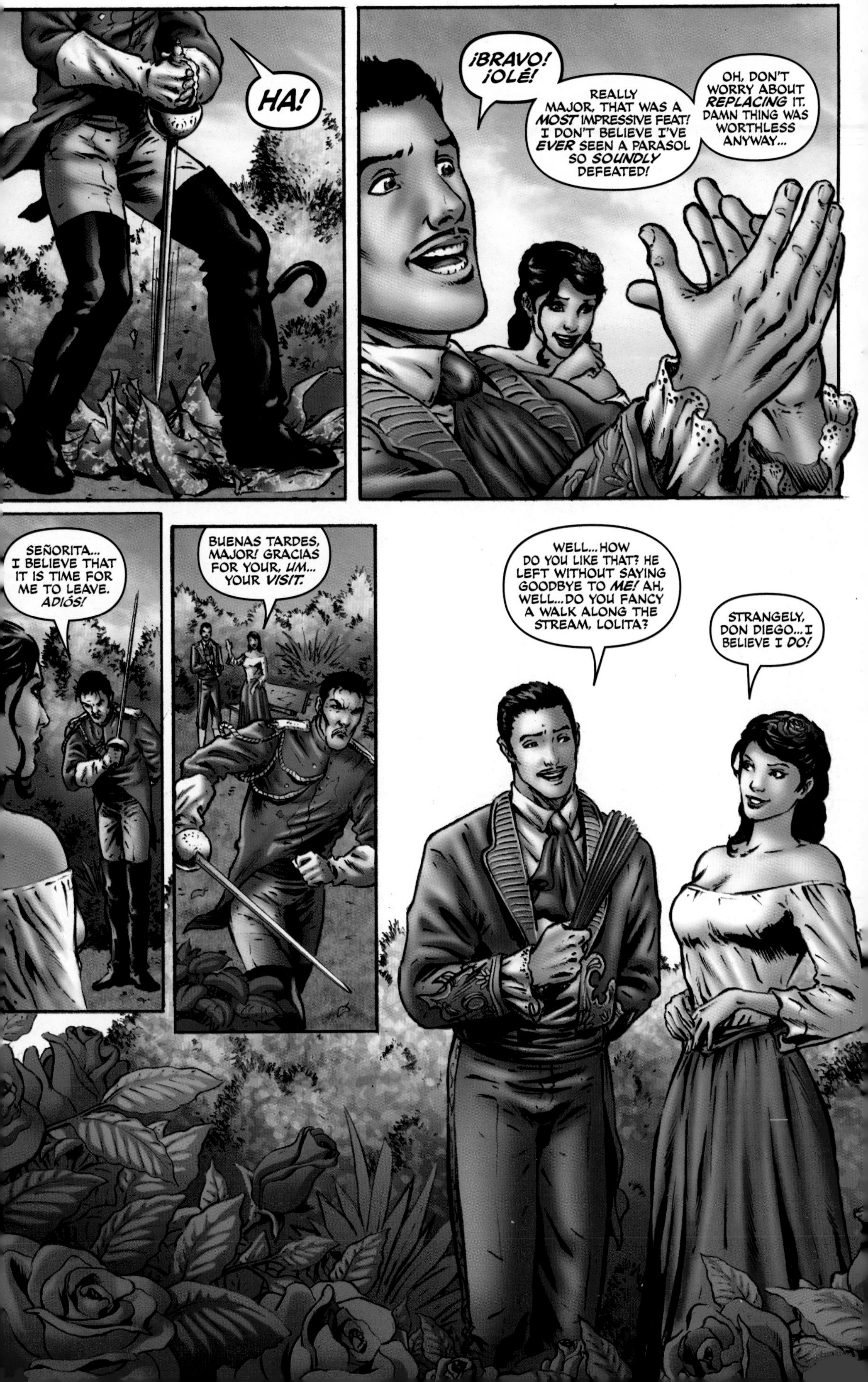
HA!
¡BRAVO! ¡OLÉ!
REALLY MAJOR, THAT WAS A MOST IMPRESSIVE FEAT! I DON'T BELIEVE I'VE EVER SEEN A PARASOL SO SOUNDLY DEFEATED!
OH, DON'T WORRY ABOUT REPLACING IT. DAMN THING WAS WORTHLESS ANYWAY...
SEÑORITA... I BELIEVE THAT IT IS TIME FOR ME TO LEAVE. ADIÓS!
BUENAS TARDES, MAJOR! GRACIAS FOR YOUR, UM... YOUR VISIT.
WELL... HOW DO YOU LIKE THAT? HE LEFT WITHOUT SAYING GOODBYE TO ME! AH, WELL... DO YOU FANCY A WALK ALONG THE STREAM, LOLITA?
STRANGELY, DON DIEGO... I BELIEVE I DO!

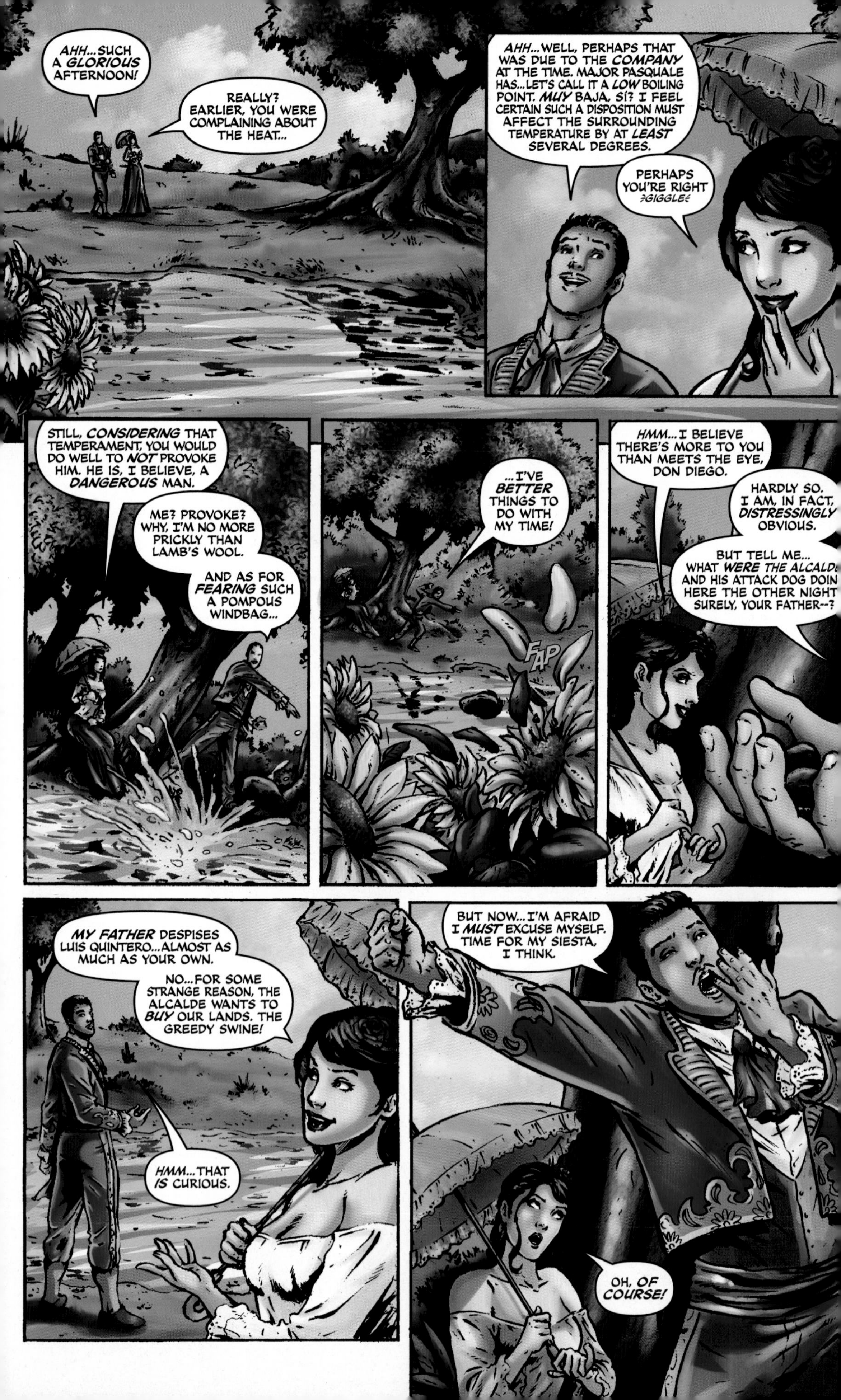
AHH...SUCH A GLORIOUS AFTERNOON!
REALLY? EARLIER, YOU WERE COMPLAINING ABOUT THE HEAT...
AHH...WELL, PERHAPS THAT WAS DUE TO THE COMPANY AT THE TIME. MAJOR PASQUALE HAS...LET'S CALL IT A LOW BOILING POINT. MUY BAJA, SÍ? I FEEL CERTAIN SUCH A DISPOSITION MUST AFFECT THE SURROUNDING TEMPERATURE BY AT LEAST SEVERAL DEGREES.
PERHAPS YOU'RE RIGHT
GIGGLE
STILL, CONSIDERING THAT TEMPERAMENT, YOU WOULD DO WELL TO NOT PROVOKE HIM. HE IS, I BELIEVE, A DANGEROUS MAN.
ME? PROVOKE? WHY, I'M NO MORE PRICKLY THAN LAMB'S WOOL.
AND AS FOR FEARING SUCH A POMPOUS WINDBAG...
...I'VE BETTER THINGS TO DO WITH MY TIME!
FAP
HMM...I BELIEVE THERE'S MORE TO YOU THAN MEETS THE EYE, DON DIEGO.
HARDLY SO. I AM, IN FACT, DISTRESSINGLY OBVIOUS.
BUT TELL ME... WHAT WERE THE ALCALD AND HIS ATTACK DOG DOIN HERE THE OTHER NIGHT SURELY, YOUR FATHER--?
MY FATHER DESPISES LUIS QUINTERO...ALMOST AS MUCH AS YOUR OWN.
NO...FOR SOME STRANGE REASON, THE ALCALDE WANTS TO BUY OUR LANDS. THE GREEDY SWINE!
HMM...THAT IS CURIOUS.
BUT NOW...I'M AFRAID I MUST EXCUSE MYSELF. TIME FOR MY SIESTA, I THINK.
OH, OF COURSE!

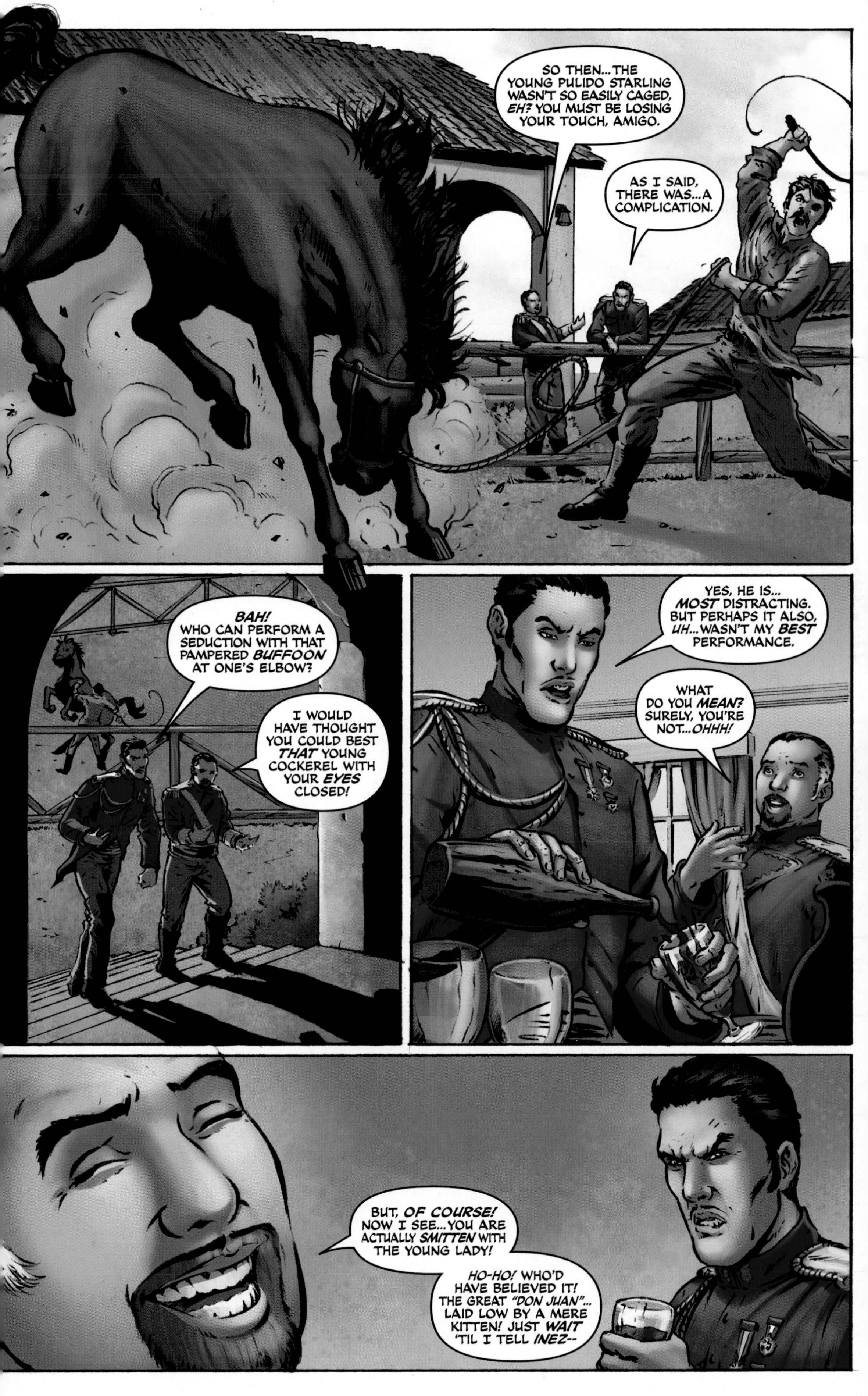
SO THEN... THE YOUNG PULIDO STARLING WASN'T SO EASILY CAGED, EH? YOU MUST BE LOSING YOUR TOUCH, AMIGO.
AS I SAID, THERE WAS...A COMPLICATION.
BAH! WHO CAN PERFORM A SEDUCTION WITH THAT PAMPERED BUFFOON AT ONE'S ELBOW?
I WOULD HAVE THOUGHT YOU COULD BEST THAT YOUNG COCKEREL WITH YOUR EYES CLOSED!
YES, HE IS... MOST DISTRACTING. BUT PERHAPS IT ALSO, UH...WASN'T MY BEST PERFORMANCE.
WHAT DO YOU MEAN? SURELY, YOU'RE NOT...OHHH!
BUT, OF COURSE! NOW I SEE...YOU ARE ACTUALLY SMITTEN WITH THE YOUNG LADY!
HO-HO! WHO'D HAVE BELIEVED IT! THE GREAT "DON JUAN"... LAID LOW BY A MERE KITTEN! JUST WAIT 'TIL I TELL INEZ--

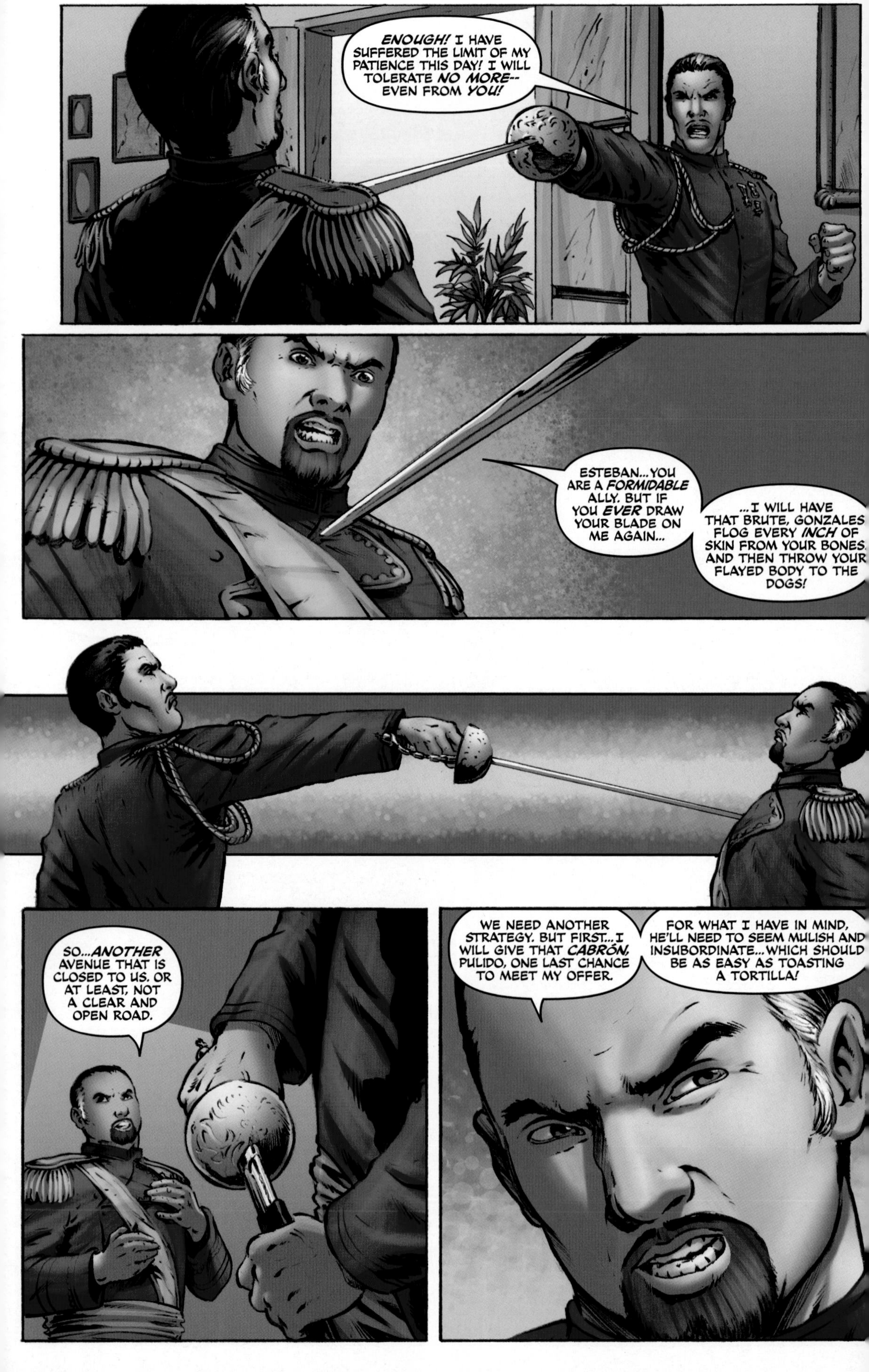
ENOUGH! I HAVE SUFFERED THE LIMIT OF MY PATIENCE THIS DAY! I WILL TOLERATE NO MORE-- EVEN FROM YOU!
ESTEBAN...YOU ARE A FORMIDABLE ALLY. BUT IF YOU EVER DRAW YOUR BLADE ON ME AGAIN...
...I WILL HAVE THAT BRUTE, GONZALES FLOG EVERY INCH OF SKIN FROM YOUR BONES. AND THEN THROW YOUR FLAYED BODY TO THE DOGS!
SO...ANOTHER AVENUE THAT IS CLOSED TO US. OR AT LEAST, NOT A CLEAR AND OPEN ROAD.
WE NEED ANOTHER STRATEGY. BUT FIRST...I WILL GIVE THAT CABRÓN, PULIDO, ONE LAST CHANCE TO MEET MY OFFER.
FOR WHAT I HAVE IN MIND, HE'LL NEED TO SEEM MULISH AND INSUBORDINATE...WHICH SHOULD BE AS EASY AS TOASTING A TORTILLA!

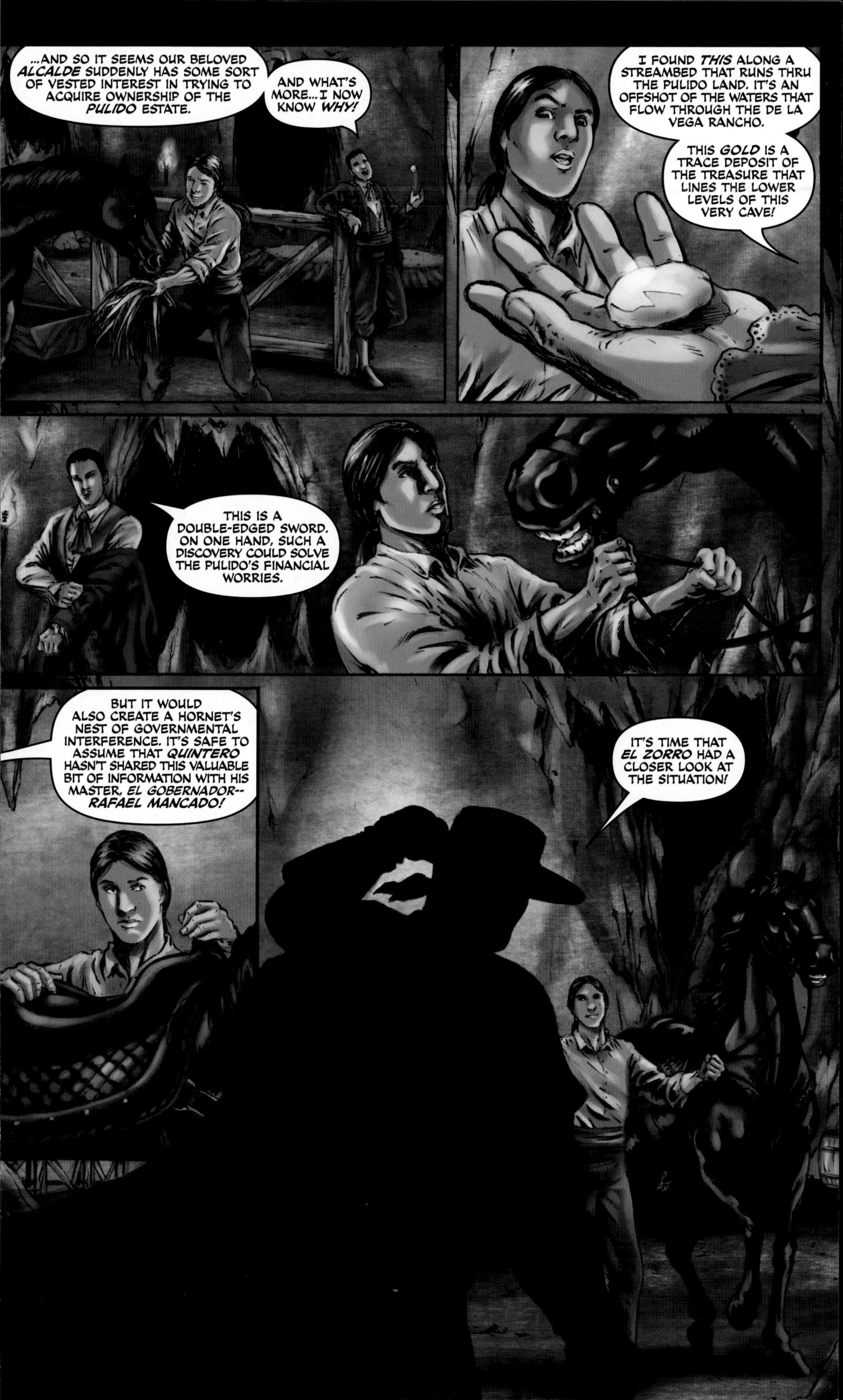
...AND SO IT SEEMS OUR BELOVED ALCALDE SUDDENLY HAS SOME SORT OF VESTED INTEREST IN TRYING TO ACQUIRE OWNERSHIP OF THE PULIDO ESTATE.
AND WHAT'S MORE... I NOW KNOW WHY!
I FOUND THIS ALONG A STREAMBED THAT RUNS THRU THE PULIDO LAND. IT'S AN OFFSHOT OF THE WATERS THAT FLOW THROUGH THE DE LA VEGA RANCHO.
THIS GOLD IS A TRACE DEPOSIT OF THE TREASURE THAT LINES THE LOWER LEVELS OF THIS VERY CAVE!
THIS IS A DOUBLE-EDGED SWORD. ON ONE HAND, SUCH A DISCOVERY COULD SOLVE THE PULIDO'S FINANCIAL WORRIES.
BUT IT WOULD ALSO CREATE A HORNET'S NEST OF GOVERNMENTAL INTERFERENCE. IT'S SAFE TO ASSUME THAT QUINTERO HASN'T SHARED THIS VALUABLE BIT OF INFORMATION WITH HIS MASTER, EL GOBERNADOR-- RAFAEL MANCADO!
IT'S TIME THAT EL ZORRO HAD A CLOSER LOOK AT THE SITUATION!

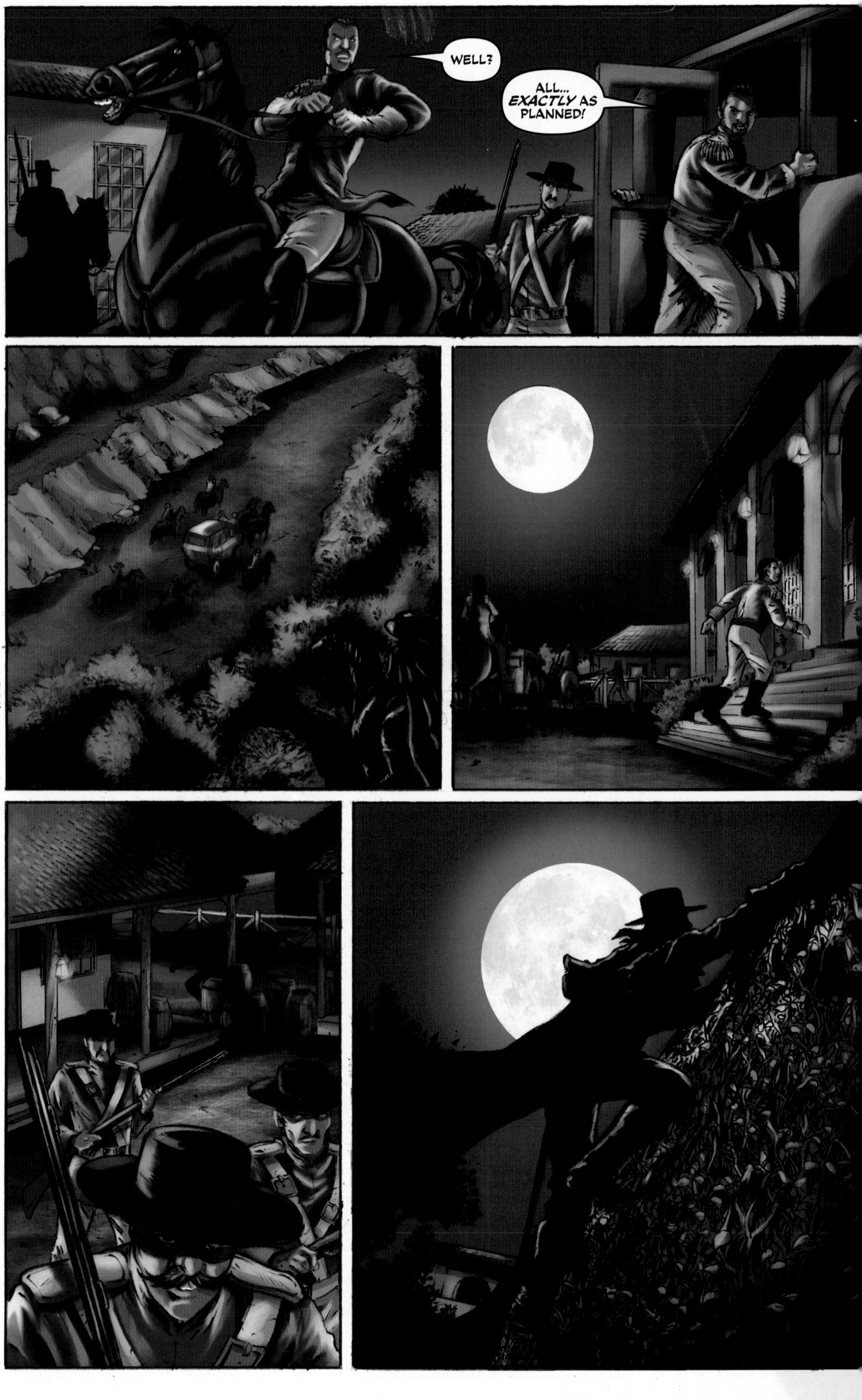

WELL?
ALL... EXACTLY AS PLANNED!

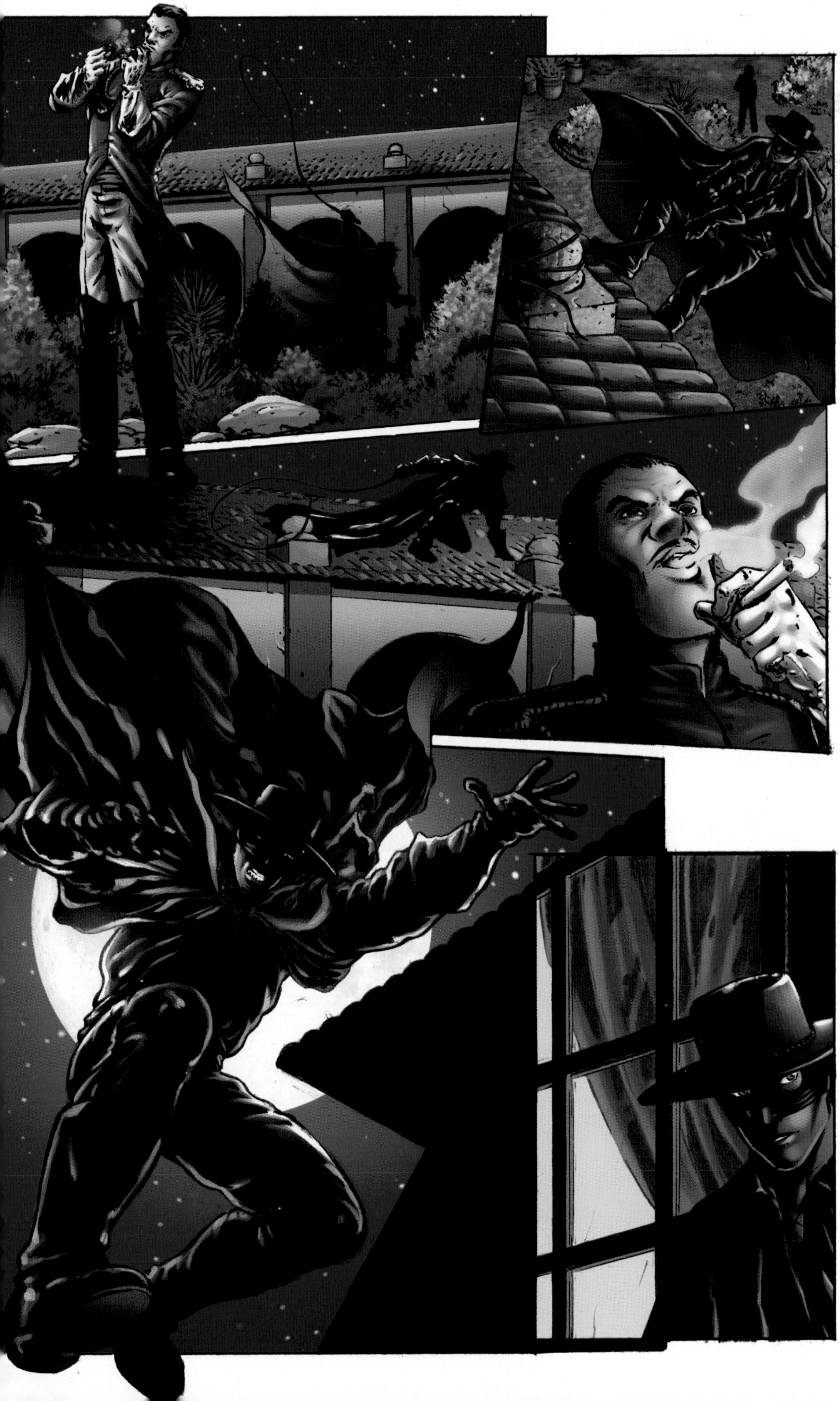

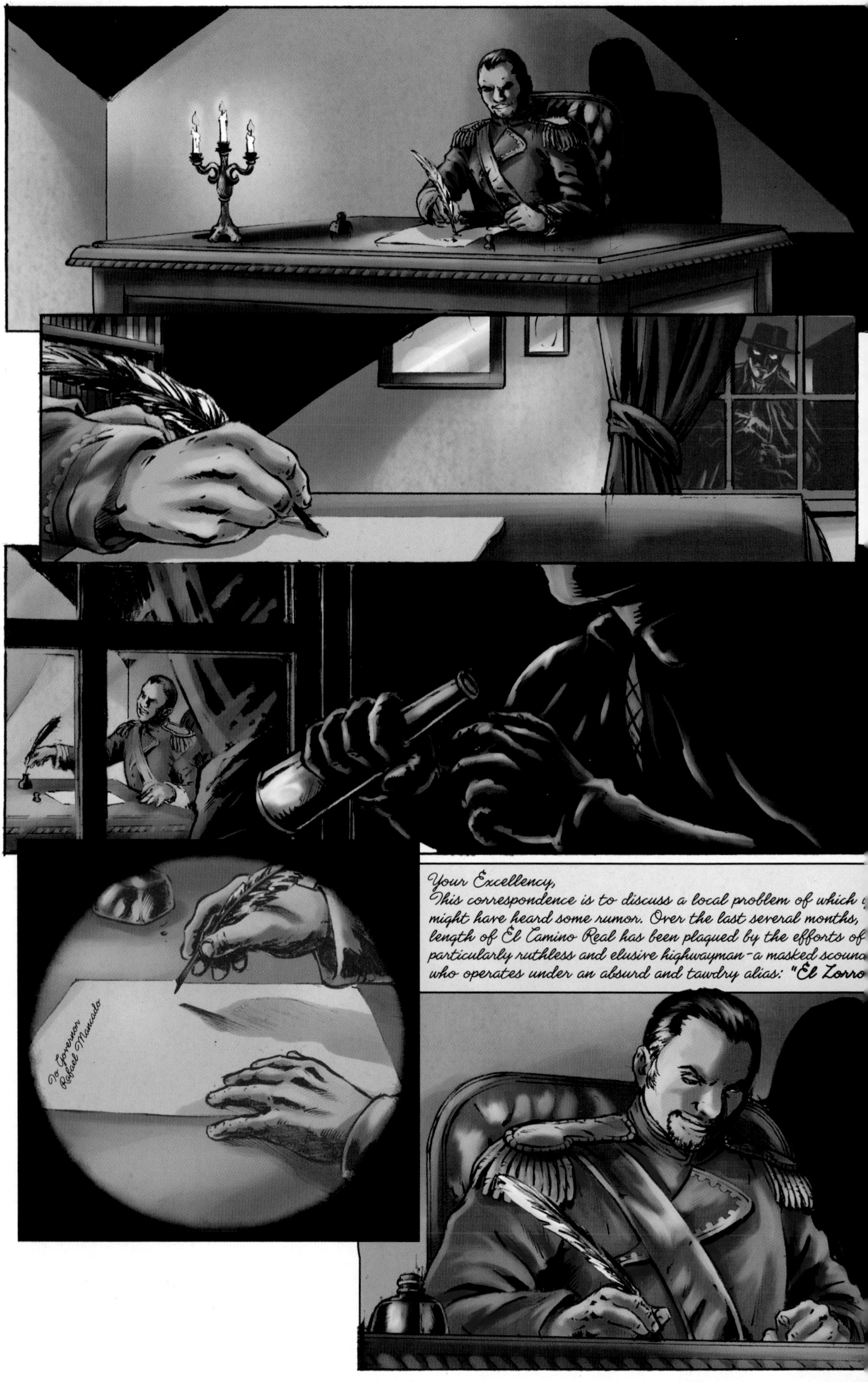
To Governor
Rafael Mancado
Your Excellency,
This correspondence is to discuss a local problem of which
might have heard some rumor. Over the last several months,
length of El Camino Real has been plagued by the efforts of
particularly ruthless and elusive highwayman–a masked scoun
who operates under an absurd and tawdry alias: "El Zorro

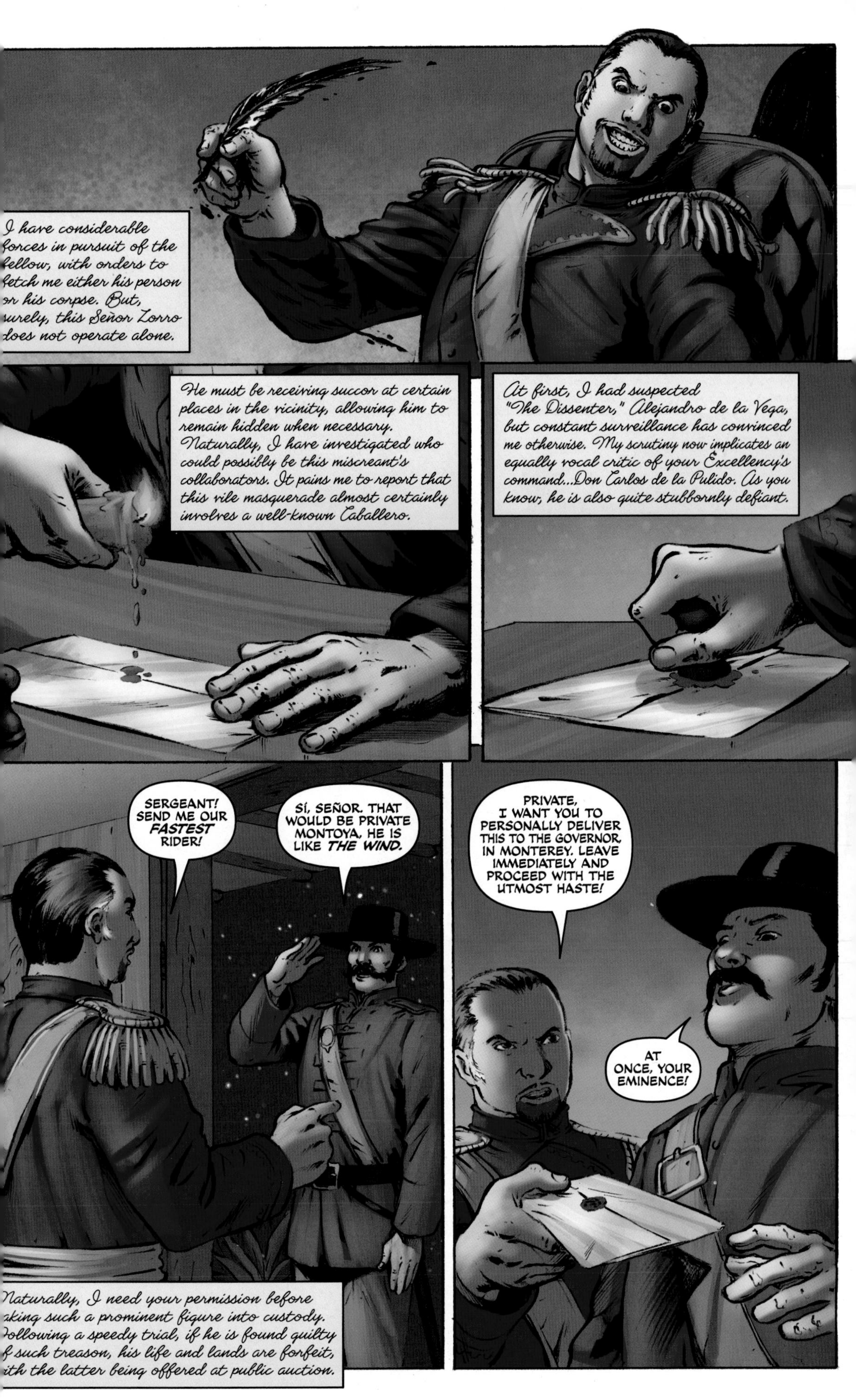
I have considerable forces in pursuit of the fellow, with orders to fetch me either his person or his corpse. But, surely, this Señor Zorro does not operate alone.
He must be receiving succor at certain places in the vicinity, allowing him to remain hidden when necessary. Naturally, I have investigated who could possibly be this miscreant's collaborators. It pains me to report that this vile masquerade almost certainly involves a well-known Caballero.
At first, I had suspected "The Dissenter," Alejandro de la Vega, but constant surveillance has convinced me otherwise. My scrutiny now implicates an equally vocal critic of your Excellency's command...Don Carlos de la Pulido. As you know, he is also quite stubbornly defiant.
SERGEANT! SEND ME OUR FASTEST RIDER!
SÍ, SEÑOR. THAT WOULD BE PRIVATE MONTOYA. HE IS LIKE THE WIND.
Naturally, I need your permission before taking such a prominent figure into custody. Following a speedy trial, if he is found guilty of such treason, his life and lands are forfeit, with the latter being offered at public auction.
PRIVATE, I WANT YOU TO PERSONALLY DELIVER THIS TO THE GOVERNOR IN MONTEREY. LEAVE IMMEDIATELY AND PROCEED WITH THE UTMOST HASTE!
AT ONCE, YOUR EMINENCE!

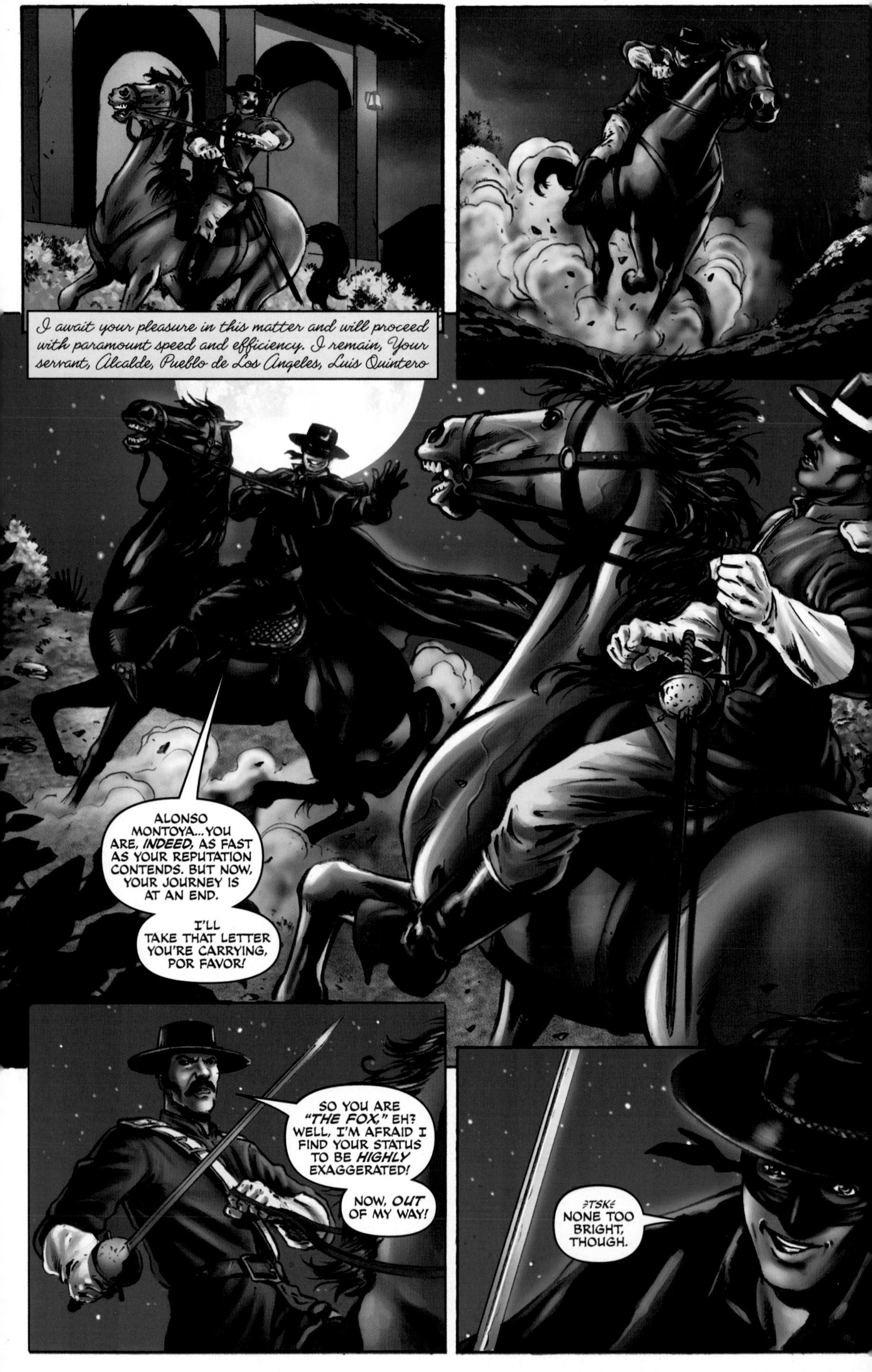
I await your pleasure in this matter and will proceed with paramount speed and efficiency. I remain, Your servant, Alcalde, Pueblo de Los Angeles, Luis Quintero
ALONSO MONTOYA...YOU ARE, INDEED, AS FAST AS YOUR REPUTATION CONTENDS. BUT NOW, YOUR JOURNEY IS AT AN END.
I'LL TAKE THAT LETTER YOU'RE CARRYING, POR FAVOR!
SO YOU ARE "THE FOX," EH? WELL, I'M AFRAID I FIND YOUR STATUS TO BE HIGHLY EXAGGERATED!
NOW, OUT OF MY WAY!
TSK
NONE TOO BRIGHT, THOUGH.

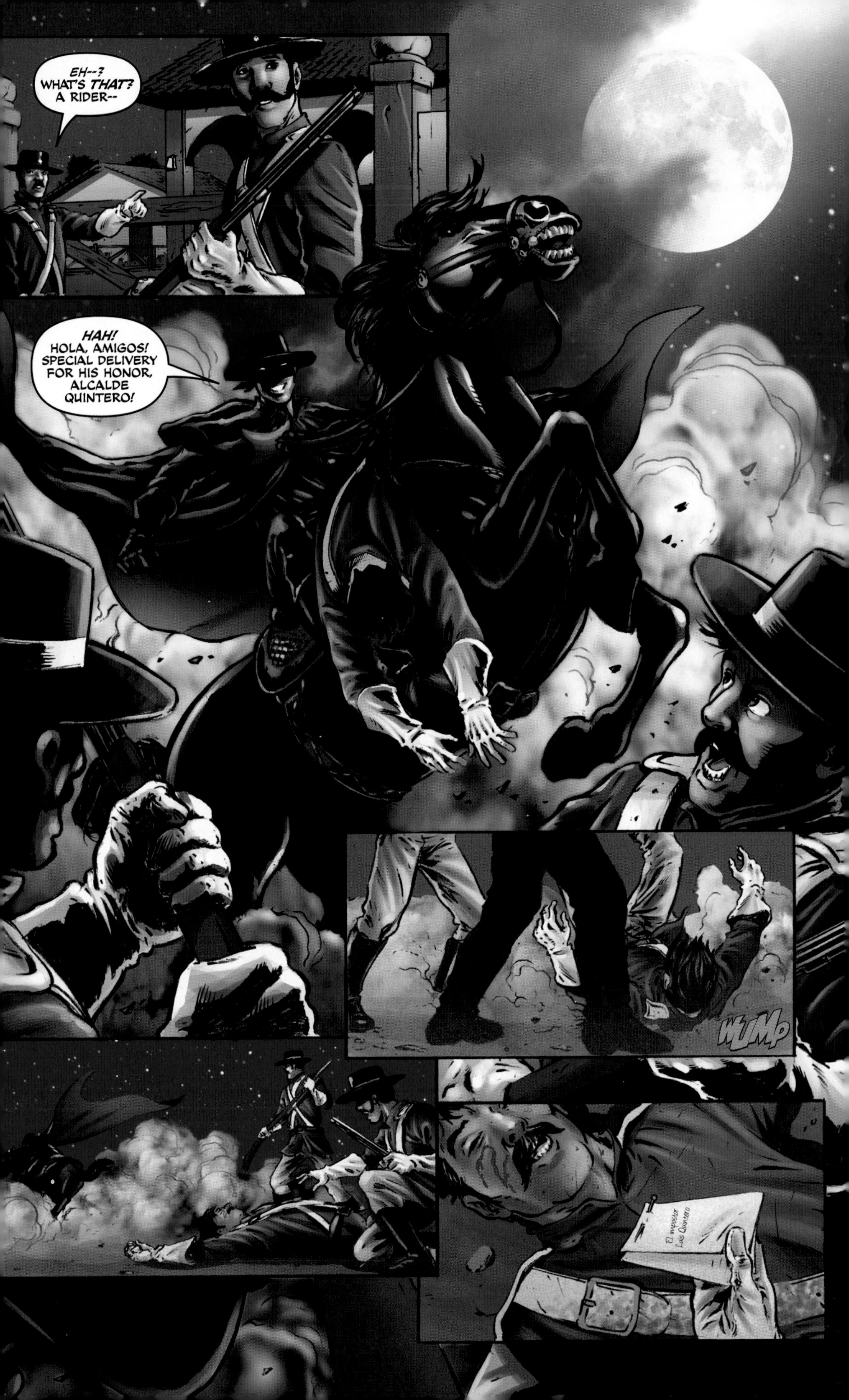
EH--? WHAT'S THAT? A RIDER--
HAH! HOLA, AMIGOS! SPECIAL DELIVERY FOR HIS HONOR, ALCALDE QUINTERO!
WUMP
El impostor Luis Quintero

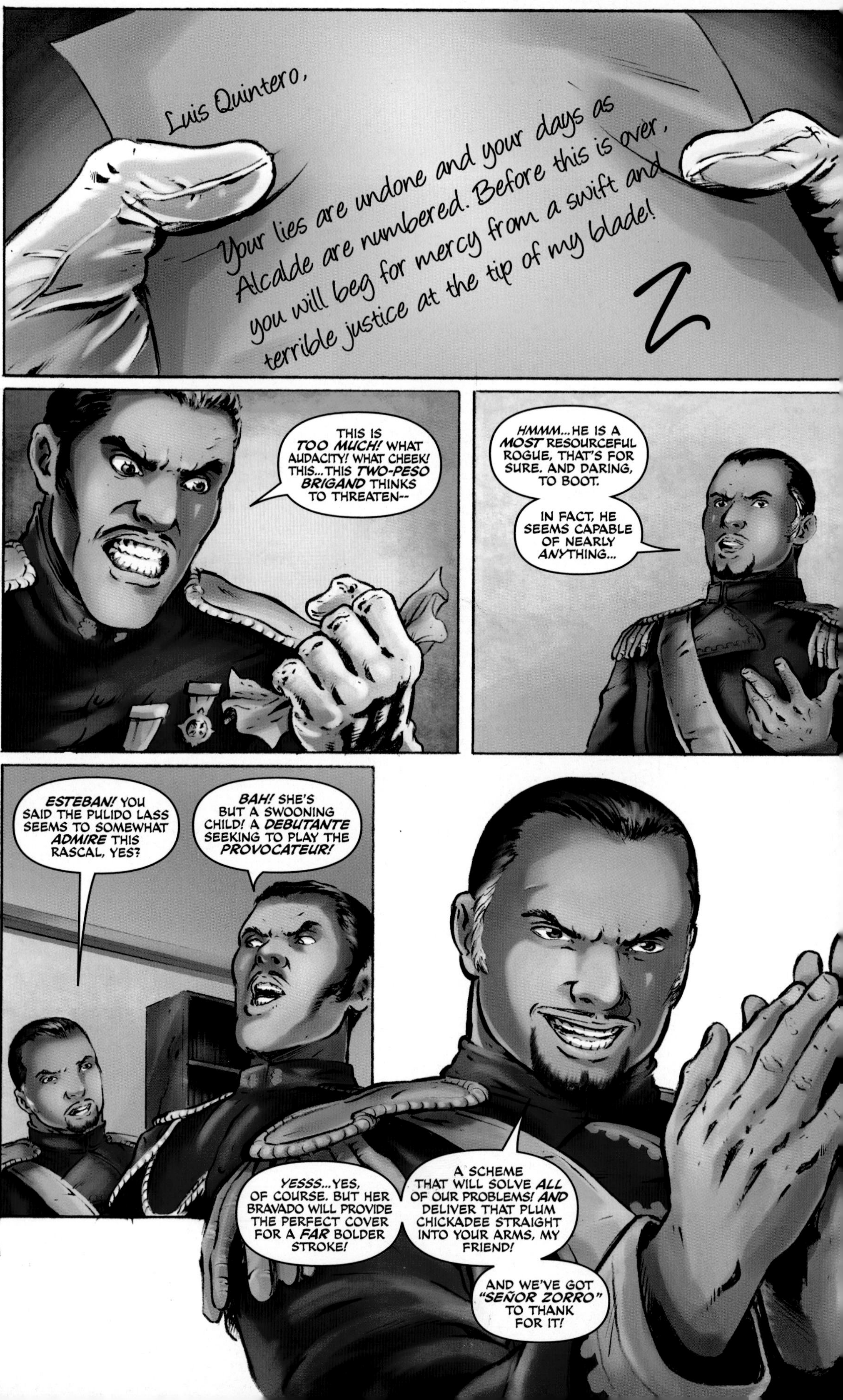

Luis Quintero,
Your lies are undone and your days as Alcalde are numbered. Before this is over, you will beg for mercy from a swift and terrible justice at the tip of my blade!
Z
THIS IS TOO MUCH! WHAT AUDACITY! WHAT CHEEK! THIS...THIS TWO-PESO BRIGAND THINKS TO THREATEN--
HMMM...HE IS A MOST RESOURCEFUL ROGUE, THAT'S FOR SURE. AND DARING, TO BOOT.
IN FACT, HE SEEMS CAPABLE OF NEARLY ANYTHING...
ESTEBAN! YOU SAID THE PULIDO LASS SEEMS TO SOMEWHAT ADMIRE THIS RASCAL, YES?
BAH! SHE'S BUT A SWOONING CHILD! A DEBUTANTE SEEKING TO PLAY THE PROVOCATEUR!
YESSS...YES, OF COURSE. BUT HER BRAVADO WILL PROVIDE THE PERFECT COVER FOR A FAR BOLDER STROKE!
A SCHEME THAT WILL SOLVE ALL OF OUR PROBLEMS! AND DELIVER THAT PLUM CHICKADEE STRAIGHT INTO YOUR ARMS, MY FRIEND!
AND WE'VE GOT "SEÑOR ZORRO" TO THANK FOR IT!

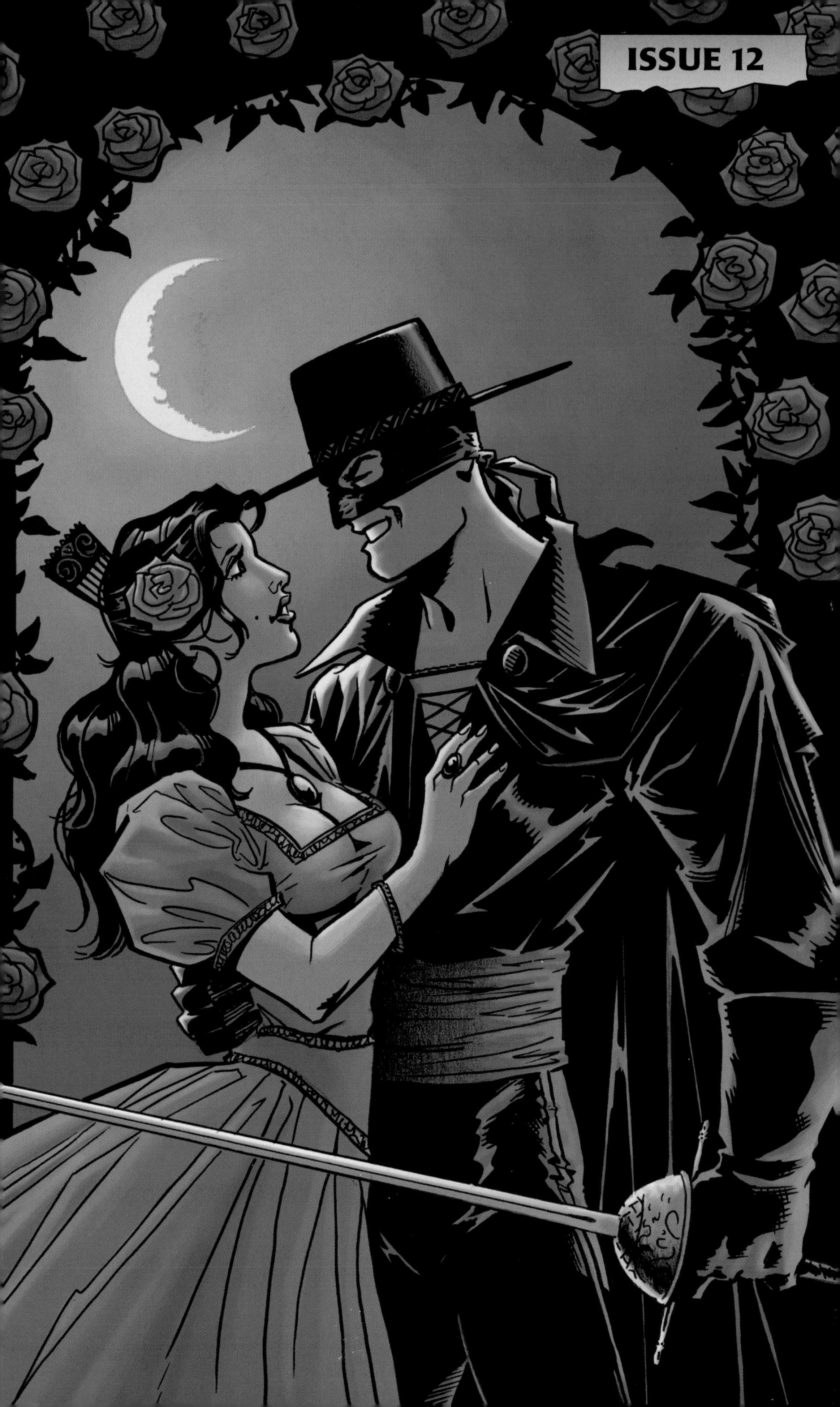
ISSUE 12

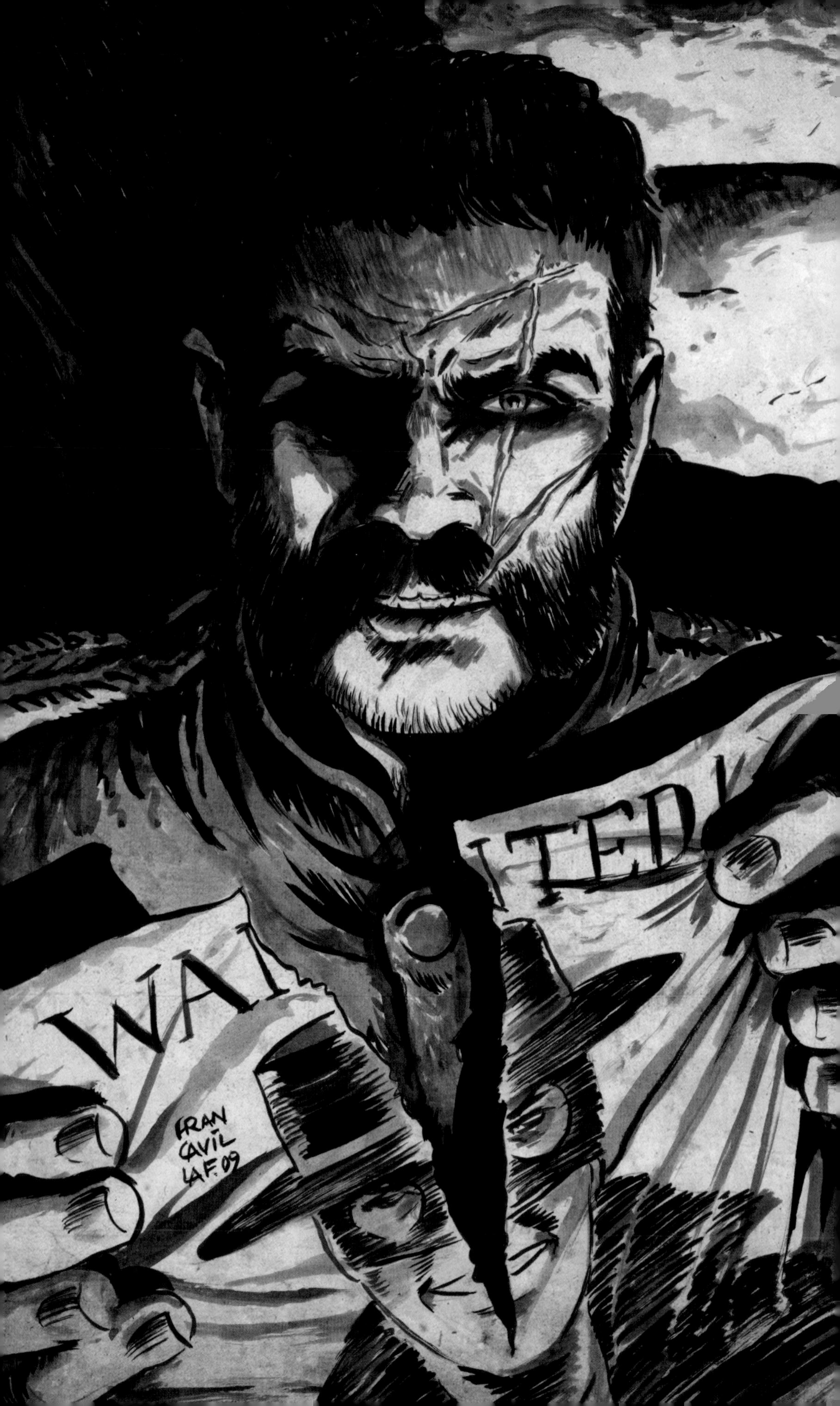
WA
TED!
FRAN
CAVIL
LAF.09

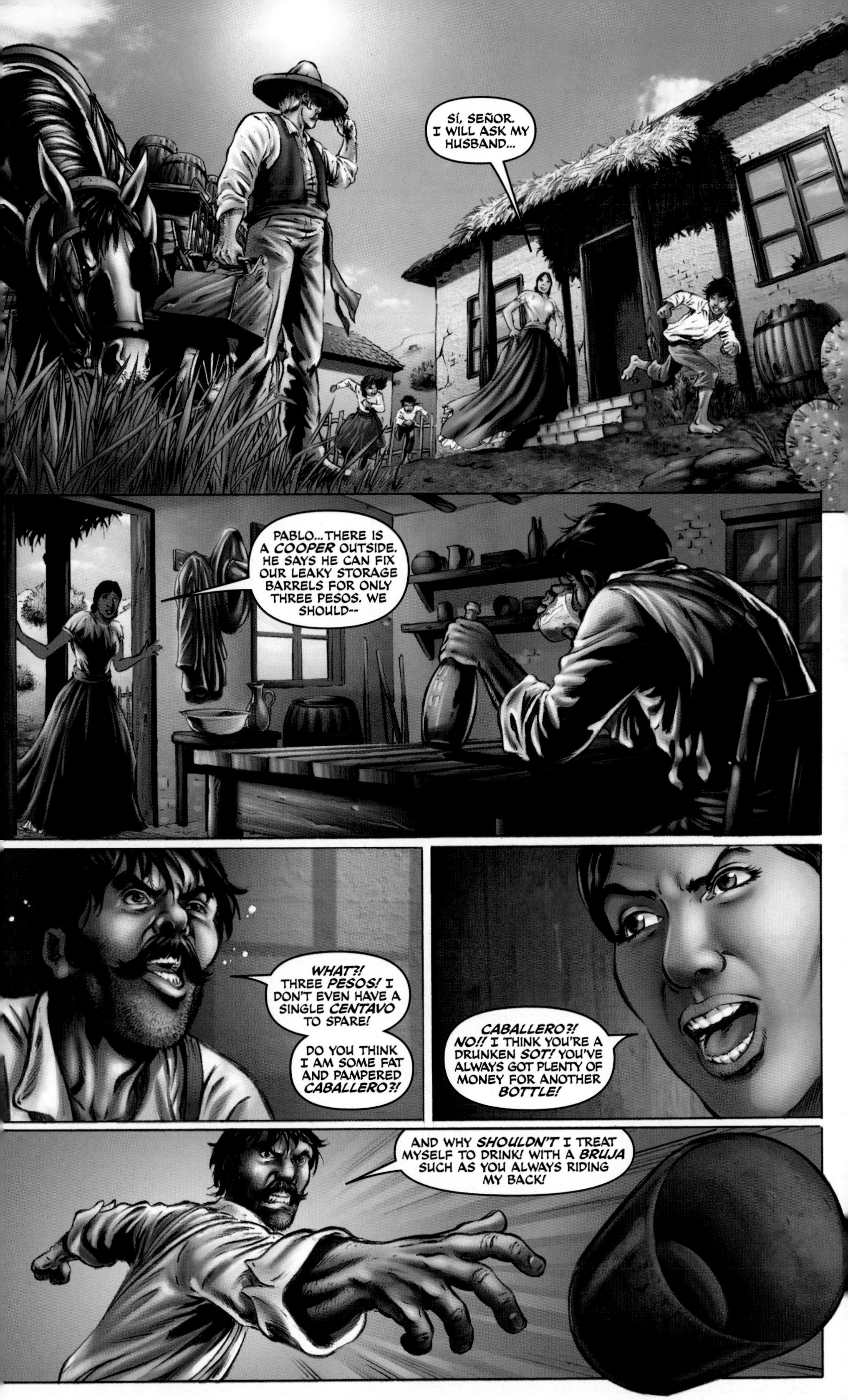

SÍ, SEÑOR. I WILL ASK MY HUSBAND...
PABLO...THERE IS A *COOPER* OUTSIDE. HE SAYS HE CAN FIX OUR LEAKY STORAGE BARRELS FOR ONLY THREE PESOS. WE SHOULD--
WHAT?! THREE *PESOS!* I DON'T EVEN HAVE A SINGLE *CENTAVO* TO SPARE!
DO YOU THINK I AM SOME FAT AND PAMPERED *CABALLERO?!*
CABALLERO?! NO!! I THINK YOU'RE A DRUNKEN *SOT!* YOU'VE ALWAYS GOT PLENTY OF MONEY FOR ANOTHER *BOTTLE!*
AND WHY *SHOULDN'T* I TREAT MYSELF TO DRINK! WITH A *BRUJA* SUCH AS YOU ALWAYS RIDING MY BACK!

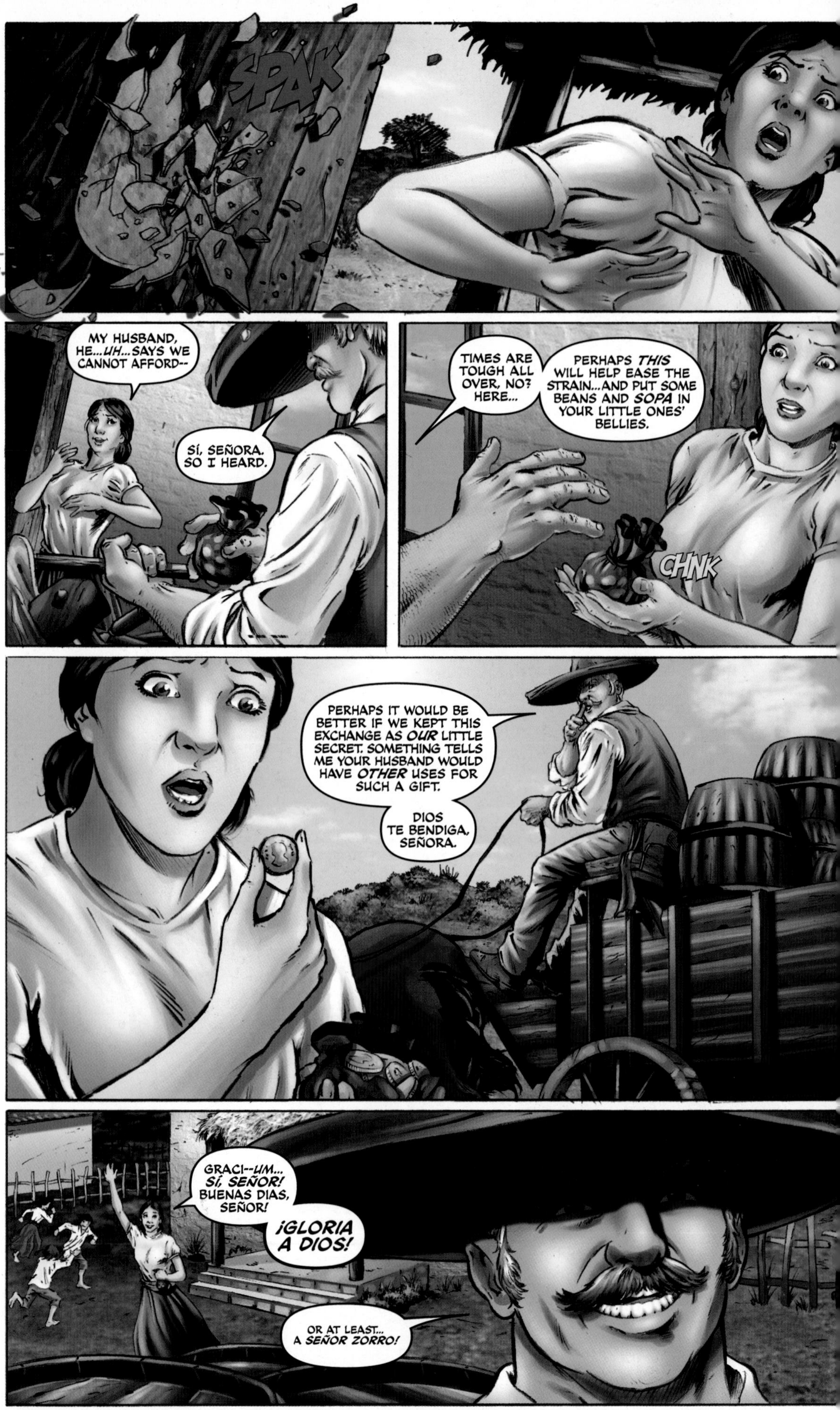
SPAK
MY HUSBAND, HE...UH...SAYS WE CANNOT AFFORD--
SÍ, SEÑORA. SO I HEARD.
TIMES ARE TOUGH ALL OVER, NO? HERE...
PERHAPS THIS WILL HELP EASE THE STRAIN...AND PUT SOME BEANS AND SOPA IN YOUR LITTLE ONES' BELLIES.
CHNK
PERHAPS IT WOULD BE BETTER IF WE KEPT THIS EXCHANGE AS OUR LITTLE SECRET. SOMETHING TELLS ME YOUR HUSBAND WOULD HAVE OTHER USES FOR SUCH A GIFT.
DIOS TE BENDIGA, SEÑORA.
GRACI--UM... SÍ, SEÑOR! BUENAS DIAS, SEÑOR!
¡GLORIA A DIOS!
OR AT LEAST... A SEÑOR ZORRO!

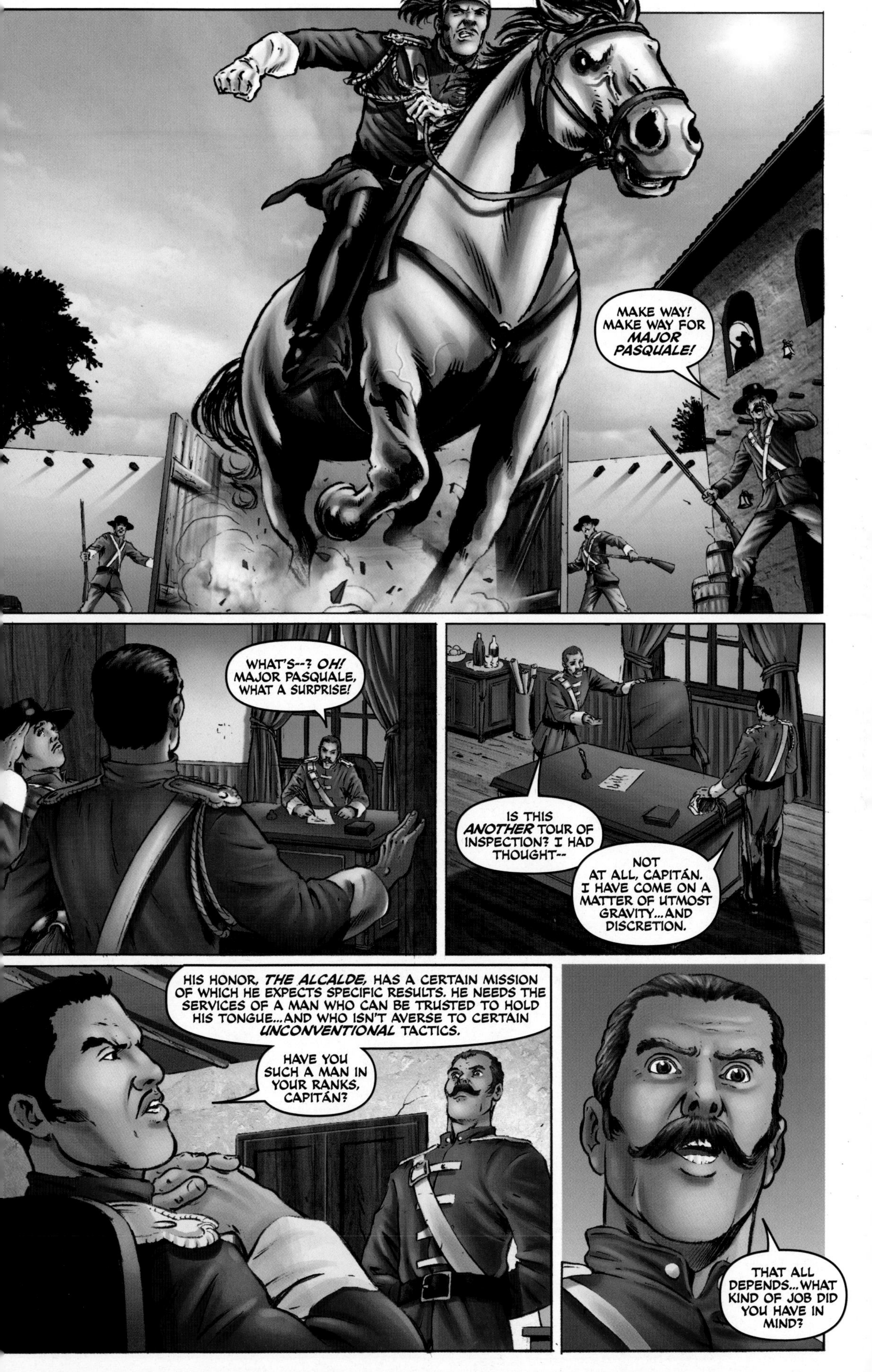
MAKE WAY! MAKE WAY FOR *MAJOR PASQUALE!*
WHAT'S--? *OH!* MAJOR PASQUALE, WHAT A SURPRISE!
IS THIS *ANOTHER* TOUR OF INSPECTION? I HAD THOUGHT--
NOT AT ALL, CAPITÁN. I HAVE COME ON A MATTER OF UTMOST GRAVITY...AND DISCRETION.
HIS HONOR, *THE ALCALDE,* HAS A CERTAIN MISSION OF WHICH HE EXPECTS SPECIFIC RESULTS. HE NEEDS THE SERVICES OF A MAN WHO CAN BE TRUSTED TO HOLD HIS TONGUE...AND WHO ISN'T AVERSE TO CERTAIN *UNCONVENTIONAL* TACTICS.
HAVE YOU SUCH A MAN IN YOUR RANKS, CAPITÁN?
THAT ALL DEPENDS...WHAT KIND OF JOB DID YOU HAVE IN MIND?

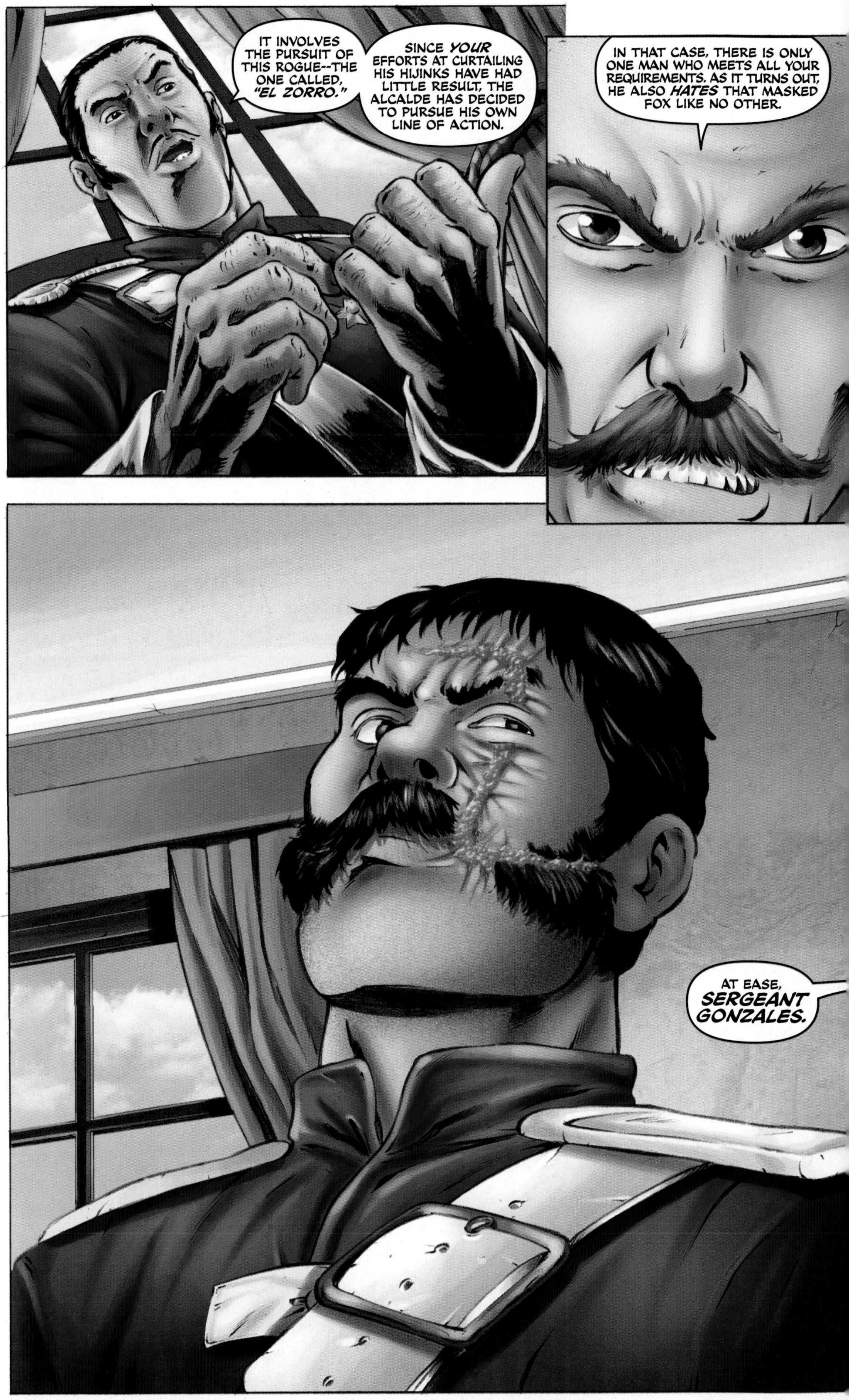
IT INVOLVES THE PURSUIT OF THIS ROGUE--THE ONE CALLED, "EL ZORRO."
SINCE YOUR EFFORTS AT CURTAILING HIS HIJINKS HAVE HAD LITTLE RESULT, THE ALCALDE HAS DECIDED TO PURSUE HIS OWN LINE OF ACTION.
IN THAT CASE, THERE IS ONLY ONE MAN WHO MEETS ALL YOUR REQUIREMENTS. AS IT TURNS OUT, HE ALSO HATES THAT MASKED FOX LIKE NO OTHER.
AT EASE, SERGEANT GONZALES.

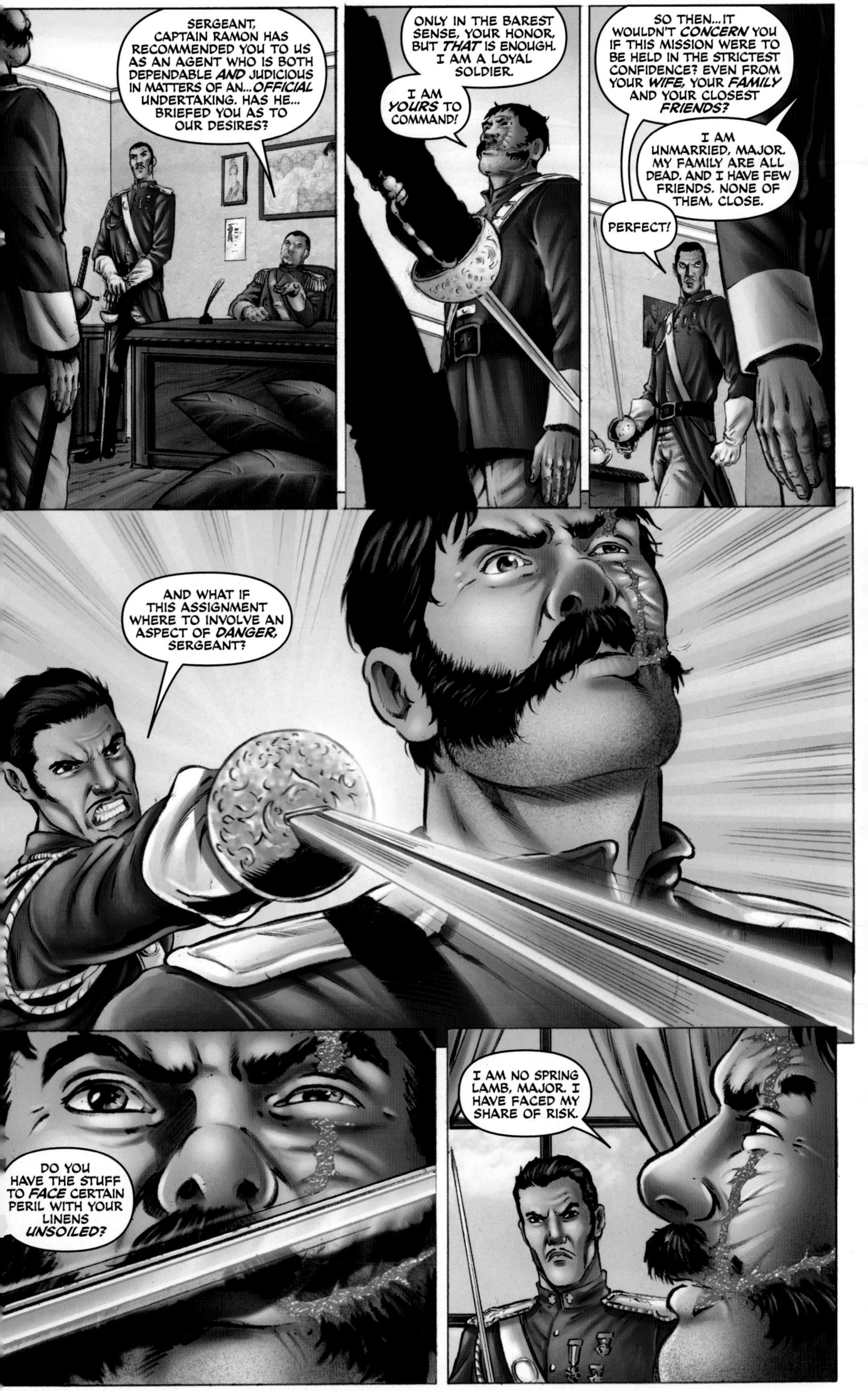
SERGEANT, CAPTAIN RAMON HAS RECOMMENDED YOU TO US AS AN AGENT WHO IS BOTH DEPENDABLE AND JUDICIOUS IN MATTERS OF AN...OFFICIAL UNDERTAKING. HAS HE... BRIEFED YOU AS TO OUR DESIRES?
ONLY IN THE BAREST SENSE, YOUR HONOR, BUT THAT IS ENOUGH. I AM A LOYAL SOLDIER.
I AM YOURS TO COMMAND!
SO THEN...IT WOULDN'T CONCERN YOU IF THIS MISSION WERE TO BE HELD IN THE STRICTEST CONFIDENCE? EVEN FROM YOUR WIFE, YOUR FAMILY AND YOUR CLOSEST FRIENDS?
I AM UNMARRIED, MAJOR. MY FAMILY ARE ALL DEAD. AND I HAVE FEW FRIENDS. NONE OF THEM, CLOSE.
PERFECT!
AND WHAT IF THIS ASSIGNMENT WHERE TO INVOLVE AN ASPECT OF DANGER, SERGEANT?
DO YOU HAVE THE STUFF TO FACE CERTAIN PERIL WITH YOUR LINENS UNSOILED?
I AM NO SPRING LAMB, MAJOR. I HAVE FACED MY SHARE OF RISK.

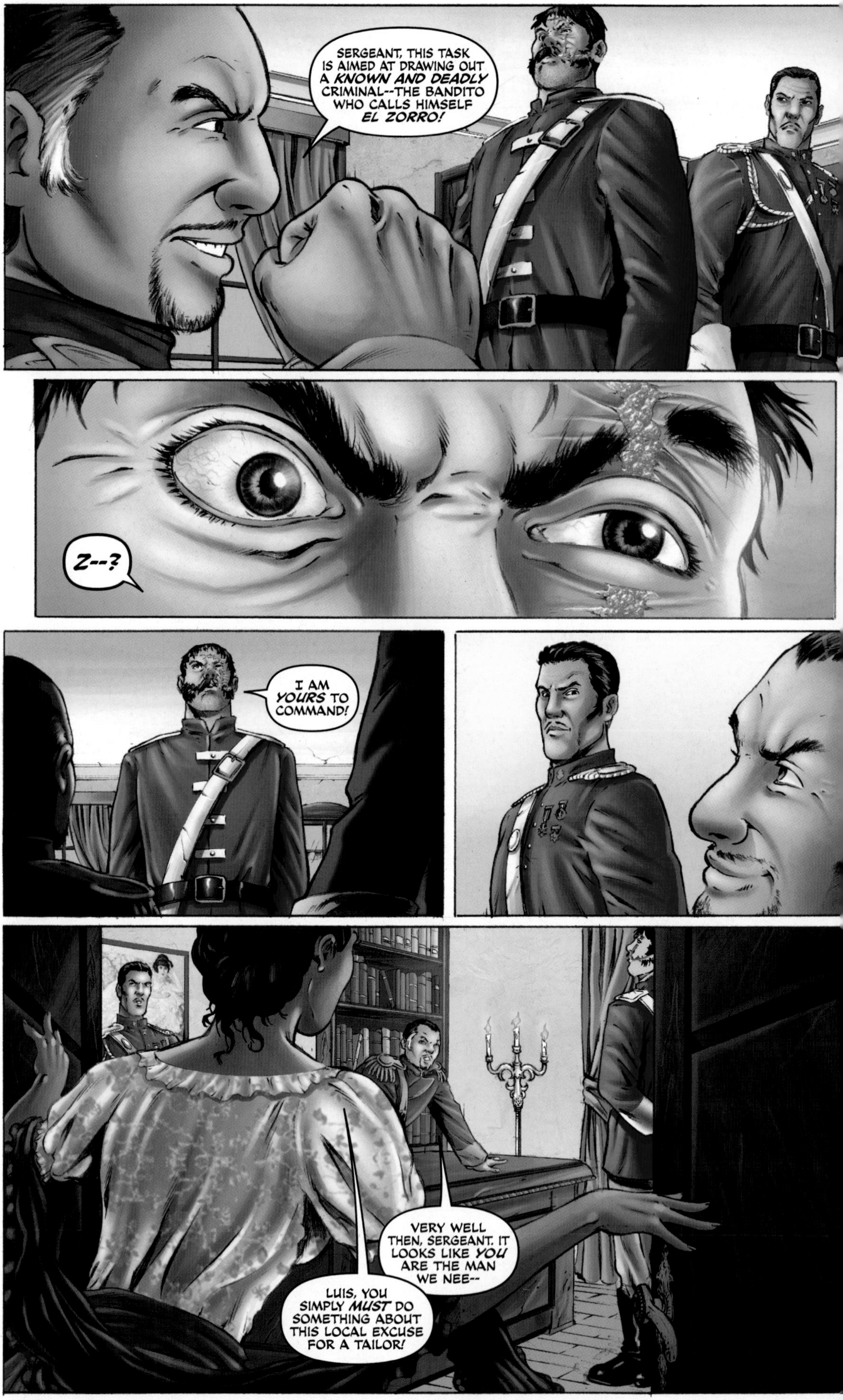
SERGEANT, THIS TASK IS AIMED AT DRAWING OUT A *KNOWN AND DEADLY* CRIMINAL--THE BANDITO WHO CALLS HIMSELF *EL ZORRO!*
Z--?
I AM *YOURS* TO COMMAND!
VERY WELL THEN, SERGEANT. IT LOOKS LIKE *YOU* ARE THE MAN WE NEE--
LUIS, YOU SIMPLY *MUST* DO SOMETHING ABOUT THIS LOCAL EXCUSE FOR A TAILOR!

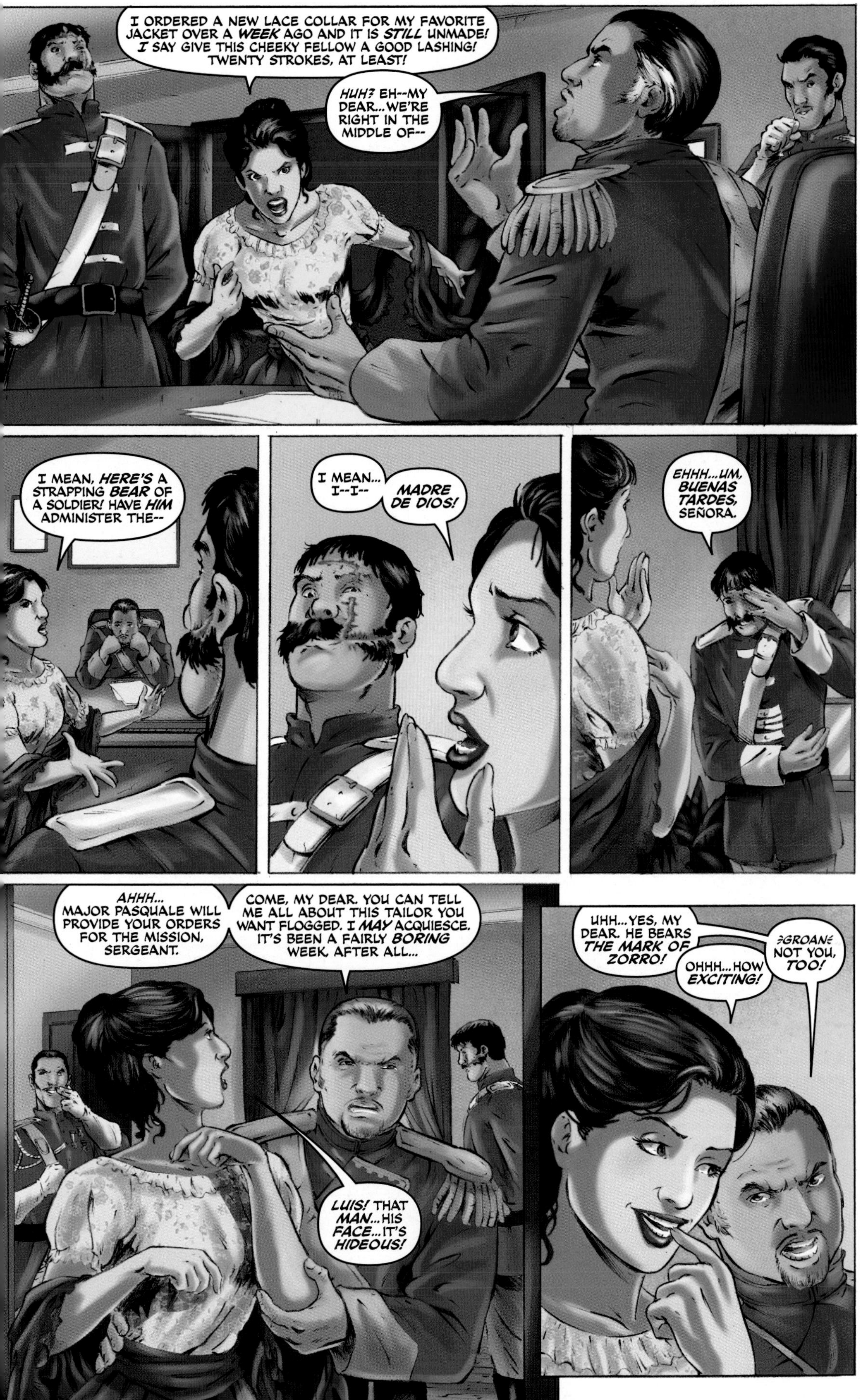
I ORDERED A NEW LACE COLLAR FOR MY FAVORITE JACKET OVER A *WEEK* AGO AND IT IS *STILL* UNMADE! *I* SAY GIVE THIS CHEEKY FELLOW A GOOD LASHING! TWENTY STROKES, AT LEAST!
HUH? EH--MY DEAR... WE'RE RIGHT IN THE MIDDLE OF--
I MEAN, *HERE'S* A STRAPPING *BEAR* OF A SOLDIER! HAVE *HIM* ADMINISTER THE--
I MEAN... I--I--
MADRE DE DIOS!
EHHH...UM, BUENAS TARDES, SEÑORA.
AHHH... MAJOR PASQUALE WILL PROVIDE YOUR ORDERS FOR THE MISSION, SERGEANT.
COME, MY DEAR. YOU CAN TELL ME ALL ABOUT THIS TAILOR YOU WANT FLOGGED. I *MAY* ACQUIESCE. IT'S BEEN A FAIRLY *BORING* WEEK, AFTER ALL...
LUIS! THAT *MAN*... HIS *FACE*... IT'S *HIDEOUS!*
UHH... YES, MY DEAR. HE BEARS *THE MARK OF ZORRO!*
OHHH... HOW *EXCITING!*
≡GROAN≡ NOT YOU, *TOO!*

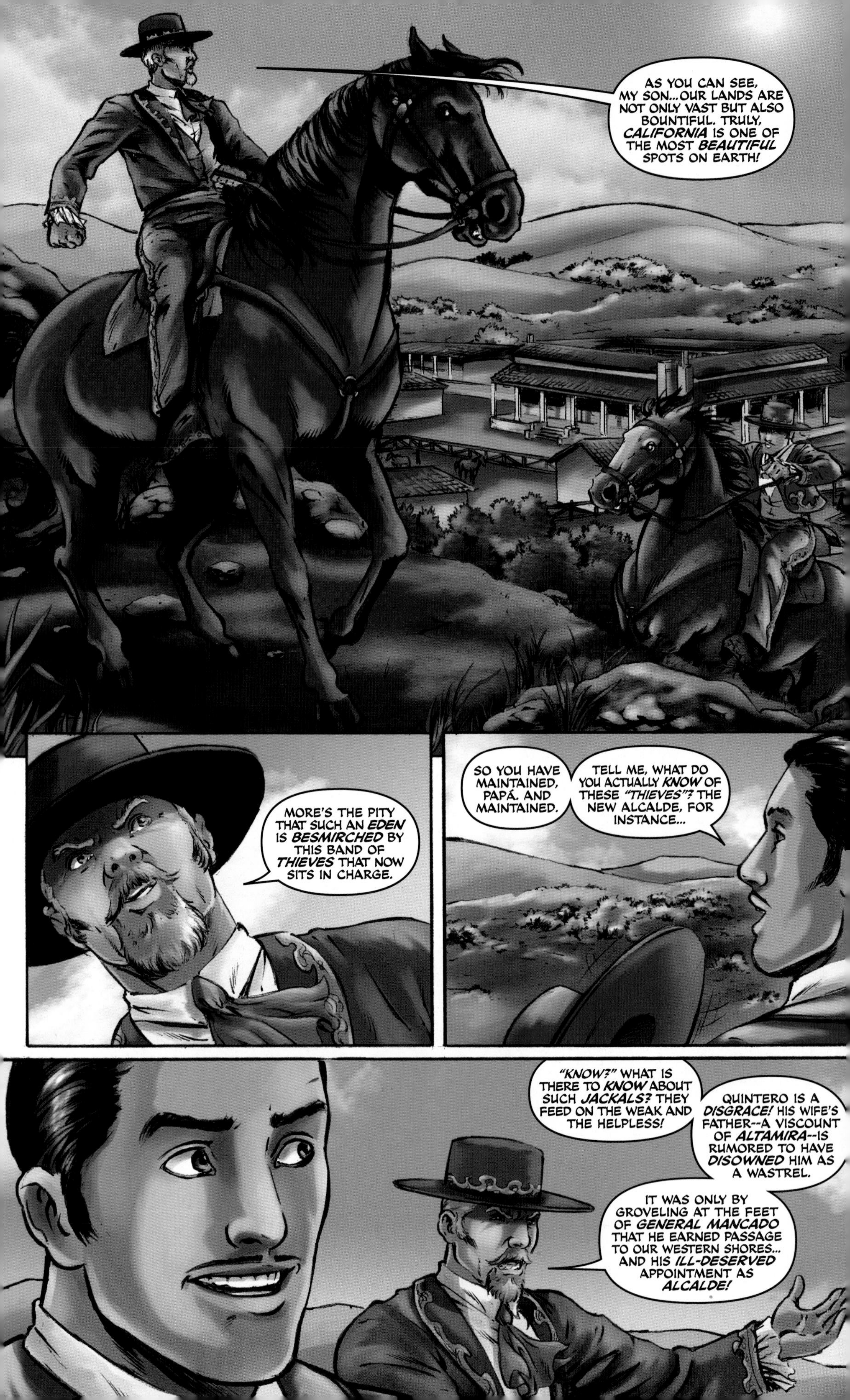
AS YOU CAN SEE, MY SON...OUR LANDS ARE NOT ONLY VAST BUT ALSO BOUNTIFUL. TRULY, CALIFORNIA IS ONE OF THE MOST BEAUTIFUL SPOTS ON EARTH!
MORE'S THE PITY THAT SUCH AN EDEN IS BESMIRCHED BY THIS BAND OF THIEVES THAT NOW SITS IN CHARGE.
SO YOU HAVE MAINTAINED, PAPÁ. AND MAINTAINED.
TELL ME, WHAT DO YOU ACTUALLY KNOW OF THESE "THIEVES"? THE NEW ALCALDE, FOR INSTANCE...
"KNOW?" WHAT IS THERE TO KNOW ABOUT SUCH JACKALS? THEY FEED ON THE WEAK AND THE HELPLESS!
QUINTERO IS A DISGRACE! HIS WIFE'S FATHER--A VISCOUNT OF ALTAMIRA--IS RUMORED TO HAVE DISOWNED HIM AS A WASTREL.
IT WAS ONLY BY GROVELING AT THE FEET OF GENERAL MANCADO THAT HE EARNED PASSAGE TO OUR WESTERN SHORES... AND HIS ILL-DESERVED APPOINTMENT AS ALCALDE!

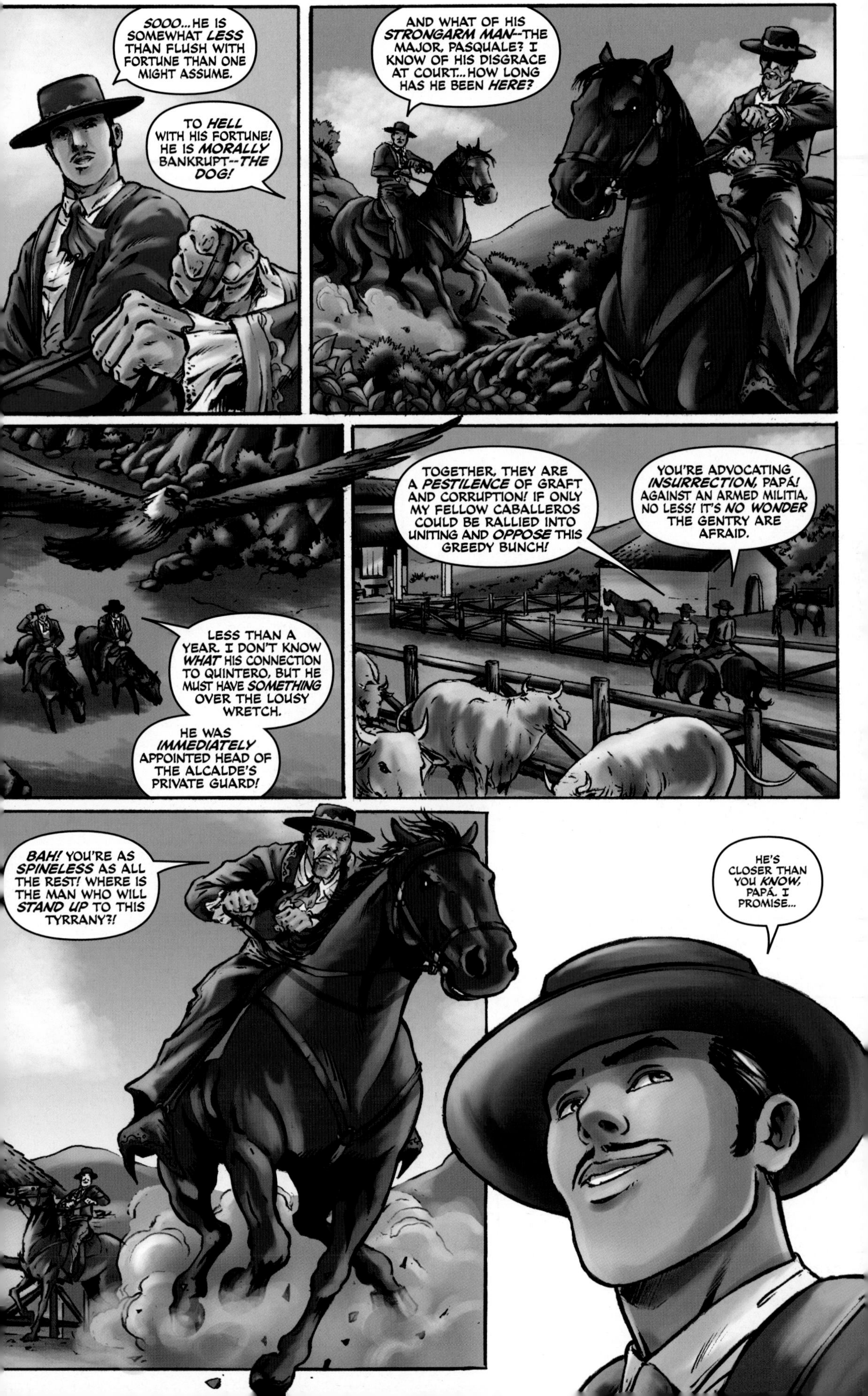
SOOO...HE IS SOMEWHAT LESS THAN FLUSH WITH FORTUNE THAN ONE MIGHT ASSUME.
TO HELL WITH HIS FORTUNE! HE IS MORALLY BANKRUPT--THE DOG!
AND WHAT OF HIS STRONGARM MAN--THE MAJOR, PASQUALE? I KNOW OF HIS DISGRACE AT COURT...HOW LONG HAS HE BEEN HERE?
LESS THAN A YEAR. I DON'T KNOW WHAT HIS CONNECTION TO QUINTERO, BUT HE MUST HAVE SOMETHING OVER THE LOUSY WRETCH.
HE WAS IMMEDIATELY APPOINTED HEAD OF THE ALCALDE'S PRIVATE GUARD!
TOGETHER, THEY ARE A PESTILENCE OF GRAFT AND CORRUPTION! IF ONLY MY FELLOW CABALLEROS COULD BE RALLIED INTO UNITING AND OPPOSE THIS GREEDY BUNCH!
YOU'RE ADVOCATING INSURRECTION, PAPÁ! AGAINST AN ARMED MILITIA, NO LESS! IT'S NO WONDER THE GENTRY ARE AFRAID.
BAH! YOU'RE AS SPINELESS AS ALL THE REST! WHERE IS THE MAN WHO WILL STAND UP TO THIS TYRRANY?!
HE'S CLOSER THAN YOU KNOW, PAPÁ. I PROMISE...

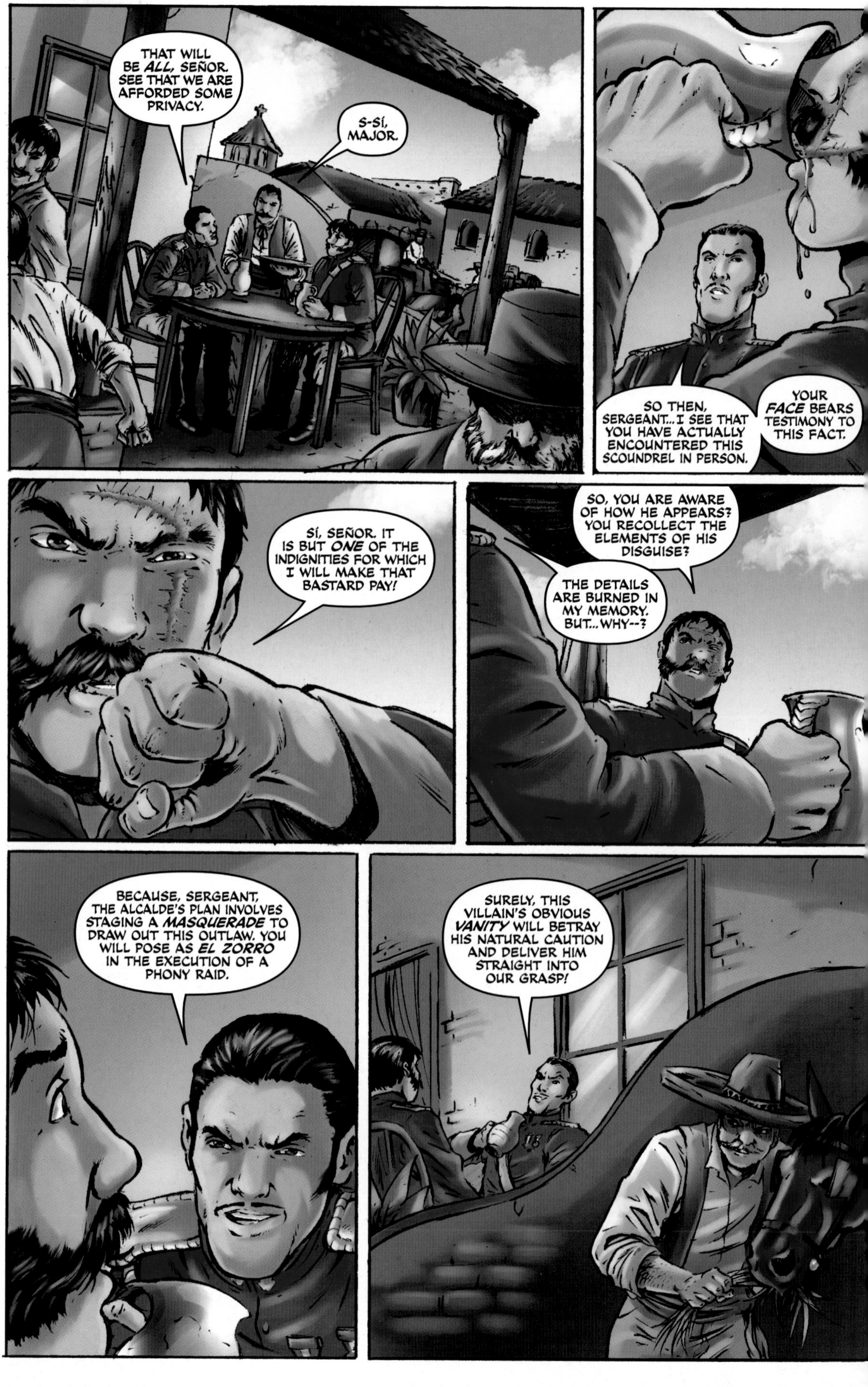
THAT WILL BE ALL, SEÑOR. SEE THAT WE ARE AFFORDED SOME PRIVACY.
S-SÍ, MAJOR.
SO THEN, SERGEANT... I SEE THAT YOU HAVE ACTUALLY ENCOUNTERED THIS SCOUNDREL IN PERSON.
YOUR FACE BEARS TESTIMONY TO THIS FACT.
SÍ, SEÑOR. IT IS BUT ONE OF THE INDIGNITIES FOR WHICH I WILL MAKE THAT BASTARD PAY!
SO, YOU ARE AWARE OF HOW HE APPEARS? YOU RECOLLECT THE ELEMENTS OF HIS DISGUISE?
THE DETAILS ARE BURNED IN MY MEMORY. BUT... WHY--?
BECAUSE, SERGEANT, THE ALCALDE'S PLAN INVOLVES STAGING A MASQUERADE TO DRAW OUT THIS OUTLAW. YOU WILL POSE AS EL ZORRO IN THE EXECUTION OF A PHONY RAID.
SURELY, THIS VILLAIN'S OBVIOUS VANITY WILL BETRAY HIS NATURAL CAUTION AND DELIVER HIM STRAIGHT INTO OUR GRASP!

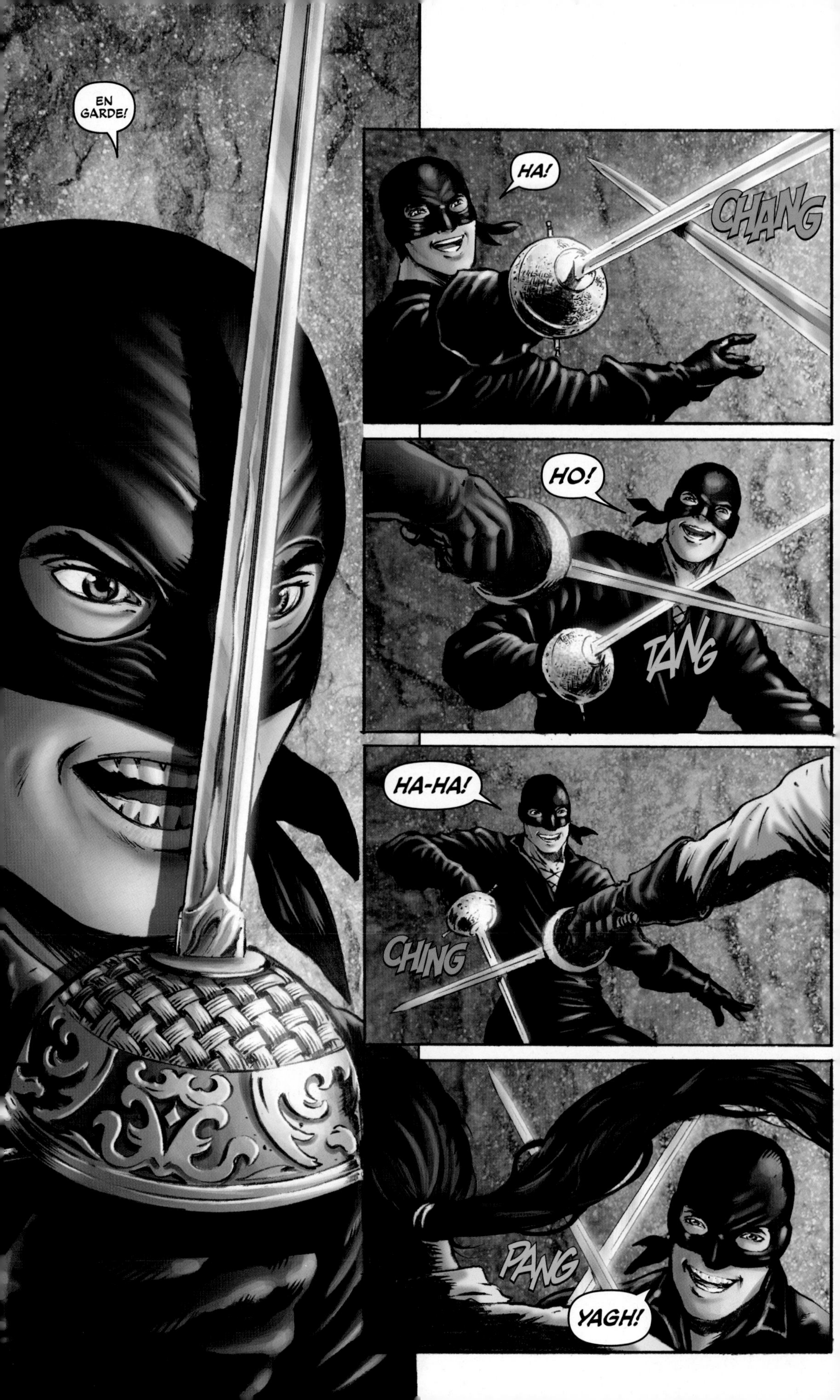

EN GARDE!
HA!
CHANG
HO!
TANG
HA-HA!
CHING
PANG
YAGH!

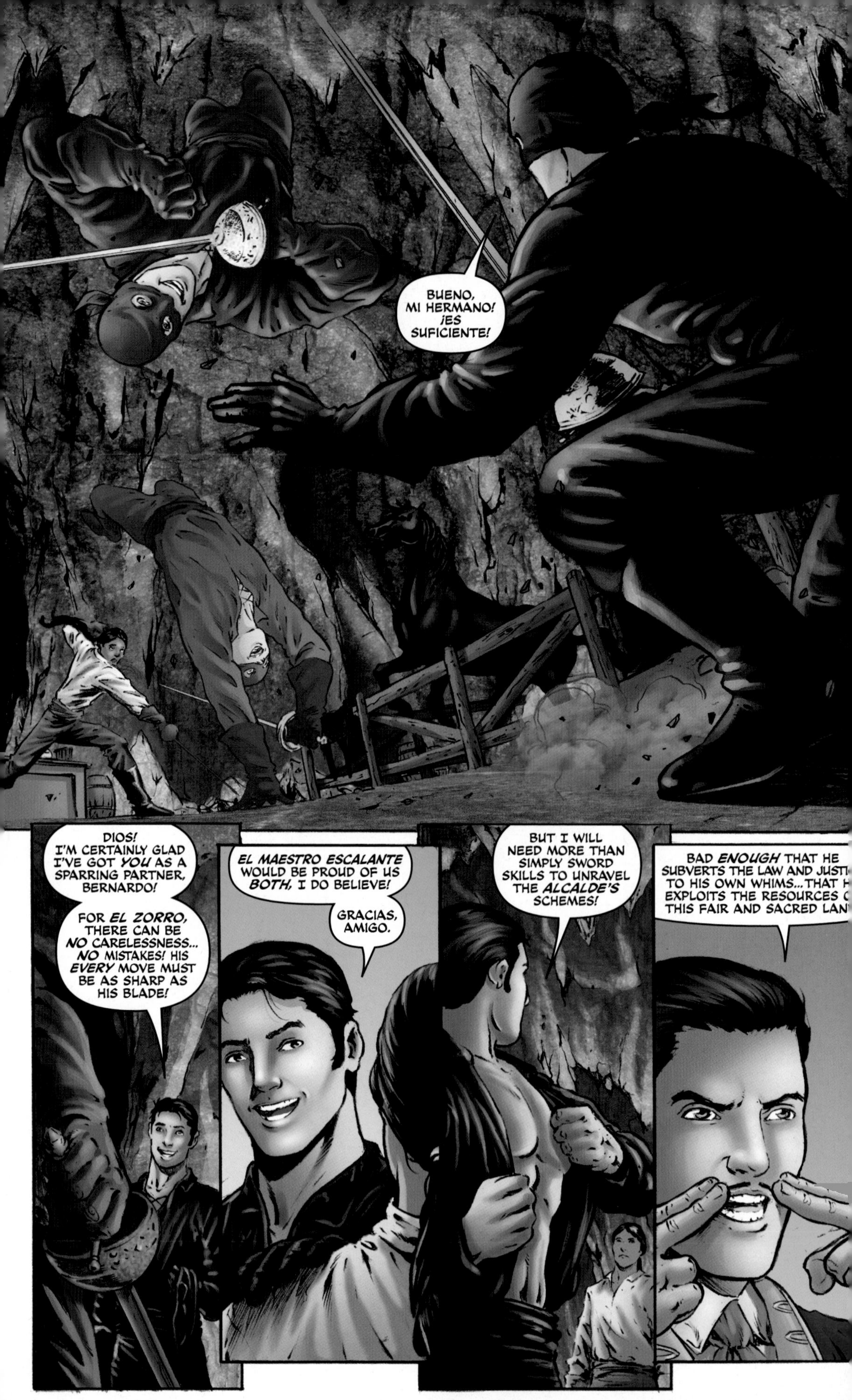

BUENO, MI HERMANO! ¡ES SUFICIENTE!
DIOS! I'M CERTAINLY GLAD I'VE GOT YOU AS A SPARRING PARTNER, BERNARDO!
FOR EL ZORRO, THERE CAN BE NO CARELESSNESS... NO MISTAKES! HIS EVERY MOVE MUST BE AS SHARP AS HIS BLADE!
EL MAESTRO ESCALANTE WOULD BE PROUD OF US BOTH, I DO BELIEVE!
GRACIAS, AMIGO.
BUT I WILL NEED MORE THAN SIMPLY SWORD SKILLS TO UNRAVEL THE ALCALDE'S SCHEMES!
BAD ENOUGH THAT HE SUBVERTS THE LAW AND JUSTI TO HIS OWN WHIMS...THAT H EXPLOITS THE RESOURCES O THIS FAIR AND SACRED LAN

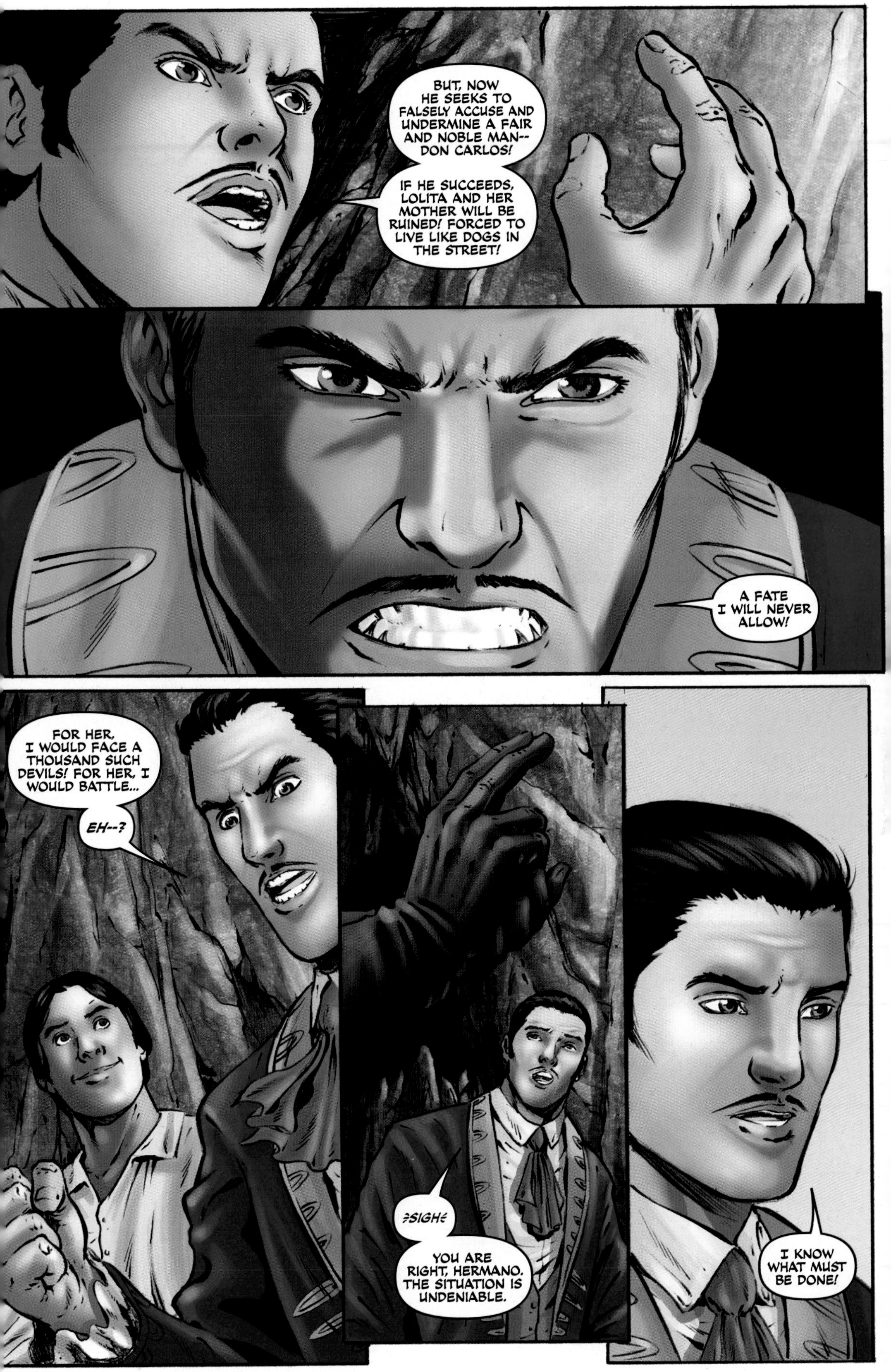
BUT, NOW HE SEEKS TO FALSELY ACCUSE AND UNDERMINE A FAIR AND NOBLE MAN--DON CARLOS!
IF HE SUCCEEDS, LOLITA AND HER MOTHER WILL BE RUINED! FORCED TO LIVE LIKE DOGS IN THE STREET!
A FATE I WILL NEVER ALLOW!
FOR HER, I WOULD FACE A THOUSAND SUCH DEVILS! FOR HER, I WOULD BATTLE...
EH--?
SIGH
YOU ARE RIGHT, HERMANO. THE SITUATION IS UNDENIABLE.
I KNOW WHAT MUST BE DONE!

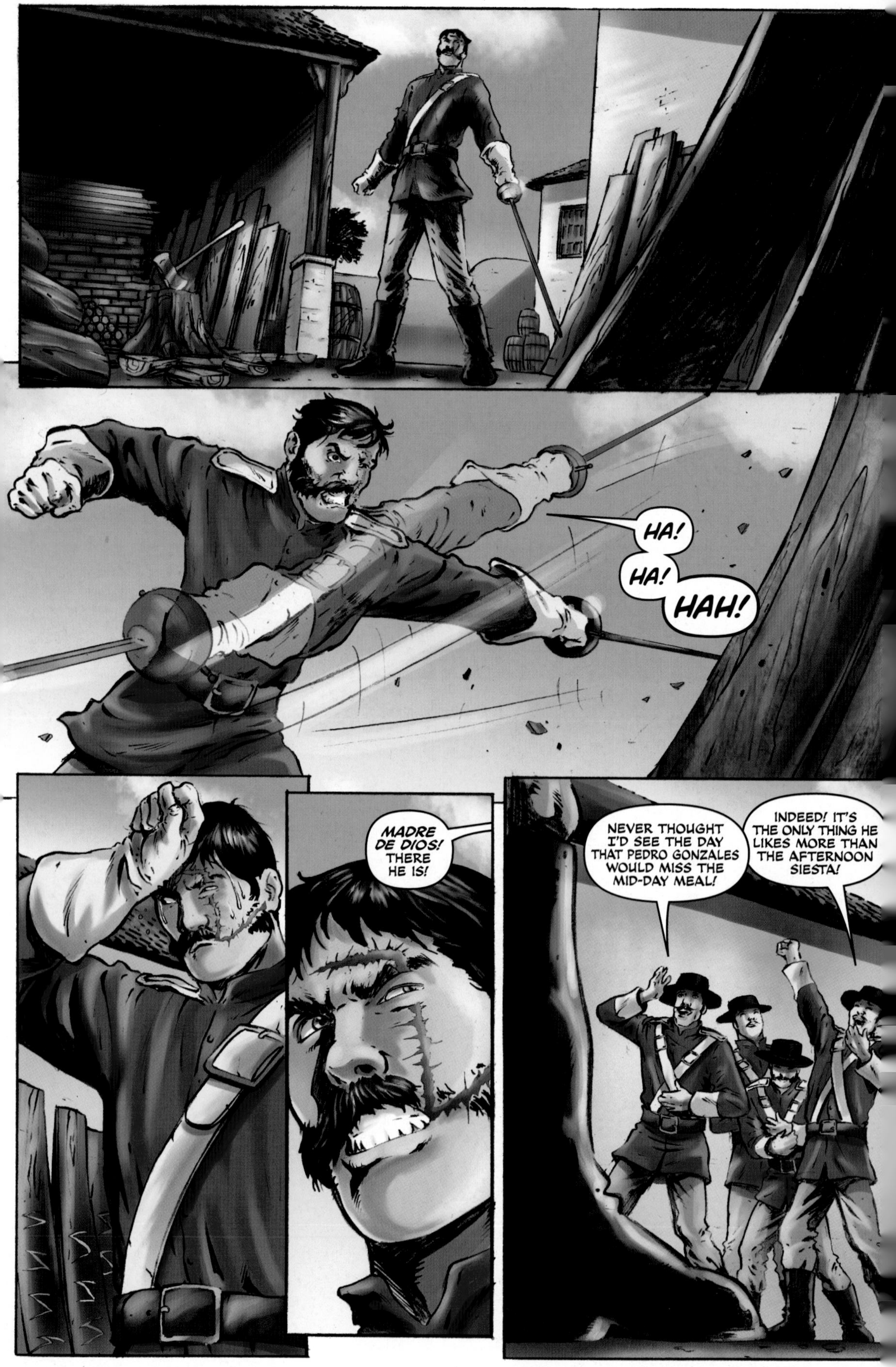
HA!
HA!
HAH!
MADRE DE DIOS! THERE HE IS!
NEVER THOUGHT I'D SEE THE DAY THAT PEDRO GONZALES WOULD MISS THE MID-DAY MEAL!
INDEED! IT'S THE ONLY THING HE LIKES MORE THAN THE AFTERNOON SIESTA!

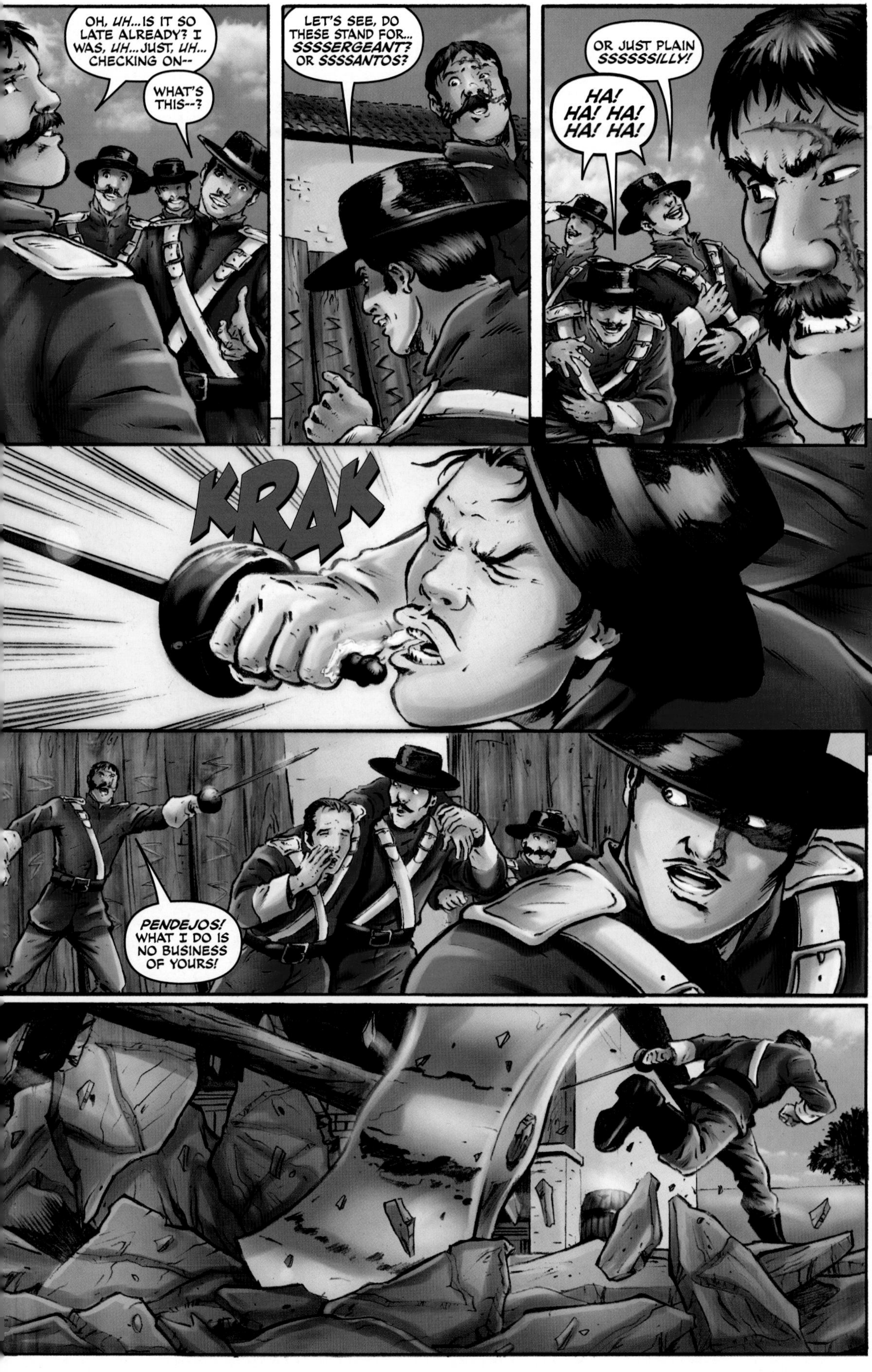
OH, UH...IS IT SO LATE ALREADY? I WAS, UH...JUST, UH... CHECKING ON--
WHAT'S THIS--?
LET'S SEE, DO THESE STAND FOR... SSSSERGEANT? OR SSSSANTOS?
OR JUST PLAIN SSSSSSILLY!
HA! HA! HA! HA! HA!
KRAK
PENDEJOS! WHAT I DO IS NO BUSINESS OF YOURS!

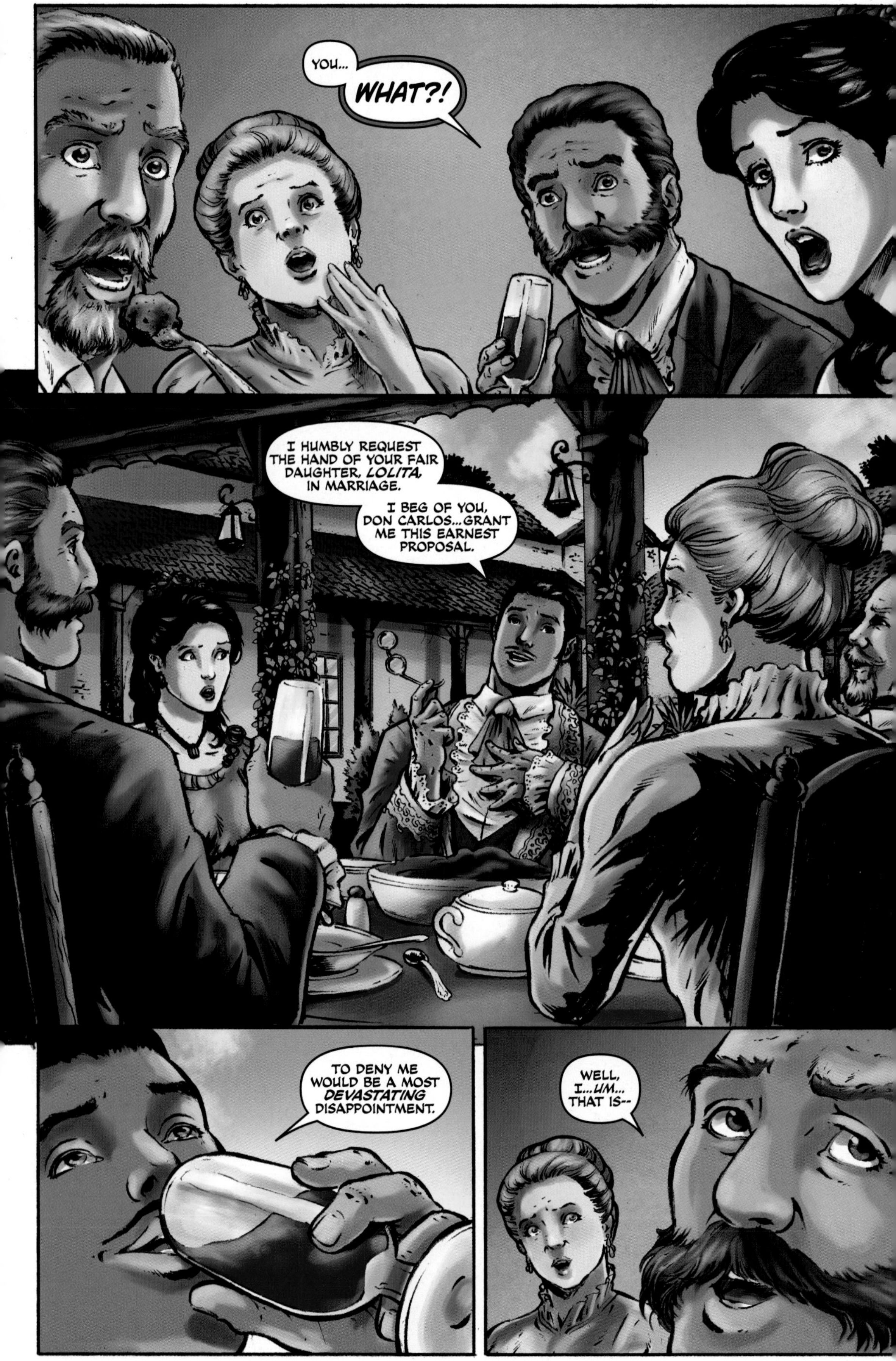
YOU...
WHAT?!
I HUMBLY REQUEST THE HAND OF YOUR FAIR DAUGHTER, LOLITA, IN MARRIAGE.
I BEG OF YOU, DON CARLOS...GRANT ME THIS EARNEST PROPOSAL.
TO DENY ME WOULD BE A MOST DEVASTATING DISAPPOINTMENT.
WELL, I...UM... THAT IS--

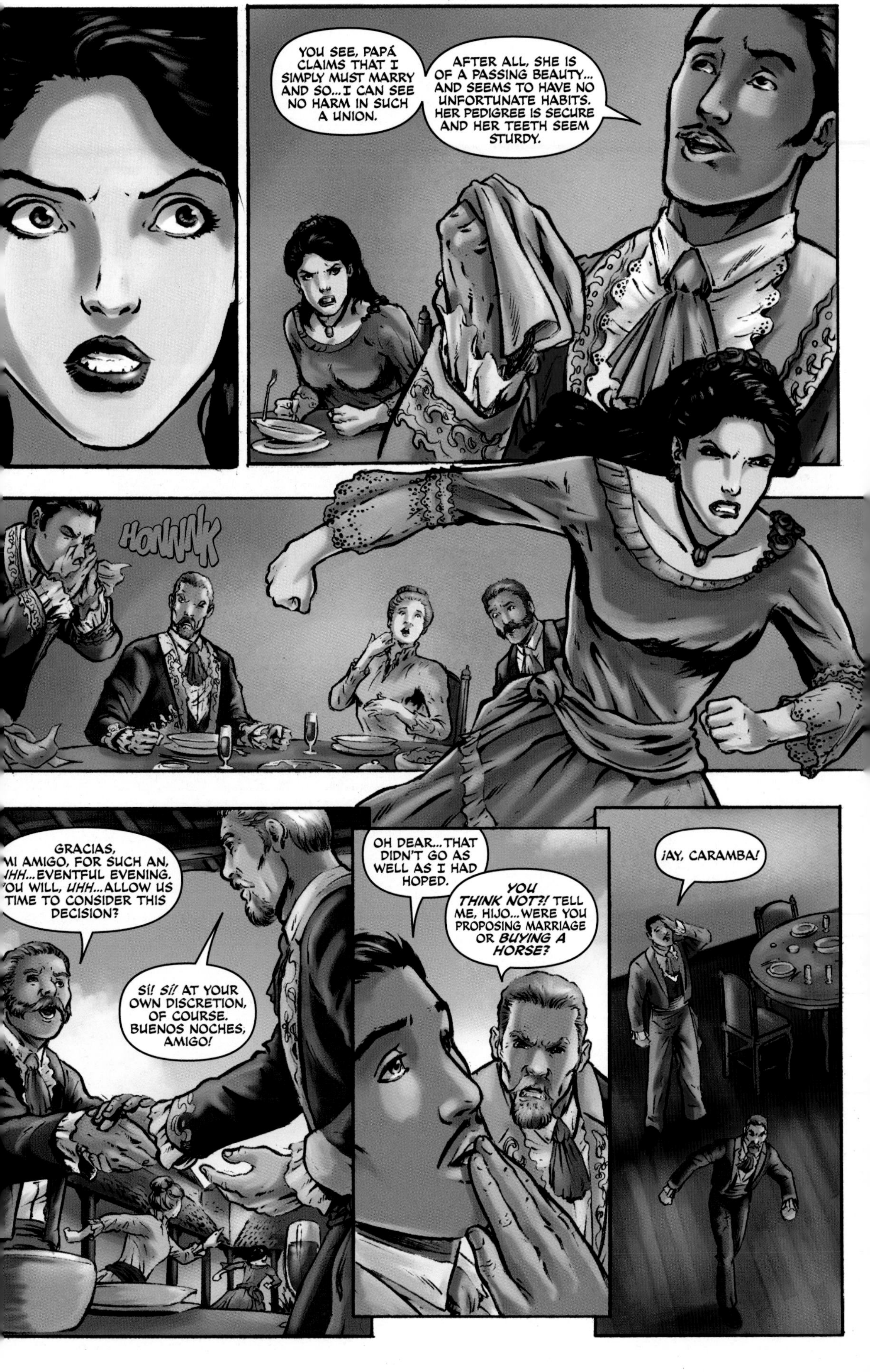
YOU SEE, PAPÁ CLAIMS THAT I SIMPLY MUST MARRY AND SO...I CAN SEE NO HARM IN SUCH A UNION.
AFTER ALL, SHE IS OF A PASSING BEAUTY... AND SEEMS TO HAVE NO UNFORTUNATE HABITS. HER PEDIGREE IS SECURE AND HER TEETH SEEM STURDY.
HONNNK
GRACIAS, MI AMIGO, FOR SUCH AN, UHH...EVENTFUL EVENING. YOU WILL, UHH...ALLOW US TIME TO CONSIDER THIS DECISION?
SÍ! SÍ! AT YOUR OWN DISCRETION, OF COURSE. BUENOS NOCHES, AMIGO!
OH DEAR...THAT DIDN'T GO AS WELL AS I HAD HOPED.
YOU THINK NOT?! TELL ME, HIJO...WERE YOU PROPOSING MARRIAGE OR BUYING A HORSE?
¡AY, CARAMBA!

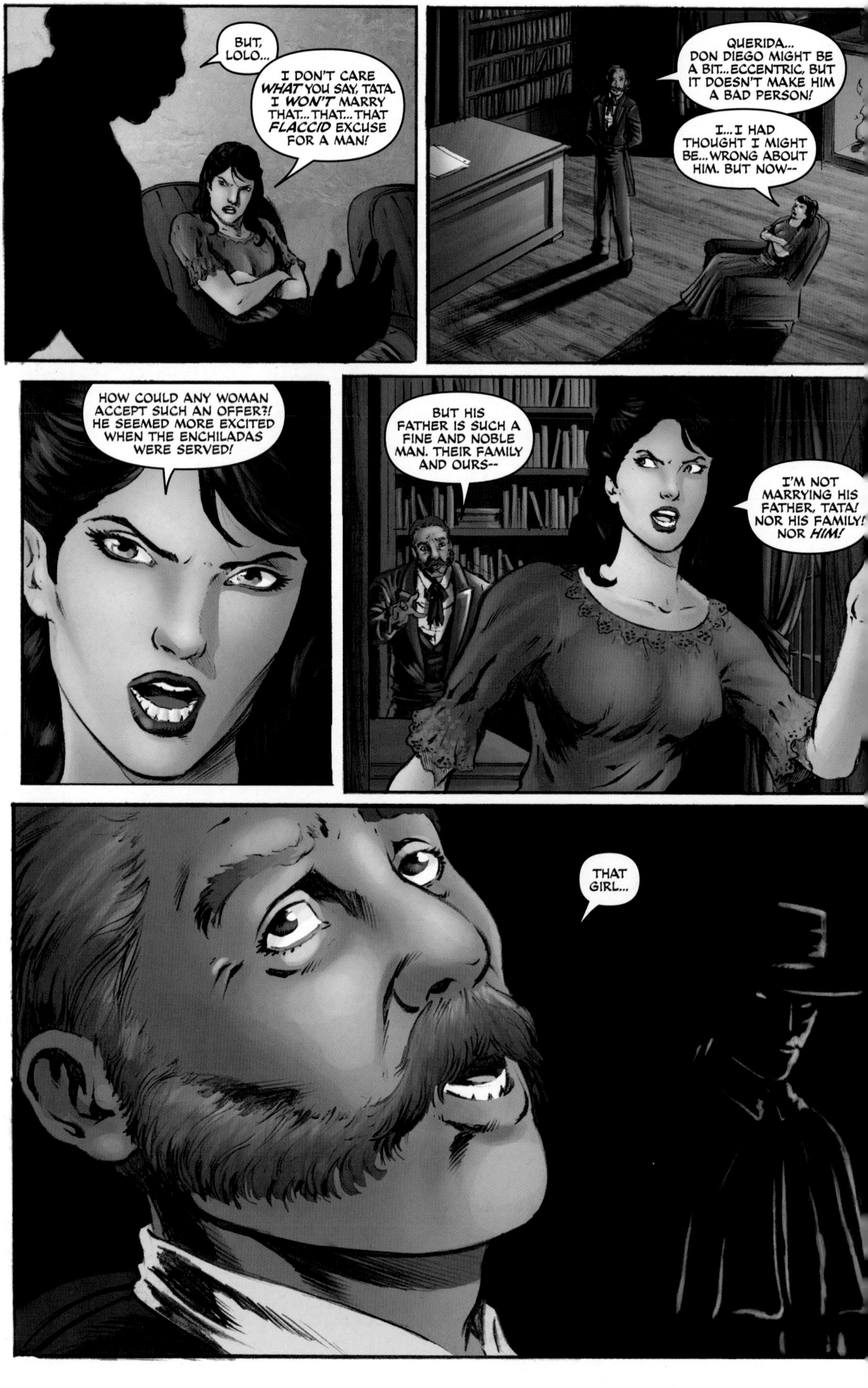
BUT, LOLO...
I DON'T CARE *WHAT* YOU SAY, TATA. I *WON'T* MARRY THAT... THAT... THAT *FLACCID* EXCUSE FOR A MAN!
QUERIDA... DON DIEGO MIGHT BE A BIT... ECCENTRIC, BUT IT DOESN'T MAKE HIM A BAD PERSON!
I... I HAD THOUGHT I MIGHT BE... WRONG ABOUT HIM. BUT NOW--
HOW COULD ANY WOMAN ACCEPT SUCH AN OFFER?! HE SEEMED MORE EXCITED WHEN THE ENCHILADAS WERE SERVED!
BUT HIS FATHER IS SUCH A FINE AND NOBLE MAN. THEIR FAMILY AND OURS--
I'M NOT MARRYING HIS FATHER, TATA! NOR HIS FAMILY! NOR *HIM!*
THAT GIRL...

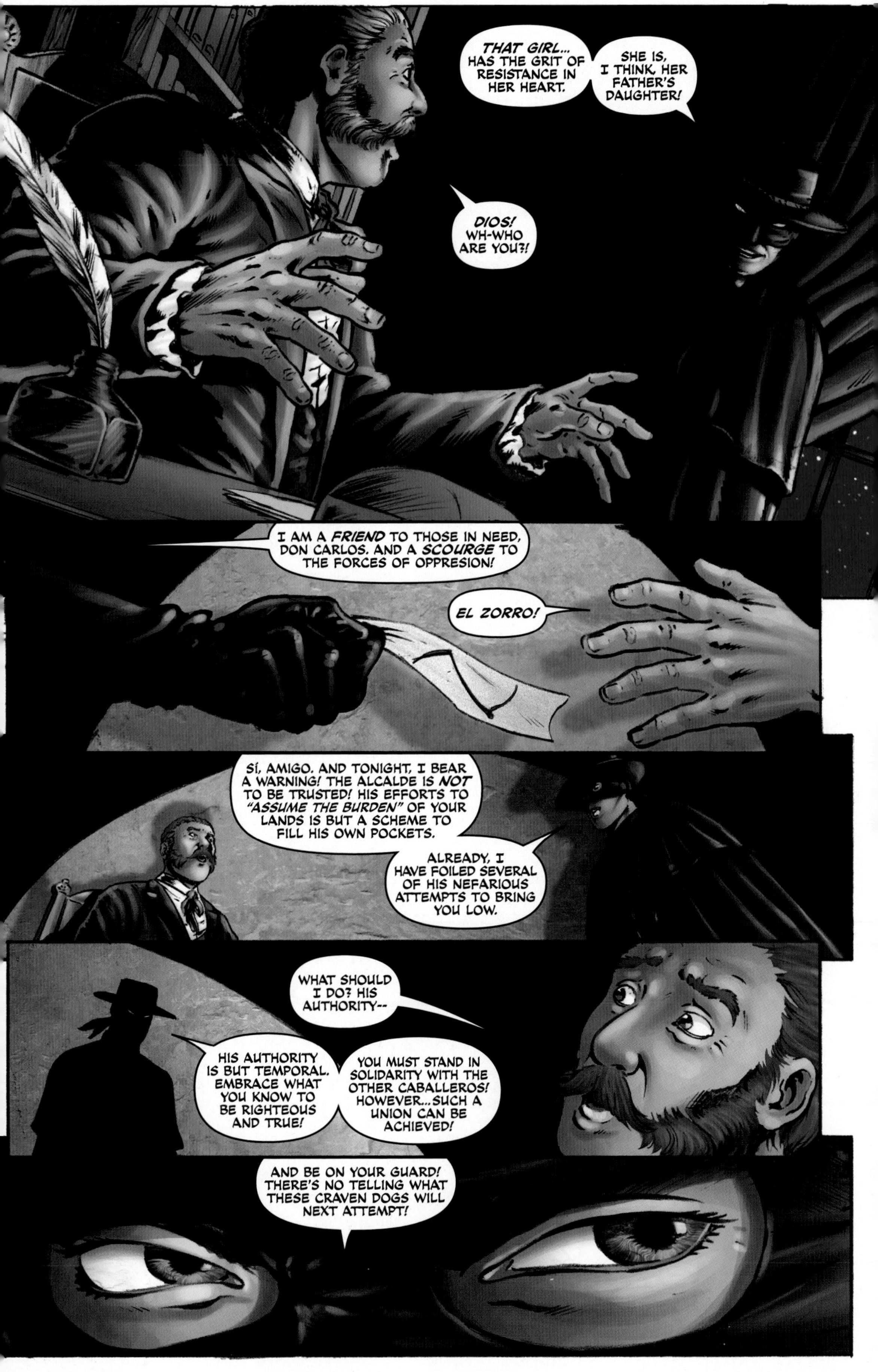
THAT GIRL... HAS THE GRIT OF RESISTANCE IN HER HEART.
SHE IS, I THINK, HER FATHER'S DAUGHTER!
DIOS! WH-WHO ARE YOU?!
I AM A FRIEND TO THOSE IN NEED, DON CARLOS. AND A SCOURGE TO THE FORCES OF OPPRESION!
EL ZORRO!
SÍ, AMIGO. AND TONIGHT, I BEAR A WARNING! THE ALCALDE IS NOT TO BE TRUSTED! HIS EFFORTS TO "ASSUME THE BURDEN" OF YOUR LANDS IS BUT A SCHEME TO FILL HIS OWN POCKETS.
ALREADY, I HAVE FOILED SEVERAL OF HIS NEFARIOUS ATTEMPTS TO BRING YOU LOW.
WHAT SHOULD I DO? HIS AUTHORITY--
HIS AUTHORITY IS BUT TEMPORAL. EMBRACE WHAT YOU KNOW TO BE RIGHTEOUS AND TRUE!
YOU MUST STAND IN SOLIDARITY WITH THE OTHER CABALLEROS! HOWEVER...SUCH A UNION CAN BE ACHIEVED!
AND BE ON YOUR GUARD! THERE'S NO TELLING WHAT THESE CRAVEN DOGS WILL NEXT ATTEMPT!

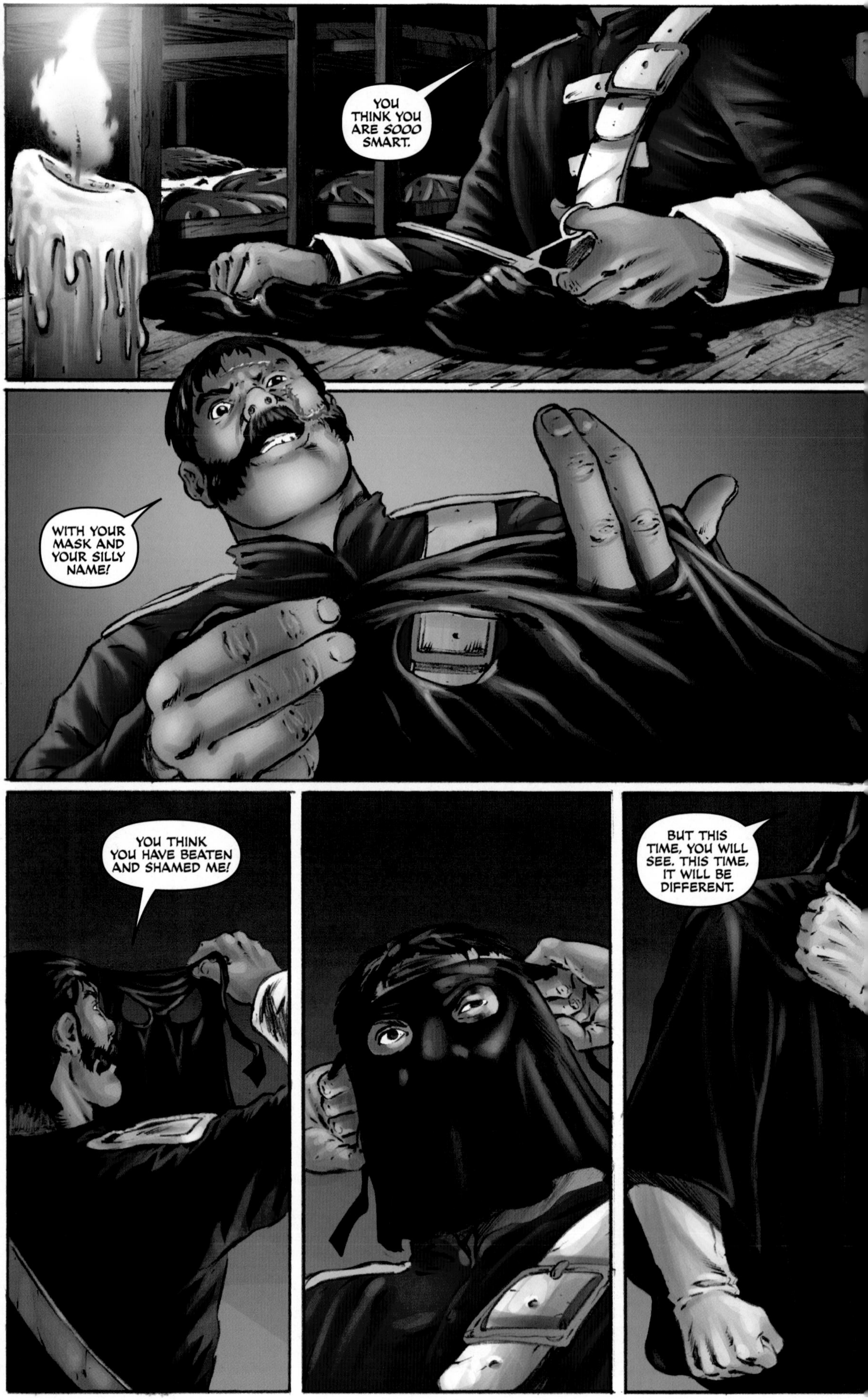
YOU THINK YOU ARE SOOO SMART.
WITH YOUR MASK AND YOUR SILLY NAME!
YOU THINK YOU HAVE BEATEN AND SHAMED ME!
BUT THIS TIME, YOU WILL SEE. THIS TIME, IT WILL BE DIFFERENT.

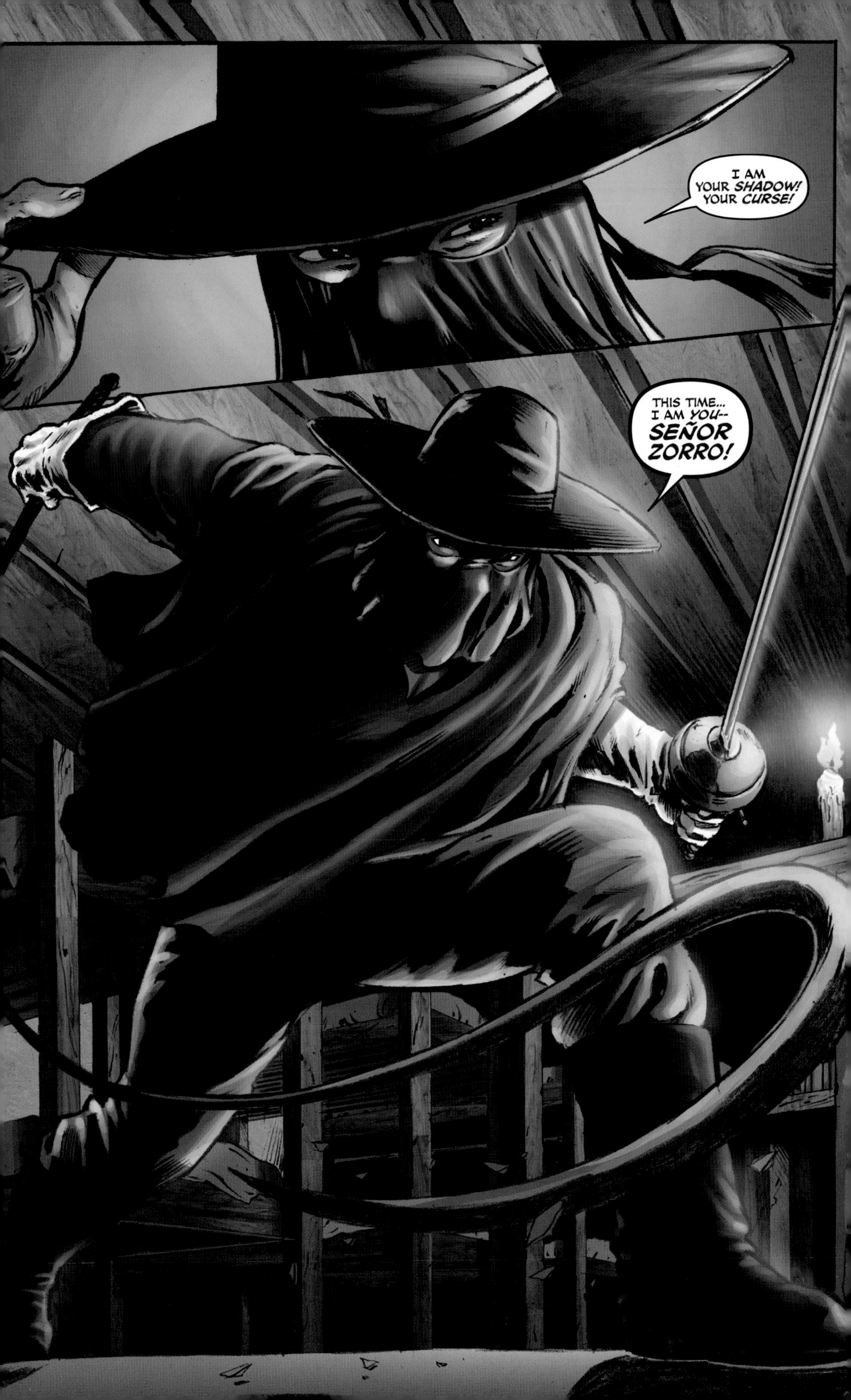
I AM YOUR SHADOW! YOUR CURSE!
THIS TIME... I AM YOU-- SEÑOR ZORRO!

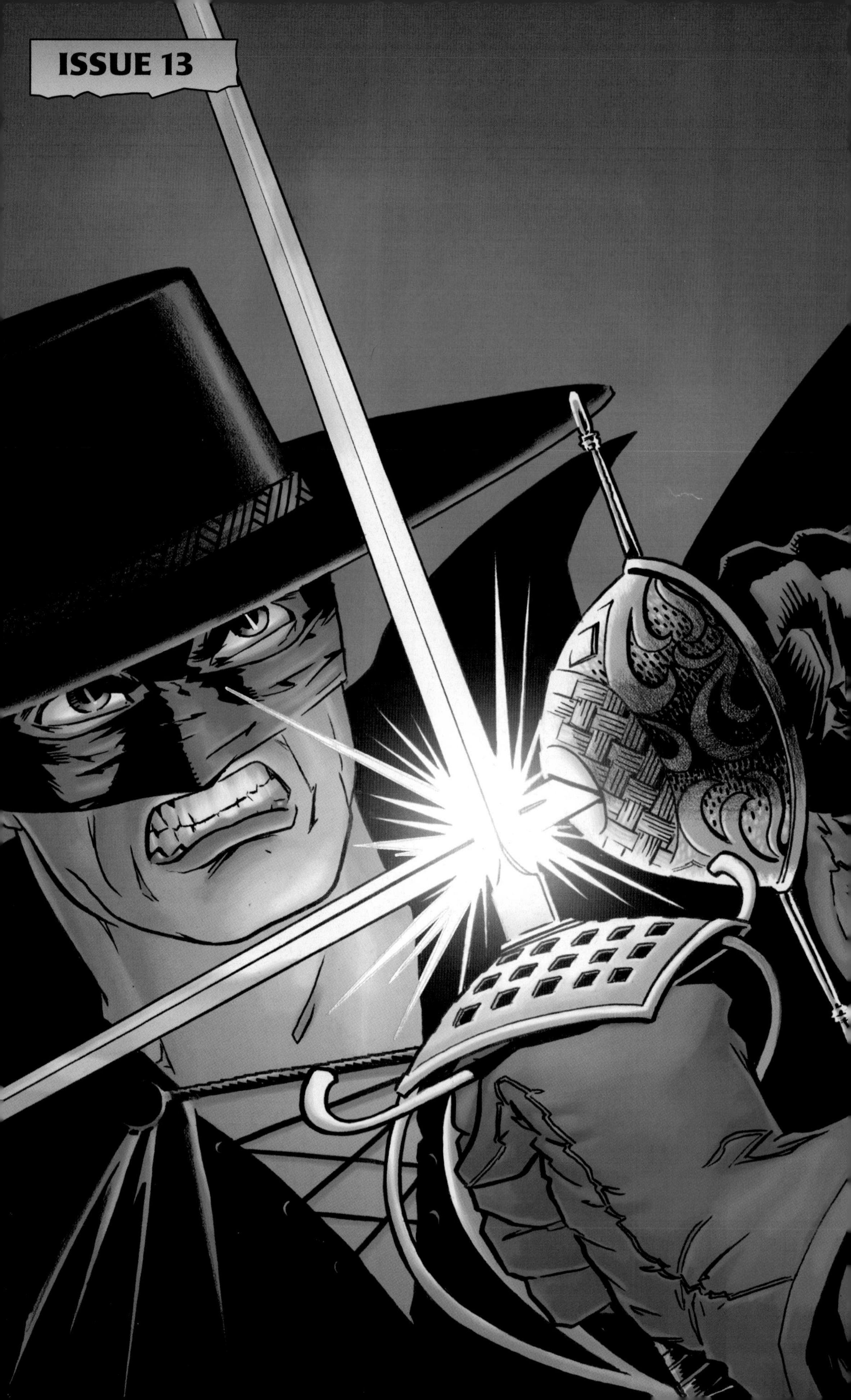
ISSUE 13

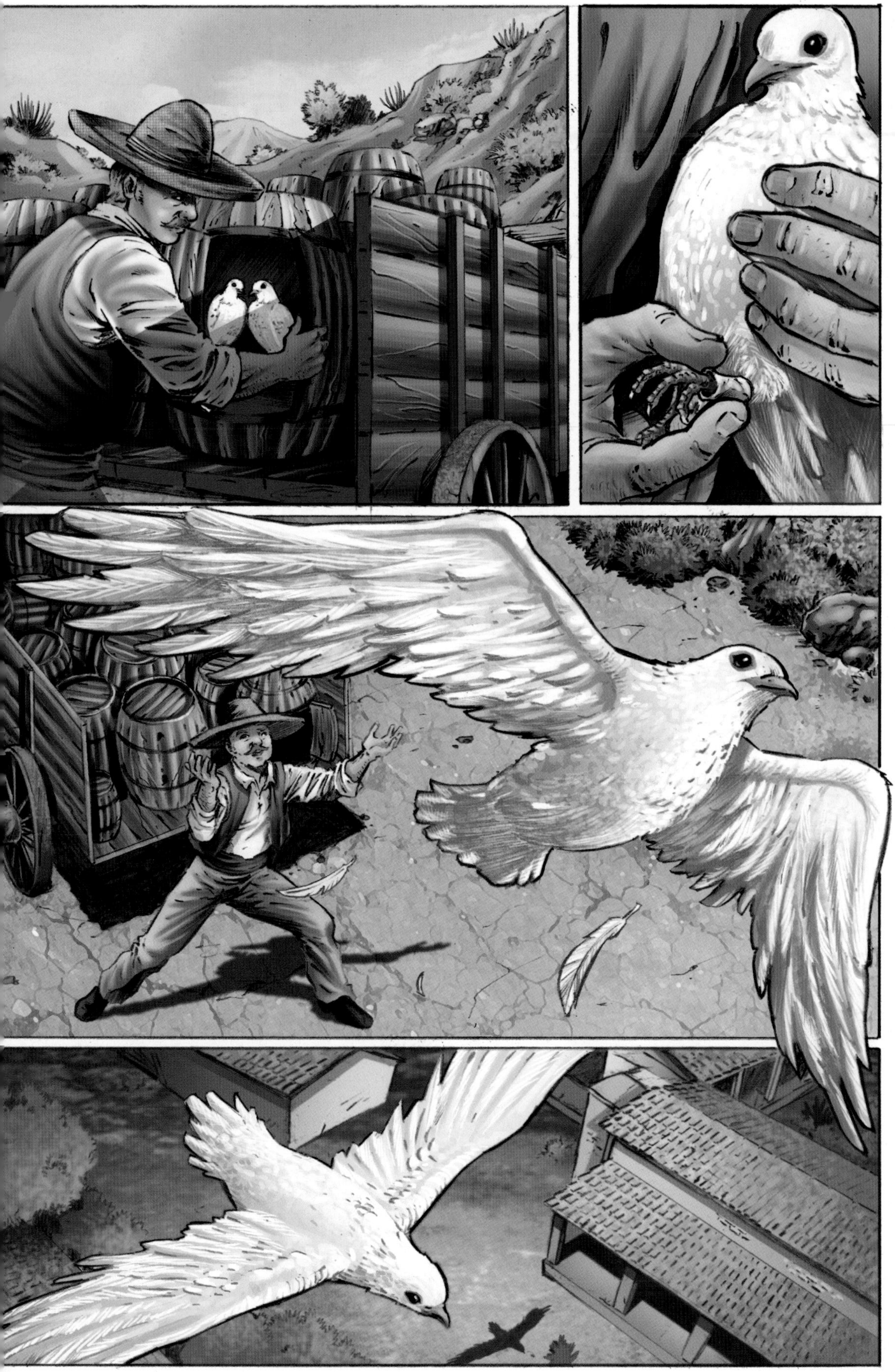

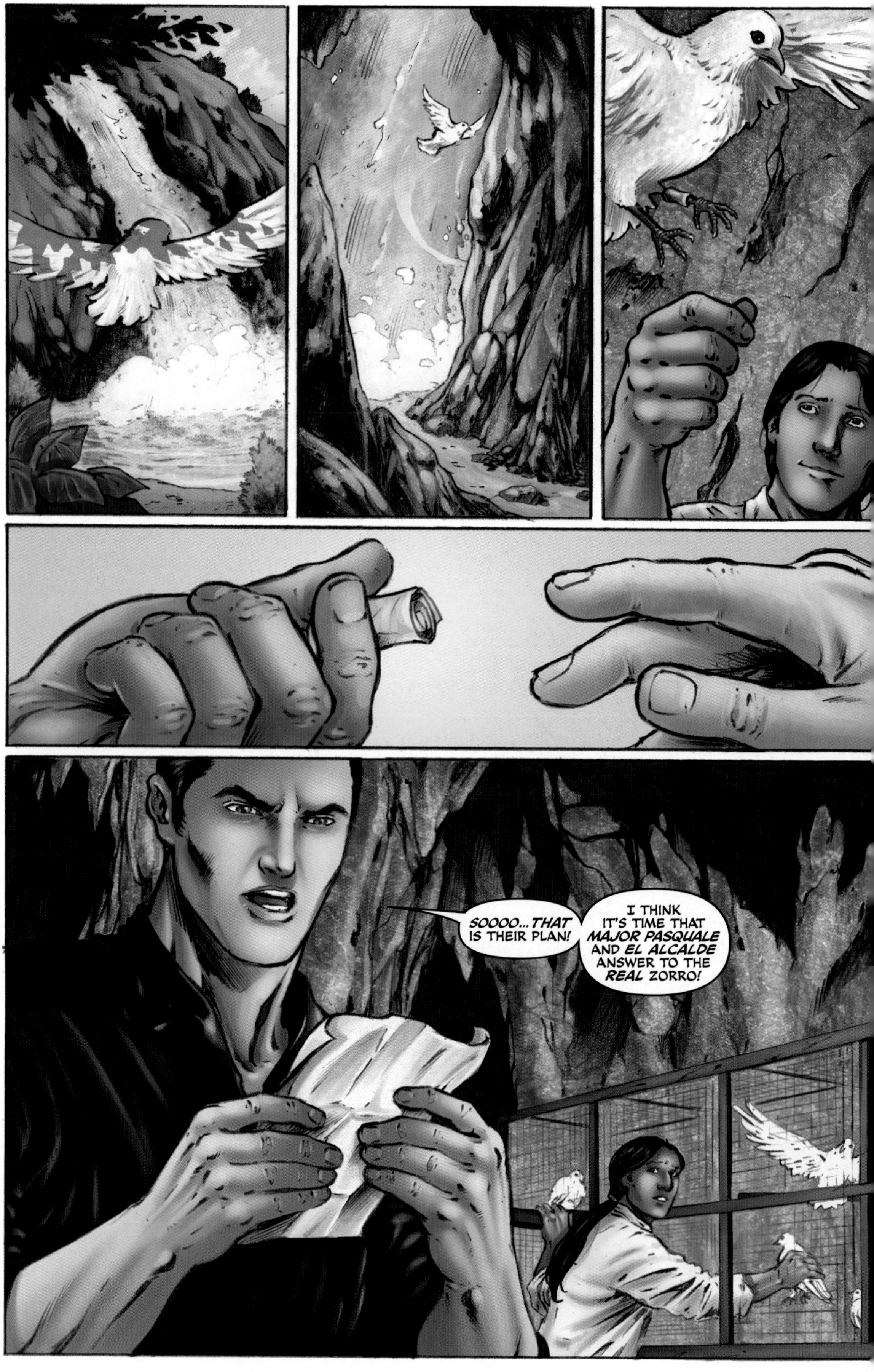
SOOOO...THAT IS THEIR PLAN!
I THINK IT'S TIME THAT MAJOR PASQUALE AND EL ALCALDE ANSWER TO THE REAL ZORRO!

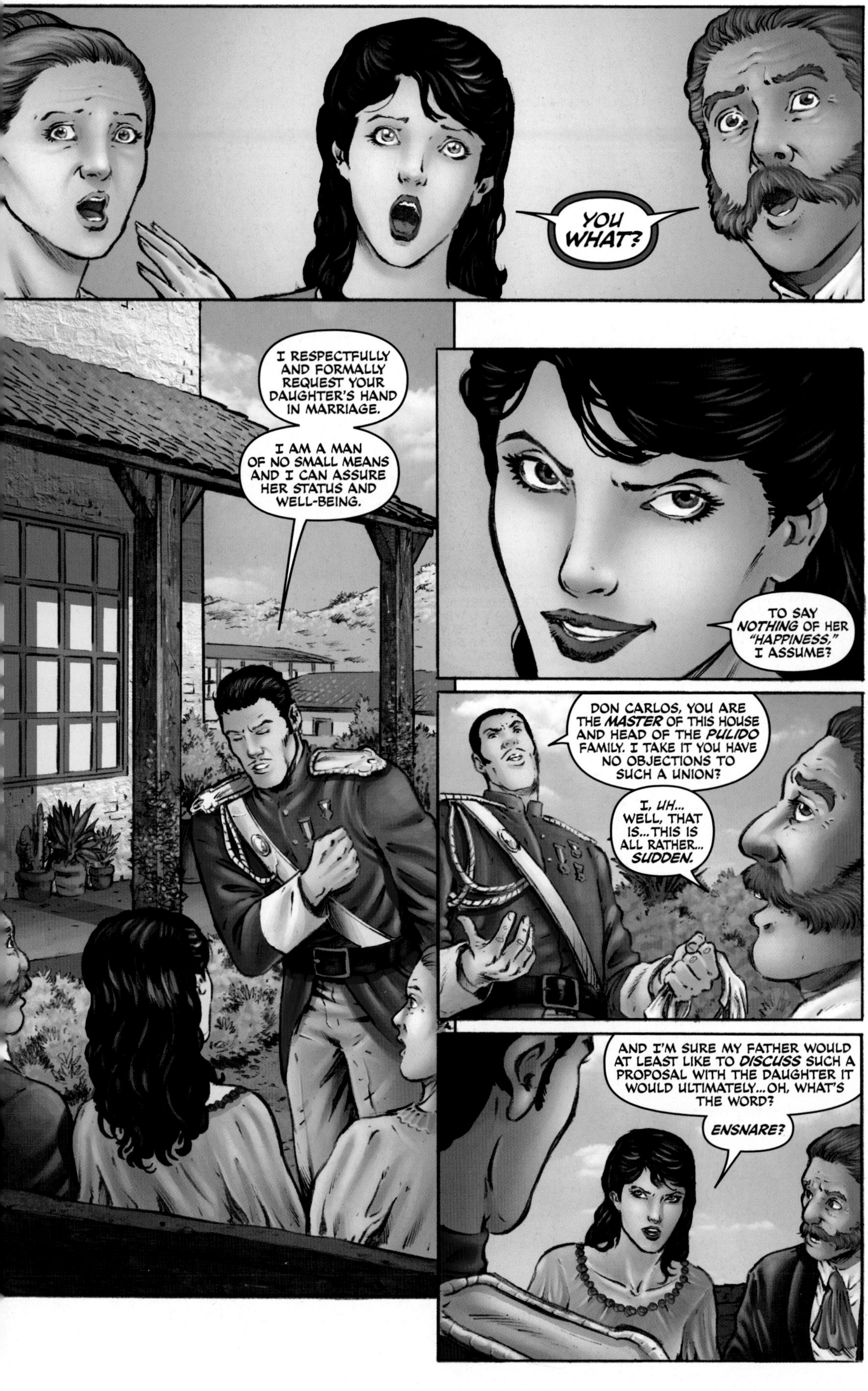

YOU WHAT?
I RESPECTFULLY AND FORMALLY REQUEST YOUR DAUGHTER'S HAND IN MARRIAGE.
I AM A MAN OF NO SMALL MEANS AND I CAN ASSURE HER STATUS AND WELL-BEING.
TO SAY NOTHING OF HER "HAPPINESS," I ASSUME?
DON CARLOS, YOU ARE THE MASTER OF THIS HOUSE AND HEAD OF THE PULIDO FAMILY. I TAKE IT YOU HAVE NO OBJECTIONS TO SUCH A UNION?
I, UH... WELL, THAT IS...THIS IS ALL RATHER... SUDDEN.
AND I'M SURE MY FATHER WOULD AT LEAST LIKE TO DISCUSS SUCH A PROPOSAL WITH THE DAUGHTER IT WOULD ULTIMATELY...OH, WHAT'S THE WORD?
ENSNARE?

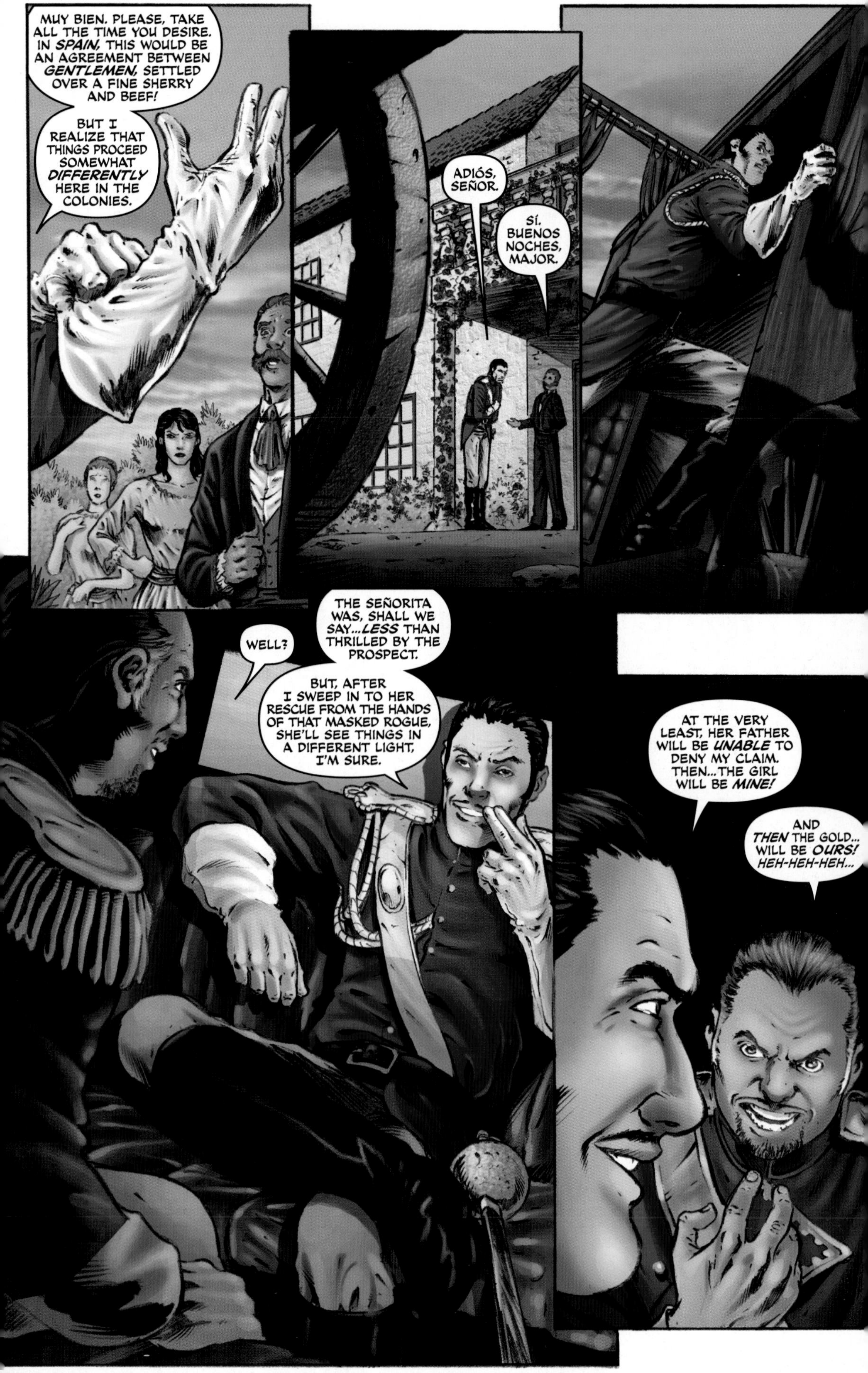

MUY BIEN. PLEASE, TAKE ALL THE TIME YOU DESIRE. IN *SPAIN,* THIS WOULD BE AN AGREEMENT BETWEEN *GENTLEMEN,* SETTLED OVER A FINE SHERRY AND BEEF!
BUT I REALIZE THAT THINGS PROCEED SOMEWHAT *DIFFERENTLY* HERE IN THE COLONIES.
ADIÓS, SEÑOR.
SÍ. BUENOS NOCHES, MAJOR.
WELL?
THE SEÑORITA WAS, SHALL WE SAY...*LESS* THAN THRILLED BY THE PROSPECT.
BUT, AFTER I SWEEP IN TO HER RESCUE FROM THE HANDS OF THAT MASKED ROGUE, SHE'LL SEE THINGS IN A DIFFERENT LIGHT, I'M SURE.
AT THE VERY LEAST, HER FATHER WILL BE *UNABLE* TO DENY MY CLAIM. THEN...THE GIRL WILL BE *MINE!*
AND *THEN* THE GOLD... WILL BE *OURS!* *HEH-HEH-HEH...*

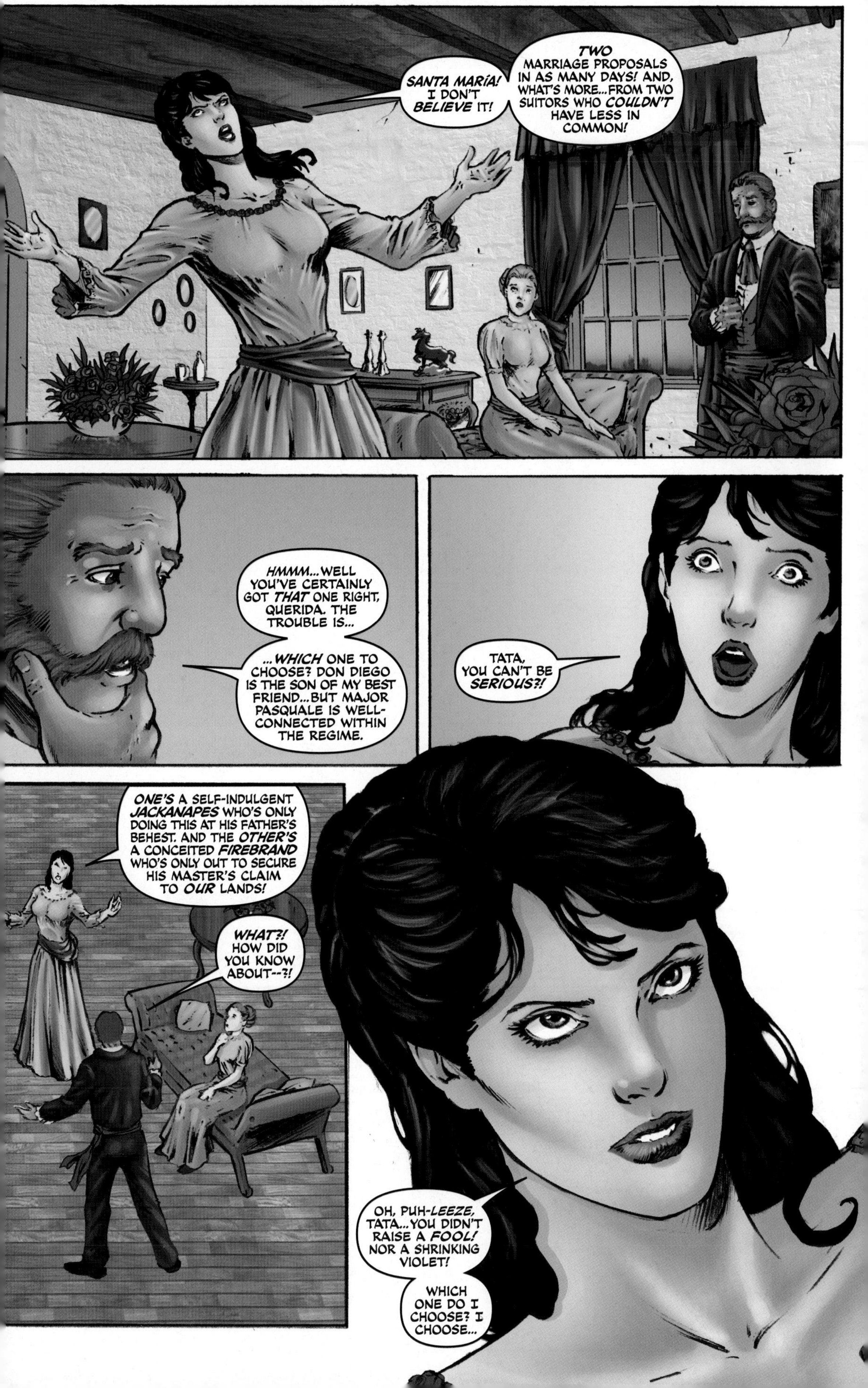
SANTA MARÍA! I DON'T BELIEVE IT!
TWO MARRIAGE PROPOSALS IN AS MANY DAYS! AND, WHAT'S MORE...FROM TWO SUITORS WHO COULDN'T HAVE LESS IN COMMON!
HMMM...WELL YOU'VE CERTAINLY GOT THAT ONE RIGHT, QUERIDA. THE TROUBLE IS...
...WHICH ONE TO CHOOSE? DON DIEGO IS THE SON OF MY BEST FRIEND...BUT MAJOR PASQUALE IS WELL-CONNECTED WITHIN THE REGIME.
TATA, YOU CAN'T BE SERIOUS?!
ONE'S A SELF-INDULGENT JACKANAPES WHO'S ONLY DOING THIS AT HIS FATHER'S BEHEST. AND THE OTHER'S A CONCEITED FIREBRAND WHO'S ONLY OUT TO SECURE HIS MASTER'S CLAIM TO OUR LANDS!
WHAT?! HOW DID YOU KNOW ABOUT--?!
OH, PUH-LEEZE, TATA...YOU DIDN'T RAISE A FOOL! NOR A SHRINKING VIOLET!
WHICH ONE DO I CHOOSE? I CHOOSE...

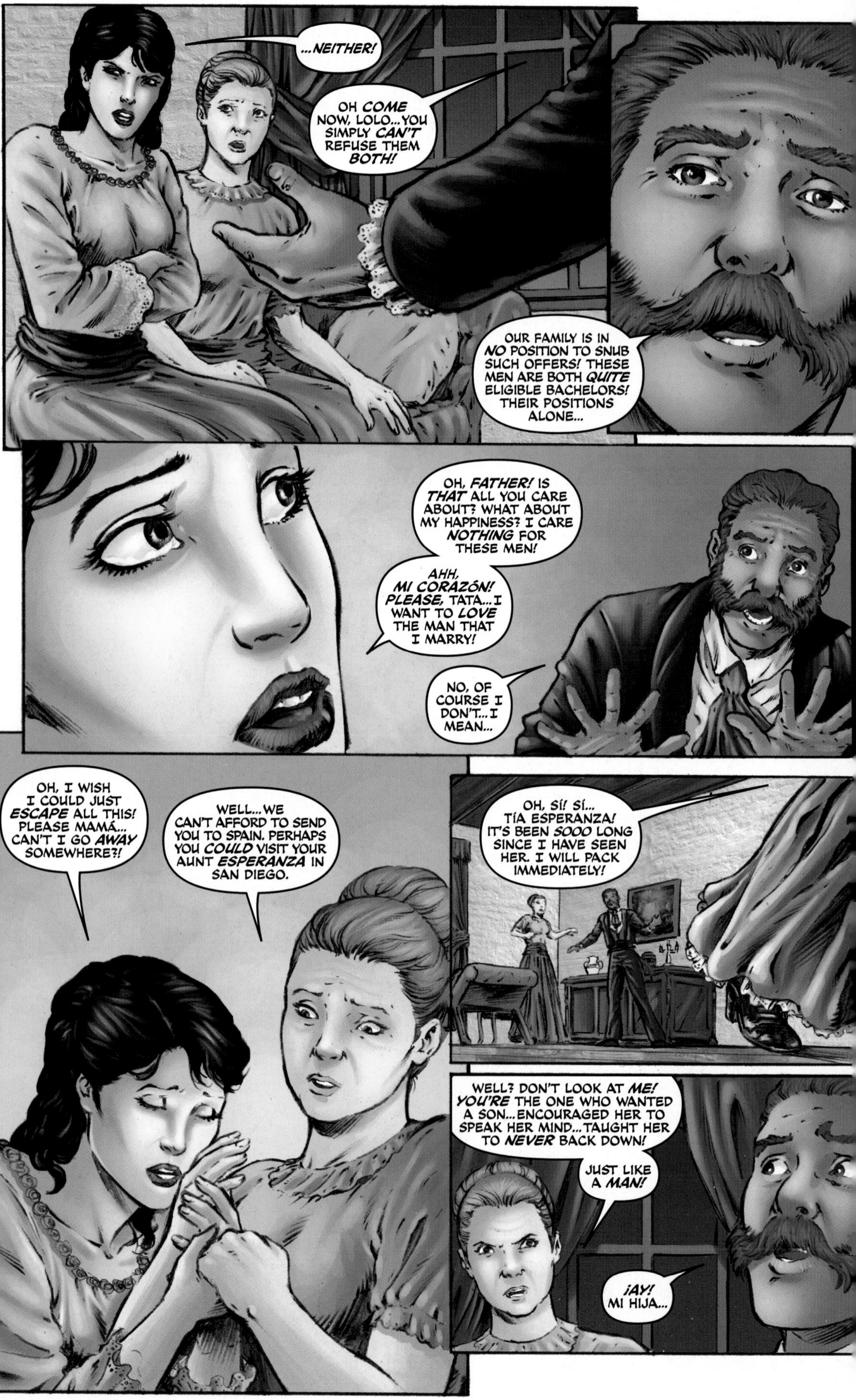
...NEITHER!
OH COME NOW, LOLO...YOU SIMPLY CAN'T REFUSE THEM BOTH!
OUR FAMILY IS IN NO POSITION TO SNUB SUCH OFFERS! THESE MEN ARE BOTH QUITE ELIGIBLE BACHELORS! THEIR POSITIONS ALONE...
OH, FATHER! IS THAT ALL YOU CARE ABOUT? WHAT ABOUT MY HAPPINESS? I CARE NOTHING FOR THESE MEN!
AHH, MI CORAZÓN!
PLEASE, TATA...I WANT TO LOVE THE MAN THAT I MARRY!
NO, OF COURSE I DON'T...I MEAN...
OH, I WISH I COULD JUST ESCAPE ALL THIS! PLEASE MAMÁ... CAN'T I GO AWAY SOMEWHERE?!
WELL...WE CAN'T AFFORD TO SEND YOU TO SPAIN. PERHAPS YOU COULD VISIT YOUR AUNT ESPERANZA IN SAN DIEGO.
OH, SÍ! SÍ... TÍA ESPERANZA! IT'S BEEN SOOO LONG SINCE I HAVE SEEN HER. I WILL PACK IMMEDIATELY!
WELL? DON'T LOOK AT ME! YOU'RE THE ONE WHO WANTED A SON...ENCOURAGED HER TO SPEAK HER MIND...TAUGHT HER TO NEVER BACK DOWN!
JUST LIKE A MAN!
¡AY! MI HIJA...

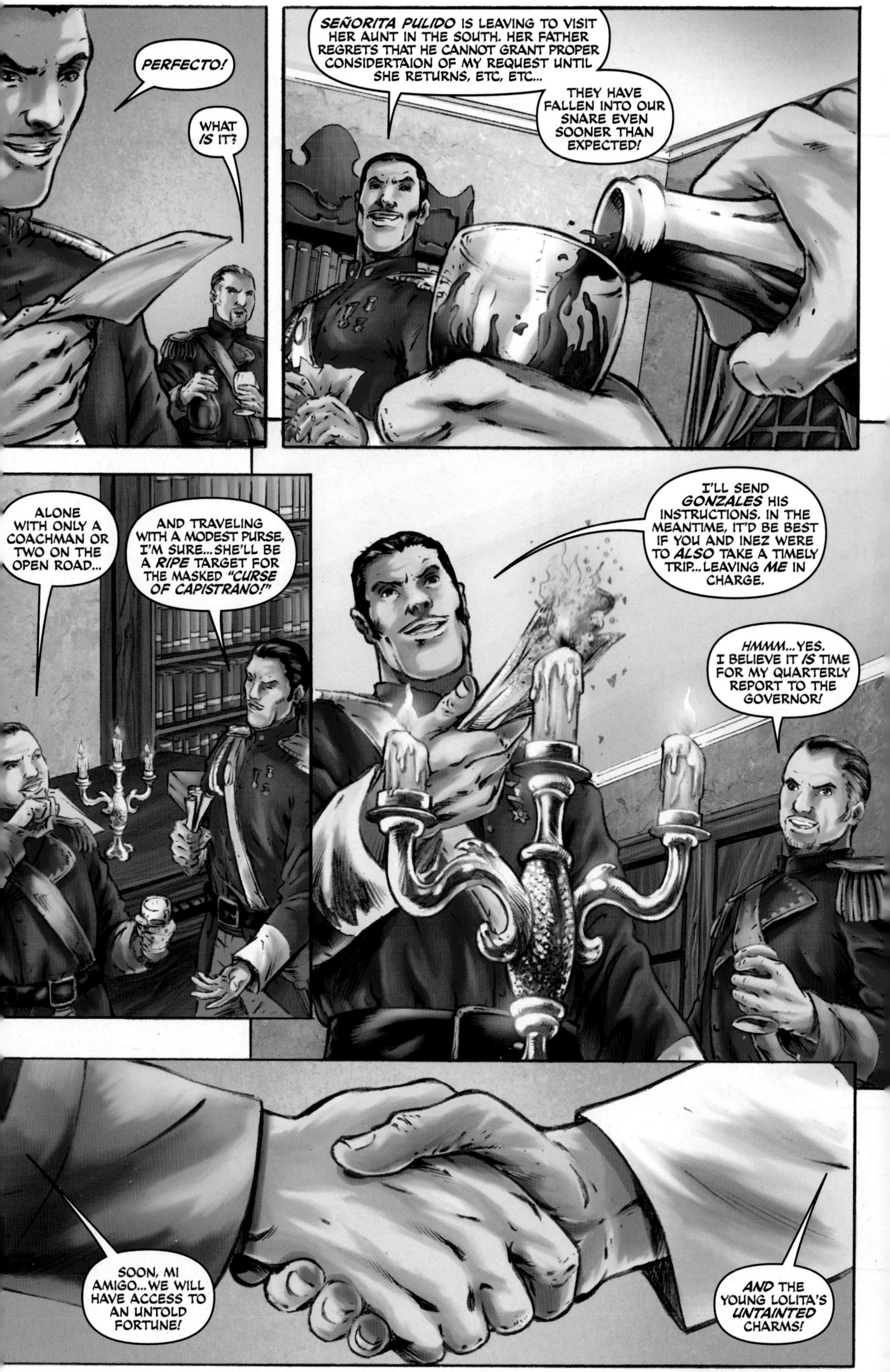
PERFECTO!
WHAT IS IT?
SEÑORITA PULIDO IS LEAVING TO VISIT HER AUNT IN THE SOUTH. HER FATHER REGRETS THAT HE CANNOT GRANT PROPER CONSIDERTAION OF MY REQUEST UNTIL SHE RETURNS, ETC, ETC...
THEY HAVE FALLEN INTO OUR SNARE EVEN SOONER THAN EXPECTED!
ALONE WITH ONLY A COACHMAN OR TWO ON THE OPEN ROAD...
AND TRAVELING WITH A MODEST PURSE, I'M SURE...SHE'LL BE A RIPE TARGET FOR THE MASKED "CURSE OF CAPISTRANO!"
I'LL SEND GONZALES HIS INSTRUCTIONS. IN THE MEANTIME, IT'D BE BEST IF YOU AND INEZ WERE TO ALSO TAKE A TIMELY TRIP...LEAVING ME IN CHARGE.
HMMM...YES. I BELIEVE IT IS TIME FOR MY QUARTERLY REPORT TO THE GOVERNOR!
SOON, MI AMIGO...WE WILL HAVE ACCESS TO AN UNTOLD FORTUNE!
AND THE YOUNG LOLITA'S UNTAINTED CHARMS!

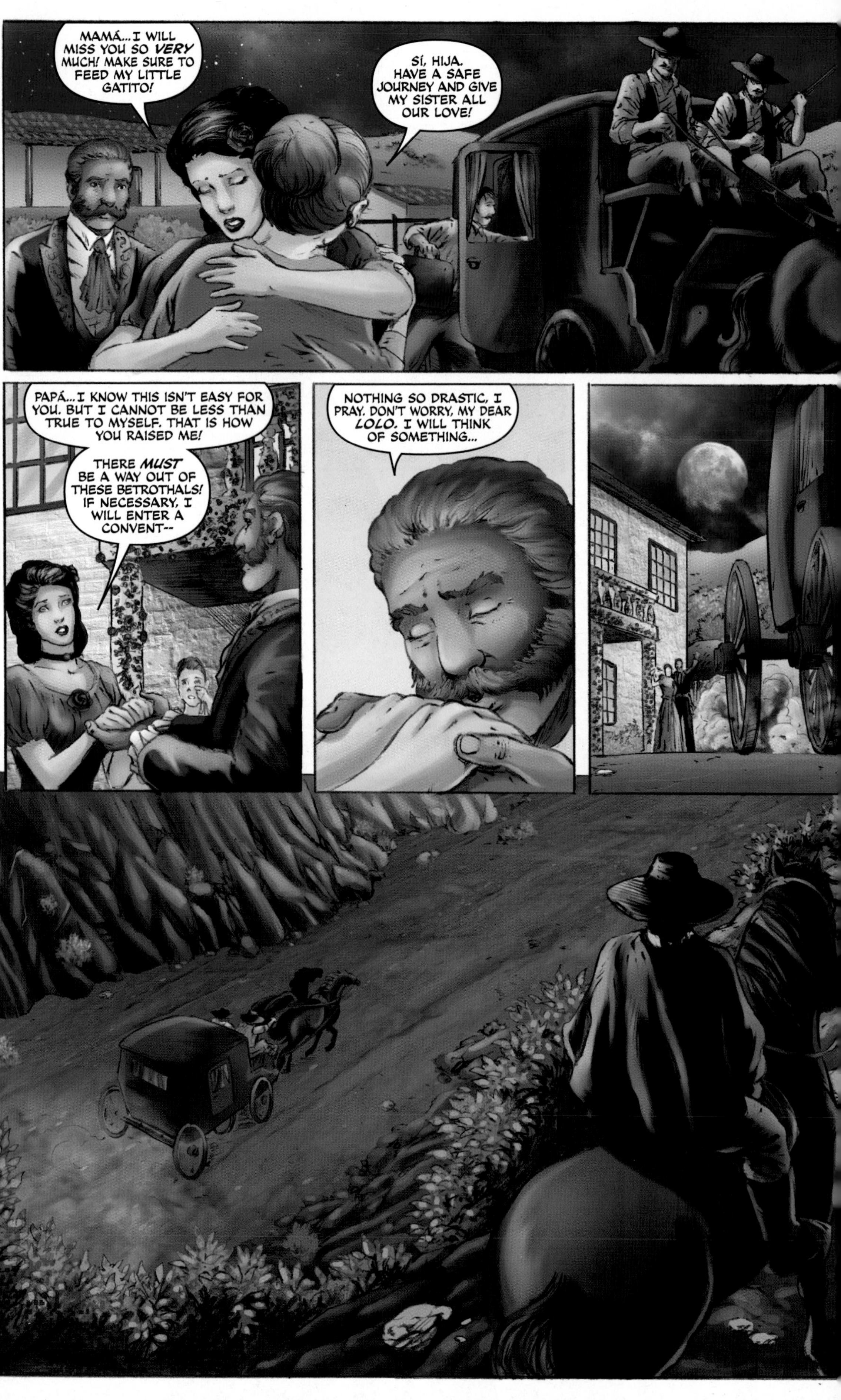
MAMÁ... I WILL MISS YOU SO VERY MUCH! MAKE SURE TO FEED MY LITTLE GATITO!
SÍ, HIJA. HAVE A SAFE JOURNEY AND GIVE MY SISTER ALL OUR LOVE!
PAPÁ... I KNOW THIS ISN'T EASY FOR YOU. BUT I CANNOT BE LESS THAN TRUE TO MYSELF. THAT IS HOW YOU RAISED ME!
THERE MUST BE A WAY OUT OF THESE BETROTHALS! IF NECESSARY, I WILL ENTER A CONVENT--
NOTHING SO DRASTIC, I PRAY. DON'T WORRY, MY DEAR LOLO. I WILL THINK OF SOMETHING...

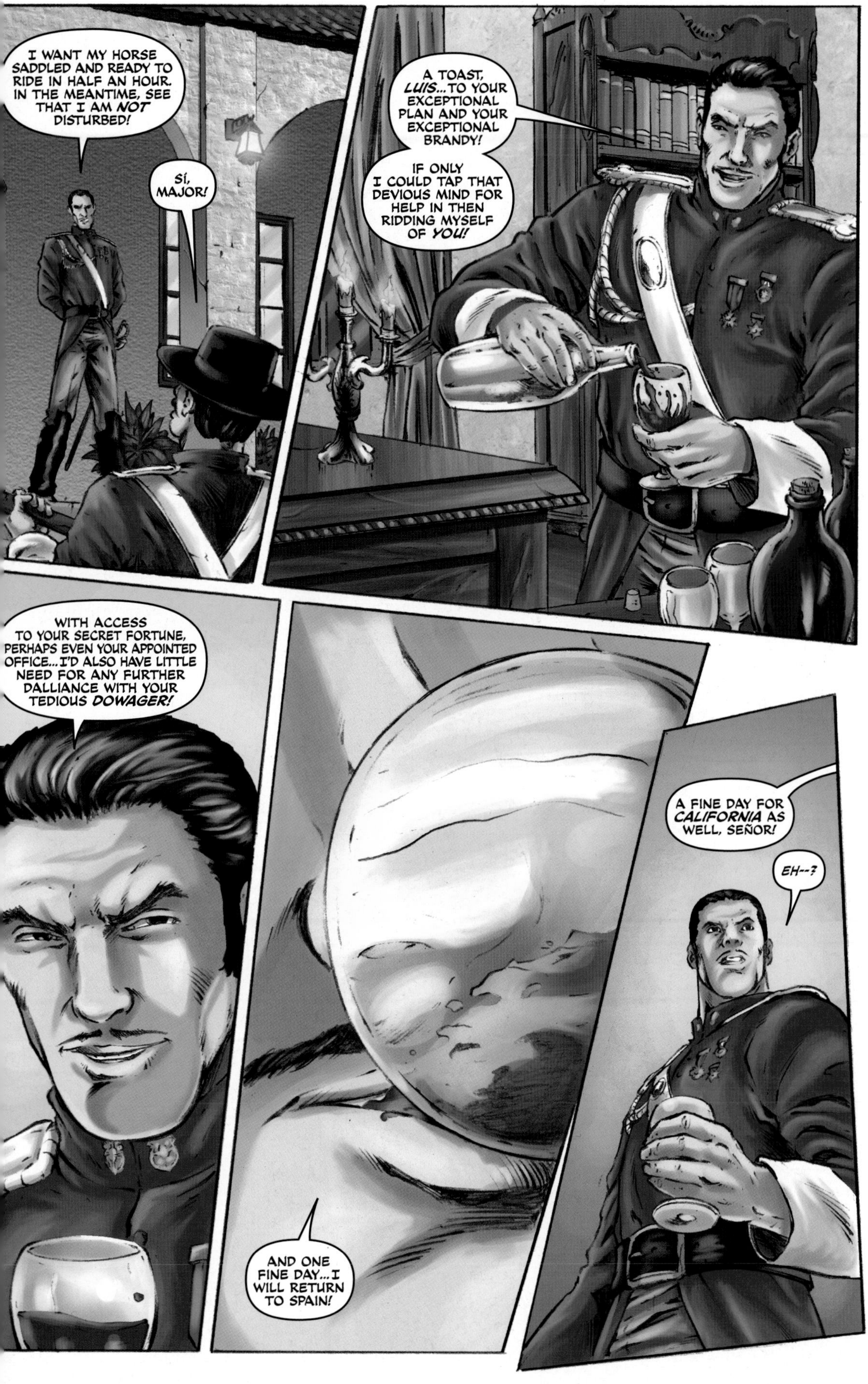
I WANT MY HORSE SADDLED AND READY TO RIDE IN HALF AN HOUR. IN THE MEANTIME, SEE THAT I AM NOT DISTURBED!
SÍ, MAJOR!
A TOAST, LUIS...TO YOUR EXCEPTIONAL PLAN AND YOUR EXCEPTIONAL BRANDY!
IF ONLY I COULD TAP THAT DEVIOUS MIND FOR HELP IN THEN RIDDING MYSELF OF YOU!
WITH ACCESS TO YOUR SECRET FORTUNE, PERHAPS EVEN YOUR APPOINTED OFFICE...I'D ALSO HAVE LITTLE NEED FOR ANY FURTHER DALLIANCE WITH YOUR TEDIOUS DOWAGER!
AND ONE FINE DAY...I WILL RETURN TO SPAIN!
A FINE DAY FOR CALIFORNIA AS WELL, SEÑOR!
EH--?

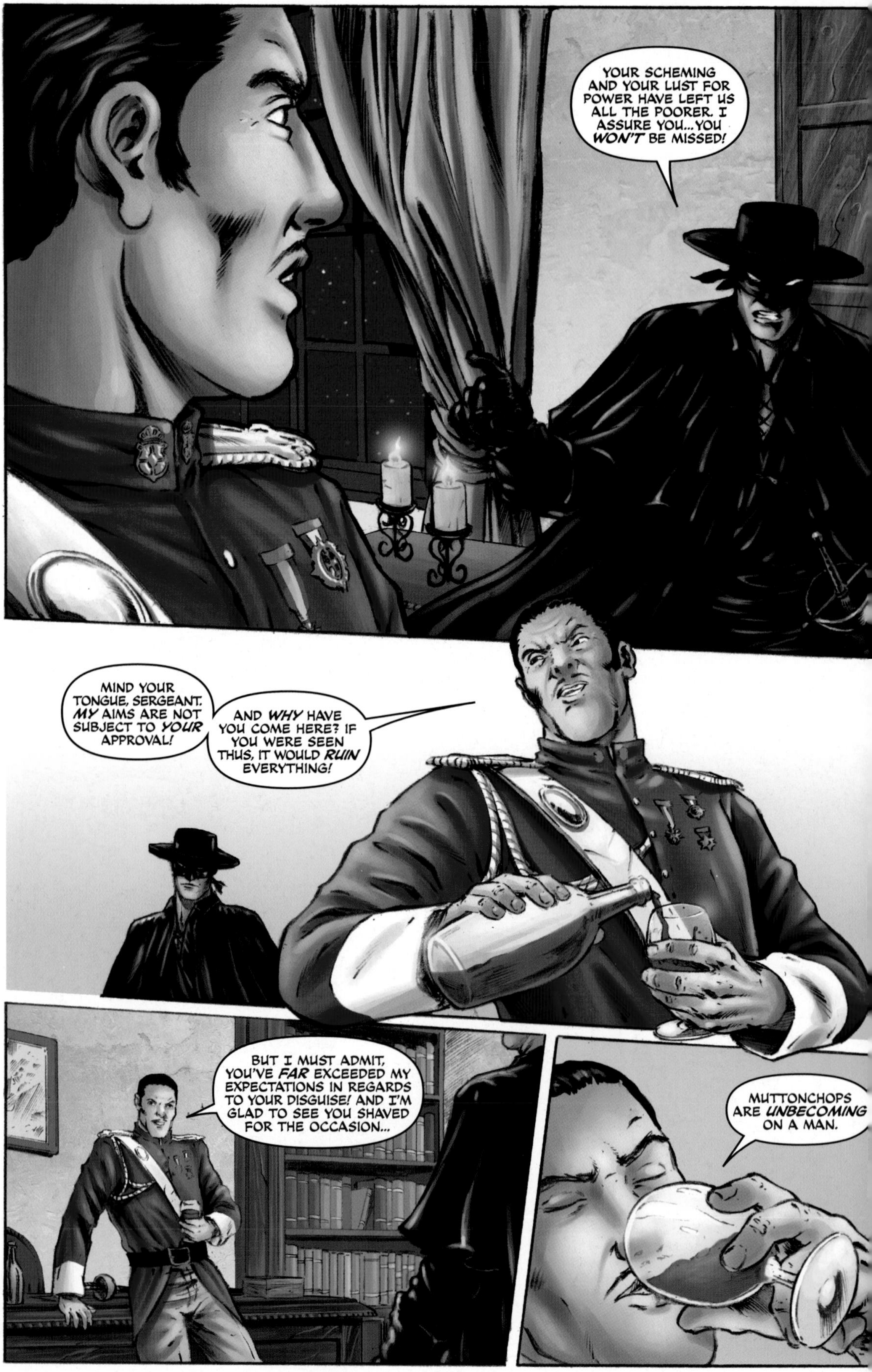
YOUR SCHEMING AND YOUR LUST FOR POWER HAVE LEFT US ALL THE POORER. I ASSURE YOU...YOU *WON'T* BE MISSED!
MIND YOUR TONGUE, SERGEANT. *MY* AIMS ARE NOT SUBJECT TO *YOUR* APPROVAL!
AND *WHY* HAVE YOU COME HERE? IF YOU WERE SEEN THUS, IT WOULD *RUIN* EVERYTHING!
BUT I MUST ADMIT, YOU'VE *FAR* EXCEEDED MY EXPECTATIONS IN REGARDS TO YOUR DISGUISE! AND I'M GLAD TO SEE YOU SHAVED FOR THE OCCASION...
MUTTONCHOPS ARE *UNBECOMING* ON A MAN.

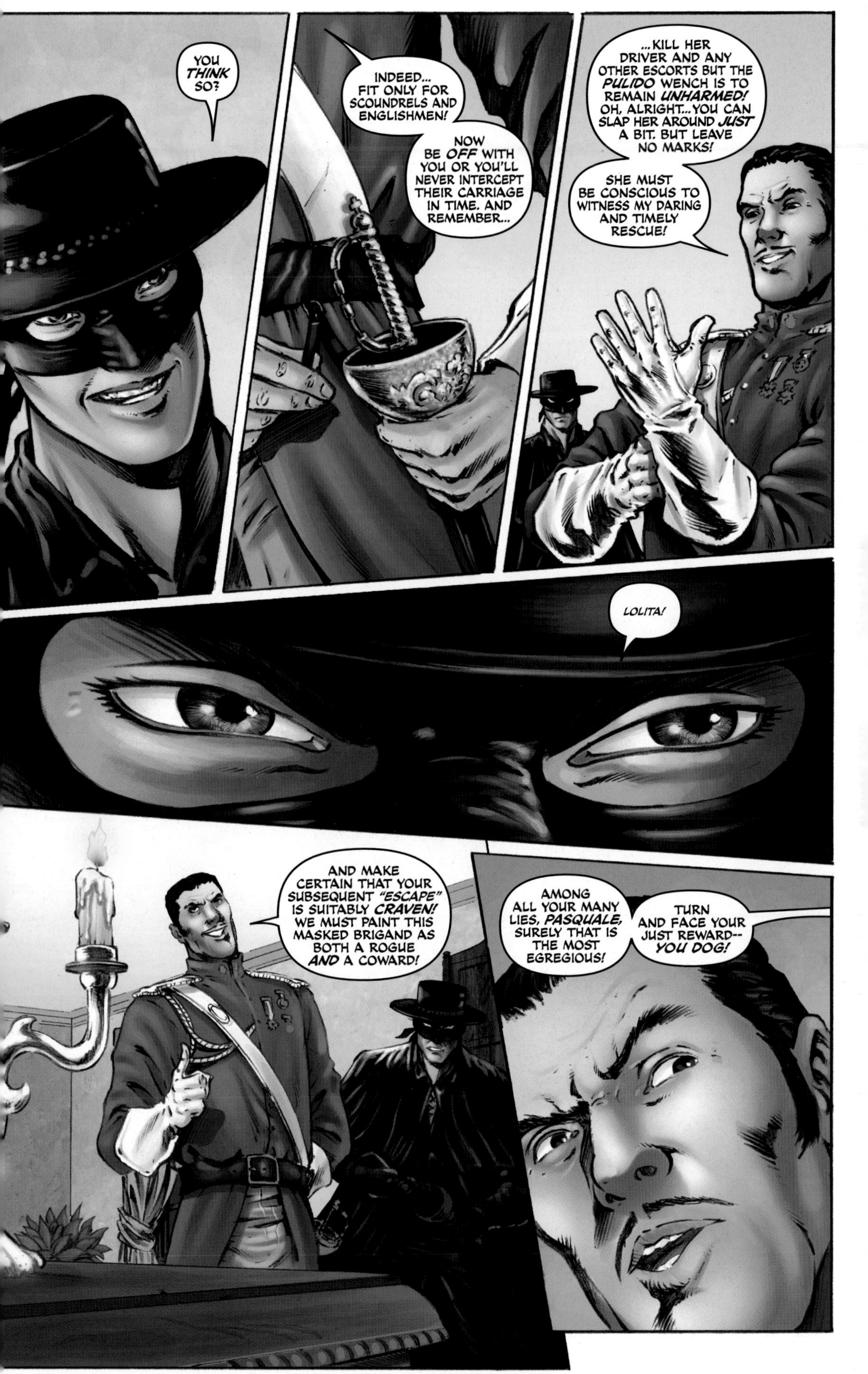
YOU THINK SO?
INDEED... FIT ONLY FOR SCOUNDRELS AND ENGLISHMEN!
NOW BE OFF WITH YOU OR YOU'LL NEVER INTERCEPT THEIR CARRIAGE IN TIME. AND REMEMBER...
...KILL HER DRIVER AND ANY OTHER ESCORTS BUT THE PULIDO WENCH IS TO REMAIN UNHARMED! OH, ALRIGHT...YOU CAN SLAP HER AROUND JUST A BIT. BUT LEAVE NO MARKS!
SHE MUST BE CONSCIOUS TO WITNESS MY DARING AND TIMELY RESCUE!
LOLITA!
AND MAKE CERTAIN THAT YOUR SUBSEQUENT "ESCAPE" IS SUITABLY CRAVEN! WE MUST PAINT THIS MASKED BRIGAND AS BOTH A ROGUE AND A COWARD!
AMONG ALL YOUR MANY LIES, PASQUALE, SURELY THAT IS THE MOST EGREGIOUS!
TURN AND FACE YOUR JUST REWARD-- YOU DOG!

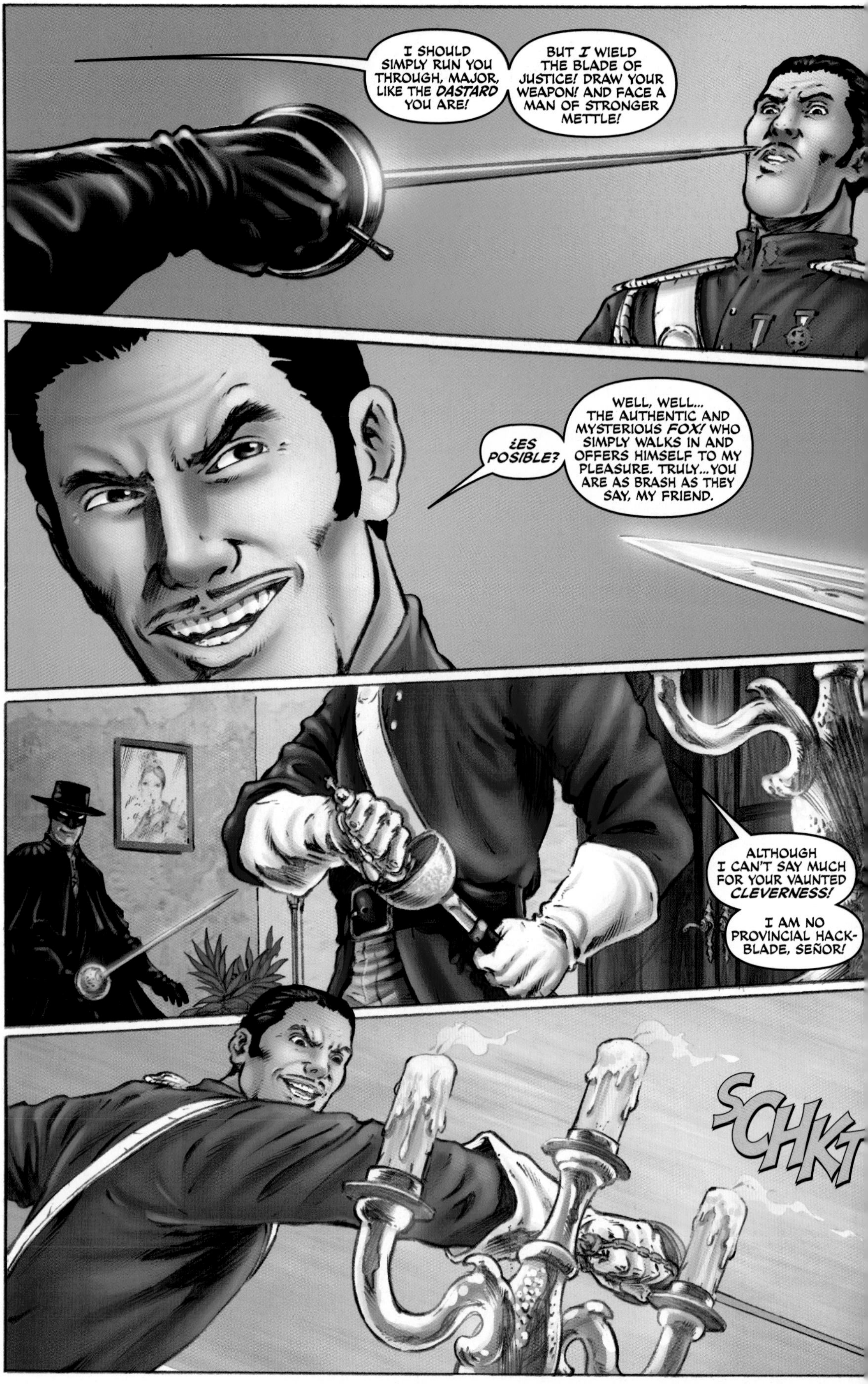

I SHOULD SIMPLY RUN YOU THROUGH, MAJOR, LIKE THE *DASTARD* YOU ARE!
BUT *I* WIELD THE BLADE OF JUSTICE! DRAW YOUR WEAPON! AND FACE A MAN OF STRONGER METTLE!
¿ES POSIBLE?
WELL, WELL... THE AUTHENTIC AND MYSTERIOUS *FOX!* WHO SIMPLY WALKS IN AND OFFERS HIMSELF TO MY PLEASURE. TRULY...YOU ARE AS BRASH AS THEY SAY, MY FRIEND.
ALTHOUGH I CAN'T SAY MUCH FOR YOUR VAUNTED *CLEVERNESS!*
I AM NO PROVINCIAL HACK-BLADE, SEÑOR!
SCHKT

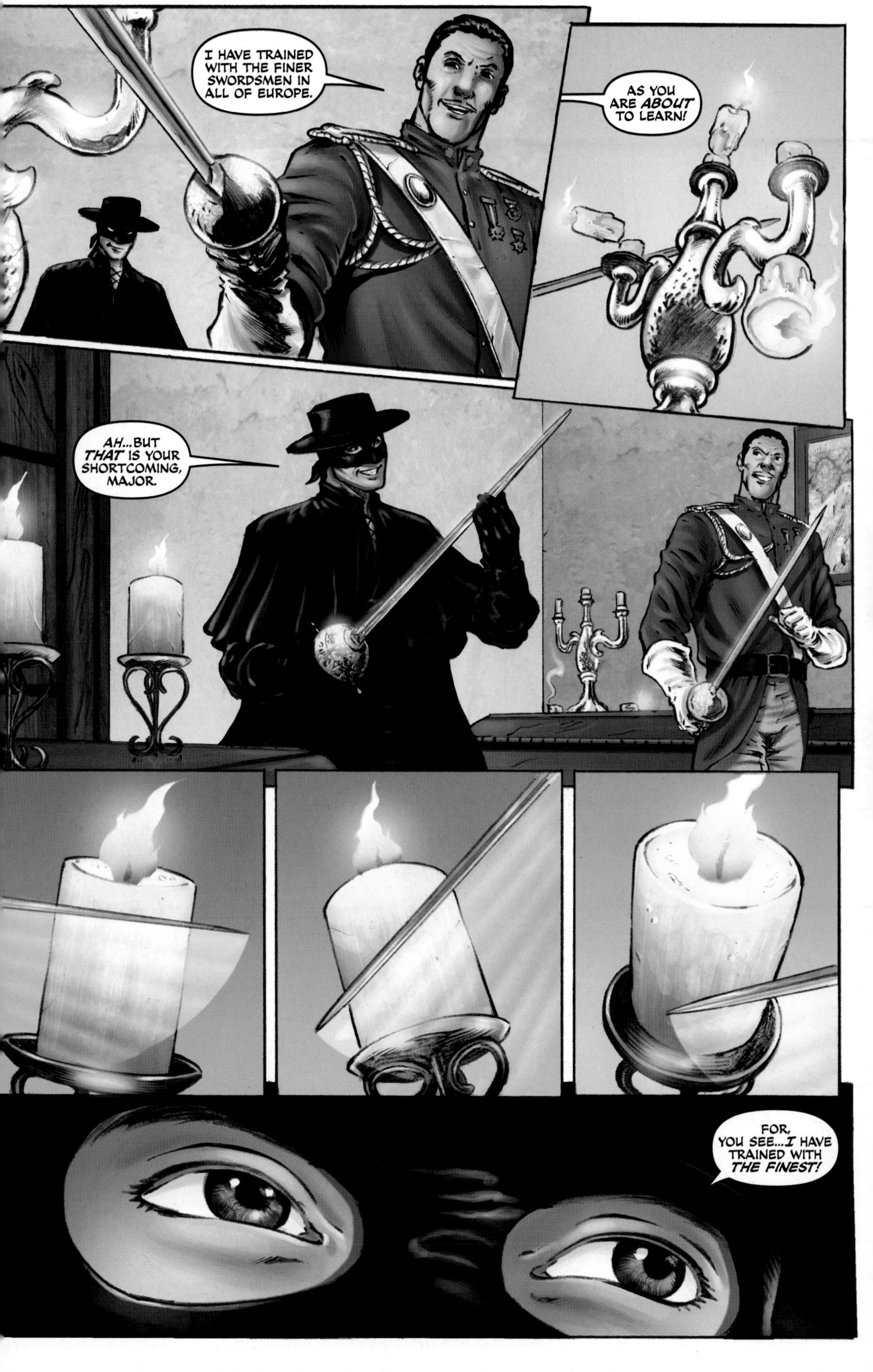
I HAVE TRAINED WITH THE FINER SWORDSMEN IN ALL OF EUROPE.
AS YOU ARE *ABOUT* TO LEARN!
AH...BUT *THAT* IS YOUR SHORTCOMING, MAJOR.
FOR, YOU SEE...*I* HAVE TRAINED WITH *THE FINEST!*

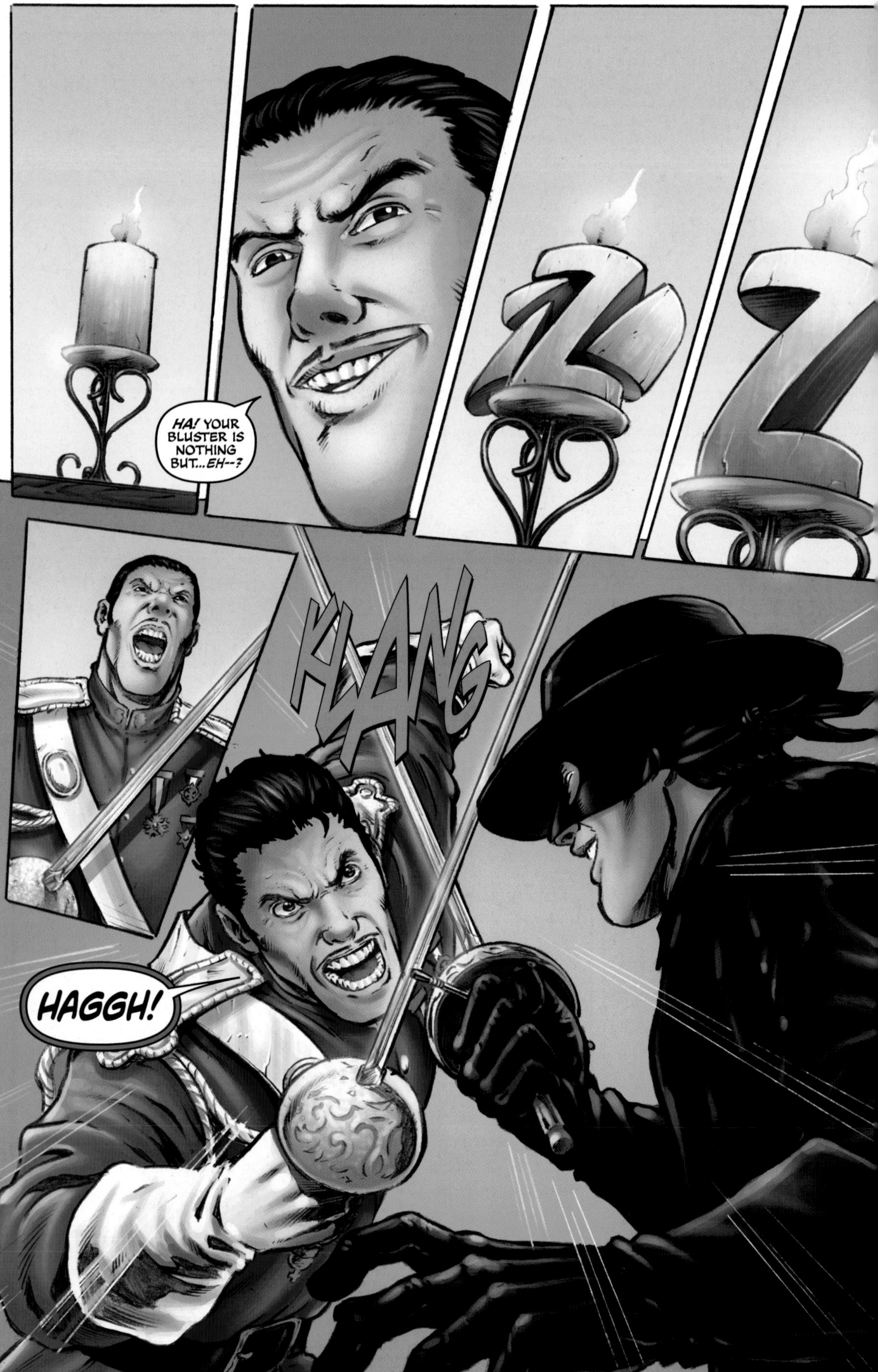
HA! YOUR BLUSTER IS NOTHING BUT...EH--?
KLANG
HAGGH!

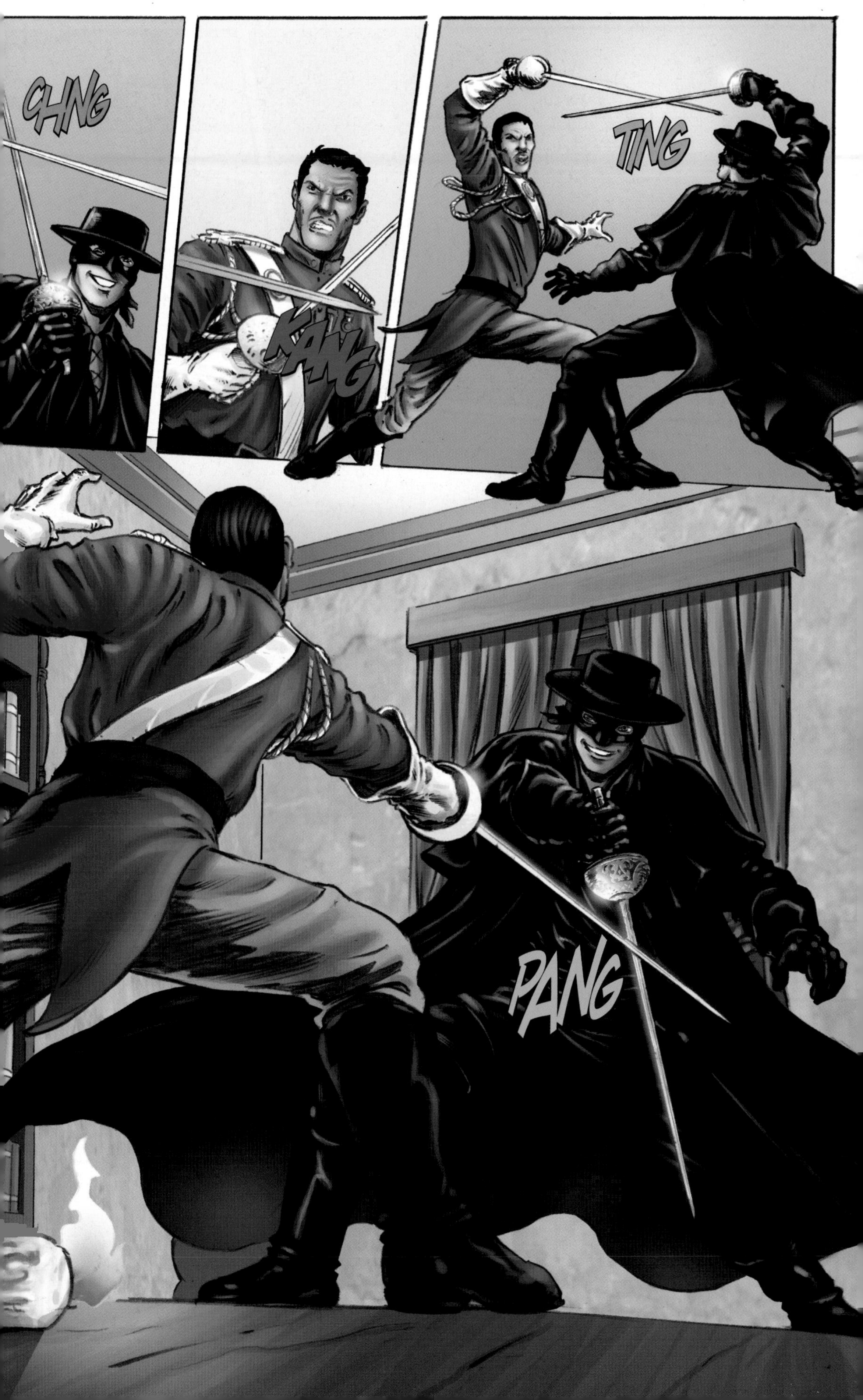
CHING
KANG
TING
PANG

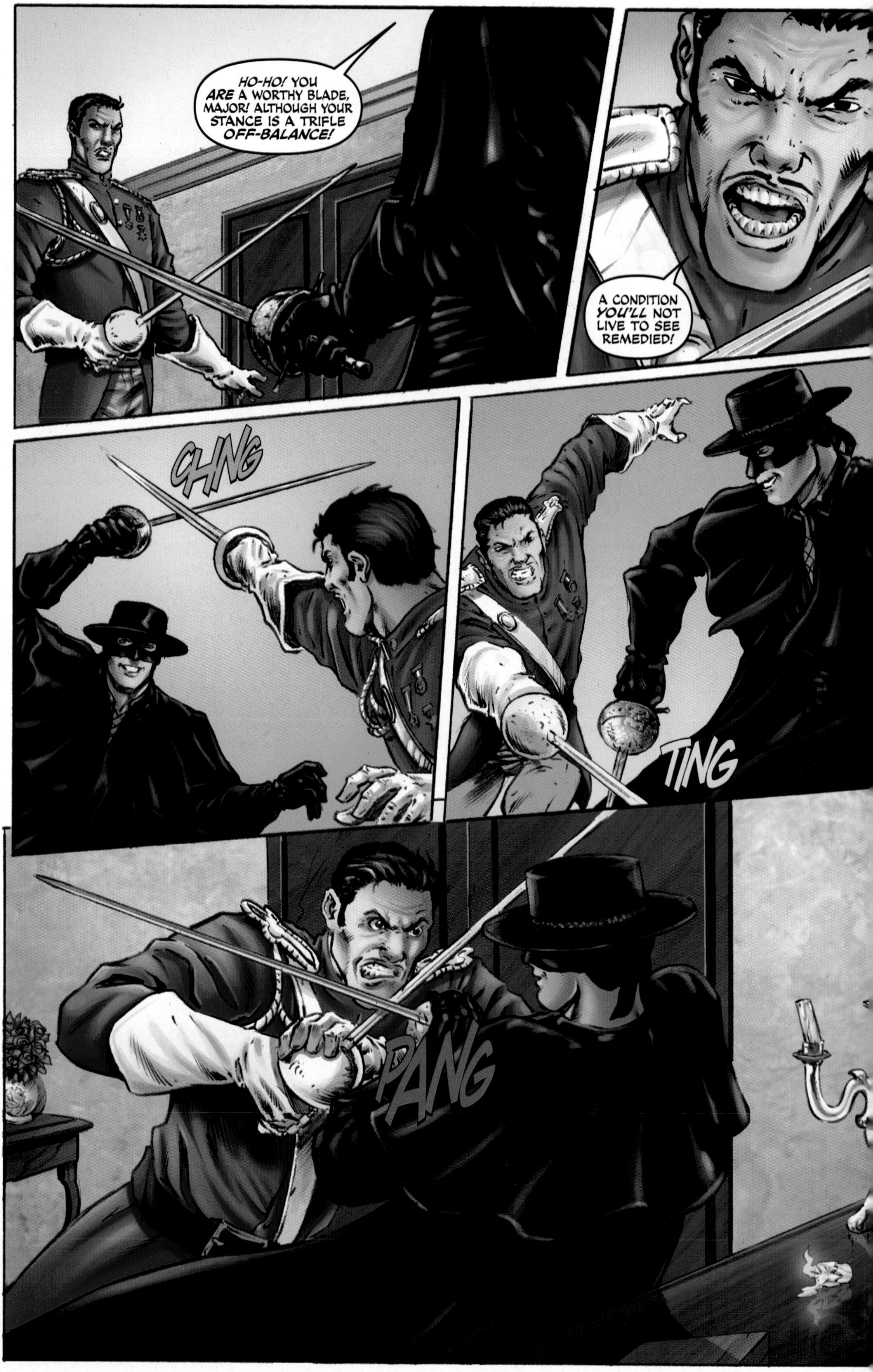
HO-HO! YOU ARE A WORTHY BLADE, MAJOR! ALTHOUGH YOUR STANCE IS A TRIFLE OFF-BALANCE!
A CONDITION YOU'LL NOT LIVE TO SEE REMEDIED!
CHING
TING
PANG

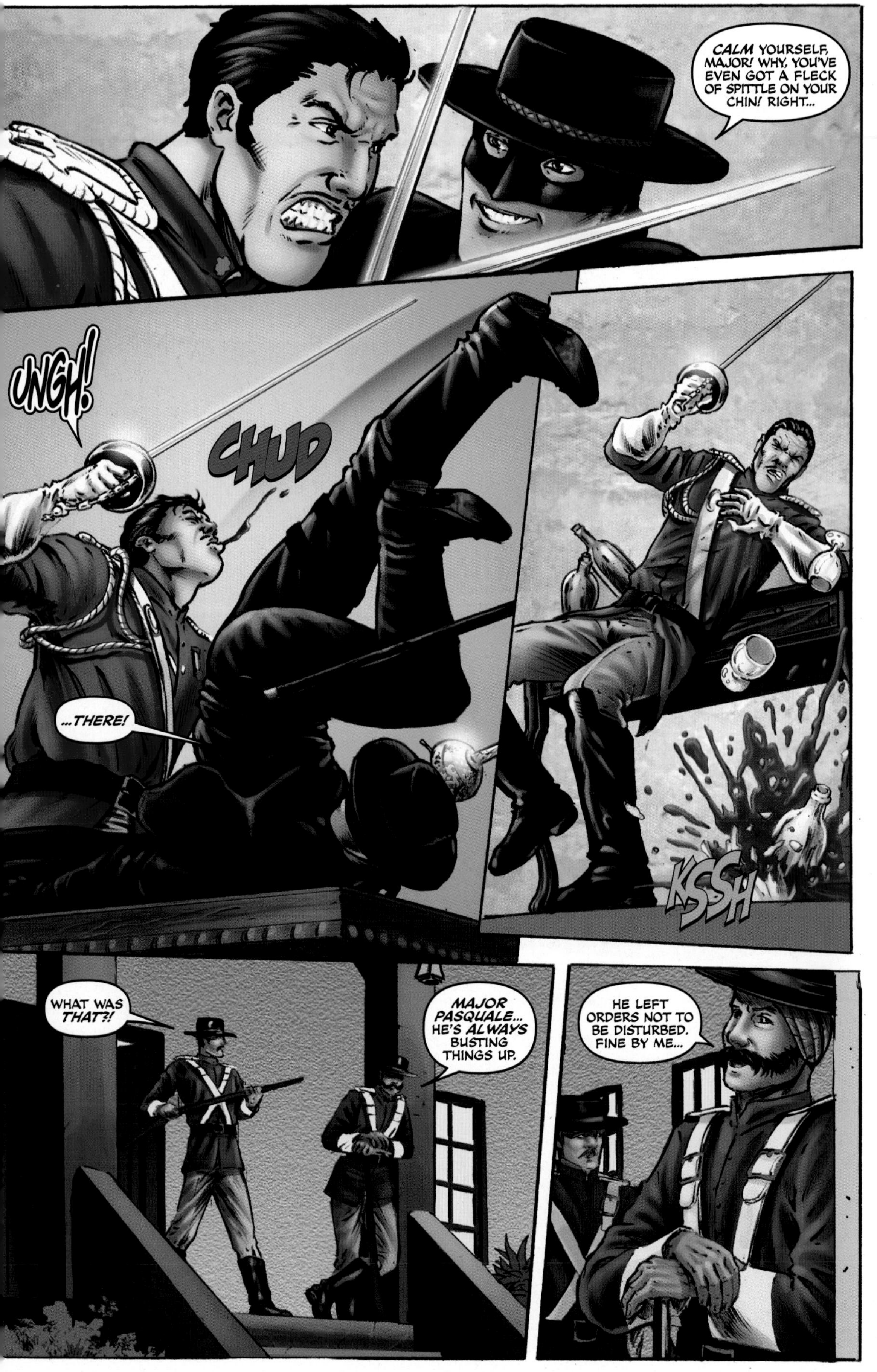
CALM YOURSELF, MAJOR! WHY, YOU'VE EVEN GOT A FLECK OF SPITTLE ON YOUR CHIN! RIGHT...
UNGH!
CHUD
...THERE!
KSSH
WHAT WAS THAT?!
MAJOR PASQUALE... HE'S ALWAYS BUSTING THINGS UP.
HE LEFT ORDERS NOT TO BE DISTURBED. FINE BY ME...

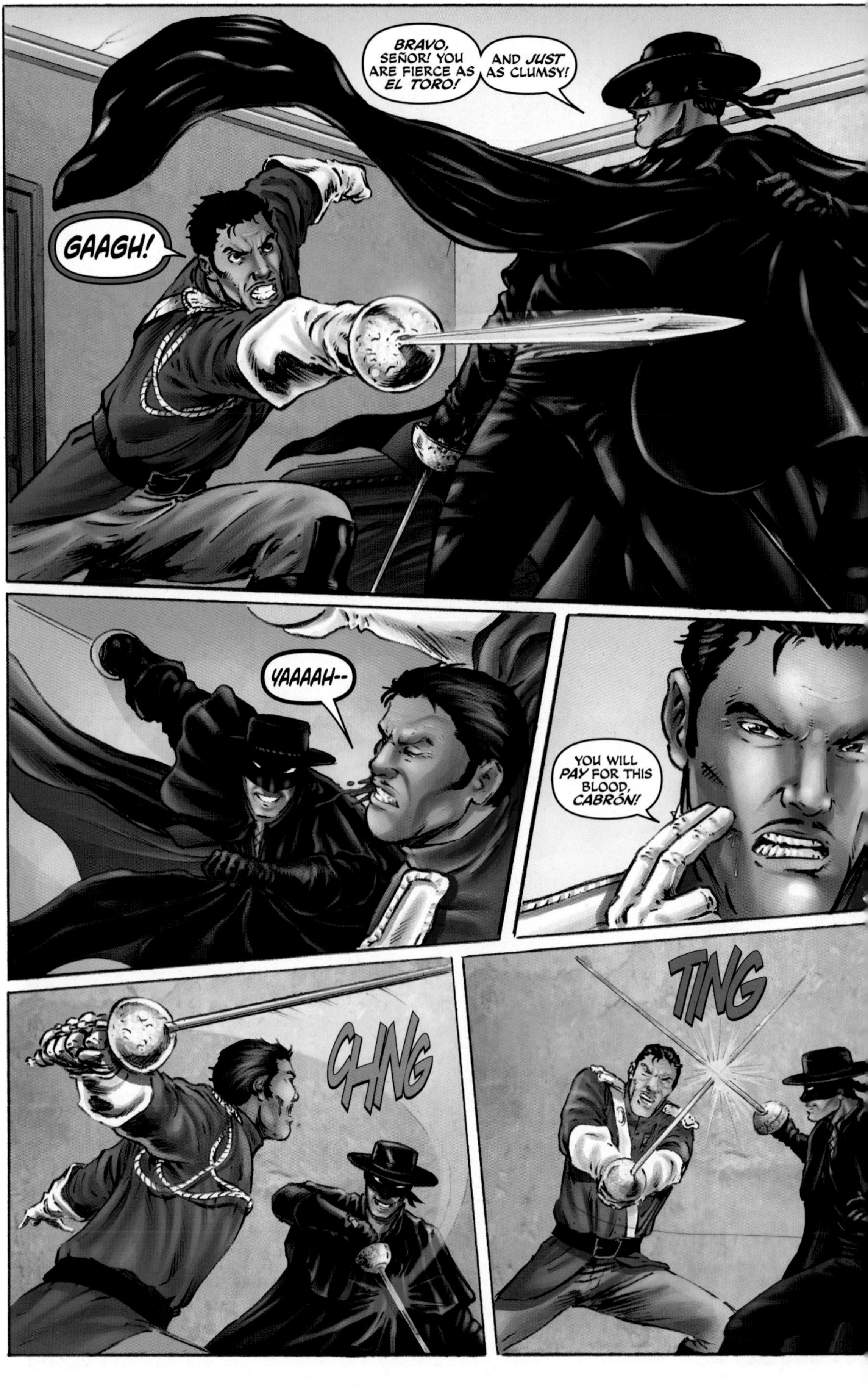
BRAVO, SEÑOR! YOU ARE FIERCE AS EL TORO!
AND JUST AS CLUMSY!
GAAGH!
YAAAAH--
YOU WILL PAY FOR THIS BLOOD, CABRÓN!
CHING
TING

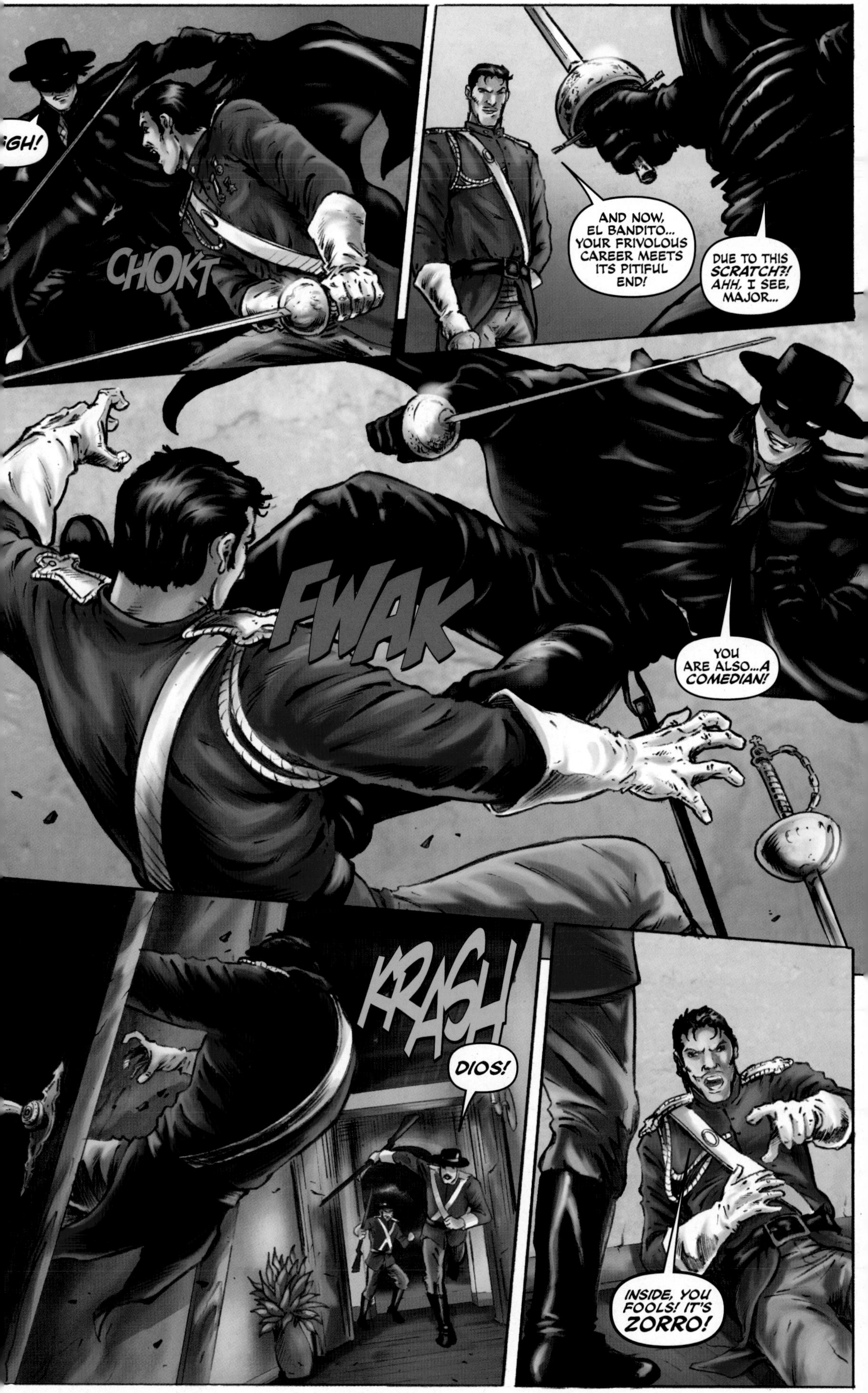

GH!
CHOKT
AND NOW, EL BANDITO... YOUR FRIVOLOUS CAREER MEETS ITS PITIFUL END!
DUE TO THIS SCRATCH?! AHH, I SEE, MAJOR...
FWAK
YOU ARE ALSO...A COMEDIAN!
KRASH
DIOS!
INSIDE, YOU FOOLS! IT'S ZORRO!

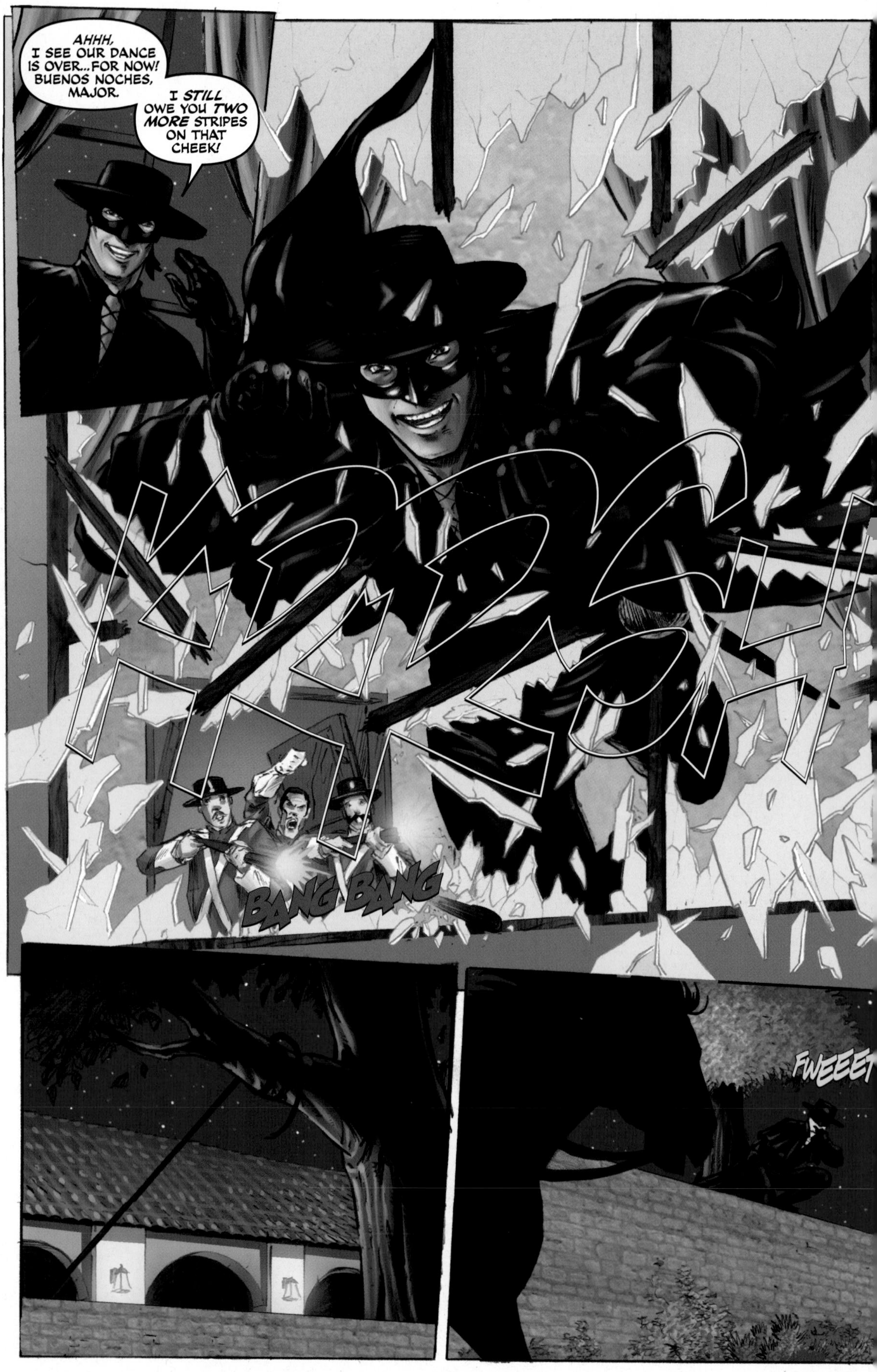
AHHH, I SEE OUR DANCE IS OVER...FOR NOW! BUENOS NOCHES, MAJOR.
I STILL OWE YOU TWO MORE STRIPES ON THAT CHEEK!
BANG BANG
FWEEET

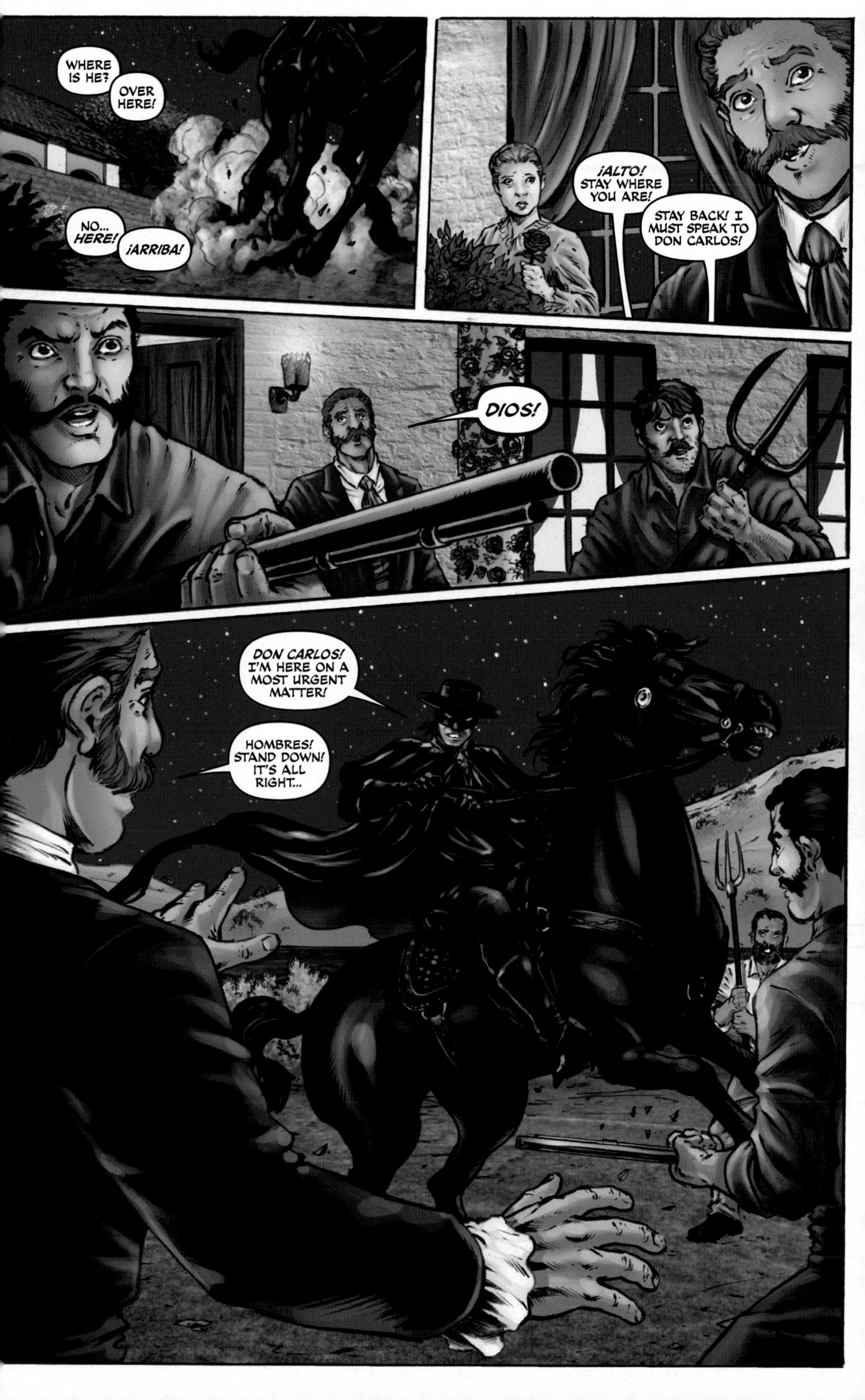
WHERE IS HE?
OVER HERE!
NO... HERE!
¡ARRIBA!
¡ALTO! STAY WHERE YOU ARE!
STAY BACK! I MUST SPEAK TO DON CARLOS!
DIOS!
DON CARLOS! I'M HERE ON A MOST URGENT MATTER!
HOMBRES! STAND DOWN! IT'S ALL RIGHT...

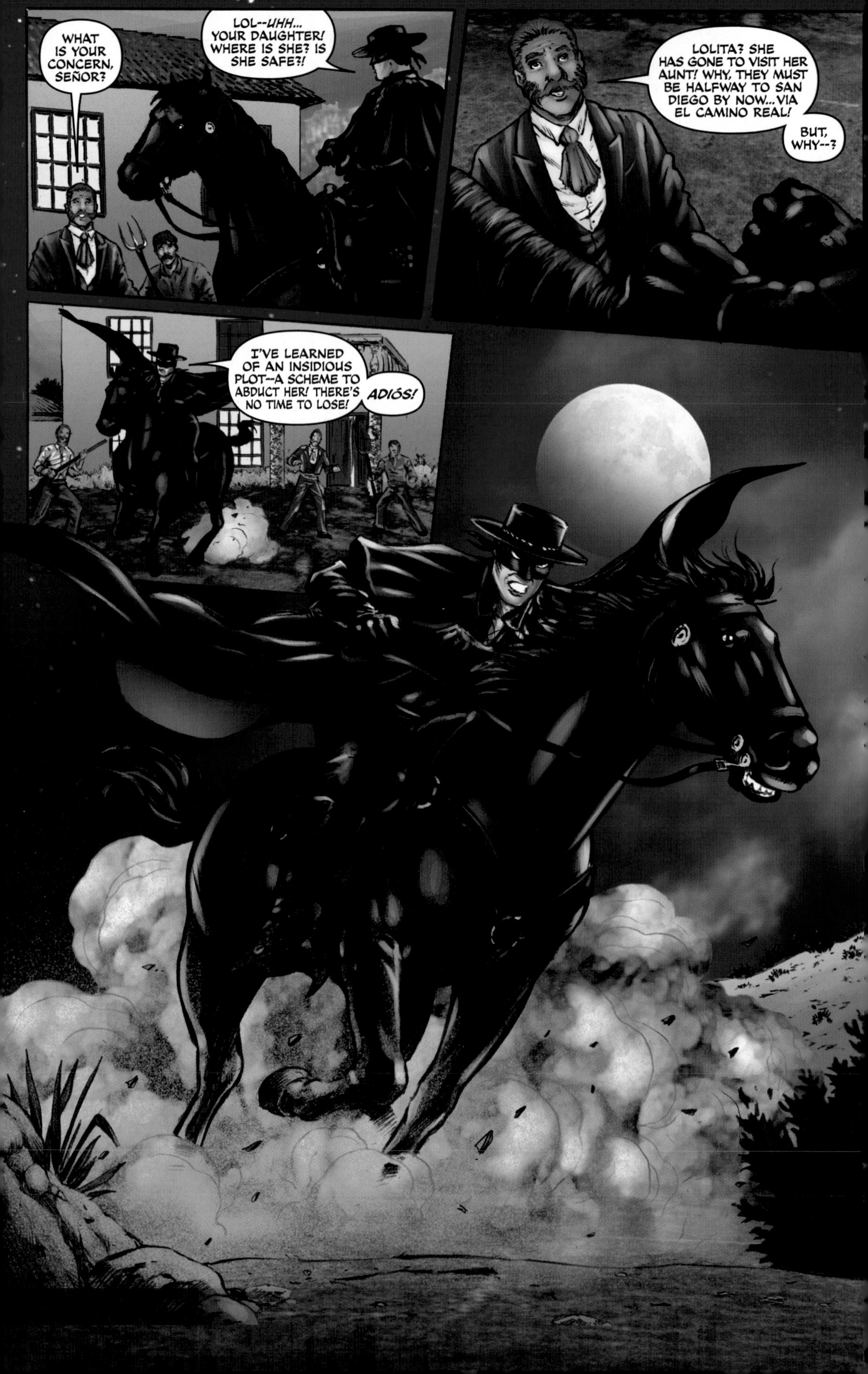
WHAT IS YOUR CONCERN, SEÑOR?
LOL--UHH... YOUR DAUGHTER! WHERE IS SHE? IS SHE SAFE?!
LOLITA? SHE HAS GONE TO VISIT HER AUNT! WHY, THEY MUST BE HALFWAY TO SAN DIEGO BY NOW...VIA EL CAMINO REAL!
BUT, WHY--?
I'VE LEARNED OF AN INSIDIOUS PLOT--A SCHEME TO ABDUCT HER! THERE'S NO TIME TO LOSE!
ADIÓS!

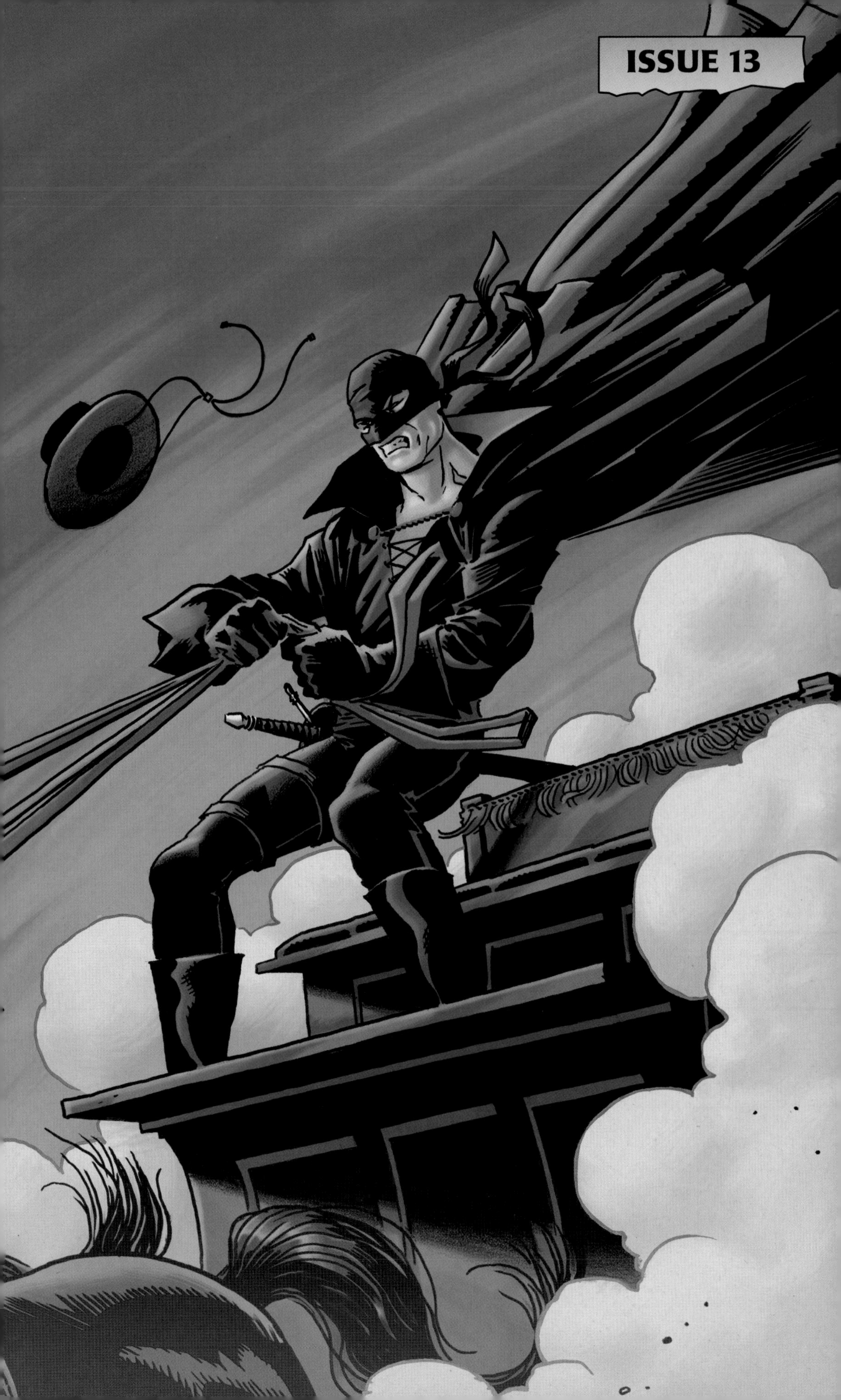
ISSUE 13

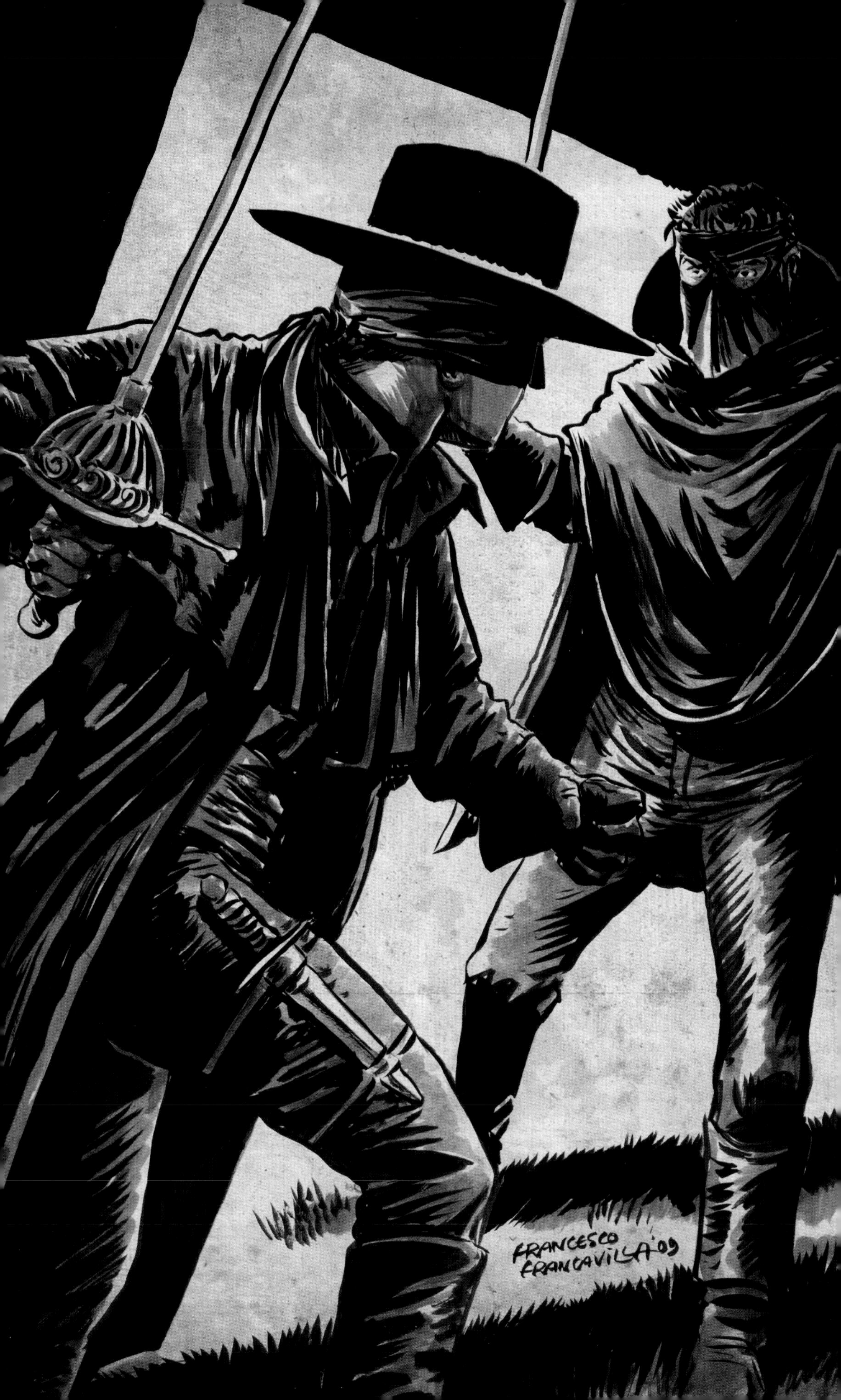
FRANCESCO FRANCAVILLA '09

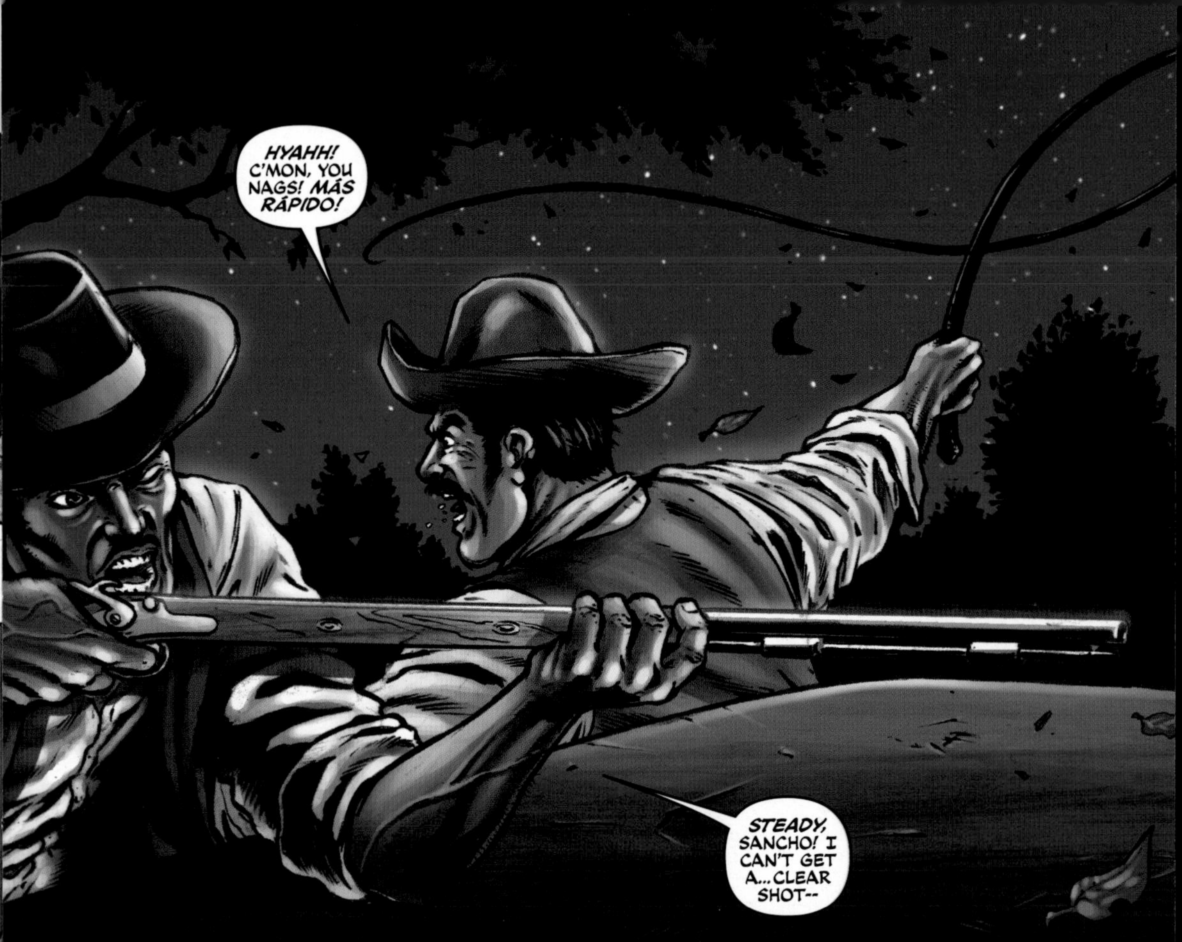
HYAHH! C'MON, YOU NAGS! MÁS RÁPIDO!
STEADY, SANCHO! I CAN'T GET A...CLEAR SHOT--

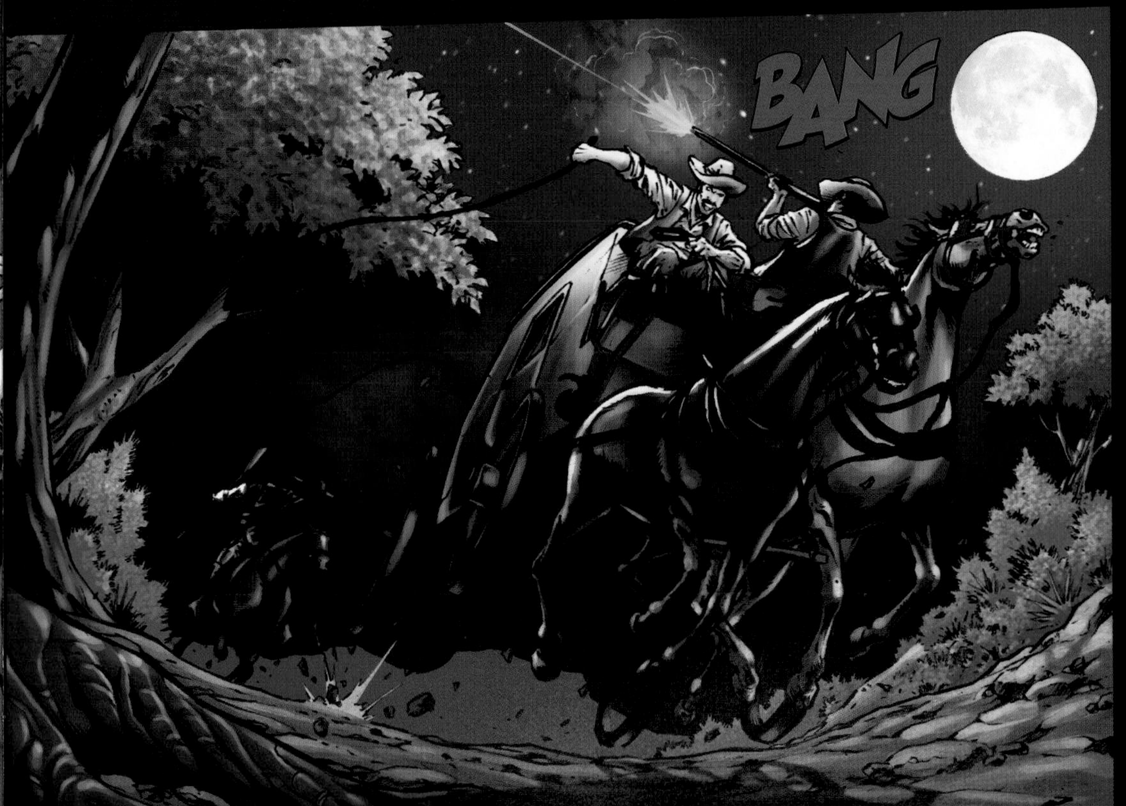
BANG

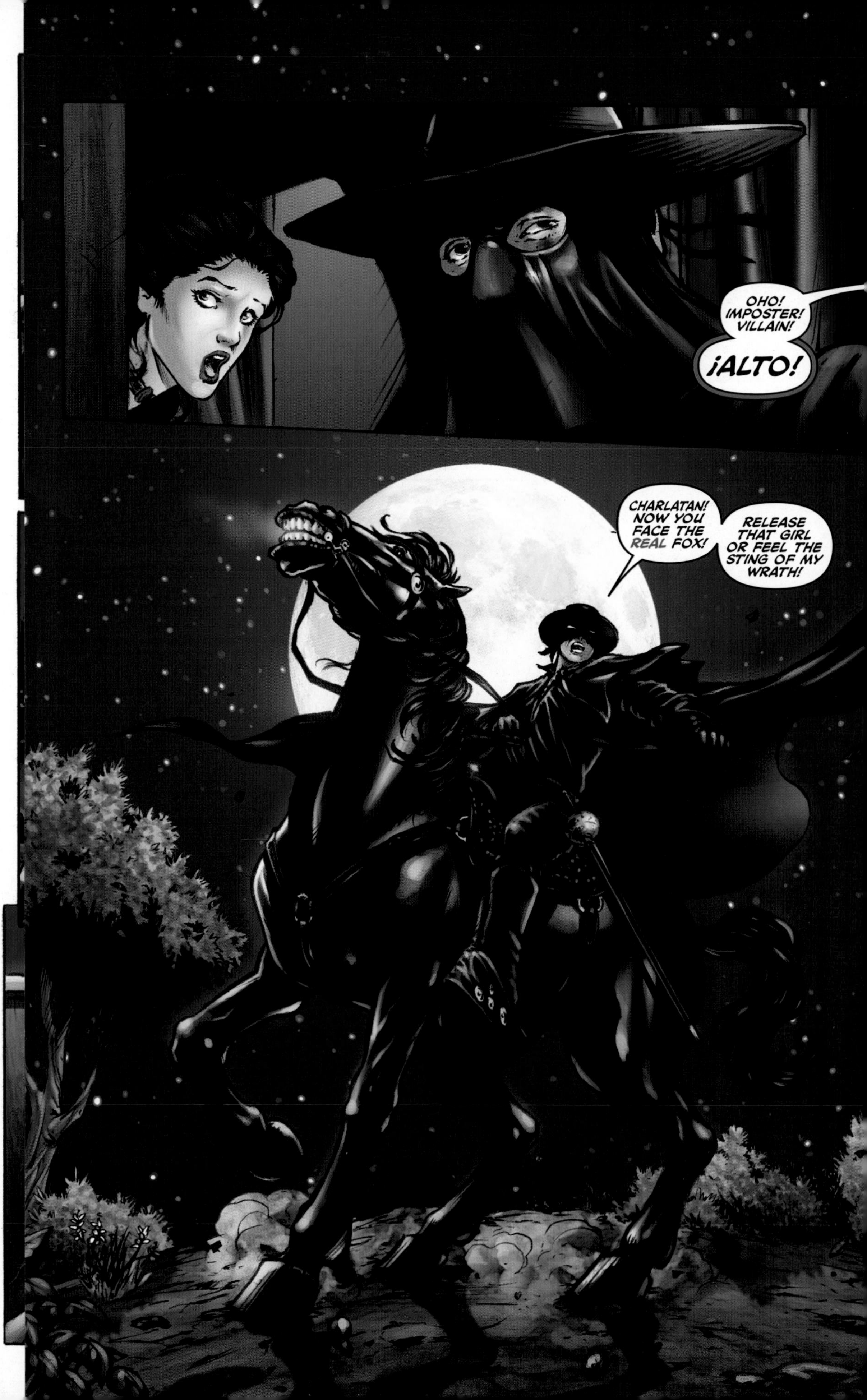
OHO! IMPOSTER! VILLAIN!
¡ALTO!
CHARLATAN! NOW YOU FACE THE REAL FOX!
RELEASE THAT GIRL OR FEEL THE STING OF MY WRATH!

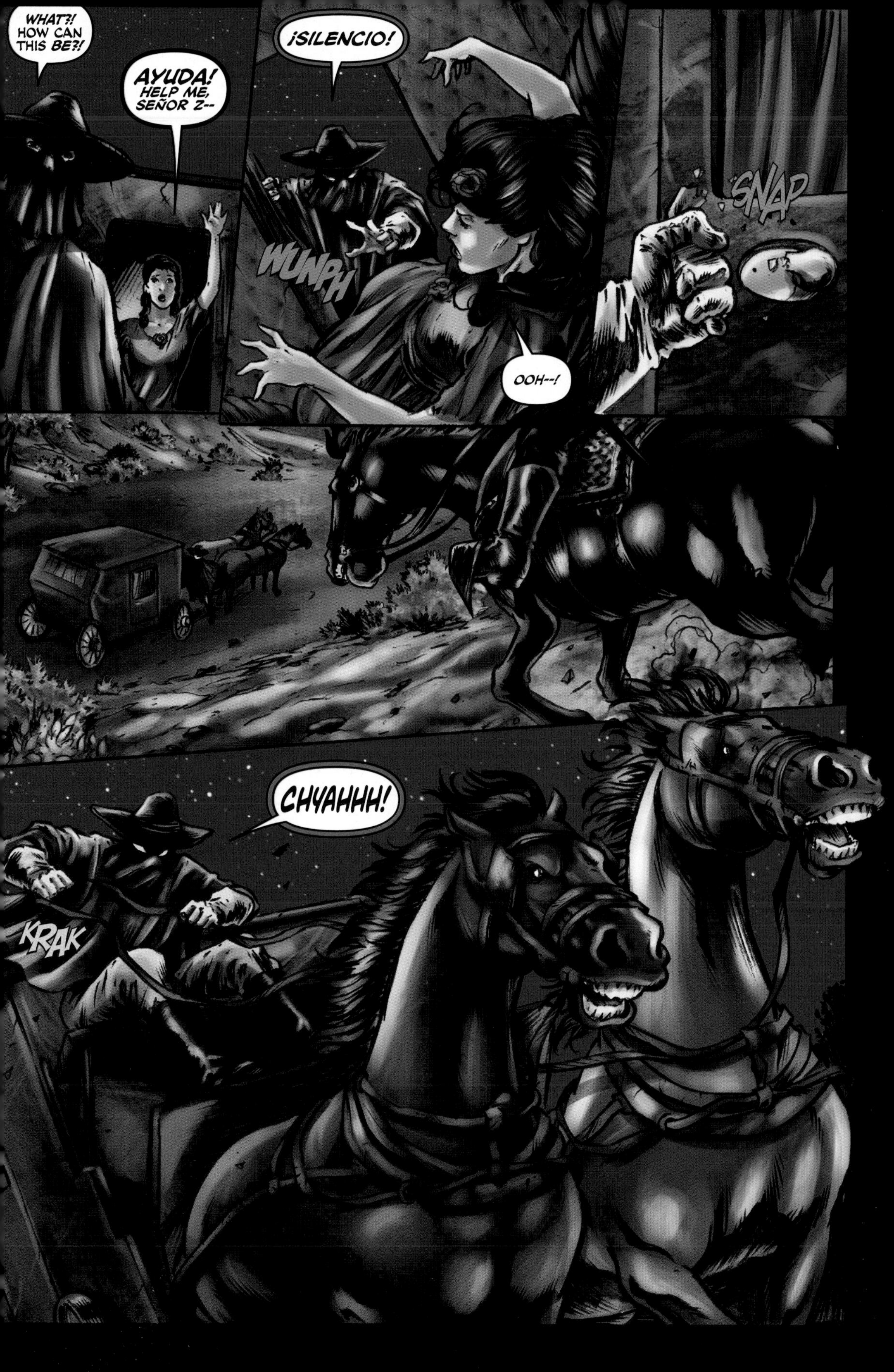
WHAT?! HOW CAN THIS BE?!
AYUDA! HELP ME, SEÑOR Z--
¡SILENCIO!
WUNPH
OOH--!
SNAP
CHYAHHH!
KRAK

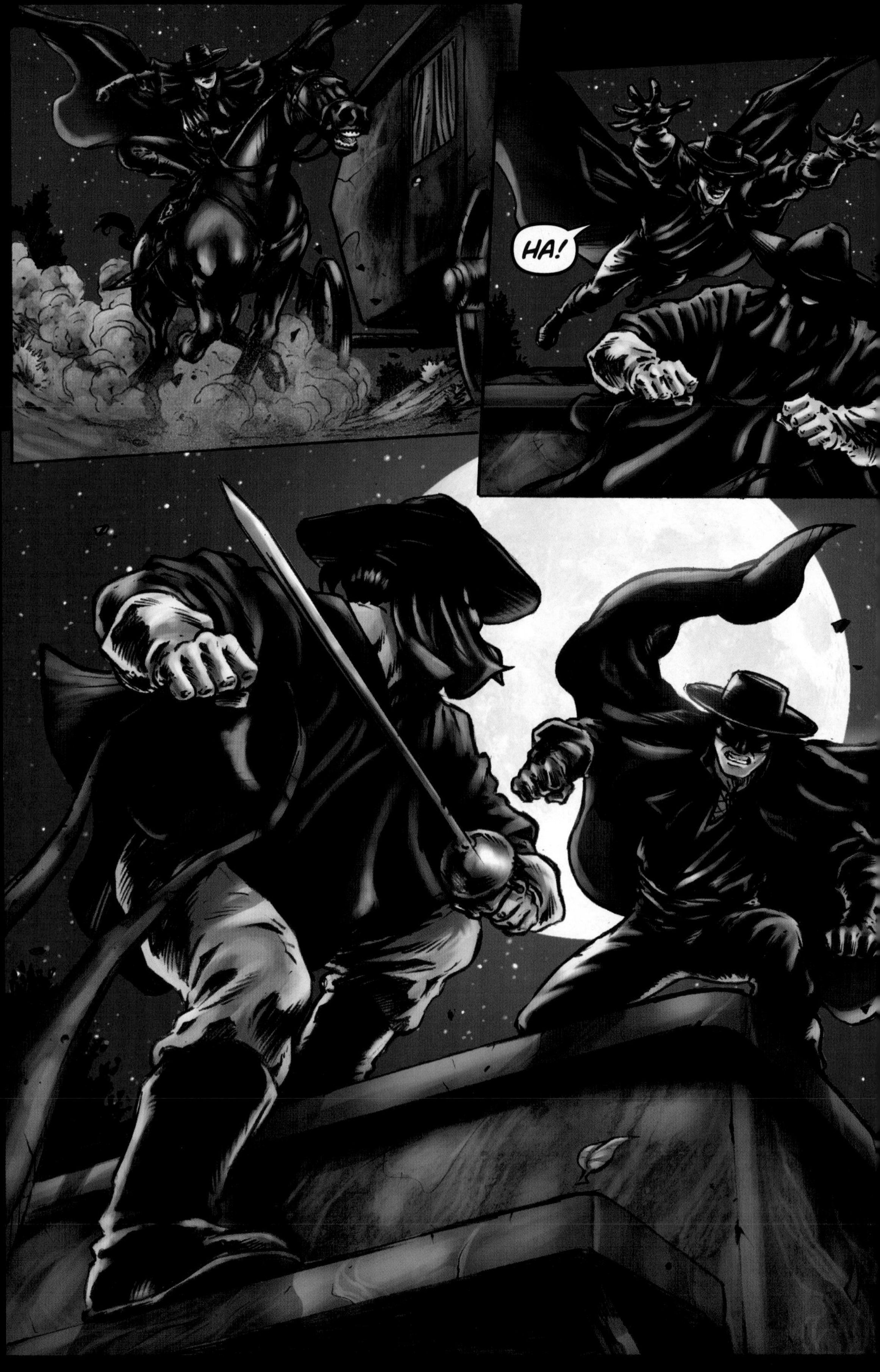
HA!

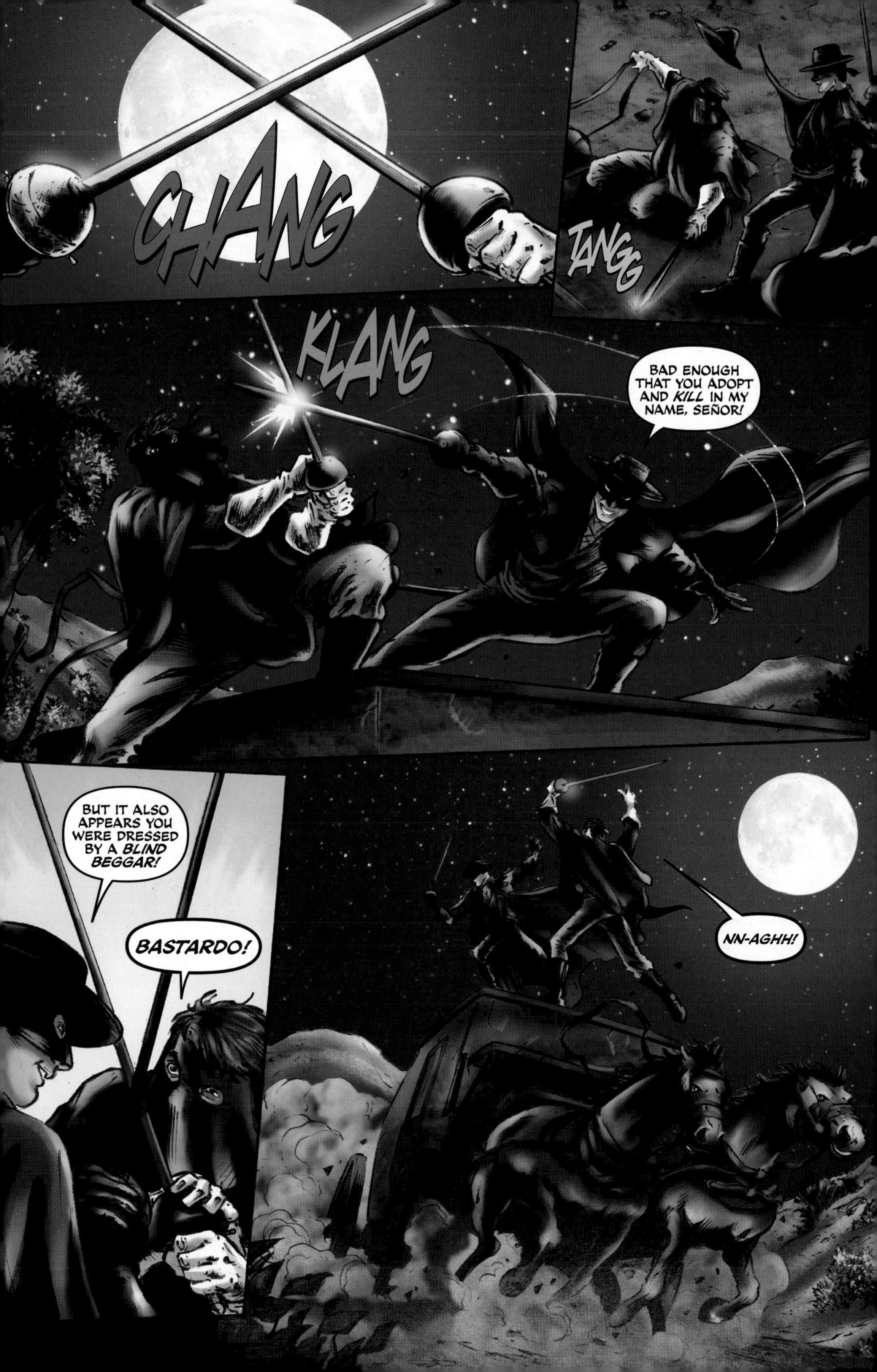
CHANG
TANGG
KLANG
BAD ENOUGH THAT YOU ADOPT AND *KILL* IN MY NAME, SEÑOR!
BUT IT ALSO APPEARS YOU WERE DRESSED BY A *BLIND BEGGAR!*
BASTARDO!
NN-AGHH!

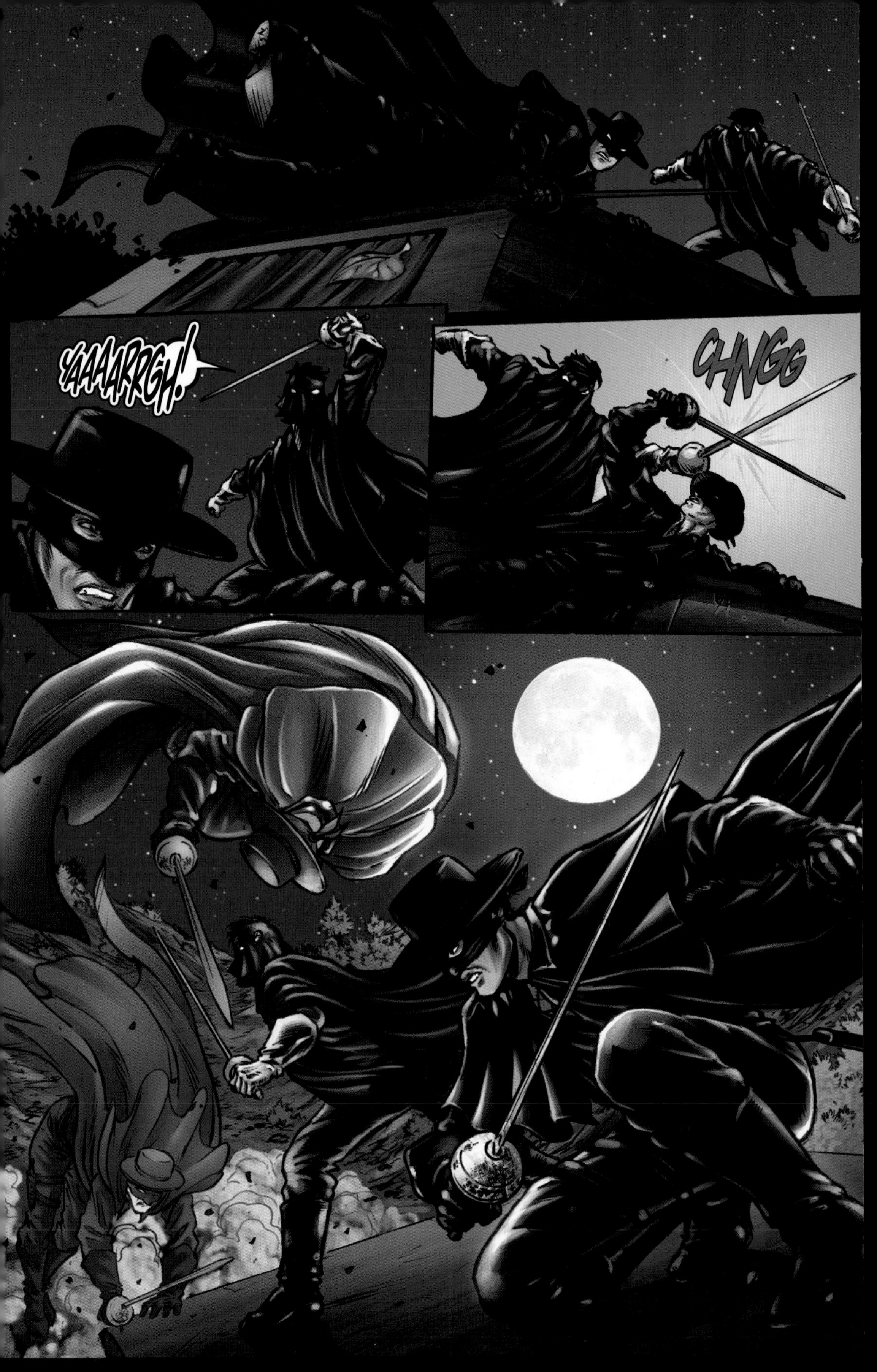
YAAAARRGH!
CHNGG

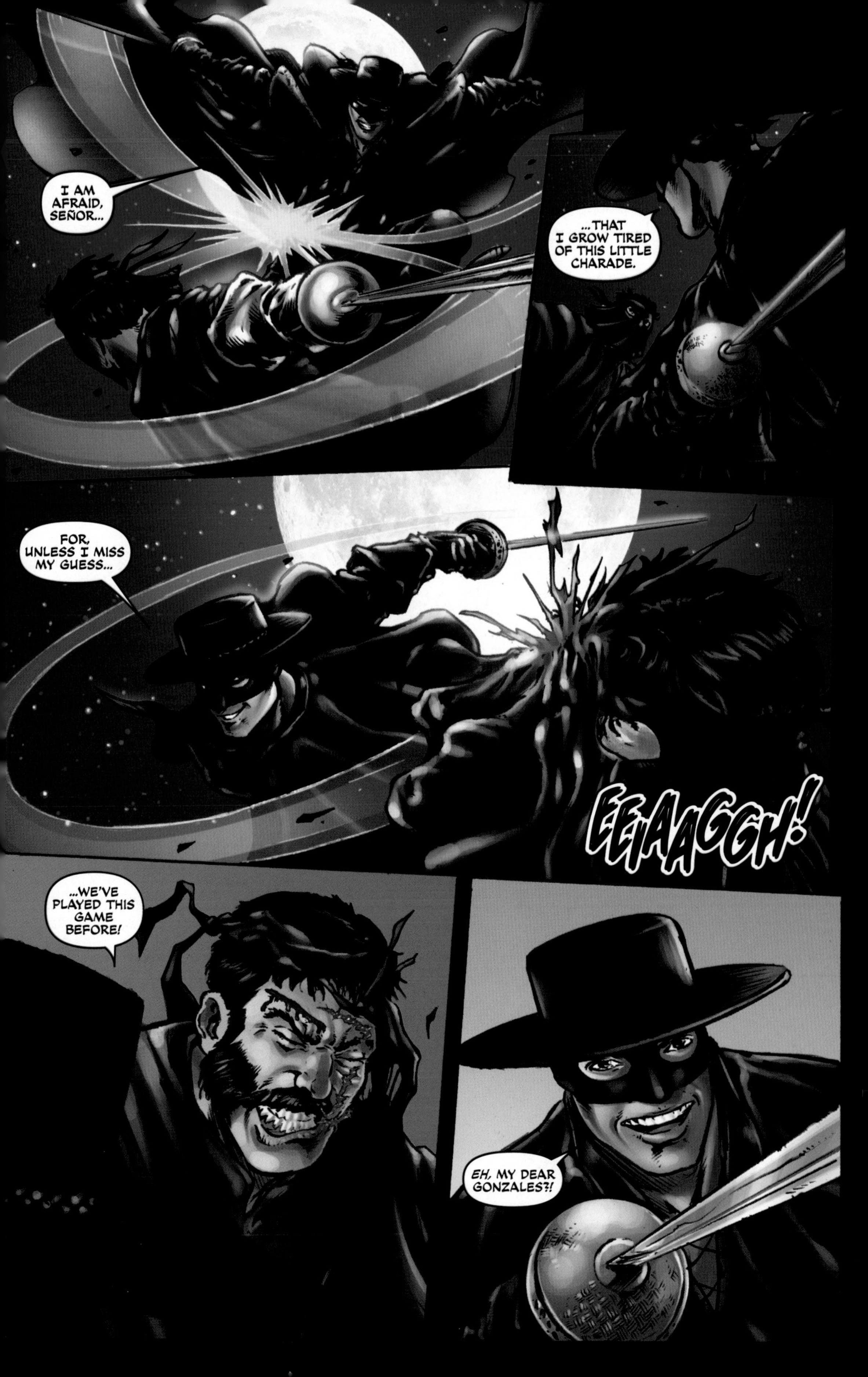
I AM AFRAID, SEÑOR...
...THAT I GROW TIRED OF THIS LITTLE CHARADE.
FOR, UNLESS I MISS MY GUESS...
EEIAAGGH!
...WE'VE PLAYED THIS GAME BEFORE!
EH, MY DEAR GONZALES?!

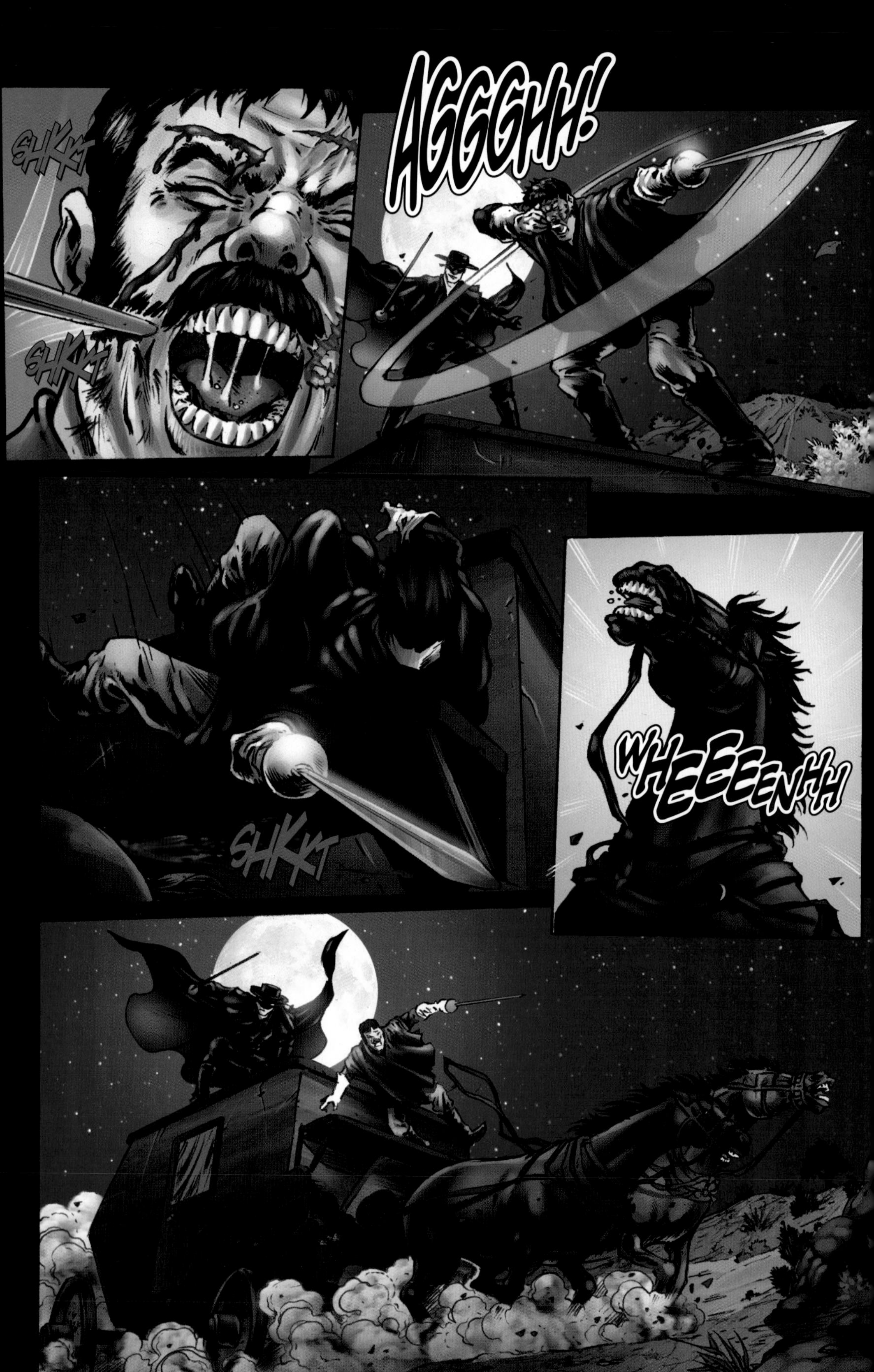
SHKKT
SHKKT
AGGGHH!
SHKKT
WHEEEEENHH

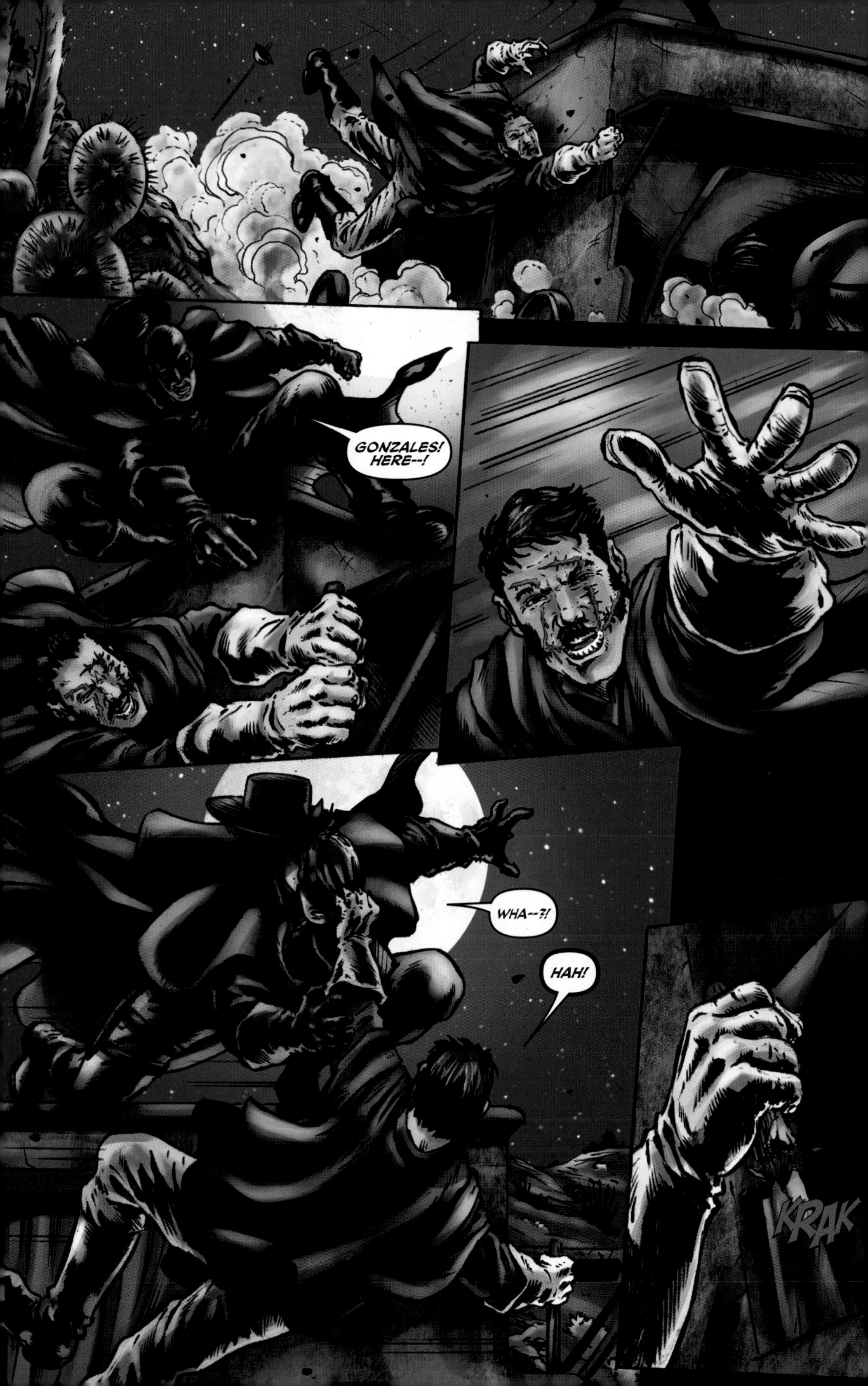
GONZALES! HERE--!
WHA--?!
HAH!
KRAK

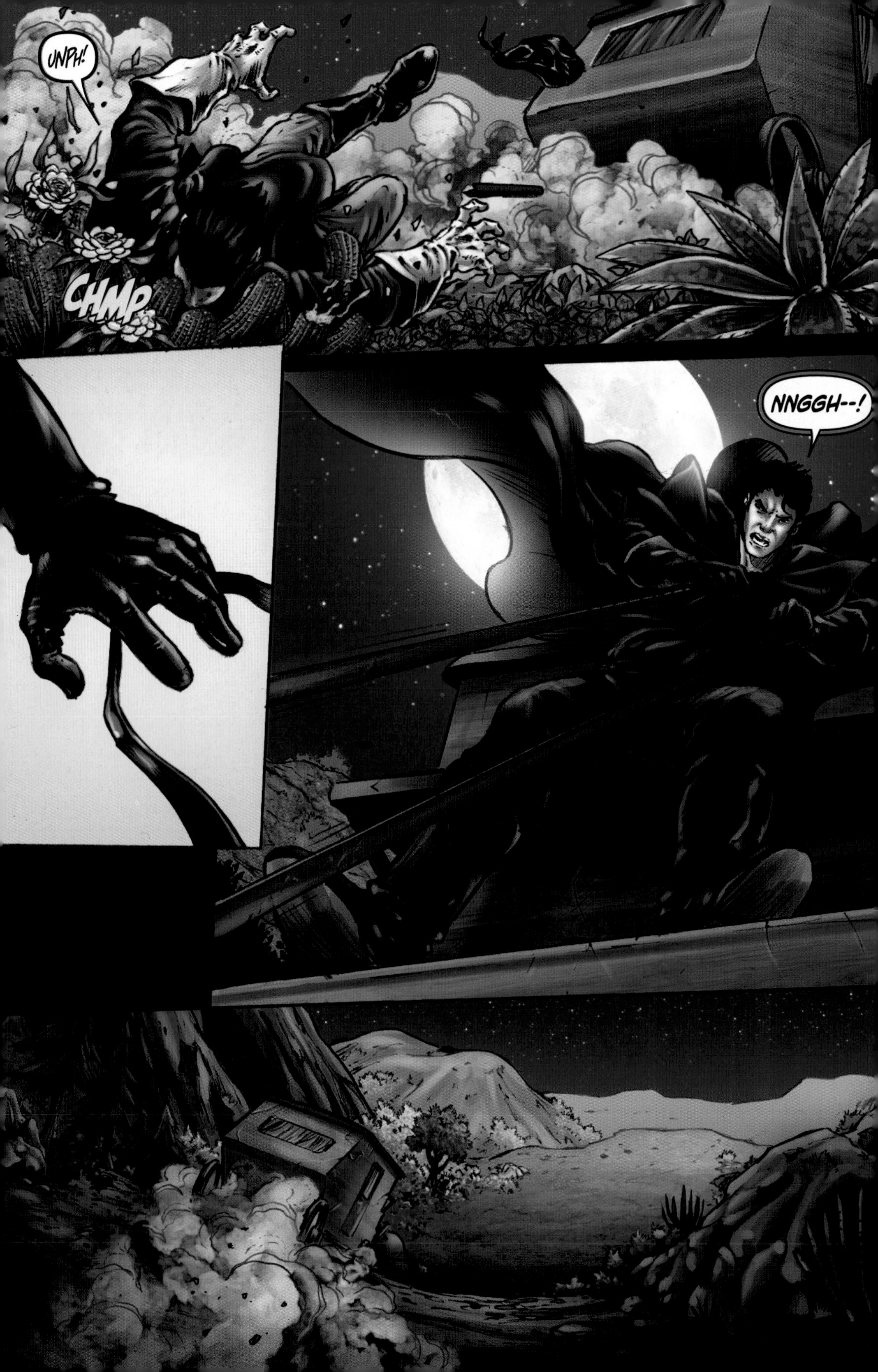
UNPH!
CHMP
NNGGH--!

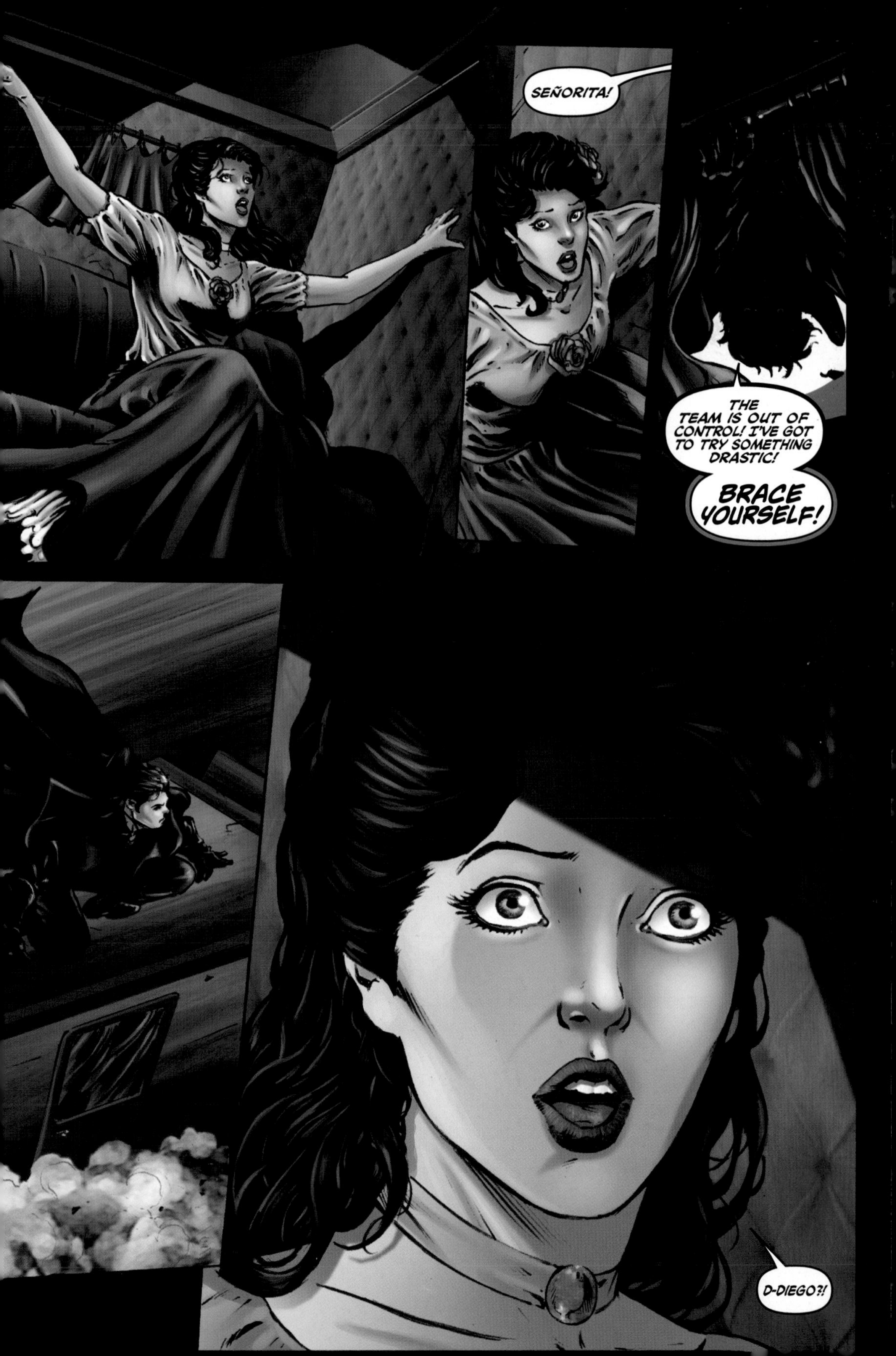
SEÑORITA!
THE TEAM IS OUT OF CONTROL! I'VE GOT TO TRY SOMETHING DRASTIC!
BRACE YOURSELF!
D-DIEGO?!

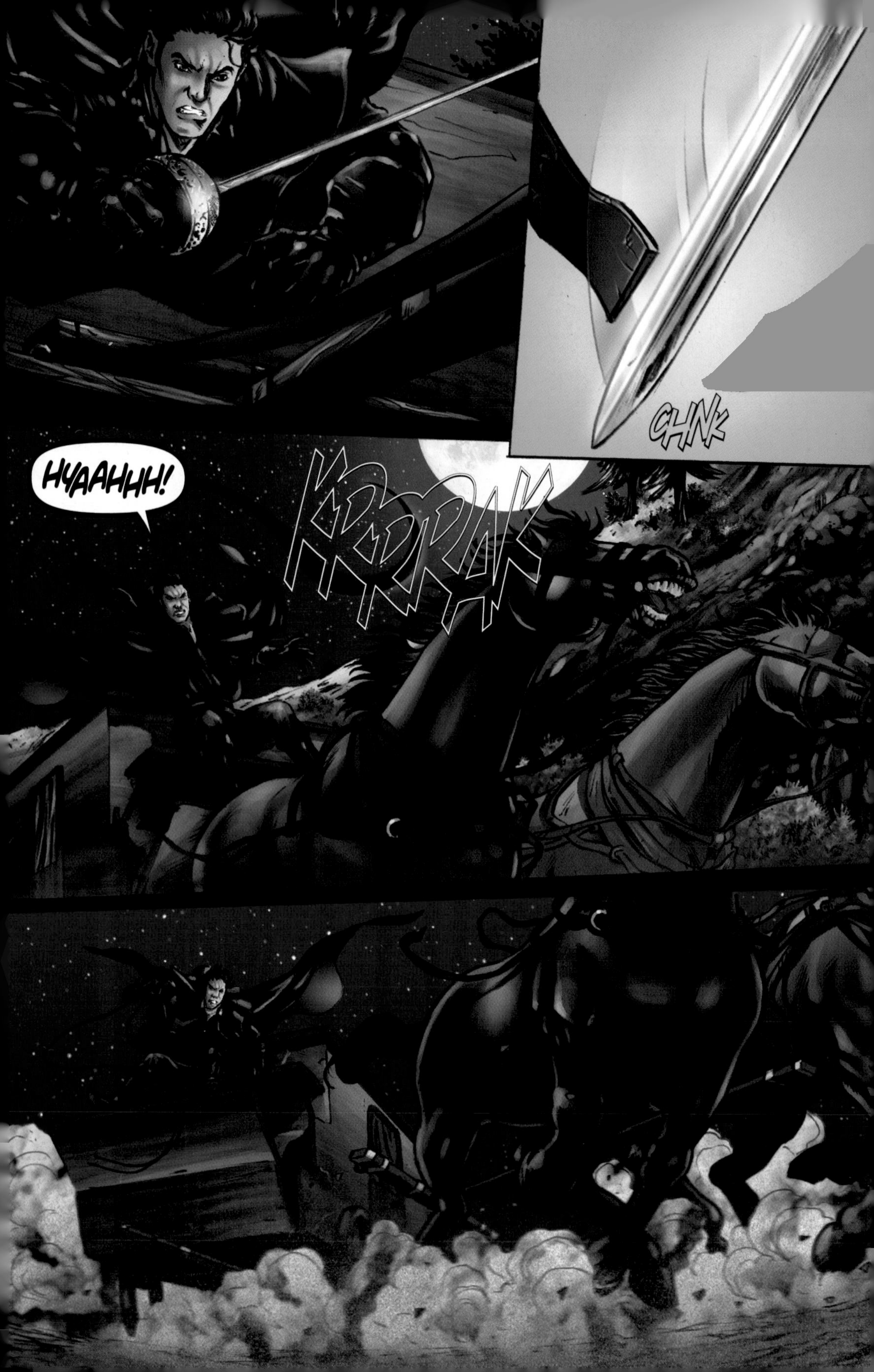
CHINK
HYAAHHH!
KRDRAK

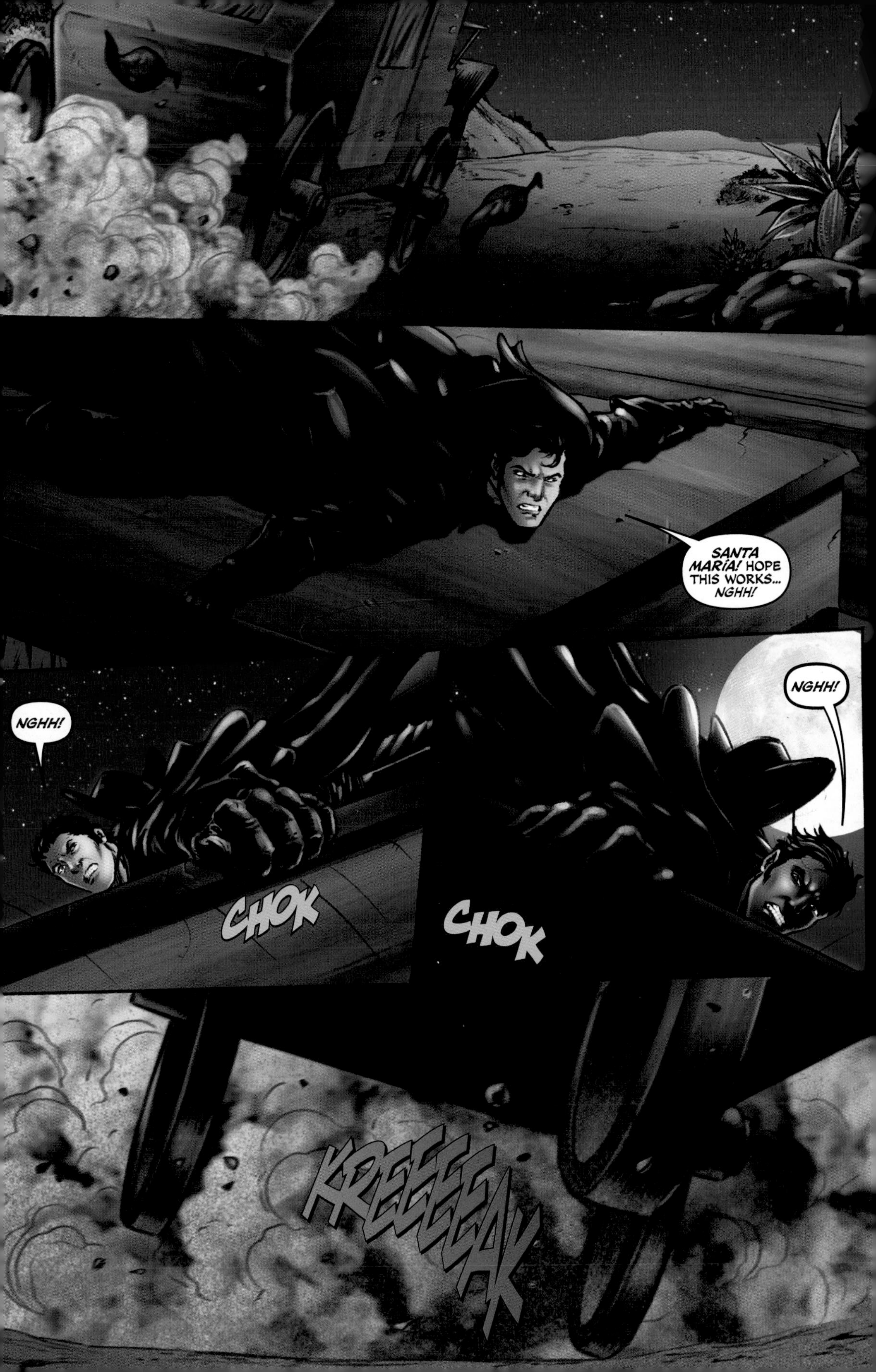
SANTA MARÍA! HOPE THIS WORKS... NGHH!
NGHH!
CHOK
NGHH!
CHOK
KREEEEAK

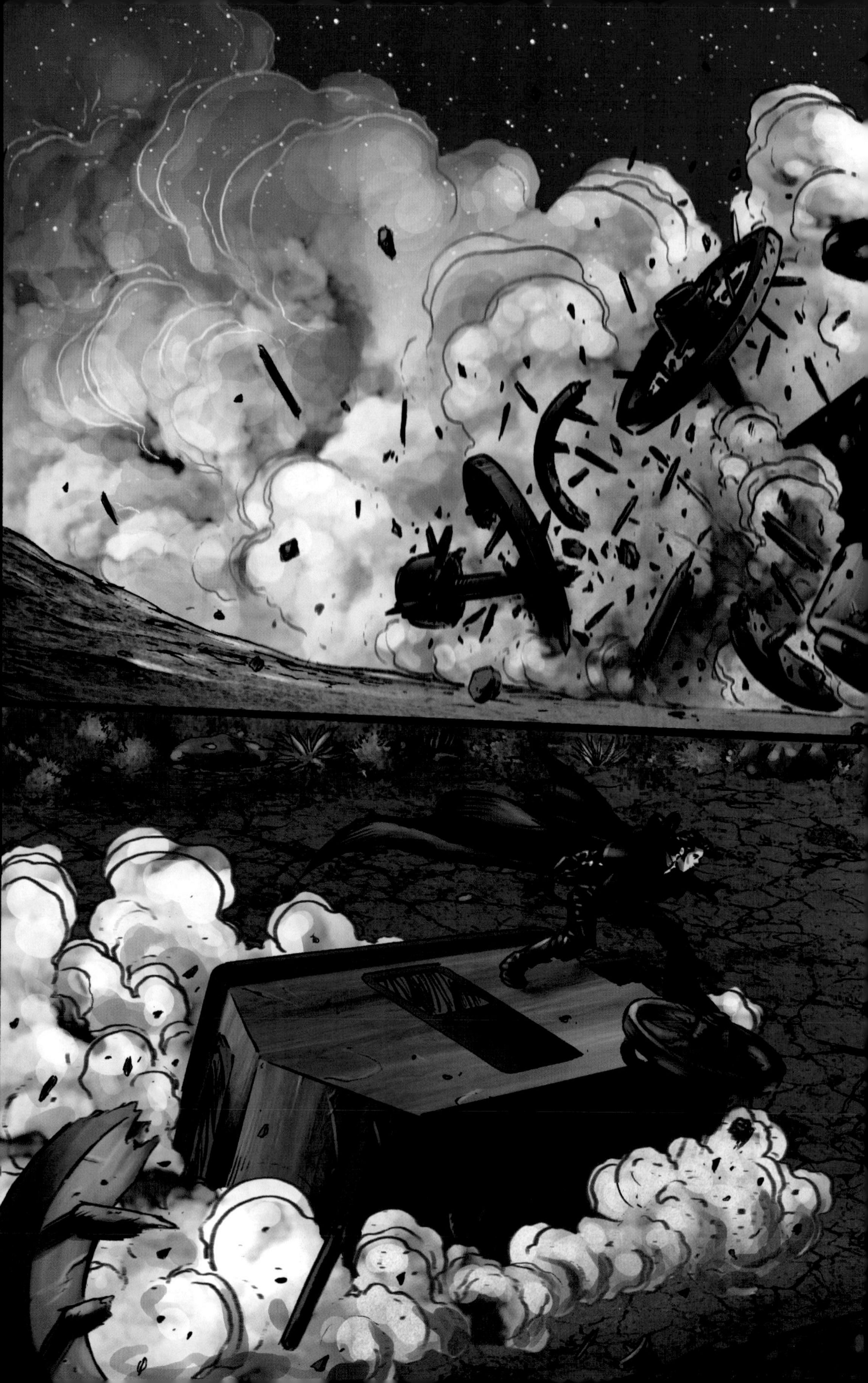

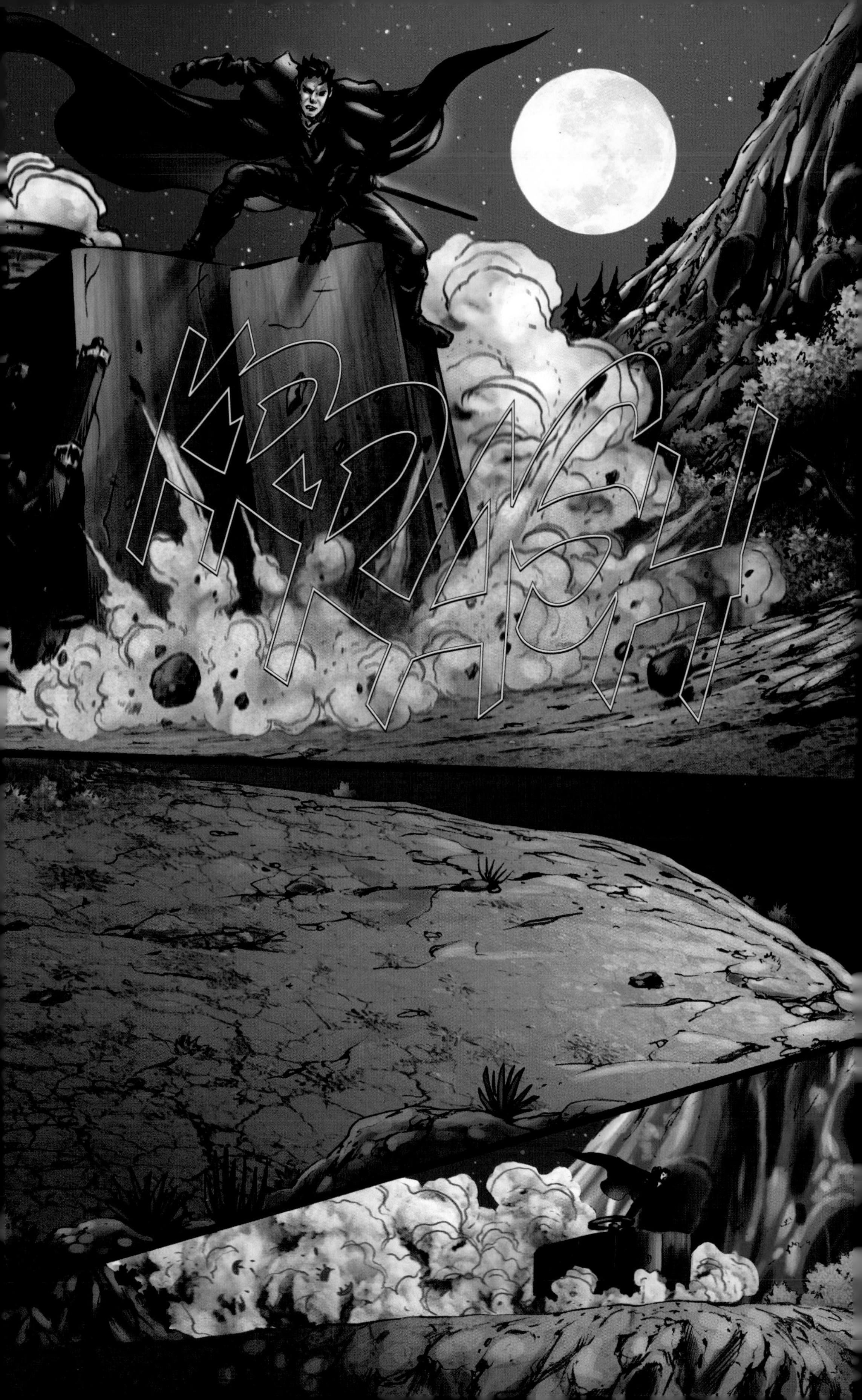
KRASH!

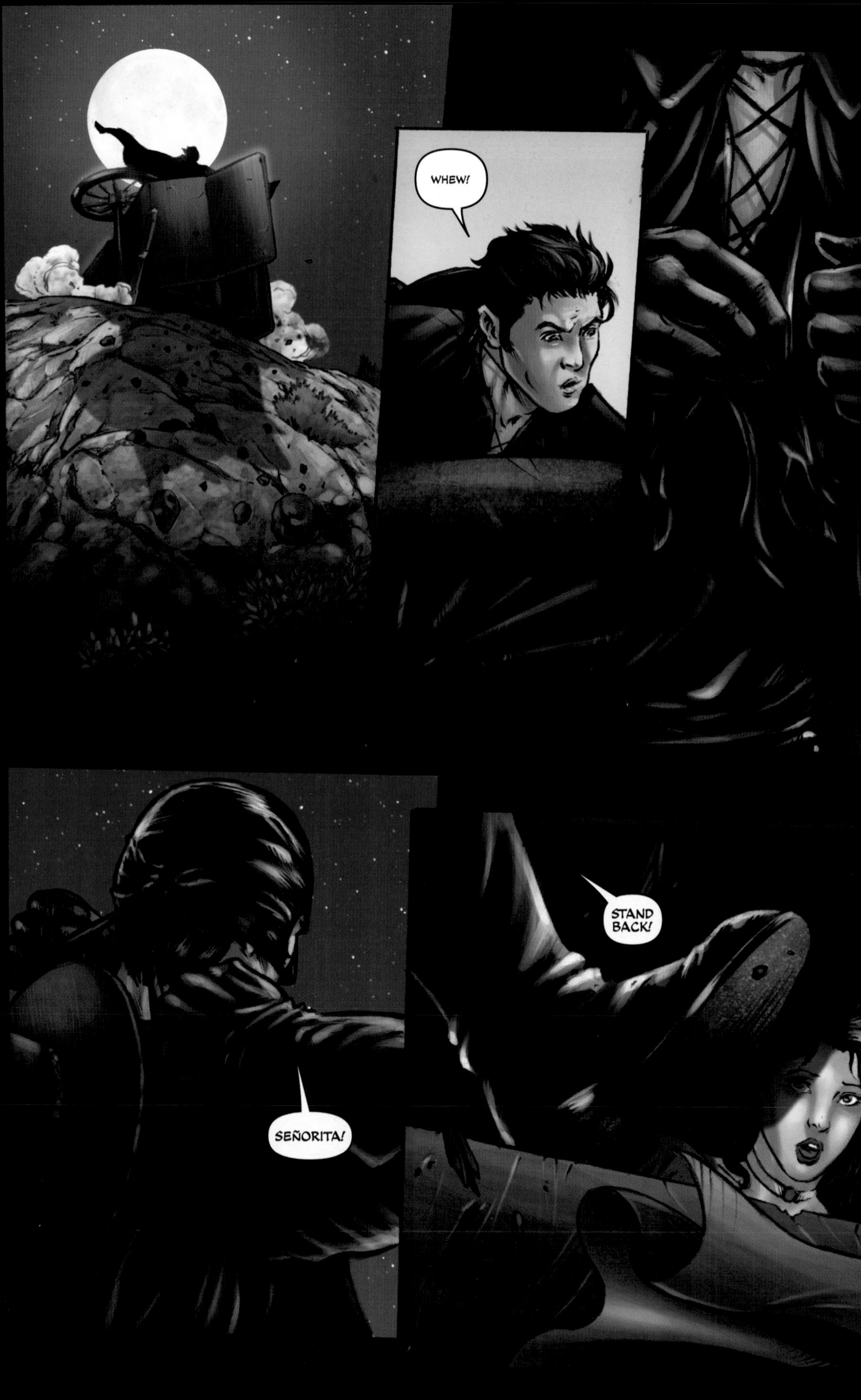
WHEW!
SEÑORITA!
STAND BACK!

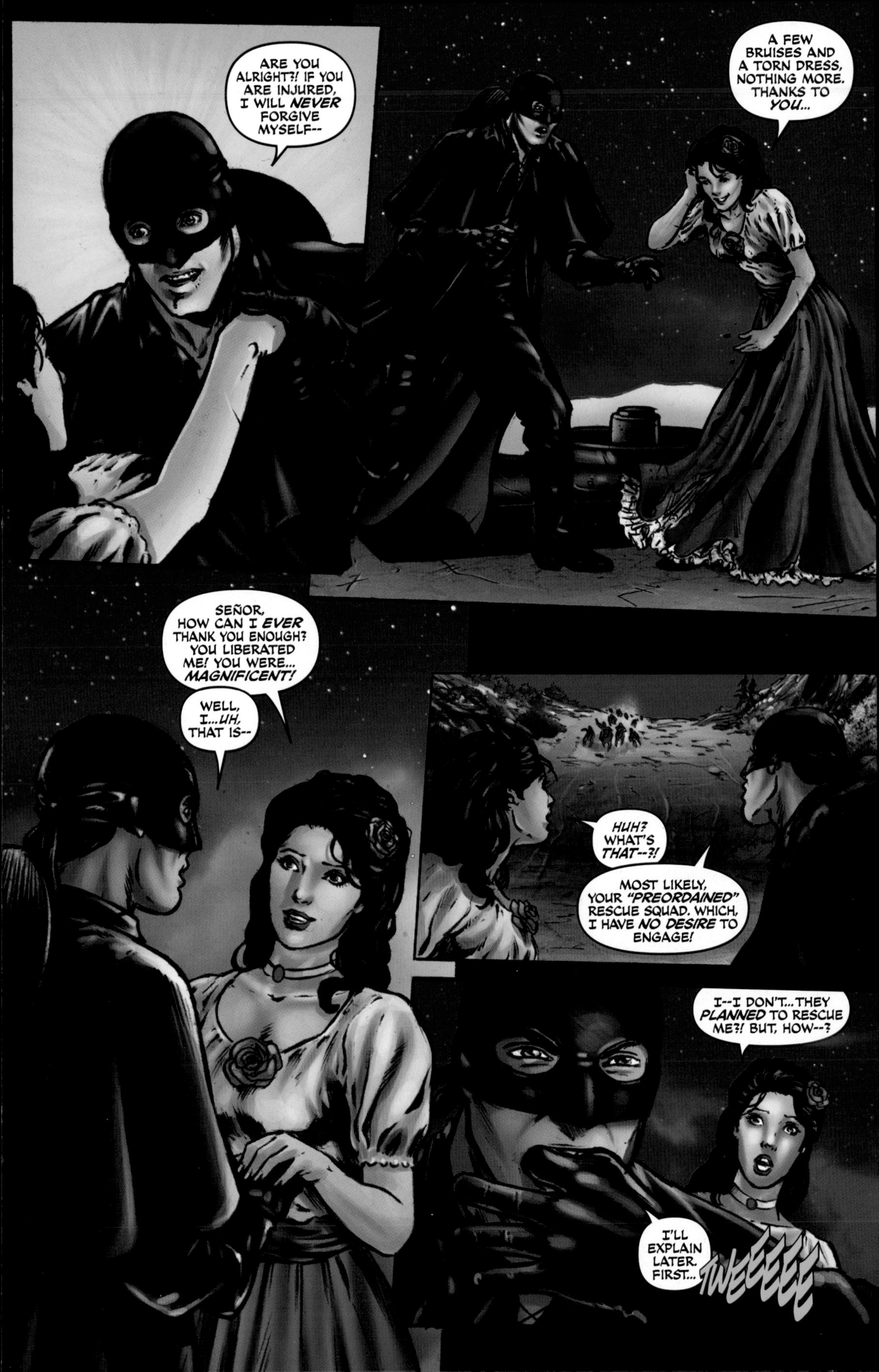
ARE YOU ALRIGHT?! IF YOU ARE INJURED, I WILL NEVER FORGIVE MYSELF--
A FEW BRUISES AND A TORN DRESS, NOTHING MORE. THANKS TO YOU...
SEÑOR, HOW CAN I EVER THANK YOU ENOUGH? YOU LIBERATED ME! YOU WERE... MAGNIFICENT!
WELL, I...UH, THAT IS--
HUH? WHAT'S THAT--?!
MOST LIKELY, YOUR "PREORDAINED" RESCUE SQUAD. WHICH, I HAVE NO DESIRE TO ENGAGE!
I--I DON'T...THEY PLANNED TO RESCUE ME?! BUT, HOW--?
I'LL EXPLAIN LATER. FIRST...
TWEEEEE

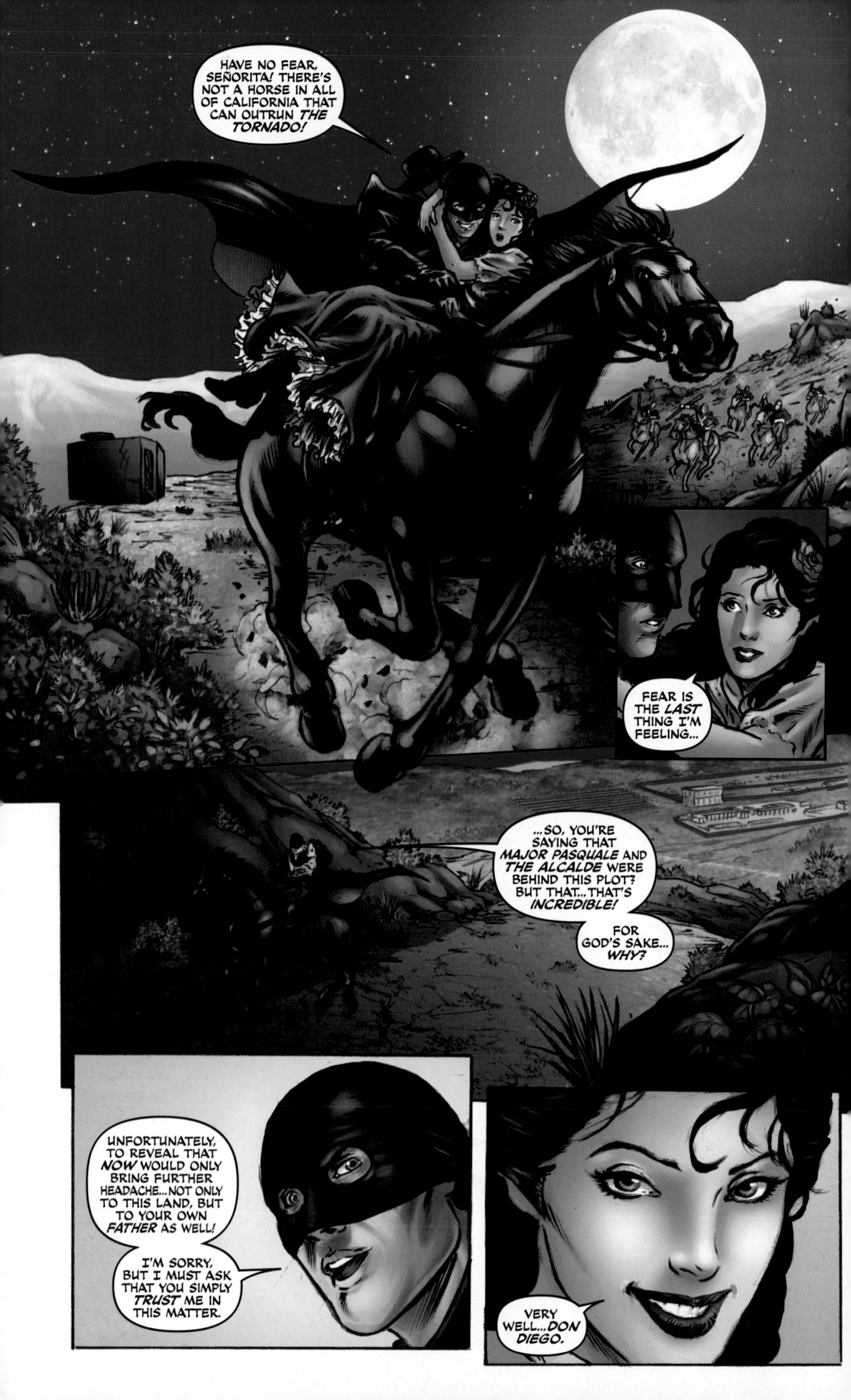
HAVE NO FEAR, SEÑORITA! THERE'S NOT A HORSE IN ALL OF CALIFORNIA THAT CAN OUTRUN *THE TORNADO!*
FEAR IS THE *LAST* THING I'M FEELING...
...SO, YOU'RE SAYING THAT *MAJOR PASQUALE* AND *THE ALCALDE* WERE BEHIND THIS PLOT? BUT THAT...THAT'S *INCREDIBLE!*
FOR GOD'S SAKE... *WHY?*
UNFORTUNATELY, TO REVEAL THAT *NOW* WOULD ONLY BRING FURTHER HEADACHE...NOT ONLY TO THIS LAND, BUT TO YOUR OWN *FATHER* AS WELL!
I'M SORRY, BUT I MUST ASK THAT YOU SIMPLY *TRUST* ME IN THIS MATTER.
VERY WELL...*DON DIEGO.*

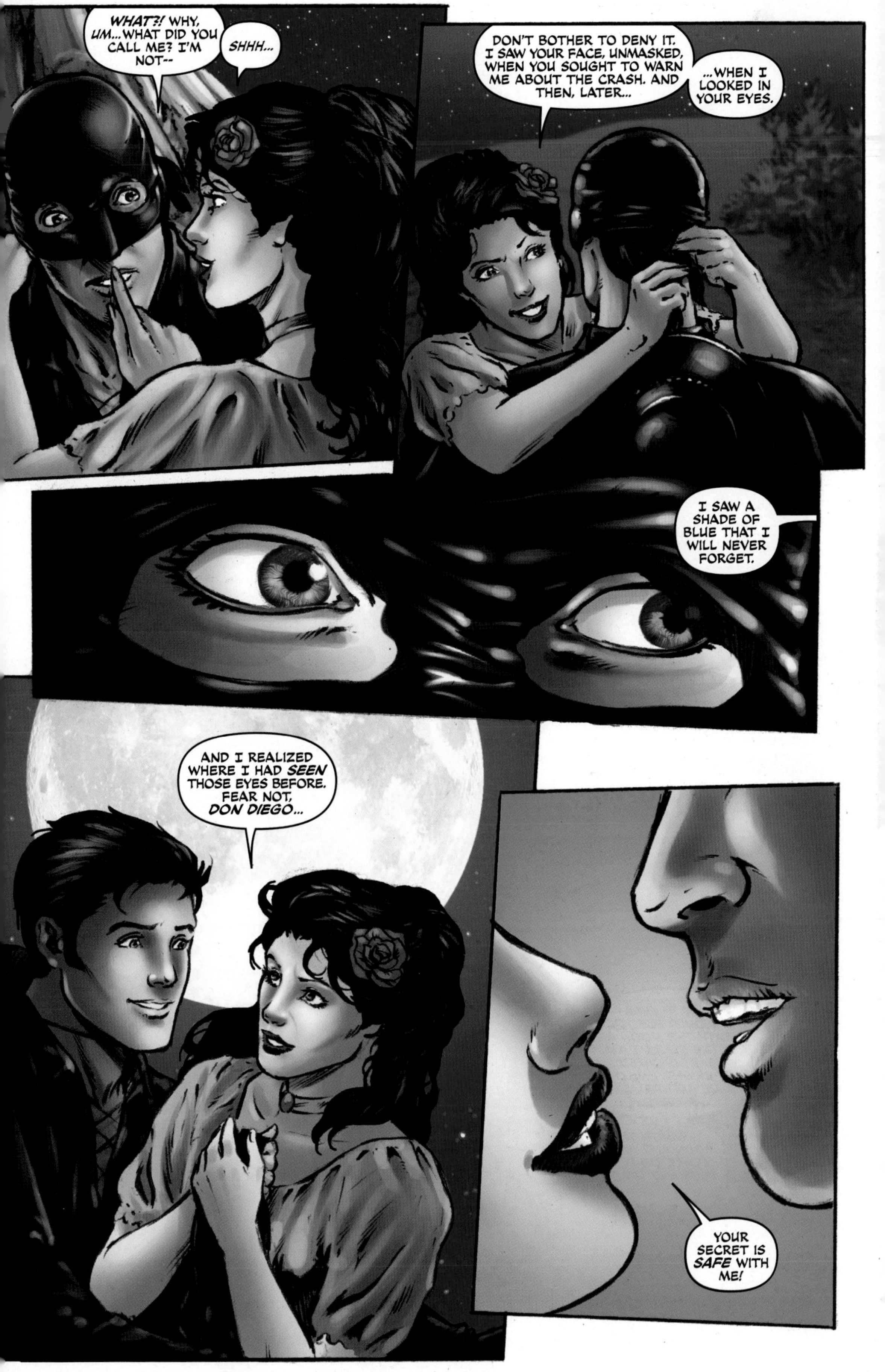
WHAT?! WHY, UM...WHAT DID YOU CALL ME? I'M NOT--
SHHH...
DON'T BOTHER TO DENY IT. I SAW YOUR FACE, UNMASKED, WHEN YOU SOUGHT TO WARN ME ABOUT THE CRASH. AND THEN, LATER...
...WHEN I LOOKED IN YOUR EYES.
I SAW A SHADE OF BLUE THAT I WILL NEVER FORGET.
AND I REALIZED WHERE I HAD SEEN THOSE EYES BEFORE. FEAR NOT, DON DIEGO...
YOUR SECRET IS SAFE WITH ME!

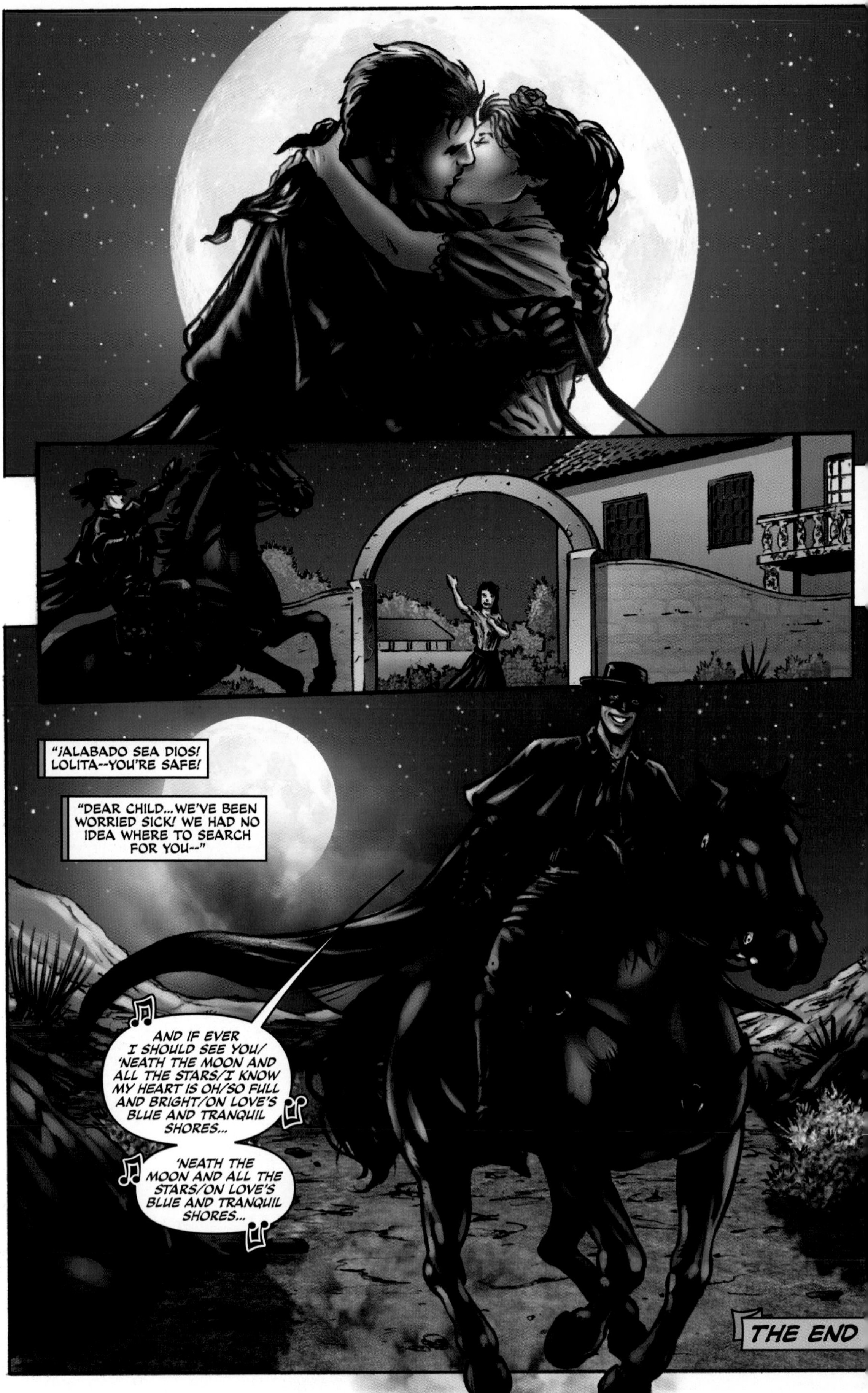
"¡ALABADO SEA DIOS! LOLITA--YOU'RE SAFE!
"DEAR CHILD...WE'VE BEEN WORRIED SICK! WE HAD NO IDEA WHERE TO SEARCH FOR YOU--"
AND IF EVER I SHOULD SEE YOU/ 'NEATH THE MOON AND ALL THE STARS/I KNOW MY HEART IS OH/SO FULL AND BRIGHT/ON LOVE'S BLUE AND TRANQUIL SHORES...
'NEATH THE MOON AND ALL THE STARS/ON LOVE'S BLUE AND TRANQUIL SHORES...
THE END

ZORRO

ALTERNATE COVER GALLERY

Page 146 • FRANCESCO FRANCAVILLA #9 COVER
Page 147 • FRANCESCO FRANCAVILLA #10 COVER
Page 148 • FRANCESCO FRANCAVILLA #11 COVER
Page 149 • FRANCESCO FRANCAVILLA #12 COVER
Page 150 • FRANCESCO FRANCAVILLA #12 BACK COVER
Page 151 • FRANCESCO FRANCAVILLA #13 COVER
Page 152 • FRANCESCO FRANCAVILLA #14 COVER

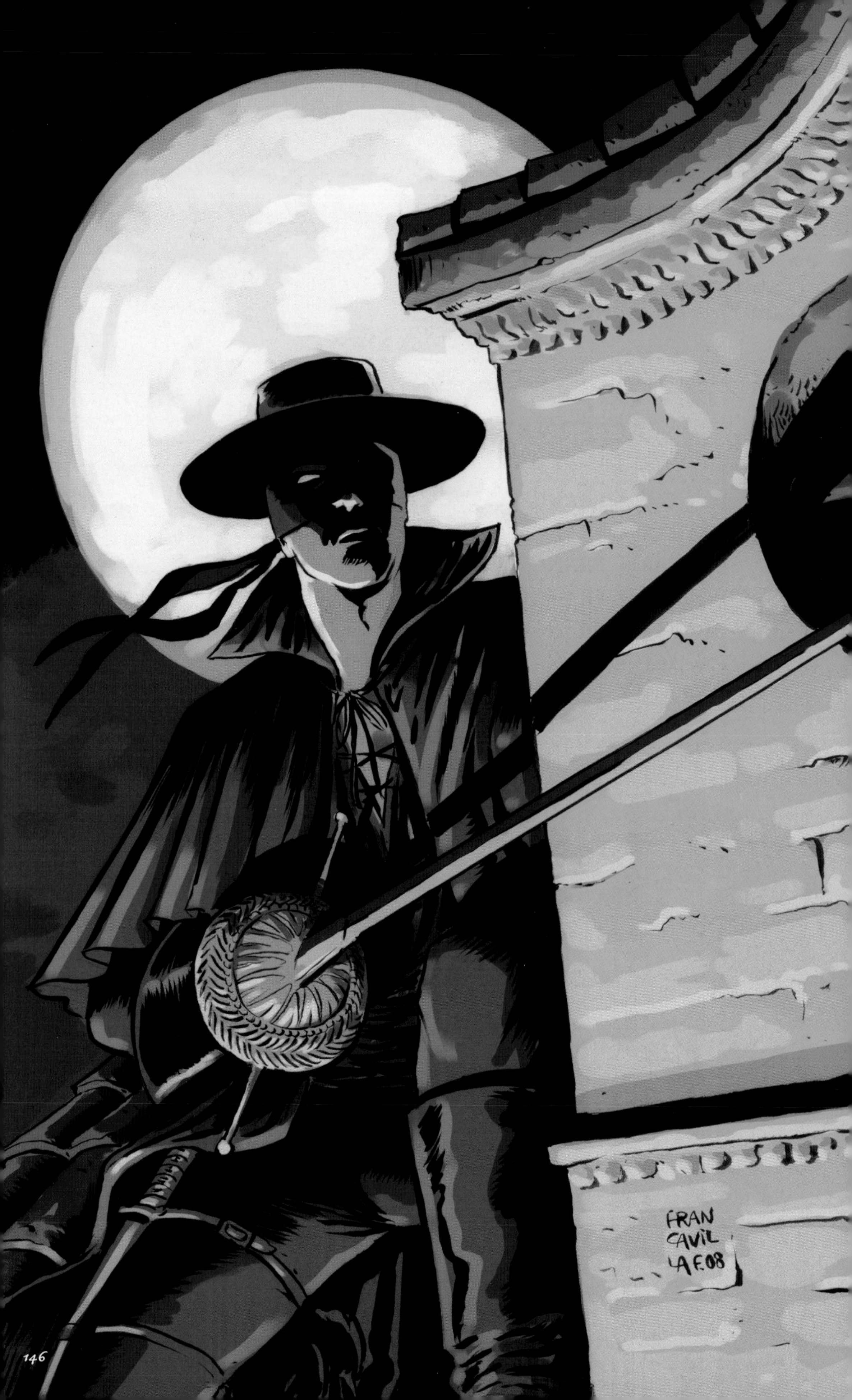
FRAN
CAVIL
LA F.08

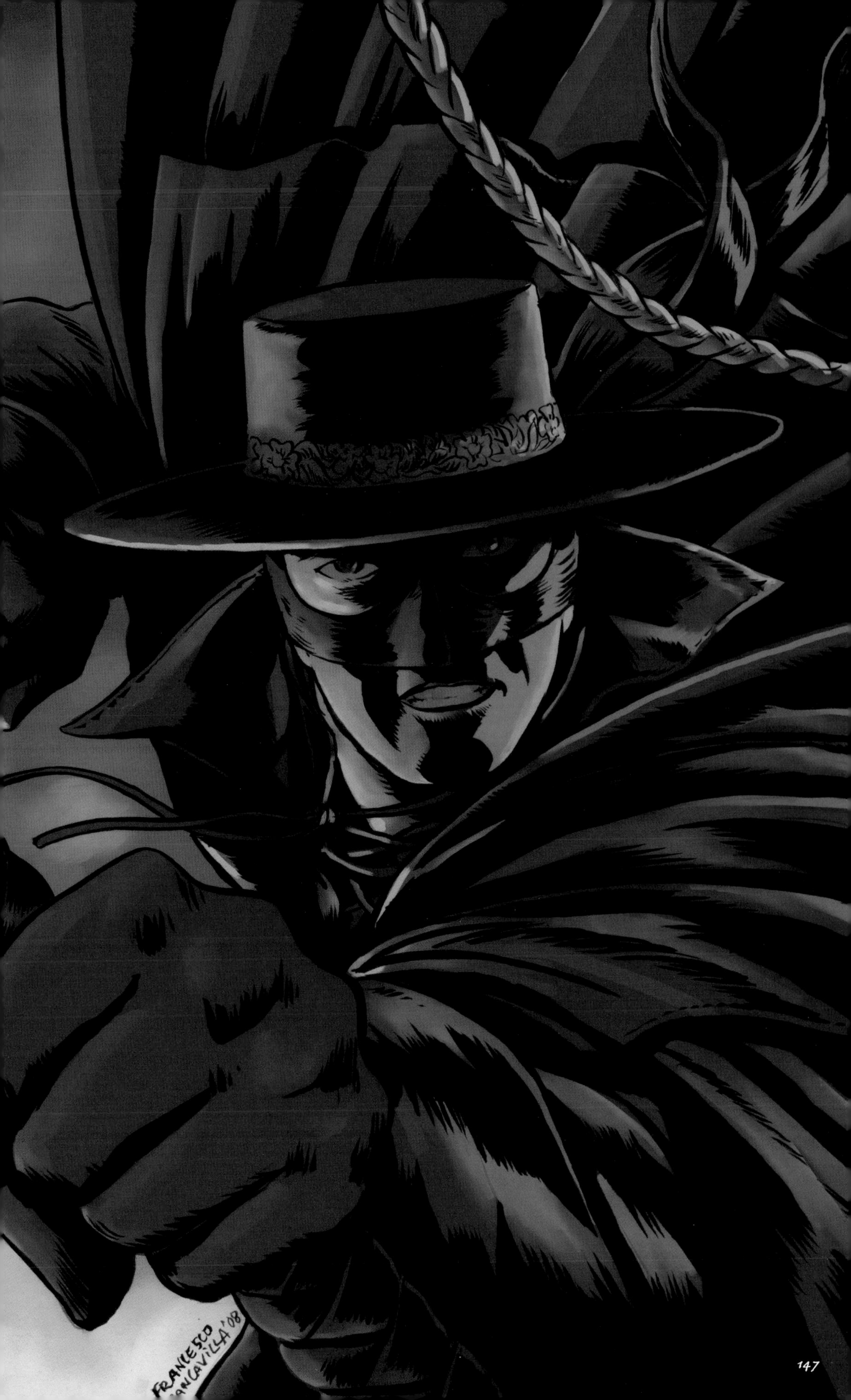
FRANCESCO

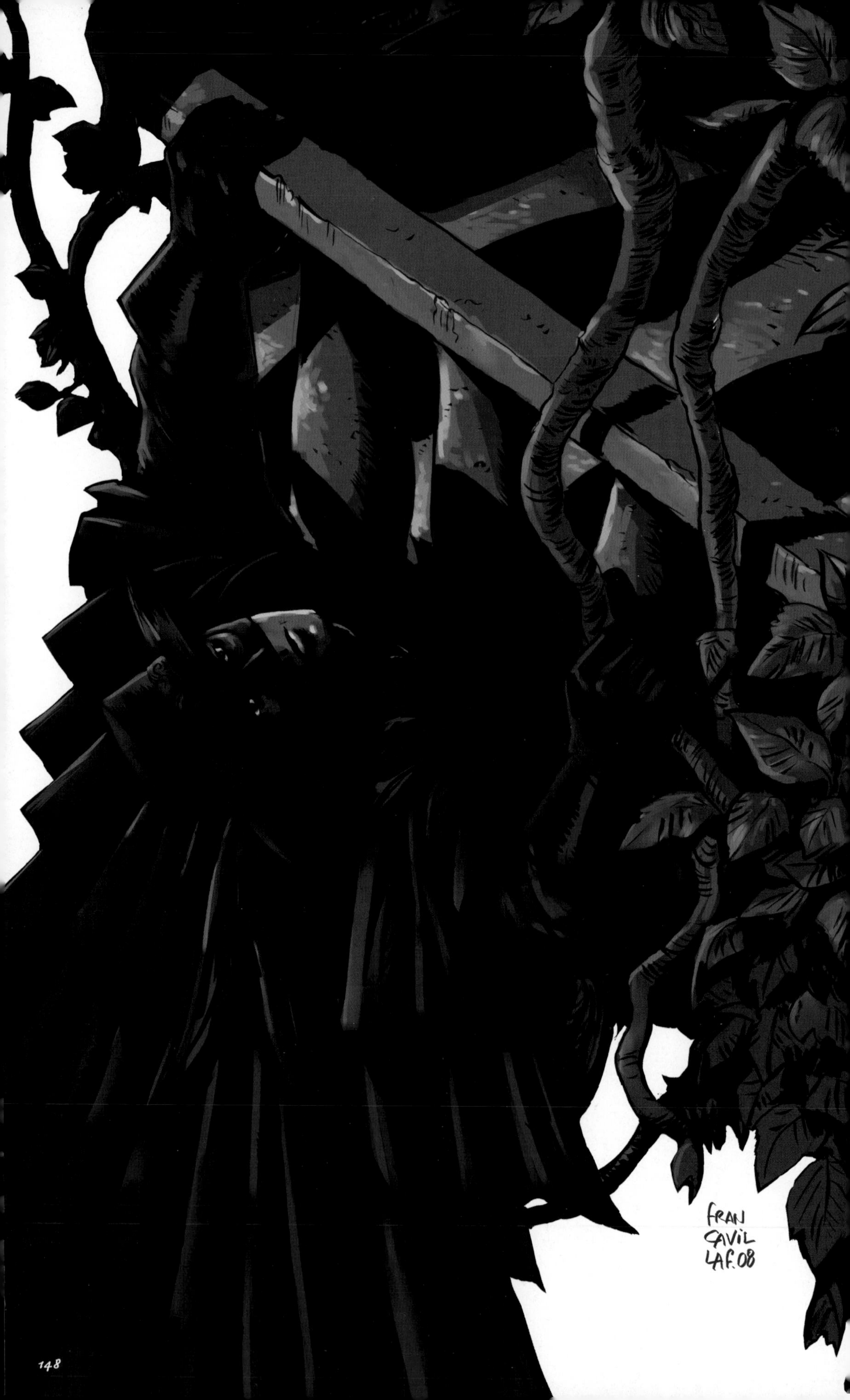
FRAN
CAVIL
LAF.08

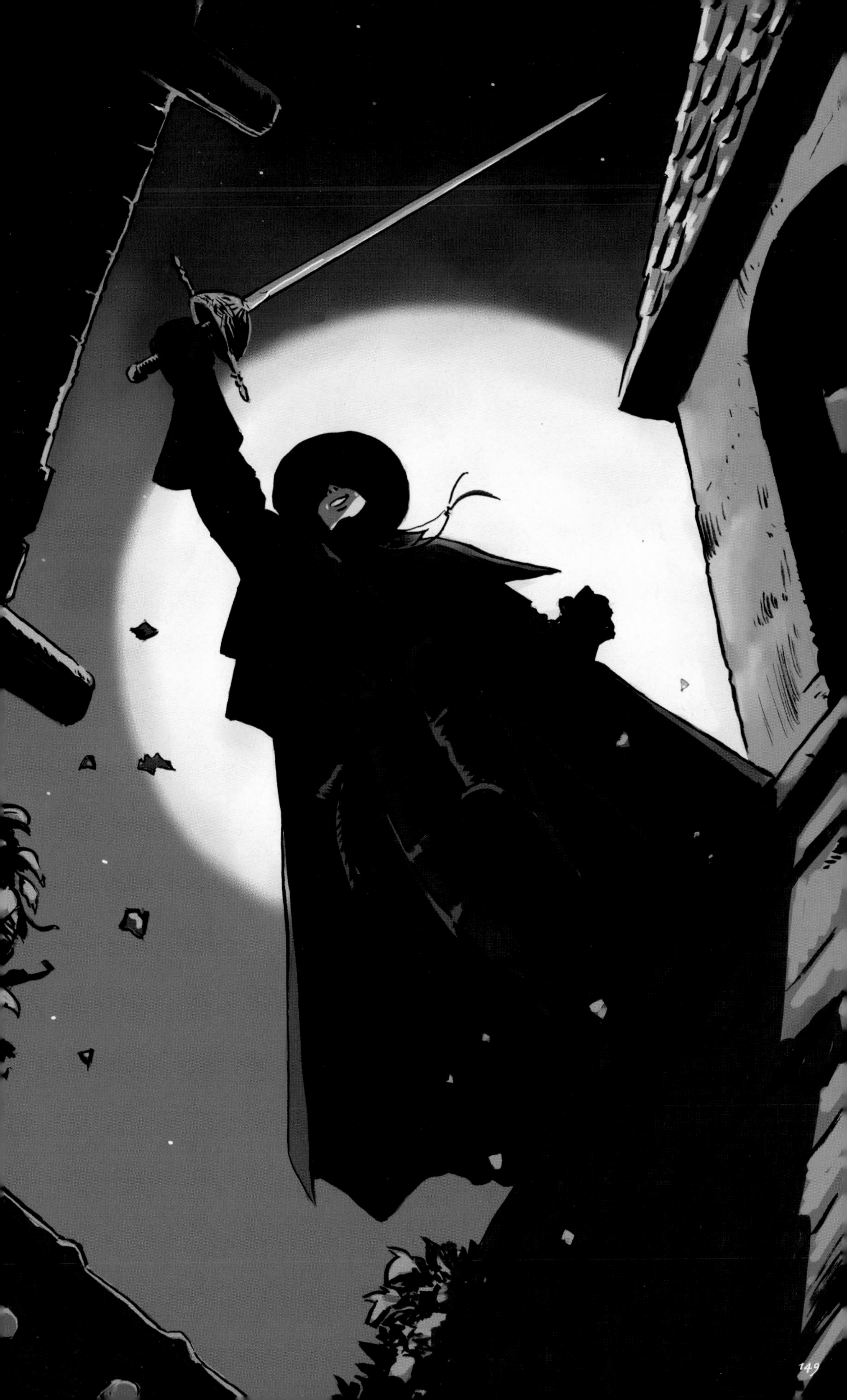

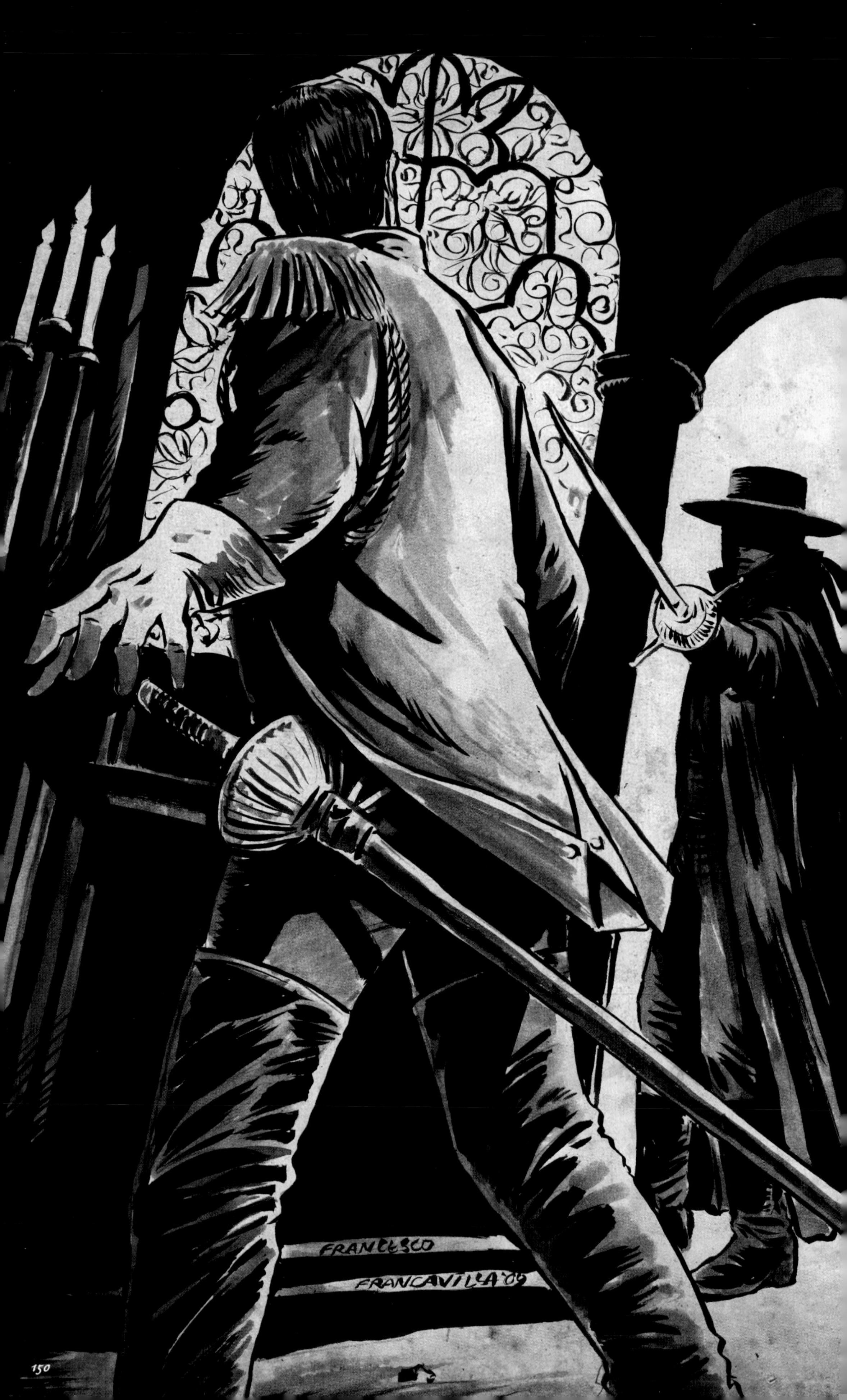
FRANCESCO
FRANCAVILLA '09

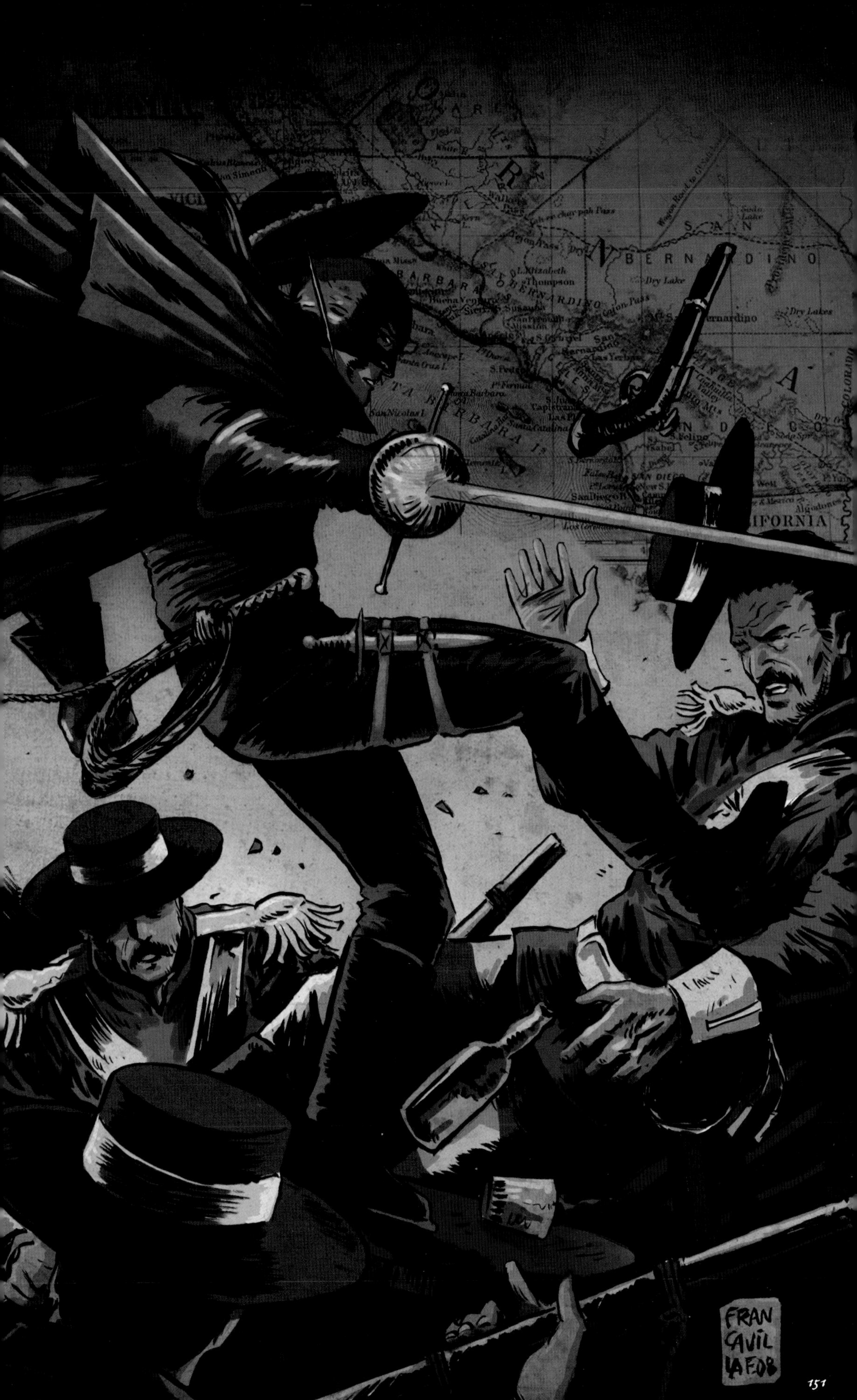
L. Elizabeth
Thompson
Dry Lake
Dry Lakes
Santa Catalina

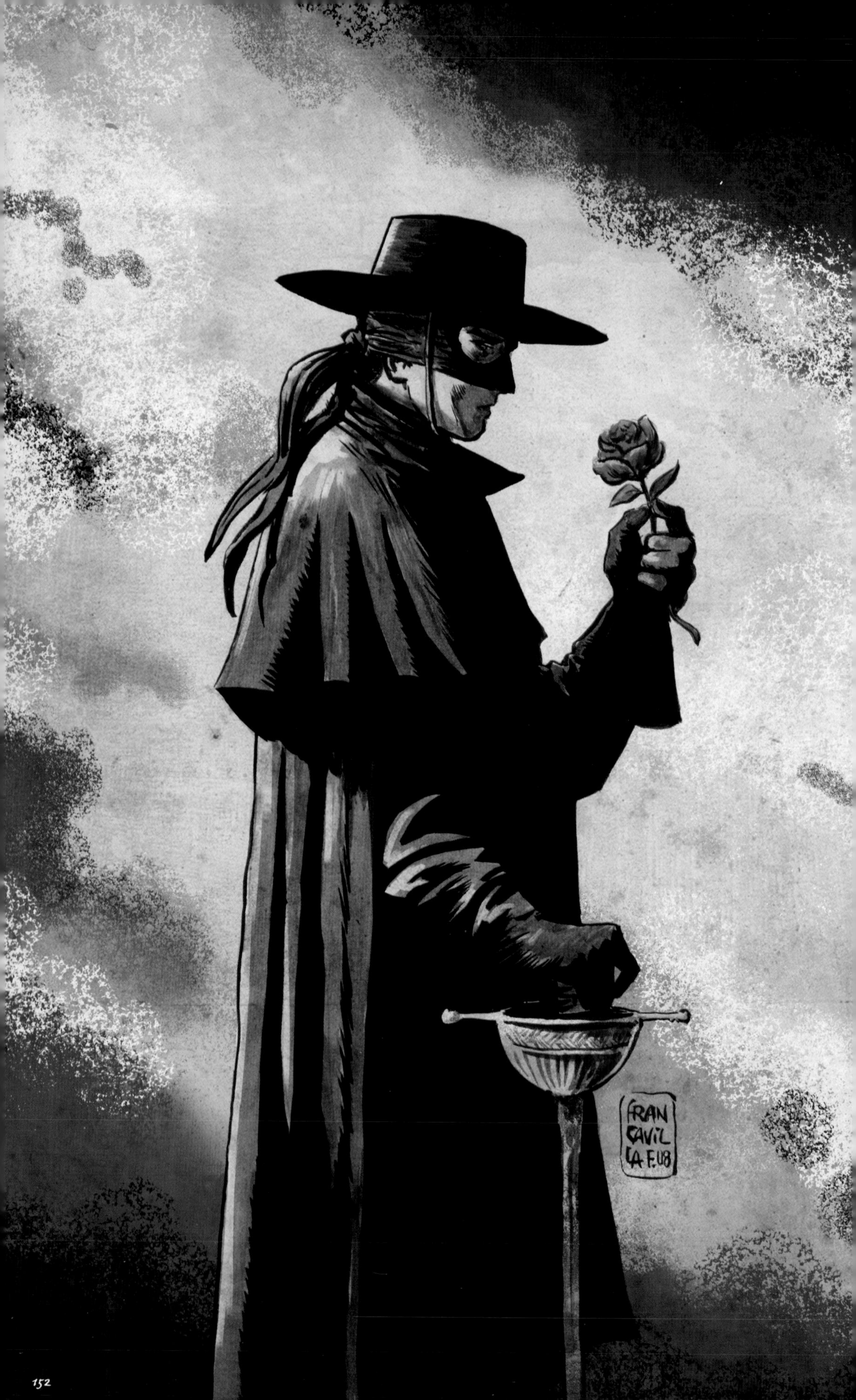
FRAN
CAVIL
LA F. 08